R . TAPSCOTT

The leasing handbook

The leasing handbook

Editors
Derek R. Soper
Robert M. Munro

with
Ewen Cameron

McGRAW-HILL BOOK COMPANY

London · New York · St Louis · San Francisco · Auckland
Bogotá · Caracas · Hamburg · Lisbon · Madrid · Mexico
Milan · Montreal · New Delhi · Panama · Paris · San Juan · São
Paulo · Singapore · Sydney · Tokyo · Toronto

Published by
McGRAW-HILL Book Company Europe
Shoppenhangers Road
Maidenhead, Berkshire, SL6 2QL, England
Telephone 0628 23432
Fax 0628 770224

British Library Cataloging in Publication data

Leasing Handbook
 I. Soper, Derek R.
 658.14242

 ISBN 0–07–707555–2

Library of Congress Cataloging-in-Publication Data

The Leasing handbook / Editors, Derek R. Soper, Robert M. Munro, with
Ewen Cameron.
  p.   cm.
  Includes bibliographical references and index.
  ISBN 0–07–707555–2
  1. Industrial equipment leases—Great Britain.   I. Soper, Derek
R.   II. Munro, Robert M.   III. Cameron, Ewen
HD39.4.L377   1992
658.15′242—dc20   92–16109

12345 CUP 95432

Typeset by TecSet Ltd, Wallington, Surrey
and printed and bound in Great Britain at the University Press, Cambridge.

Contents

Foreword

The first authoritative book produced on what was then a fledgeling industry in the UK, *Leasing* by Tom Clark, published in August 1978, stimulated two thoughts: firstly, what an excellent job had been done and, secondly, how did he find the time to write it?

It was with some trepidation, therefore, that Bob Munro and I accepted an invitation from the publishers and the Equipment Leasing Association to oversee the second publication. Once the outline of the book had been agreed, we approached various members of the leasing industry to 'contribute' sections of the book. The time taken to do this and the wide differences in style of the many contributors, led us to ask Ewen Cameron, who had recently retired from NWS BANK, to restyle the whole book into a single cohesive work. He has done this to a very high standard, ably assisted in several of the statistical and factual sections by Andy Thompson of the Equipment Leasing Association.

While it is clear that the pre–1984 tax system together with off-balance sheet financing prior to SSAP 21 had a catalytic effect in creating a large and vibrant leasing industry, in the absence of these factors the major leasing company groups have continued to find a major market for leasing in its own right.

The innovation and marketing ability that has characterized the industry throughout its history will continue to ensure that it has a significant contribution to make. The limitation is likely to be the total of fixed investment in UK industry and commerce which, in turn, is dependent on the performance of the UK as an industrial country.

Leasing now accounts for some 30 per cent of UK investment in equipment. With the growth expected to flow from the single European market, we are seeing many new entrants to the industry — both companies and individuals — attracted by the opportunities. I commend this book to each of them as well as to existing participants.

Derek Soper
Chairman
AT&T Capital Holdings

1. *What is leasing?*

The term 'leasing' can have a number of meanings. All are concerned, however, with the use of an asset of some sort by a party who does not own that asset in the full sense.

For the purpose of this book, leasing has a more particular meaning, as defined by its industrial and commercial context. There is in the United Kingdom — more so than in some other industrialized countries — a distinct leasing industry. It consists, mainly, of companies operating in the broad financial services sector of the economy, particularly within banking, who are the leasing or lessor companies and who acquire assets in order to lease them to lessee businesses spread across the whole spectrum of industry and commerce.

Because there is such a distinct leasing industry in the UK, there is a tendency to define leasing in sector or 'status' terms: i.e. to say that leasing is what leasing companies do or, at any rate, some of the things they do. This is the general perception of leasing within the industry. However, as a definition — particularly in a country like the UK where no rigid rules restrict certain types of company to particular types of activity — this is less than satisfactory. There are too many overlaps within and between leasing companies and between that which is, and that which is not, within the usual concept of leasing.

A possible definition of leasing, which is functional rather than status-based but which, nevertheless, defines the scope of the UK leasing industry as it generally sees itself, would be:

> *The leasing of capital assets for substantial periods to commercial users who do not require, or obtain, title to the assets.*

Such a definition would not be universally accepted. For example, some leasing companies who are to some degree engaged in the business of land and property leasing as well as asset leasing, might well regard the former as part of their leasing activities. Indeed, the Equipment Leasing Association (ELA), as the representative body for the UK leasing industry (see Chapter 7), has not attempted an authoritative definition of the concept of leasing and includes property leasing within its aggregate statistics for the leasing activity of member companies.

In the UK, it is above all the system of corporate taxation which sets the boundaries of the leasing industry. Where assets are leased by one company to another, without the opportunity for the latter to acquire ownership, the tax system recognizes the lessor as owner of the assets, using them in its trade — i.e. the trade of leasing — and thus entitled to

1

offset the cost of acquisition, by way of capital allowances, against its tax liability on the rental income from the lease. If, on the other hand, the user can acquire legal title to the assets at some point within a hiring agreement, the tax system regards that party as the owner.

If it is not clear at the outset whether ownership of the assets is to be transferred to the lessee or hirer — i.e. user — during the course of an agreement or on its termination, the consequent uncertainties in tax treatment could rule out any capital allowance entitlement for either party, thus rendering the cost of the transaction prohibitive. Commercial hiring arrangements, therefore, tend to divide clearly into two categories:

1. The leasing agreement, where the lessor claims capital allowances on the understanding that at no stage will title in the assets pass to the lessee.
2. The hire purchase agreement, which provides for the user — in this case known as the hirer rather than the lessee — to acquire title.

In the case of hire purchase the passing of title, giving ownership to the user, could well occur only at the end of the agreement, when the hirer has completed the instalment payments representing capital and interest. However, because there is only a nominal option fee for the passing of title itself, while the hirer is in any event committed to the substantive cost of capital and interest payments, the tax system recognizes at the outset that the structure involves a purchase rather than a lease. The hirer rather than the financier can, in this case, claim capital allowances at the commencement of the agreement under Section 45 of the Finance Act 1971, even though the hirer does not have legal title at this stage.

There may be no essential difference in the commercial structure of these two types of asset-based finance arrangements. For any given asset financed at a particular time, the pattern of instalment payments for capital and interest under the hire-purchase structure may match quite closely those of the rental payments under a lease. However, the tax system follows the legal principle in recognizing a critical distinction between the two — treating the financier or lessor as owner in the leasing case, and the hirer as owner in the case of hire purchase.

Most of the major leasing companies offer facilities for assets to be leased or hired for business use. Whether the finance is taken on lease or on hire purchase may depend largely on which of the two parties, the lessor or the hirer, can make the best use of capital allowances at the time, in the light of the current tax position. In spite of this factor of interchangeability with other forms of finance, leasing is nevertheless regarded as a quite separate form of commercial activity and indeed as a specific industry under the established principles of economic analysis, where the boundaries of category sectors and subsectors cut across those of the large corporate groups.

Because of the taxation factors described above, equipment leases are so structured that the lessee never acquires ownership of the assets even where that party wishes to have the use of them for an indefinite period. The agreement is for an initial or primary lease period, at the end of which the equipment will revert to the possession of the lessor if no other arrangements are made.

Beyond these common principles, there are distinct types of leasing structure, the most significant of which are the *finance lease* and the *operating lease*.

The finance lease structure is closest in its economic nature to the hire-purchase alternative, though without crossing the dividing line related to the passing of title, which distinguishes leasing from other forms of finance. The finance lease effectively transfers to the lessee most of the risks and rewards of ownership of the asset, without making the lessee the legal owner. The lessor, which will usually be a financial sector company, will expect to recover the full capital cost of the asset from the primary lease rentals and the primary lease period will cover almost the whole expected useful life of the asset. The arrangements for the distribution of sale proceeds at the end of a lease, and early terminations or secondary lease periods, where the lessee eventually wishes to have use of the assets for a shorter or longer period than the primary lease period originally agreed, are all structured to reserve the principle of full recovery of the lessor's cost from the primary lease (see Chapter 9).

With the operating lease there is a commercial rationale, as well as a possible fiscal reason, for the lessee not to acquire ownership. The asset may be required for a shorter period than its expected useful life. The lessor in this case takes a substantial interest in the residual value of the asset from its sale in the second-hand market at the conclusion of the primary lease period and does not recover the whole of his or her capital investment from the primary lease rentals.

Short-term hiring arrangements,where there is no single extended primary lease period and the owner of the asset relies upon a succession of assignments to a variety of users over the life of the asset, fall outside the accepted definition of leasing. For these types of facility, such as plant hire in the construction industry, the party who owns the assets is much more actively involved in their management than is the case in either the finance or the operating lease, which are both essentially financing facilities.

The operating lease, which is particularly important in respect of such assets as vehicles, computers and aircraft for which there is a viable second-hand market, by its nature owes little to fiscal benefits, though lessors in this sector have been able to take advantage of the features of the taxation system which have generally assisted leasing. The same could be said of the small-ticket sector of leasing (see Chapter 24) in general — regardless of whether the lease agreements take the finance or operating form — if only because the lessees in this sector have seen other advantages of leasing as more important than any fiscal benefits.

In defining the institutional limits of the leasing industry — confined as it is to agreements between commercial parties rather than private individuals — taxation factors are once again quite critical. The value added tax (VAT) system generally inhibits the use of leasing, as opposed to hire purchase, in credit sales of consumer durables for the personal sector. In leasing, the gross lease rentals carry VAT at the current rate, but in hire purchase only the capital cost of the asset is taxed while the financing charges or interest payments are VAT-exempt. For the commercial sector lessee, who will generally be a VAT-registered trader entitled to claim 'input tax relief' on all VAT paid on his supplies, the higher VAT liability on leasing compared with hire purchase usually makes no practical difference. However, for the final consumer who cannot reclaim VAT paid, the difference is sufficient to ensure that hire purchase predominates over leasing or hiring agreements except for certain categories of assets that have overriding attractions on other grounds. Where it does occur — as, for example, in television and video equipment — the leasing of assets to consumers is regarded as essentially a retailing activity, quite outside the commercial leasing industry.

The leasing of assets by individuals to commercial sector lessees was once a factor of some importance, when favourable capital allowances offered an attractive 'tax shelter' against the higher rate of personal income tax. However, new rules introduced in the Finance Act 1980 precluded capital allowances for assets leased by an individual, unless that person devotes 'substantially the whole of his time' to the trade of leasing, and is thus operating as an unincorporated commercial lessor. The general advantages of trading with limited liability status are such that leasing as a business has usually been carried on through companies. The 1980 Act, therefore, put an end to the use of occasional leases by private individuals for tax deferral purposes.

The leasing of property, as distinct from plant and equipment, is usually regarded as a separate activity from that of the leasing industry. Land and buildings are by nature long-life assets, offering investors a mixture of income and capital growth, while plant and machinery represent depreciating assets offering a limited term exposure, with the lessor able to claim capital allowances that can be set against rental income receivable over the life of the asset. The latter type of exposure is more attractive to a banking sector lessor both because of the fiscal system and as a result of features of banking supervision (see Chapter 23). The former is attractive to specialist property companies, and to financial institutions such as pension funds who look for a proportion of longer term investments within their portfolios.

However, one area where plant- and equipment-leasing companies find property leases an attractive proposition is in the enterprise zones — i.e. certain particular inner urban areas where fiscal incentives are available for investment in immovable assets (see Chapter 24). In these areas, the ownership of industrial and commercial buildings attracts highly favourable capital allowances, whereas elsewhere in the UK there are only very limited tax write-offs for industrial buildings and none at all for commercial buildings — on the grounds that the latter are not depreciating assets. Financial lessors, therefore, find it attractive to acquire and lease property in the enterprise zones, whereas, in the remainder of the country, this activity is dominated by other types of companies and institutions.

It is, therefore, probably appropriate to regard property leasing as outside the general conceptual scope of the leasing industry. There is, nevertheless, a substantial amount of leasing of fixed plant within buildings, such as lifts and heating systems, which can be subject to leasing agreements independent of the interests in the property itself, and which are treated under the tax system as plant rather than integral parts of buildings. Fixture leasing is very much a part of the equipment-leasing activity (see Chapter 21).

There are, therefore, a variety of factors which together determine the effective limits of leasing as an economic activity in the UK. It is largely commercial factors which mark out the distinction between longer term leases and short-time hiring, while legal and fiscal factors mark the difference between leasing and other forms of asset-based finance. It is essentially the tax system which separates commercial leasing from other forms of leasing or hiring to private individuals, while a mixture of taxation and commercial factors generally demarcate between plant and property leasing.

The net result of all these factors is to set the bounds of an equipment-leasing industry, which has come to play a major role in asset finance and is of considerable significance within the UK economy.

2. *What leasing offers*

The form that leasing takes evolves constantly in response to market demand and changes imposed by legislation. Yet its advantages to the customer remain much the same as they were when leasing was first developed. Quantitative illustrations of the financial implications of leasing are given in later chapters. The essential advantages of leasing, from the respective standpoints of lessee and lessor, are summarized briefly in this chapter.

Advantages to lessees

For the users of assets, leasing offers firstly an additional source of finance with no initial outlay other than the first rental. It extends the range of methods of financing the acquisition of capital equipment and allows companies to adopt a mixed financing strategy using leasing as one of several facilities that can be employed simultaneously to finance capital investment.

Leasing also offers flexibility in the financing of fixed assets. Lease rentals can be tailored to match the anticipated income generated by the use of an asset, thus making the investment 'self-funding' with payment periods broadly matching the economic life of the asset. This applies particularly when assets will not generate income evenly, as a result of seasonal trade or delays in commencement of production. Lessors may also build into a lease some form of sharing arrangement with the lessee in relation to the residual value of the assets.

Then, there is certainty of access to credit where a lease is a medium-term facility. Unlike some forms of loan finance, which are repayable on demand, or subject to annual review, leasing finance cannot be withdrawn or curtailed in the event of a credit squeeze or a change in economic conditions. Except as a consequence of default by the lessee, the lessor cannot seek to accelerate the payment of lease rentals during the primary lease period.

Leasing can also have advantages in terms of pure availability of finance. It may on occasion be the only suitable form of external finance available to a company. Leasing facilities on fixed terms can be obtained at times when it may not be possible for a company to arrange a comparable loan for a five-year period, or longer either at a fixed interest rate or on any other terms.

Leasing gives fiscal efficiency for the lessee as well as the lessor. Lease rentals are fully deductible by the lessee for tax purposes. A lease may be structured to provide after-tax savings for both tax-paying and non-tax paying companies. The capital allowances that are currently available on the purchase of most types of plant and machinery are claimed by the lessor and the benefits of the resultant tax deferment are normally reflected in the calculation of the rentals. A competitively priced rental stream is attractive to those companies whose taxable profits are insufficient to obtain immediate and full benefit from the allowances to which they would be entitled if purchasing the equipment.

Short-term leasing can also be tax efficient for companies with taxable profits. By entering into a three-year lease the full rental may be offset against the lessee's profits over the period of the lease, rather than the lessee purchasing the equipment and claiming the allowances over a longer period.

Leasing may also help to preserve the lessee's debt capacity. Leasing facilities are freely available in the market, and as such can be used as additional sources of finance to those available from the lessee's bankers. Debt-raising capacity may thus remain available to meet working capital or other needs deriving from internal growth or acquisition. A lease is not a loan, and as such may not come under the type of borrowing restrictions that are sometimes found in a company's Articles of Association, debentures, bond or other loan agreements. A lessor's sole security is the asset financed and, from the lessee's standpoint, this may be preferable to the creation of a fixed or floating charge over held assets.

The principal attraction of leasing turns on its price competitiveness when compared with alternative sources of finance. The practice of competitive bidding for business by lessors tends to ensure that leasing transactions are keenly priced with fixed rate terms normally available for periods of up to seven years. When tax benefits are included in the calculations, leasing rates often provide significant cost advantages over traditional forms of borrowing.

Advantages to lessors

The way in which various types of companies have entered the UK leasing market as lessors is set out in Chapters 4, 5 and 7. A consistent feature of the attractions seen by lessors in recent years has been the ability to utilize capital allowances available on leased assets against their own taxable profits, whether derived from leasing or other activities.

Leasing may also provide financiers with the additional security or reward necessary to encourage them to offer asset financing facilities for new types of risk, such as the financing of communication satellites. Ownership of an asset may be preferable to a mortgage or charge, the enforcement of which may be difficult and the cost of registration, if available, high. In this respect leasing differs from most, though not all, forms of finance. A hire-purchase facility can, however, be used to give the financier the same type of security as with a lease; so in this respect leasing is not unique.

Financial institutions who offer traditional lending such as overdraft facilities, term loans and acceptance credit financing can enhance their service by offering leasing facilities, thus retaining customer loyalty. New customers attracted by the leasing company can be offered the full range of financial services offered by the lessor's financial sector parent.

For the lessor, margins achieved on leasing transactions can, through the use of fiscal benefits, be greater than those achieved on traditional forms of lending, especially where the leasing option is attractive to the lessee.

Furthermore, as leasing is an asset-based form of finance, additional security is required less often than with other forms of finance and the resulting administration costs can be reduced.

There are also certain specialized forms of leasing — notably sales-aid leasing (see Chapter 24) — where substantially higher margins can be achieved than in the leasing market generally. Where the lessee is offered a lease as part of the package for the supply of equipment, the effective cost of the leasing finance, as opposed to the capital cost of the equipment, may be a less sensitive factor in the overall transaction.

3. *Economic and industrial impact*

Leasing has come to play a major role in the overall UK economy, particularly in the financing of investment by British industry. Official statistics show that of the total fixed investment in UK manufacturing industry in 1986, assets leased from financial institutions alone — which do not account for the whole of the leasing industry — accounted for 11.4 per cent (*British Business*, 25 September 1987).

Total fixed investment, of course, includes investment in buildings — in which the leasing industry plays only a limited part — as well as in plant and machinery. The leasing industry's own statistics show that in 1990 leasing (without purchase option) of equipment, excluding buildings, accounted for 20.3 per cent of total UK investment in equipment, across all sectors of the economy (see Table 3.2 below). This equipment-leasing activity amounted to some 2.2 per cent of total gross domestic product (GDP), i.e. of all capital and current expenditure in all economic sectors.

Tables 3.1–3.4 show how UK leasing activity has grown over recent years. Table 3.1, column (a), gives the statistics produced by the ELA for new leasing business in each year from 1971 to 1990. In column (b) the adjustment of these figures by an indicator of inflation, which converts them to a constant price basis, gives the trend of business over the period in real terms.

The ELA statistics reflect the business written by members of the association in each year. The number of lessors in membership has varied from year to year but the major leasing companies were included throughout the period and the combined leasing business of all ELA member companies has always been estimated at close to 90 per cent of UK leasing business. The varying membership factor, therefore, does not give rise to any major distortion in the overall picture.

Table 3.2 shows the extent of leasing penetration, within the overall market for UK capital equipment financing over the 11 years to 1990.

In Table 3.2, ELA statistics for all leasing by member companies, excluding leasing of buildings, are expressed as a percentage of CSO figures for investment for all UK economic sectors in 'plant and machinery, vehicles, ships and aircraft' (from *UK National Accounts*, HMSO). The figures should be seen as approximations, since the ELA statistics include a small amount of leasing of second-hand equipment, while on the other hand they account for less than the whole of leasing business due to the membership factor. It is likely that these two factors broadly balance out.

9

Table 3.1 The trend of leasing business, 1971–1990

Year	New leasing business written by ELA members (£ million)	
	(a) *at current prices*[1]	(b) *at constant 1990 prices*[2]
1971	159	982
1972	130	744
1973	288	1,541
1974	321	1,493
1975	330	1,210
1976	421	1,341
1977	675	1,890
1978	1,214	3,049
1979	1,802	3,959
1980	2,359	4,330
1981	2,674	4,410
1982	2,834	4,342
1983	2,894	4,213
1984	4,012	5,581
1985	5,757	7,576
1986	5,182	6,589
1987	6,024	7,293
1988	7,836	8,882
1989	9,641	10,232
1990	10,314	10,314

1. From ELA statistics (excluding leases with purchase options.
2. Figures from column (a) adjusted to a cconstant price basis on the Central Statistical Office (CSO) 'implied GDP deflator'.

Sources: *ELA Annual Report* (various years); and *Economic Trends*, HMSO.

Tables 3.1 and 3.2, taken together, show the three distinct phases of growth in UK leasing — in the early 1970s, the late 1970s, and the mid–1980s (see Chapter 5). Tables 3.3 and 3.4, taken from the *ELA Annual Report 1991*, show the breakdown of member companies' leasing business in 1990, firstly by type of asset (in each case covering all economic sectors) and secondly by sector (covering all plant categories).

For the banking sector, the flow of funds to industrial and commercial companies through leasing represents a significant part of overall banking business. It can, therefore, be seen that leasing business being undertaken in the UK represents a major part of the overall economic activity.

Table 3.2 Leasing of equipment as percentage of all UK investment in equipment

Year	(a) Without purchase options (%)	(b) Total including purchase options (from 1988) %
1980	11.1	
1981	11.1	
1982	13.3	
1983	12.9	
1984	15.3	
1985	18.5	
1986	16.7	
1987	16.9	
1988	18.0	26.3
1989	20.0	28.6
1990	20.3	28.5

Source: *ELA Annual Report 1991*

Table 3.3 Leasing in 1990 by type of asset

	£m
Plant and machinery	3,317
Computer and office equipment	2,543
Oil exploration and extraction equipment	69
Cars	4,970
Commercial vehicles	1,563
Aircraft	355
Ships	268
Industrial and commercial buildings	854
Other	356
Total	14,295

Source: *ELA Annual Report 1991.*

Table 3.4 Leasing in 1990 by type of customer

Energy and water supply industries	636
Extraction of minerals other than fuel, manufacture of metals, mineral products and chemicals	301
Metal goods, enginering and vehicl industries	1,528
Other manufacturing industries	2,086
Construction	674
Banking, finance, insurance and business services and leasing for own use	2,205
Banking, finance, insurance and business services and leasing for on-leasing[1]	194
Distribution, hotels and catering	1,616
Transport and communication	2,067
Central and local government	1,004
Agriculture, forestry and fishing	44425
Other services	1,559
Total	14,295

1. On-leasing, where the identity of the lessee cannot be identified.

Source: ELA Annual Report 1991.

4. *The early history of leasing*

In one form or another, leasing has existed since the beginning of civilized society. The essential condition for a lease is commercial confidence in a system of law that can guarantee the lessor's entitlement to a rental income and the ultimate return of the assets held by the lessee.

It was not, however, until comparatively recently that equipment leasing as it is now known could come into being, for in early times there was relatively little capital equipment to supplement the use of human labour. The first recorded leases were therefore largely confined to agricultural land, cattle and, indeed, slaves. Records nevertheless exist, almost as old as the art of writing itself, from the ancient Sumerian kingdoms in what is now southern Iraq, from around the year 3000 BC, of ploughs and other agricultural implements, as well as land and oxen, being leased to farmers by templar authorities.[1] Private enterprise lessors first appear rather later, though in the same area, in Babylonian times at around 500 BC, where a banking house with the corporate name of Murashu is recorded as having leased agricultural land and oxen.[2]

A little later, in and around Athens at about 370 BC, there are extensive records of the leasing of silver mines, and — in the first recorded instance of an industrial property lease — that of a factory making shields in the port of Piraeus.[3]. Similar types of transactions are recorded later in the Roman Empire.

The first large-scale leases of movable equipment appear in the military field. The vessels used for the Norman invasion of England in 1066 were leased to William the Conquerer by Norman nobles from various places in continental Europe; and the first recorded equipment lease in Britain was of a suit of armour for use in the Seventh Crusade, in the year 1248.[4]

Large-scale commercial leasing first appeared in the maritime trades in the Baltic states. The leasing of merchant ships in the city of Stockholm was recorded in 1345.[5] In the same city in a later period, one of the earliest examples of the privatization of a state enterprise took the form of an industrial property lease. In 1694 King Charles XI of Sweden granted a 10-year lease of the royal shipyard in Stockholm, with all its equipment and buildings, to a group of merchants, having 'agreed and conceded that the use of the City's shipyard be granted to private persons, for in this way it is believed that the yard can be managed with greater zeal than would otherwise be the case'.[6]

The leasing of equipment in the British Isles, as in other countries, grew out of the leasing of land and buildings. The first statutory reference to equipment leasing came in the Statute of Wales in 1284, where it was declared that the legal action of covenant derived from land law was also available for leases of moveable property. By the Elizabethan era, both land and chattels were being leased as a way of secretly transferring property with the intention of defrauding creditors who had relied on the strength of the apparent ownership of the property. These devices were prohibited by the Fraudulent Conveyances Act of 1571, which provided that, except for leases that were bona fide and for good consideration, 'any conveyance, lease, rent . . . of land, tenements, hereditaments, goods and chattels . . . shall from henceforth be deemed to be clearly and utterly void'.

Matthew Bacon, in his treatise on leases published in 1798, noted that once the advantages of leasehold interests had been recognized, men found it desirable to extend this type of property 'to all sorts of interests and possessions whatsoever, being led thereto by that known rule that whatsoever may be granted or parted with for ever, may be granted or parted with for a time; and therefore not only lands and houses have been let for years, but also goods and chattels'.[7]

Equipment leasing in its modern form came about as a result of the industrial revolution after the mid-eighteenth century. Commercial companies were not permitted to trade with limited liability until 1855. Capital-intensive undertakings were therefore restricted to ownership by wealthy individuals, through sole proprietorships or in generally closely controlled companies with unlimited liability. No such business structure was in a strong enough position to capitalize a railway network, so that ownership and control of the first railways were divided between (a) the railway promoters, who developed the track and charged tolls for it use, (b) the original railway companies, who operated the trains with their own locomotives and passenger rolling stock, and (c) private colliery owners, who provided the coal wagons. As both the coal industry and the railways expanded in the early nineteenth century, a role quickly appeared for private investors to finance the construction of coal wagons to be leased to the coal owners for use on the railways.

When limited liability for the corporate sector was finally introduced, this type of leasing business was among the first commercial activities to be the subject of share subscriptions for public companies. One such instance was recorded in the prospectus for the Birmingham Wagon Company:

> By far the greater number of wagons used upon the railways by coal and other mineral proprietors, are leased for a fixed term of years, at rentals varying from £13 to £20 per annum, according to their capacity and cost of construction — the latter ranging from £65 to £110 each. Such wagons, being the property of private capitalists, and supplied by few individuals, have proved unequal to the demands; it is therefore considered by the promoters of this undertaking, that a legitimate field is open for a joint-stock company, and hence the 'Birmingham Wagon Company' is proposed to be formed.[8]

One of the earliest of these specialized wagon-leasing companies was the North Central Wagon Company of Rotherham, established in 1861, which eventually became part of Lombard North Central plc (see Chapter 7), the largest of the UK leasing companies today.

The railway companies and collieries were, of course, able to expand their capital base through the use of limited liability company status, and were thus better able to acquire rolling stock on their own account. The early wagon finance companies retained their economic role as asset-based financiers, but in the 1860s their facility was oriented much more towards hire purchase rather than leasing. Their own next major development was to be consumer hire purchase, with the mass-production of the motor car in the twentieth century, though with leasing and industrial hire purchase remaining very important throughout.

Over the 100 years up to 1960, a number of specific strands can be identified in the growth of equipment leasing in new directions. Some of these were to be permanent features, while others were of a more temporary nature. One significant development, which was not to prove durable, came towards the end of the nineteenth century in the shape of leasing as a restrictive trade practice, supported by what was then tight patent protection for producers of machinery who faced only limited competition. In some instances, machinery manufacturers made their products available solely on lease rather than for sale, in order to control the resale market.

The classic example of the use of leasing for this purpose in the UK involved boot- and shoe-manufacturing equipment, leased by the British United Shoe Manufacturing Company. By 1919, one research study showed that 80 per cent of shoe factories in Britain were tied by machinery-leasing agreements to one machinery firm in perpetuity.[9] An official committee of inquiry at the time reported on:

> . . . (the) ingenious and elaborate method of leasing shoe machinery, under which the user of any machine made by the company became restricted not merely as to the hire or purchase of similar machines but was also debarred for all practical purposes from purchasing any other machinery necessary for the purpose of his business from any firm other than the organisation in question.[10]

Other early, though less widespread, examples of leasing as a restrictive practice involved looms for the Lancashire cotton industry, telephone systems, electricity and gas meters, accounting machines and some types of vehicles.

Later examples of restrictive leasing involved attempts by manufacturers to monopolize products other than capital equipment, by controlling patented machinery used in manufacture. One instance of this was the Metal Box Company's practice, introduced in the 1930s, of making available on lease only, at excessive rates, machinery used in the manufacture of cans, to prevent other companies from competing effectively in that market. Another, which became important for a period after the Second World War, was the attempt by the British Oxygen Company to manipulate the industrial gases market by controlling the leasing of machinery.

However, this type of use — or abuse — of leasing has effectively been eliminated since the 1950s, as a result of: (a) some diminution in the extent of patent protection in most industrial sectors; (b) the operation of legislation against monopolies and restrictive trade practices; and, not least important (c) international moves towards freer trade in industrial products and the much stronger international competitive challenge to the UK manufacturing sector, both in capital goods and in the 'downstream' product markets.

Another important historical development, of limited duration in most market sectors, was the adaptation of leasing to the consumer sector, initially as a means of avoiding legislative restrictions applied to consumer hire-purchase. This first appeared after the move to protect consumers from onerous hire-purchase terms in the Hire Purchase Act 1938. It received a fresh impetus with the application of statutory price controls to hire-purchase agreements in the Second World War; and again with the use of hire-purchase controls for monetary policy reasons from 1952 onwards. Leasing to consumers survived permanently to a large extent only in the television rental market, though it has, of course, now been extended in the associated area of home video equipment.

Tax-based leasing started in a very small way in the 1920s. Lessors, like commercial enterprises using their own equipment, had been entitled to depreciation allowances on machinery since these were first introduced in 1878. However, until the First World War, tax rates on corporate profits and personal incomes were sufficiently low for taxation considerations not to be a major factor in commercial decisions generally. Moreover, even after much higher tax rates were introduced in later periods, tax factors could not provide leasing with a clear advantage, compared with alternative forms of finance, until the phenomenon of 'tax exhaustion' on the part of potential commercial lessees began to manifest itself in the 1970s (see Chapter 5).

In terms of corporate structure, leasing until the late 1950s remained in the hands of specialized asset-based finance companies, which, with the rapid advance of living standards and consumer spending in the post-war period had, for the time being, become much stronger in the consumer hire-purchase field than in any other form of industrial finance. However, the transfer of the larger of such companies into the clearing bank sector in the late 1960s and early 1970s through corporate takeovers, changed the pattern (see Chapter 7) and the industrial finance sector progressed rapidly.

NOTES

1. Livijn, C.-O., *Studies in Financial History*, Saljfinans AB, Stockholm, 1971.
2. Ibid.
3. Ibid.
4. *Documents Inédits sur le Commerce de Marseille au Moyen Age*, Marseille, 1884.
5. Livijn, C.-O., *Studies in Financial History*, Saljfinans AB, Stockholm, 1971.
6. Ibid.
7. Bacon, M., *A Treatise on Leases and Terms for Years*, London, 1798.
8. *The Railway Times* and *The Mining Journal*, August 1854.
9. 'A study of trade organisations and combinations in the United Kingdom', annexed to the *Report of the Committee on Trusts*, Cmd 9236, 1919.
10. *Report of the Committee on Trusts* (see note 5).

5. *The last 25 years*

The UK leasing industry began to evolve into its present form in the early 1960s. The type of facilities involved included both medium- to large-ticket business and sales aid programmes marketed through manufacturers and dealers, particularly in office equipment. However, a common feature at that time was leasing to highly credit-worthy companies, who would not normally have considered the alternative of hire purchase. Typical lease structures in those days involved either no initial payments or only one quarterly rental payable in advance. Leasing was sold to lessees as offering clear advantages in terms of simplifying budgeting, improving liquidity and freeing working capital.

The first UK leasing company of the modern type was Mercantile Leasing Company, incorporated in June 1960 as a joint subsidiary of the Mercantile Credit finance house, which held 80 per cent of the shares, and United States Leasing (see Chapter 25) with 20 per cent. Other early participants in the market as lessors included a variety of companies with established business in asset-based or corporate finance, sometimes with other partners as minority shareholders. These included Astley Industrial Trust (which was eventually to be taken over by Mercantile Credit in 1970) and the merchant bank Hambros.

Computer leasing was one of the major growth areas of the middle and late 1960s. In the 1963–64 period the two major British mainframe computer manufacturers (which were later to become constituent parts of International Computers Ltd) each set up leasing subsidiaries, in one case as a joint venture with three finance houses. Towards the end of the 1960s, a number of American leasing companies began to move into the UK computer-leasing market. The initial computer leases consisted mainly of two-year operating leases, based on minimizing the user's exposure to the risks of obsolescence. However, finance leases for periods as long as five to seven years also began to become important in this field.

Though still on a very small scale in relation to the overall UK economy, leasing activity grew strongly throughout the 1960s. It has been estimated that the total book value of equipment held on lease by UK finance houses and accepting houses (i.e. merchant banks) rose from £56 million at the end of 1965 to £165 million at the end of 1969.[1]

In this period, the regulatory framework was broadly neutral as between leasing and alternative forms of finance. On the fiscal side capital allowances for plant and machinery investment were relatively favourable prior to 1966, but since both potential lessees and lessors were in a tax-paying position, the allowances had little impact on the decision to 'lease or buy'. The introduction of investment grants in 1966, replacing some of the more favourable elements in capital allowances in the preceding period, at first gave rise to some uncertainty where leasing was concerned. However, this was largely resolved by a Board of Trade ruling that lessors would be entitled to receive grants in respect of leased assets, where a lease was for a minimum three-year period and the standard grant conditions were met.

The impact of credit controls

Of more importance at the time was the impact of governmental controls on credit upon the funding of leasing, both by the clearing banks and the specialist finance houses. Between 1965 and 1971 the Bank of England laid down quantitative restrictions on the level of bank lending. The finance houses were also covered by the controls, but in addition faced direct restrictions on their hire-purchase business in the consumer sector through the imposition of 'terms controls' providing for minimum down payments and maximum repayment periods for specified types of business.

This package of credit controls affected leasing in a variety of ways as a consequence of the structure of the industry at the time. The major lessors were either finance houses, offering a range of specialized asset-based finance facilities to both the consumer and corporate sectors, but within which consumer hire purchase still tended to predominate, or banks which offered leasing as part of a range of corporate finance facilities, often through separate leasing companies as wholly owned subsidiaries. Most of the major finance houses had not yet been wholly owned by the clearing banks, though the latter had taken minority stakes in many of them in an earlier period of rapid consumer credit growth in the late 1950s, and the clearers were now largely funding the finance houses' activities. The 1965 controls on lending affected both the funding of clearing banks and of finance houses to their leasing company subsidiaries, and thus restricted the funding of the major UK lessors, though in a few cases — such as Hambros Bank where the leasing business was undertaken within the bank rather than through a subsidiary company — the leasing activity escaped the controls. For the finance houses, the controls on consumer hire purchase business meant that their financing of leasing and other corporate sector credit could be maintained in spite of the finance houses' funding from the banks being caught by the controls on bank lending.

The authorities eventually accepted that, although it had never been intended to exclude leasing from the general scope of controls on credit, the impact on leasing was nevertheless operating in a quite arbitrary fashion, depending on the corporate structures involved. In 1969 the Bank of England agreed to accept arrangements — which had to be negotiated individually between itself and each banking institution — in which banks and finance houses could extend a certain amount of lending to subsidiary or associated companies in the leasing business, outside their ceilings on overall lending. This concession gave a stimulus to the establishment of new leasing companies as joint subsidiaries of banking and non-banking parent company groups.

In 1971 the system of credit controls first introduced in 1965 gave way to a new form of indirect regulation of credit, in which all banking institutions (clearing banks, merchant banks and finance houses) were to be governed by ratios of 'reserve assets' to 'eligible liabilities' which were designed to limit the overall growth of credit without constraining free competition for business between the banking groups and without arbitrary distortions between different types of lending. Though there was a return to a more active policy of credit control through the 'corset' restrictions on bank lending in the 1973–80 period, the authorities' credit control policy did not again impinge on the size and structure of the leasing industry in such a direct manner as in the 1960s.

The new credit control regime removed the need for some of the earlier special arrangements in the structure of leasing companies linked to the banking sector. In 1972, Barclays, Williams & Glyns and Royal Bank of Scotland set up their own wholly owned subsidiaries to provide leasing finance for the full range of capital equipment items, with the emphasis on large-ticket business but also making use of their parent banks' branch networks to attract a variety of small- to medium-sized leasing transactions. These developments, combined with the already existing clearing bank holdings in finance houses and a further round of such acquisitions in the 1970s (see Chapter 7), set the scene for the developing structure of the leasing industry up to the present time, with the largest leasing companies falling within the clearing bank sector.

The tax factor

The growth of leasing finance throughout the 1970s was stimulated by some critical factors that have now become rather less important. The first and most important of these was the corporate tax system which operated throughout the 1972–84 period, with 100 per cent first-year allowances (FYAs) for plant and machinery investment.

The new system of capital allowances (first announced in October 1970 and fully effective from March 1972) replaced the earlier system of investment grants. It meant that all businesses purchasing equipment in the general category of 'plant and machinery' could charge the full cost of the assets against their taxable income in the year of acquisition, however long the actual or expected life of the plant might be. This included leasing companies acquiring equipment for use in the trade of leasing, as well as other companies acquiring plant for their own use. The system was thus ostensibly neutral as between leasing and other forms of finance. In practice, however, 100 per cent FYAs greatly favoured the development of leasing by financial sector companies, since for a variety of reasons industrial and commercial companies (ICCs) lacked the taxable capacity (i.e. the availability of sufficient taxable income against which allowances could be utilized) that existed in the banking sector.

The most important factor here was a distinctly depressed level of profitability among UK non-financial companies in the 1970s. This resulted from a general weakening of the British industrial performance in the face of growing competitive pressure from established and newly emerging industrial countries overseas, combined with the effect of the worldwide economic recession in the mid-1970s following the disturbance caused by the first OPEC oil price increase of 1973. It has been estimated that the real rate of return on capital — defined as pre-tax profits net of stock appreciation and capital consumption — for ICCs fell from 12 per cent in 1964 to around 9 per cent in the 1970–73 period, and then to 4 per cent in 1975; and that if the North Sea oil sector is excluded, this real rate of return fell to only 3 per cent in the depth of the next UK recession in 1981.[2]

The factor, coupled with the accelerated tax write-down of plant from 1972 and the advent in 1974 of corporation tax stock relief (which removed a previous feature of the tax system where the then very high inflation rate was producing increased taxable profits from stock appreciation), removed many of the ICCs — as potential lessees — from liability for 'mainstream' corporation tax (i.e. tax on profits exceeding the advance corporation tax payable on dividends). Indeed, it has been officially estimated that by 1984 the ICC sector was carrying forward cumulative tax losses totalling as much as £25,000 million.[3]

This fiscal and economic environment was uniquely favourable to the development of finance leasing. The banking sector had not been affected by all the factors that had eroded the profitability of ICCs and it was not itself a major user of plant and machinery qualifying for 100 per cent FYAs. It thus had the taxable capacity that the ICCs lacked. Leasing offered a way for the ICCs to obtain the benefit of tax allowances through lessors, as owners of the plant, setting the FYAs against their own taxable income, where ICCs purchasing the equipment would merely have built up unusable tax losses. As a result of competitive conditions in the leasing market, the benefit of accelerated tax depreciation was largely passed on by lessors to lessees through reduced lease rentals.

Part of the rationale for replacing investment grants with increased capital allowances had been to concentrate incentives on profitable companies, making productive use of their plant. The authorities, nevertheless, appeared to be prepared to accept that investment incentives could effectively be made available to less profitable industrial companies through leasing.

In addition to the 100 per cent FYAs factor, another feature of the tax system — which has itself outlived FYAs but which increased their impact while they lasted — also favoured leasing. This was the use of timing advantages under corporation tax group relief. Financial sector group companies found that, by maintaining a corporate structure in which individual subsidiaries had a variety of accounting years ending at different dates within the calendar year, equipment newly leased could be purchased by a group company with its accounting year about to end, thus accelerating the date when the benefit of capital allowances would be obtained. The lessee company, even if it had sufficient taxable capacity to absorb the allowances, might have a much later year-end, resulting in additional delay before receiving the benefit of capital allowances on the equipment if it were purchased. Even if the lessee company was itself part of a complex corporate group, the tax system would not give it discretion to assign the plant to a company other than the one making use of it; whereas the lessor, being in the trade of leasing, could arrange the purchase of leased assets by any one of a number of leasing companies in its own group. During the 1970s, when the inflation rate at one time exceeded 20 per cent and bank borrowing rates were often around 15 per cent, the timing advantage of accelerating the benefit of capital allowances by a period of some months was appreciable.

In this era of 'tax-based leasing' the volume of business grew very rapidly, but on a rather uneven pattern, which can be attributed to identifiable factors coming into effect at different times. The major jumps in the real volume of leasing business came in the year 1973, and over the 1976–80 period. The first year or so of 100 per cent FYAs coincided with the introduction of another change in the corporation tax system which, by itself, served to inhibit new leasing business. The switch from the 'classical' to the 'imputation' system of corporation tax, which was announced in March 1971 and became fully effective from April 1973, involved an increase from 40 to 50 per cent in the rate of corporation tax, balanced by the removal of the effective double taxation of dividend payments under the previous system. This meant that lessors writing new business in the 1971–72 period, while claiming capital allowances largely at the 40 per cent tax rate, could face a tax burden at 50 per cent on the lease rental income in later years. It had the effect of delaying until 1973 the first major increase in leasing activity in response to 100 per cent FYAs.

In the 1975–79 period, car-leasing business was stimulated by an interpretation of the availability of capital allowances which, while it continued, distinctly favoured the leasing option. In general, business cars had been excluded from the 100 per cent FYAs extended to the general category of plant and machinery in 1972. Cars used for short-term rental were, however, recognized as plant used in the trade of car hire, and attracted FYAs. Following a decision of the Special Commissioners in 1975, lessors were able to take advantage of the same treatment as the car rental trade with 100 per cent FYAs available as compared with writing-down allowances at the 25 per cent 'reducing balance' rate where business cars were purchased by the companies using them. The Inland Revenue did not take this case to appeal at the time but it was eventually overtaken by new legislation in the Finance Act 1979. In the interim period, the level of car-leasing business had mounted to a very high peak. It, also, received a more lasting benefit from the ending in 1977 of the former credit controls applying to business car leasing, which had laid down a minimum advance payment equivalent to 42 weeks' rental.

By around 1980 the level of total leasing activity appeared to reach a plateau, with the real volume of new business remaining broadly constant over the three years to 1983. By that time, even some of the financial sector lessors were running close to the position of 'tax exhaustion' (i.e. the full utilization of taxable capacity against FYAs and other reliefs and allowances) which, when it had earlier been reached by potential lessees, had first persuaded many of them to decide in favour of the leasing option. For example, in 1980 the 'Big Four' English clearing banks, largely because of capital allowances available on leasing undertaken within their groups, incurred a combined mainstream corporation tax liability of only £66 million, compared with total pre-tax profits for the year of £1,456 million.[4]

Off-balance sheet finance

The second major perceived advantage of leasing in the period up to the mid-1980s, apart from tax factors, was its attraction to lessees as a form of 'off-balance sheet' finance. By leasing, instead of purchasing, a lessee company could keep the assets concerned off its balance sheet — and thus out of the reckoning in its apparent capital financing commitments — even though it could in reality have been as much committed to meeting rental payments and maintenance costs as it might have been with the corresponding costs in the case of its own assets funded from net borrowings, which would appear as balance sheet liabilities. The leasing option could thus help such a company in its access to credit lines and, particularly in the case of publicly quoted companies, in some of its key financial performance indicators such as return on capital employed.

Throughout the 1960s and 1970s, the awareness of this off-balance sheet aspect of leasing grew steadily among the financial directors of industrial and commercial companies, and was actively promoted by some leasing companies. Some concern began to grow within the accountancy profession, and among media financial commentators and analysts in the equity markets, about the off-balance sheet leasing commitments of some major lessee companies. (The collapse in 1974 of the Court Line tour operator and airline group, whose published accounts at the time gave no information on the group's non-cancellable leasing obligations in respect of aircraft and ancillary equipment costing £40 million, was an extreme example of 'off-balance sheet' financing.)

Eventually the UK accountancy profession, following precedents established in the USA, proposed new rules for the preparation of public company accounts, designed to address what they considered to be off-balance sheet distortions arising from leasing arrangements. The Accounting Standards Committee (ASC), representing the four major UK bodies of professional accountants, proposed that certain leased assets be capitalized as part of the assets of lessee companies, appearing in their balance sheets just as if they had belonged to the company as its own assets.

Lessors, as represented by the ELA, resisted the concept of lessee capitalization, on the grounds that leased assets were the property of lessors rather than lessees. Lessors maintained that it was misleading for lessees to have assets in their balance sheets to which they did not have, nor indeed would ever have, legal title. The correct place of record, it was felt, was the notes to the accounts. After discussions lasting some years between the ELA and other interested bodies, the ASC finalized its Statement of Standard Accounting Practice (SSAP) No. 21, for leasing and hire-purchase contracts. SSAP 21, which is dealt with in greater detail in Chapter 15, requires assets leased by means of a finance lease to be capitalized, while those the subject of operating leases remain off-balance sheet — with a finance lease being defined for this purpose as one where the lessor will recover at least 90 per cent of his or her own costs from the discounted value of future rental income from the primary lease period, rather than from that of the residual value of the leased equipment accruing to the lessor at the end of that period.

SSAP 21 was published in 1984, and its lessee accounting requirements came into effect for accounting years commencing on or after 1 July 1987. In September 1987, the Institute of Chartered Accountants in England and Wales issued a 'technical release' for the guidance of lessees' external auditors, drawing attention to the fact that the 90 per cent rule in SSAP 21 is not a strict mathematical rule and that some discretion is left to auditors in taking a 'true and fair view' of a leasing contract. It is, however, clear that for full payout finance leasing, the off-balance sheet attraction of the leasing option no longer applies. The major effect of SSAP 21 has been to encourage the use of operating leases, where the lessees' commitments remain off-balance sheet, within the total quantity of leasing business.

Evolution to the present day

With the enactment of the 1984 corporate tax changes, and to some extent the adoption of SSAP 21, two of the major factors which boosted the growth of leasing in the 1970s have wholly or partly ceased to exist. Yet in many respects the present shape and structure of the leasing industry, and of the facilities it offers to customers, as it evolved in the 1970s, remain just as relevant today in spite of the changes.

The 1970s saw a number of commercial innovations in leasing, such as flexible rental structures designed to tailor the pattern of the lessee's rental payments to that of income over the leased period; new termination options; and variation clauses to allow for fluctuations in the lessor's interest costs and changes in tax rates affecting the lessor's rate of return, during the life of the lease. The interest variation clauses came about as a result of the sharp fluctuations in market rates of interest in the 1970s which — particularly in the case of longer term leases — would have left lessors highly exposed to any increased funding costs where assets had been leased at fixed rates. With the finer margins on leasing business since 1984, variation clauses — both for interest rates and for tax rates — are seen by lessors as important protection, even when the financial market conditions are more settled. Interest rate variation clauses are now the general rule in leases for periods of more than five years. These have proved acceptable to lessees, since their adoption coincided with general moves towards floating rather than fixed rates in bank lending to the corporate sector — for precisely the same reason as to uncertainty in respect of the banks' future funding costs.

Since the mid-1970s leasing has clearly established a major role in capital financing for British industry and commerce, which it has subsequently retained. It has carved out particular niches in certain types of plant that lend themselves especially to the leasing option. The company car fleet market has remained a very important area of leasing activity, within which fleet users now have a choice of a range of options from long-term finance leases to short-term contract hire (see Chapter 24). In the aircraft and computer sectors specialist leasing companies, by building up their own expertise on residual values in second-hand markets, have been able to develop the operating lease as a critically important source of finance for new equipment. However, finance leasing has at the same time played a major part in relation to general industrial plant. In one of the largest privately funded capital projects ever undertaken in the UK — the

Essochem Olefins petrochemical plant at Mossmorran in Fife, which came on stream in October 1985 — £400 million of plant and buildings was leased by a consortium of five leasing companies.

The early 1980s saw a brief but interesting development in the phenomenon of the 'corporate lessor' where for a time profitable companies outside the financial sector moved into the finance-leasing market as general lessors of plant in which they had no interest as suppliers, with a view to absorbing spare taxable capacity.

The major changes in the corporate tax system in 1984–86 are described in some detail in Chapter 6. At the time of their announcement in 1984, the combination of reduced tax rates and reduced capital allowances was generally seen as posing problems for the long-term future of leasing, since it was felt that a key element of the existing system that had favoured leasing had been removed. One of its direct effects was to crystallize tax liabilities of lessors which could otherwise have been deferred through the accumulation of FYAs on new leasing business.

However, the initial impact of the tax changes on the value of leasing business was positive and leasing rates became highly competitive compared with other types of finance. In 1985 in particular, an increased volume of business — as shown by Table 3.1 on page 10 — was achieved, albeit at substantially reduced lessors' margins. Table 5.1, which compares leasing rates with the general level of market interest rates, as exemplified by the clearing banks' base lending rates, shows the position over a 10-year period before, during and after the phased changes in corporate taxation.

Table 5.1 Annual average leasing rates and bank base rates, 1982–1991

Year	Average leasing rates[1] %	Average bank base rate %
1982	8.5	11.9
1983	8.0	9.8
1984	4.9	9.7
1985	8.4	12.2
1986	10.5	10.9
1987	10.6	9.7
1988	11.4	10.0
1989	13.4	13.8
1990	14.3	14.8
1991	12.2	11.7

1. Rates quoted for plant and machinery on five-year leases with rent payable quarterly.

Source: Saturn Lease Underwriting Ltd; Quadrex Securities Ltd; Integrated Computer Systems and Cybernetics Ltd; National Leasing & Finance Co; Financial Statistics, HMSO.

The sharp drop in leasing rates in 1984 accounts for the strong increase that year in leasing business. Yet perhaps the most striking development is the continuing high level of leasing business since April 1986, when the new tax system was finally in place. In the fiscal year 1986/87, with writing-down allowances at the 25 per cent rate, the total of new leasing business written by ELA member companies, at £5,063 million, was 66 per cent higher in cash terms than in 1983/84 when 100 per cent FYAs were available. Allowing for inflation over the three-year period, the increase in real terms was still over 40 per cent.

The leasing of computer equipment to financial sector lessees was a major growth area in 1986, connected with the 'Big Bang' developments in the institutional structure of securities trading in October of that year. The available statistics for 1990 (see Chapter 3) indicate a continuing strong trend of business.

A pointer to the future is the rapid growth of the operating lease in the aircraft, computer and vehicles sectors. The ELA's own statistics, based on a restricted definition of the operating lease, indicate that operating lease business increased from £73 million in 1985 to £270 million in 1986. Operating leases generally are clearly a major growth area, where leasing companies are now able to offer their customers a service based on expertise about equipment as well as finance, to provide an attractive financing package for equipment subject to high risks of obsolescence.

While it is clear that the 1972–84 tax regime, together with off-balance sheet financing prior to SSAP 21, had critical catalytic effects in transforming the role of the leasing industry, that role has continued to be maintained in the absence of those factors. The major leasing company groups, having built up the leasing facility as a specialized area of financial services, now find that there is a major market for it in the absence of previously favourable external factors. While before 1984 the scale of leasing activity appeared to be constrained by the 'supply side' factor of taxable capacity, in the post-1986 environment it is responding more clearly to the demands of the marketplace. Given a continuation of a broadly neutral fiscal framework, which neither greatly encourages nor inhibits leasing compared with other financing options, the leasing industry appears poised for a future, in which the level of activity will be limited only by the total of fixed investment in UK industry and commerce — which in its turn depends on a sound economic performance by the UK as an industrial country.

NOTES AND REFERENCES
1. Derived from *Board of Trade Journal* and various finance house sources.
2. *Bank of England Quarterly Bulletin*, August 1987.
3. Parliamentary Written Answers, 30 March 1984, Hansard col.
4. Times, 4 March 1982.

6. *The current outlook*

The Finance Act 1984 made sweeping changes to the level of capital allowances and to the rates of corporation tax. First-year allowances in respect of plant and machinery were phased out on the following basis:

Expenditure between 13 March 1984 and 1 April 1985 — 75 per cent
Between 1 April 1985 and 1 April 1986 — 50 per cent
From 1 April 1986 — nil

First-year allowances were replaced by annual writing-down allowances of 25 per cent, calculated on the reducing balance method.

The other major change was to the rate of corporation tax. From a rate of 52 per cent the rates were reduced as follows:

Year 1983 — 50 per cent
Year 1984 — 45 per cent
Year 1985 — 40 per cent
Year 1986 — 35 per cent

Transition to the new tax system

The period between March 1984 and April 1987 was extremely active for the leasing industry which found itself able to offer rates reflecting a most unusual set of circumstances. Although FYAs were being progressively eroded, the opportunity to absorb these allowances at a high corporate tax rate and to pay at a much lower rate on the resultant rental income produced extremely low rental charges.

With expert tax planning, coupled with precise timing of purchases of new equipment, it was possible to offer leases that had a negative effective interest rate. The results were predictable: not only did industry in general take advantage of the opportunity and increase its capital expenditure, in many cases bringing forward planned projects, but the leasing industry enjoyed a boom period.

The other major impact for the leasing industry was the effect of the new rates of corporation tax on existing leases.

Since the early 1970s most middle market and large-ticket leases have contained tax clauses. These clauses were drafted to enable the lessor to change the level of rental to reflect any alteration in the level or nature of tax in order to preserve a constant rate of return. Therefore, a major reduction in the rate of corporation tax, phased over a known period, allowed lessors to make rental rebates to their customers. Most reputable lessors made a major effort to ensure that their customers derived the full benefit of the changed regime, although there were a number of different methods used for redistribution of the excess rentals.

Many lessors recalculated the rental stream using the new tax assumptions and either reduced future rentals due or gave a one-off rebate. Some, who were not totally assured of the declared future tax rates, gave a rebate only at the expiry of the contract. The result of this was that leasing companies made rebates of rental to their customers of many millions of pounds.

At the time of these tax changes a small number of lessors, mainly the leasing subsidiaries of the large UK clearing banks, or in some cases the banks themselves, were found to be lacking in respect of their tax equalization reserves. These banking groups had seen an opportunity to continue sheltering their group profits with the 100 per cent FYAs available to their leasing subsidiaries. Anticipating the continuance of FYAs and also having a considerable need for capital, they took the opportunity of substantially eliminating their tax equalization reserves by moving the surplus into 'general reserves' where it would be treated as shareholders' funds.

The tax equalization reserve is the recognition by lessors of the substantial timing differences that arise in the flow of taxable income and the claiming of allowances. Basically, the 100 per cent FYA sheltered immediate profits, but the need to provide for tax on future rental income was important. The major lessors who decided to ignore this precept and anticipated the continuance of their leasing companies' ability to shelter tax, found the decision reacted adversely on them. The four UK clearing banks between them had to make special provisions of over £1.7 billion for deferred taxation from general reserves.

Leasing in the new environment

The leasing industry has always had a reputation for ingenuity and flexibility in addition to an aggressive approach to selling their products. Knowledge of applying after-tax cash-flow mathematics to asset-financing arrangements is the lifeblood of the industry.

The 1984 changes were greeted with an understandable reaction based upon an instinctive feeling in the industry that capital allowance incentives had made a central contribution to the continued expansion of the UK's capital investment base.

The industry, in the form of the ELA, commissioned a report from the University of Bath to see what manufacturing industry thought of the new allowance structure. This report did not indicate any strong reaction against the new tax structure but rather a desire to await the outcome of the new measures.

Two major reactions from within the established leasing industry emerged very quickly. Firstly, the margins on new business fell rapidly to nearer those being charged for similar banking loans, indicating that a premium was no longer being charged for the use of tax capacity. Secondly, a large number of lessors became interested in the small-ticket market, many new companies were formed and the competition in this sector has become acute.

It is clear that the leasing industry survives in two main parts. Small unit leasing, which is not tax sensitive, is sold on the grounds of an easily understood and flexible alternative to other forms of finance. Rentals are usually fixed for rate and for tax and through the medium of 'sales aid finance' are frequently quoted by the equipment supplier. It is difficult to envisage any alteration to the corporate tax system that could disturb this type of business, which thrives in almost all corporate tax environments throughout the industrialized world.

The other part of the industry, however, remains tax-sensitive. The middle- to large-ticket leasing industry in the UK continues to thrive by recognizing that advantageous borrowing rates can be provided to customers owing to the fact that the incidence of tax may not be identical for the two parties to a transaction. It is this tax timing asymmetric effect on transactions which enables lessors to continue to produce effective rates at levels below alternative borrowing costs.

Rather than becoming less important, the effects of tax on a lease structure have become in some ways more important than during the years to 1984. Pre-1984, the major customer category for lessors was the 'tax loss' or 'tax exhausted' company. The reason was that such a company could not obtain any current value from the 100 per cent tax allowance available whereas a company paying tax on current profits could; and the banks, which were in the latter category, had large amounts of taxable profits with which to absorb the allowances.

In the current environment of 25 per cent annual allowances, which means that it takes upwards of eight years to recover the major portion of expenditure, companies who are tax payers also find the tax deductibility of rentals over a short lease period attractive. This new group of tax-paying lessees has meant that the customer base for leasing has widened.

Lessor groups have built up considerable expertise and flexibility in the management of their tax affairs and clearly this development will continue.

As shown in Table 3.1 (see page 10), UK leasing business, having dipped in 1986 at the end of the transitional period of the tax changes, subsequently resumed a strong upward path.

At the time of writing, the acute economic recession which commenced in the UK in the second half of 1990 is having adverse effects on leasing business with forecasts of an annual reduction in 1991 of up to 14 per cent in the volume of fixed investment in manufacturing industry. The number of insolvencies among small firms, and some larger industrial and commercial companies, has risen sharply during the recession and, as a result, banks have had to make major provisions for UK bad debts, and to be particularly cautious about their exposures on new business. This will have its effects on the volume of leasing business, as on bank lending generally. In this context, it is interesting to note the following extract from an article on The Leasing Industry which appeared in the *Bank of England Quarterly Bulletin* in February 1991:

> A number of factors should underpin new leasing business . . . Leasing may, in the current climate, become an increasingly attractive way to acquire the services of capital. Cash flow constraints on investment may be eased by using leasing. Moreover, leasing may involve less risk, both to the lessee and the lessor/lender, than debt finance at a time when companies are already highly geared. Finally, lower profits in the industrial sector are likely to raise the number of tax-exhausted companies, thereby increasing the demand for leased assets. This could, however, be offset by a contraction in the funds available if lessors themselves come under financial pressure.

One significant development that has been positive for leasing has been the privatization of major public utilities which, while in the nationalized sector, were constrained by Treasury rules on capital expenditure that inhibited leasing. Now that these undertakings are in the private sector, they are free to appraise leasing propositions in the same way as other potential corporate sector lessees. The electricity and water supply industries in particular, being highly capital-intensive, have been a major source of new leasing business in 1990–91 and are expected to continue to be so in the future.

Though the structure of leasing has evolved in response to changes in taxation and the regulatory environment, the pre–1984 tax system appears to have had a catalytic effect, initially creating a largely tax-based leasing industry that can now survive on the inherent commercial attractions of the leasing option.

7. *The structure of the industry*

Leasing companies in the UK comprise a variety of types of enterprise. Most of them, particularly the larger ones, are within the financial sector of the economy, being subsidiaries of banks or other financial institutions, whether UK or foreign owned. Some others, however, are within industrial company groups, the leasing function having developed as an extension of the parent company's sales function. Others again are unconnected with financial groups or with the suppliers of the equipment they lease, being independent specialist leasing companies or members of 'conglomerate' holding companies spanning a range of industrial activities.

The clearing banks

The various UK clearing banks — i.e. major commercial banking groups that provide cheque-clearing facilities and whose operations are central to the banking system — account for around two-thirds of all ELA members' leasing business, in their own corporate groups. The location of the leasing activities within these groups varies, but in most cases a finance house subsidiary of the clearing bank plays an important part.

The term 'finance house' in this context denotes a company concerned with asset-based finance of a variety of types. The major finance houses within some clearing bank groups offer all types of leasing facilities — finance and operating leases, and vehicle contract hire — but also hire purchase and a variety of consumer-lending facilities. The latter include hire purchase for cars and household goods, and other types of consumer credit facility that are not asset-based, such as credit cards and revolving loans.

The Midland Bank (through Forward Trust Group Ltd), and some of the smaller UK clearing banks, channel virtually all their equipment-leasing business through their finance house subsidiaries. Though the finance houses may have complex corporate structures, in most cases the leasing business written by all companies within the group is managed by the finance house subsidiary of the bank.

The Barclays Bank group moved away from this type of structure in 1991, disposing of most of the consumer credit and retail motor finance activities previously combined with leasing in the Mercantile Credit finance house. All this bank's leasing business is channelled through its specialized corporate finance arm Barclays Mercantile Business Services Ltd.

Other clearing banks each have more than one subsidiary company actively involved in leasing, with the finance house undertaking a range of small- to medium-sized leasing transactions, along with its consumer credit activities, while a separate subsidiary of the bank writes large-ticket leases. This is the structure in the case of Lloyds Bank, National Westminster Bank, Royal Bank of Scotland, Bank of Scotland, and the Trustee Savings Bank group.

Other lessors in the clearing bank sector include Yorkshire Bank and Investors in Industry (3i). The latter institution is jointly owned by several UK clearing banks, and operates as a specialist vehicle to provide finance for medium-sized industrial and commercial companies, in which leasing plays a part.

Each of the main clearing banks undertakes a range of different types of leasing activity, reflecting the major volume of their overall business. Nearly all are involved in vehicle contract hire and in large-ticket finance leases. A few are also involved in small-ticket leasing, and all of them in the middle sector of the leasing market, with individual transactions around the range of £100,000 to £1 million. Some are also major participants in specialized sectors of operating leases, such as aircraft. A large number of leasing transactions come from the contacts of branch-based marketing staff — either of the banks or of the finance houses — with client businesses.

Other participants in the market

The next significant category of lessors is among the merchant banks or accepting houses. These institutions offer leasing facilities as part of their specialized role in providing banking credit to corporate sector clients. Together, they cover the full range of point-of-sale leasing activities, with the emphasis on motor vehicles and the large-ticket sector — though individually there is a degree of specialization. One merchant bank in particular, Schroders, specializes in the small-ticket leasing sector. Kleinwort Benson, Lazards, Hambros, and Hill Samuel are involved in medium- to large-ticket leasing; while others, such as Warburgs and Morgan Grenfell, are in both the small- and the large-ticket sectors.

Foreign banks, through their UK subsidiaries, are now a major force in the British leasing market. They tend to lease mainly to the most credit-worthy lessees, whose names are known world wide. In 1987, a total of 12 banks based outside the British Isles — with parent companies located in a variety of countries including the USA, Japan, France, Scandinavia, and Saudi Arabia — were members of the ELA, on the strength of their involvement in leasing to UK-based customers. In addition, two specialist non-bank international leasing companies — United States Leasing and Orient Leasing of Japan — also have UK subsidiaries who are members of the ELA.

Other types of banking lessor are represented by Standard Chartered Bank, and Abbey National Leasing Services. Standard Chartered is a British-owned international bank without major UK retail banking interests, but which undertakes leasing in the UK, through separate subsidiaries in Standard Chartered Merchant Bank and the Chartered Trust finance house. Abbey National was one of the largest UK building societies and entered the large-ticket leasing market when it became a quoted company following its change of status to a bank.

A significant category of lessors outside the banking system are the computer specialists. These companies are involved principally in the supply of computer equipment, particularly of mainframe computers manufactured by IBM, but moved into writing leases on their own account on the strength of their expertise in second-hand market values of this equipment, which enables them to take an interest in residual values of computer equipment leased to their customers. These companies include Dataserv Limited, a subsidiary of Bellsouth Corporation of the USA, and IBM UK Financial Services, which is wholly owned by the manufacturer.

Outside the computer sector, there are a number of other lessors, sometimes described as captive lessors, who lease a relatively limited range of equipment in which they are involved as manufacturers or suppliers. In the motor car sector, each of the main UK manufacturers, and some of the leading importers, have specialist finance companies wholly or partly owned by the manufacturer, that offer contract hire and leasing facilities for fleets, as well as hire purchase in the consumer sector, for their own makes of car — though in most cases these companies account for a relatively small part of the financing market in their own models, which they share with the major finance houses and lessors.

Examples of significant 'captive lessors' in other industries include JCB Finance in earth-moving and construction machinery, and Hewlett-Packard and Pitney Bowes in office equipment.

A number of financial sector companies outside the clearing bank sector have substantial leasing operations, mainly concentrated in the middle-ticket sector of finance leasing. These include one of the major discount houses, Union Discount, and two insurance-related companies (Norwich Union and the Frizzell Group).

Finally, there are diverse types of company which do not fit easily into any one of the above categories, but which also have substantial leasing operations and are members of the ELA. These include Lease Plan UK, which specializes in vehicle leasing and is part of a Dutch-owned international group, and AT&T Capital Corporation Ltd, which is building up major leasing books in the UK and other European countries as part of a diversification of the worldwide activities of the parent company, which were originally concentrated in telecommunications in the USA.

The great diversity of types of leasing company underlines the open, competitive nature of the leasing industry.

Some major leasing companies

Some of the UK leasing companies, which are significant in terms of either their size or their type, and the development of their corporate involvement in leasing over the years, are described briefly below.

Lombard North Central plc is the largest of all the leasing companies, being also the largest of the finance houses and owned by the largest clearing bank. Its activities in the modern type of general equipment leasing can be traced back to 1963; though one of its antecedents, in the shape of North Central Wagon and Finance Company, was involved in the leasing of railway rolling stock as early as 1861 (see Chapter 4). As a finance house in the instalment credit business, North Central came into the clearing bank sector in 1958 when it was acquired by the National Provincial Bank. The latter's merger in 1970 with the Westminster Bank brought North Central into the National Westminster Bank Group. In the following year Natwest acquired Lombard Banking, a previously independent finance house and international bank, and the two finance houses, with their leasing activities, were merged to become Lombard North Central.

Through its various subsidiaries, Lombard now offers leasing facilities in cars and commercial vehicles, general industrial plant and machinery, and office equipment. Its wholly owned Farming and Agriculture Finance Ltd subsidiary is one of the four major UK specialists in the leasing of agricultural equipment. The company also has jointly owned motor finance subsidiaries with the two major British-based motor manufacturers, Rover Group and Jaguar, and offers specialist contract hire facilities for fleet cars (through Lex Vehicle Leasing, a subsidiary jointly owned with Lex Service Group) and for commercial vehicles (through Transfleet (UK) Ltd).

Barclays Mercantile Business Finance Ltd is the second largest UK lessor. Its involvement in leasing commenced as early as 1960 when the independent finance house Mercantile Credit Co. Ltd formed a new subsidiary, Mercantile Leasing Co. Ltd, in which a 20 per cent minority stake was taken by US Leasing Co. Major new leasing interests were acquired by Mercantile in 1970 through the acquisition of Astley Industrial Trust Ltd, including the vehicle contract hire specialist, Dial Contracts. Following the 'secondary banking' crisis of the early 1970s when Mercantile Credit, in common with other independent finance houses, faced difficulties the company was acquired in 1975 by Barclays Bank, which already had a leasing activity of its own through Barclays Export Finance Company. Subsequently, the combined leasing activities of the Barclays Group increased steadily. The company's current leasing specialities include large-ticket business in aircraft, ships and oil rigs, as well as vehicle contract hire, office equipment and (through its Highland Leasing subsidiary) agricultural equipment.

Forward Trust Group Ltd first entered the leasing business in 1969, as a finance house that had been acquired by Midland Bank in 1958. After Midland's acquisition of the Samuel Montagu merchant bank, its leasing interests — the finance house leasing arm, Forward Leasing, Samuel Montagu Leasing and Midland Bank Finance Corporation which had undertaken some leasing operations from within the clearing bank — were merged in 1974 to form Midland Montagu Leasing. In 1979 Midland's main leasing operations were transferred back into the Forward Trust Group finance house. The company today covers the full range of leasing business, including finance and operating leasing and contract hire, ranging from the small-ticket sector, to general plant and equipment, vehicles and industrial and commercial buildings.

Lloyds Leasing Ltd was formed in 1973 as the leasing arm of Lloyds Bank, and has continued with the same corporate structure ever since, though the company took in new UK leasing activities previously within Lloyds Bank International in 1985. Lloyds Leasing provides a full range of leasing facilities, being a major participant in large-ticket finance and operating leases, property leasing, and also some larger car fleet business. Within the same corporate group is Lloyds Bowmaker Ltd, a finance house wholly owned by Lloyds Bank since 1984 when it was formed from a merger of two separate finance houses, Lloyds and Scottish and Bowmaker Finance, both of which had some established leasing business. Lloyds Bowmaker concentrates on small- and medium-ticket leasing, including office equipment and car fleet markets.

Kleinwort Benson Ltd is one of the leading merchant banks in the leasing field, which it entered in 1969 with the establishment of two specialist leasing subsidiaries within the group, Robert Benson Lonsdale & Co. and Airlease International Management. Additional subsidiaries were established in 1981 to service a growing client base, and in 1984 the group moved into vehicle leasing. Kleinwort Benson now operates throughout the large- and middle-ticket leasing market, and its specialities include ships, computer equipment, industrial and commercial buildings and vehicle fleets.

S. G. Warburg & Co. Ltd, another major merchant banking group, entered the leasing market rather later, but has steadily expanded its involvement over the years. It commenced in 1979 both with leasing business on its own account and in an arrangement and advisory role in assembling leasing packages to be financed by the clearing banks. Warburgs entered the small-ticket leasing market in 1983 with the establishment of Pallas Leasing Ltd, which has continued subsequently as a specialist wholly owned subsidiary. The group thus operates within both the large- and small-ticket sectors. It also plays a significant advisory role in the large-ticket sector both in the UK and internationally, arranging a number of deals for aircraft leases; and assembled a significant leasing package in the mid–1980s for the new Nissan motor car factory in Washington, Co. Durham.

Anglo Leasing plc is perhaps the archetypal small-ticket leasing specialist. This company has been active in the UK leasing market since the first days of leasing in its modern form, with the establishment of Anglo-African Leasing Ltd as a subsidiary of Anglo-African Shipping. The company entered the merchant banking sector in 1973, when it was acquired by Rothschild Investment Trust (now J. Rothschild Holdings plc), and adopted its present name in 1977. It is now part of the Summit Group (in which the UK industrial group GEC is a major shareholder). The company operates in sales aid finance, through both leasing and hire purchase for office and business equipment particularly for small professional computer users. It has a number of joint finance subsidiaries with manufacturers and distributors of business equipment. A major new venture of this type, Cannon Finance Ltd, was established in 1985 to provide finance for Cannon electronic business products.

The corporate breakdown of the market

Table 7.1 shows the breakdown of the total new leasing market in 1990 between the major leasing companies and the others.

The remaining members of the ELA as at 1 January 1991, in addition to those listed in Table 7.1, were: Abbey National Treasury Services Ltd; Anglo Leasing plc; AT&T Capital Corporation Ltd; BAII Leasing Ltd; Baring Brothers & Co. Ltd; BCMB Leasing Ltd; BNP Finance Ltd; Canadian Imperial Bank of Commerce; Capital Leasing Ltd; Carolina Leasing Ltd; Causeway Equipment Finance Ltd; Chartered Trust plc; Chartered WestLB Ltd; Chase Leasing Ltd; City Leasing Ltd; Co-operative Bank plc; Dana Commercial Credit Ltd; Dataserv Ltd; Den

Table 7.1 The largest UK leasing companies, 1990 (in order of value of assets acquired in 1990)

	Assets acquired for leasing in 1990[1]	Income receivable in 1990[1]	Net book value of leased assets at 31 December 1990[2]
	£m	£m	£m
Lombard North Central plc[3]	3,324	3,097	4,150
Barclays Mercantile Business Finance Ltd	1,943	1,995	4,001
Lloyds Leasing Ltd[4]	1,586	1,828	2,625
NWS BANK plc[5]	1,250	748	1,616
TSB Group Ltd[6]	792	622	1,273
Forward Trust Group Ltd	742	1,173	2,478
S. G. Warburg & Co. (UK) Ltd	448	270	828
Royal Bank Leasing Ltd	360	337	1,071
All other ELA members	3,850	2,640	6,765
Total ELA members	14,295	12,710	24,807

1. Includes purchase option business as well as pure leasing.
2. Leasing only (no purchase option).
3. Including the business of National Westminster Bank plc.
4. Including the business of Lloyds Bowmaker Finance Group.
5. Subsidiary of Bank of Scotland Group.
6. TSB Group Ltd comprises two ELA member companies, Hill Samuel Asset Finance Ltd and United Dominions Trust Ltd.

Norske Leasing Services Ltd; EFT Finance Ltd; Electronic and Medical Instruments Property Ltd; Euro Commercial Leasing Ltd; Fork Truck Rentals Ltd; GKN Sankey Finance Ltd; Guinness Yokohama Leasing Ltd; Hambros Bank Ltd; Hewlett-Packard Finance Ltd; 3i plc; IBJ Leasing (UK) Ltd; IBM UK Financial Services Ltd; Japan Leasing (UK) Ltd; Kleinwort Benson Ltd; Kredietlease (UK) Ltd; Kodak Finance Ltd; Landhurst Leasing plc; Lazard Equipment Leasing Ltd; Lease Management Services Ltd; Lease Plan UK Ltd; London Financial Group (Services) Ltd; Nikko Bank (UK) Ltd; NHL Leasing Ltd; Norwich Union Leasing Ltd; OKO Finance Ltd; Orix Europe Ltd; Parc International Ltd; Philips Finance Services Ltd; Pitney Bowes Finance plc; Rank Xerox Finance Ltd; Sanwa Business Credit (UK) Ltd; Saturn Asset Finance Ltd; Scandinavian Leasing Ltd; Schroder Leasing Ltd; SocGen Lease Ltd; Sovereign Leasing plc; TAF Group Ltd; UFB Humberclyde plc; Union Discount Finance and Leasing Ltd; US Leasing Ltd; Woodchester Equipment Leasing Ltd; and Yorlease Ltd.

The Finance and Leasing Association

The first representative body for the UK leasing industry was the Equipment Leasing Association (ELA), formed in January 1971 as an offshoot from the Finance Houses Association. The 13 founder-member companies of the ELA grew in number to 20 in the following year and 33 by 1973, by which time the association accounted for the bulk of the rapidly growing business. Additional member companies joined the ELA later in the 1970s, as leasing business grew to new levels, with the number of members eventually exceeding 70. The membership was strengthened further in the 1984–86 period, when several of the specialist computer lessors joined the association, and a change in its rules for the first time permitted membership by the 'captive' lessors. A number of specialist office equipment lessors joined the association for the first time in 1990–91. Other companies, particularly foreign banks with various types of banking business in the UK, moved in and out of the association from time to time, reflecting the extent of their involvement in the UK leasing market.

As of 2 January 1992, a new association — the Finance and Leasing Association (FLA) — was formed by a full merger of the ELA and FHA. Both associations had arrived at the view that, with tax considerations less critical to some leasing structures than in the 1970s, and with traditional barriers breaking down all over the financial service sectors, it no longer made sense for leasing to be represented separately from other types of asset-based finance for business sector customers. It was also felt that a single association would enjoy stronger lobbying power with the authorities and an enhanced standing in public perception.

The FLA is structured in two principal divisions, with the Asset Finance and Leasing Division (AFLD) representing both leasing and other forms of finance for the business sector, while the Consumer Finance Division (CFD) represents consumer business. A separate Motor Finance Group within the FLA focuses specifically on vehicle financing business. Companies in membership of the FLA may belong to either or both of the divisions, depending on their activity in the market. At the end of 1991 there had been 73 full member companies in the ELA, and nearly all of these joined the new association. There are now 86 full member companies in the AFLD, and 108 altogether in the FLA.

The FLA has no regulatory or policing role in the industry, although it has Codes of Practice binding members to act with integrity in dealings with customers. There is, however, no obligation for leasing companies to join. Its essential purpose is as a trade association and most of its activity is directed towards making representations to the authorities on matters of mutual concern to members. It therefore has extensive contacts with government departments and agencies such as the Inland Revenue and

HM Customs and Excise on taxation; with the Department of Trade and Industry and the Office of Fair Trading on matters of commercial law; with the Bank of England on the banking supervision systems as it affects those lessors who are regulated as deposit takers under the Banking Act (see Chapter 23); and with HM Treasury, as the department with general oversight of the financial sector of the economy. The association is also involved in discussions with the Accounting Standards Board and the professional accountancy institutes in the UK.

On the international level, the FLA represents the UK in the Leaseurope federation, which brings together the corresponding bodies representing lessors in each country in western Europe and, increasingly since 1989, a number of countries in eastern Europe. Leaseurope plays a similar representative role to that of the FLA in the national context, in monitoring decisions and proposals of the European Community, as they affect the leasing industry in EC member states. International conferences, which provide a useful framework for the exchange of information among practitioners concerning leasing market developments world wide, are held under the aegis of Leaseurope and through the World Leasing Conference, which brings together national leasing associations and continental federations representing existing and newly emerging countries with active leasing industries throughout the world.

The FLA is not a professional body, although it has associate membership principally for legal and accountancy firms. It does not in general provide commercial services for members. However, in 1987 the ELA instituted training courses for practitioners in leasing, which continue under the FLA and in which the employees of a number of member companies participate.

Other trade bodies

While the FLA is recognized as the premier representative body for lessors, some other trade associations also have an interest in the industry.

Among some more specialized but smaller bodies, the British Vehicle Rental and Leasing Association (BVRLA) constitutes another trade association, also within the leasing and contract hire industry. The BVRLA has as many as 1,400 full member companies — most of whom are small motor dealers undertaking a certain amount of contract hire business on their own account — as well as 55 associate members among the vehicle suppliers.

The European Computer Leasing and Trading Association (ECLAT), which is UK-based, seeks to represent the computer leasing sector, but its members include lessees and suppliers as well as a few lessors.

The British Bankers Association (BBA) represents banking institutions of every kind, and therefore has some overlap of membership with the FLA. The former is, however, concerned with the full range of banking business and not principally with asset-based finance.

The FLA is, therefore, the principal trade body for the leasing industry, with an interest in all types of leasing activity, and is focused exclusively on leasing.

8. *Commercial framework*

It is appropriate to examine the basic concept and outline of the various forms of leasing that have evolved from the core concept of 'use without ownership'.

Definitions of leasing vary slightly from one country to another in line with their own particular regulatory practices, taxation or accounting regimes. A widely used definition of leasing in the UK is as follows:

> A lease is a contract between a lessor and lessee for the hire of a specific asset selected from a manufacturer or vendor of such assets by the lessee. The lessor retains ownership of the asset. The lessee has possession and use of the asset on payment of specified rentals over a period.

There are, however, a number of ancillary factors surrounding a lease which may throw into question the condition of ownership, although even this principle has recently been eroded in the UK with the introduction of the 'deemed lease' provisions of Schedule 17 of the Finance Act 1985 (see Chapter 21).

Within this general definition of a lease, there are two main subfamilies of leasing which are internationally recognized and referred to as 'finance leases' and 'operating leases'.

A finance lease, often referred to as a 'full payout' lease, is one which requires payment by the lessee over an obligatory period of specified rentals sufficient in total to repay the capital outlay of the lessor and give a profit margin after the deduction of interest costs.

An operating lease is generally regarded as one that does not meet the full payout criteria of a finance lease. However, with the introduction of accounting standards for leasing (see Chapter 15), more precise definitions have been introduced.

In the UK, the Statement of Standard Accounting Practice (SSAP 21), while setting out the parameters as regards the quantum of obligatory rentals suitably discounted, omits any conditions of the lease's duration. The accounting definition of an operating lease has commanded considerable attention since the decision (also contained in SSAP 21) that lessees should capitalize all finance leases.

There is a growing discussion in the UK as to whether the substance of a lease should override its legal form as more and more complex structures are devised to avoid the requirement for lessees to capitalize leased assets.

SSAP 21 is, however, unlikely to be changed materially and the financially engineered operating lease, where a lessor or a third party accepts a part of the residual value risk, is already providing lessors with a significant new area of development and will test the skills of investment analysts in future interpretation of statutory accounts.

In addition to the above classifications, leases will normally be described as either 'tax based' or 'non-tax based'. The latter are often referred to as 'lease with option to purchase' agreements and differ only very slightly from a hire-purchase contract.

Salient features of a lease

Whatever the form, the substance of the most common form of a finance or full pay-out lease is usually evident from the following characteristics:

1. The asset is selected by the lessee, although the order may often be placed in the lessor's own name.
2. The lessor retains ownership. In the UK, for a lessor's claim to capital allowances to be successful, no right or opportunity should exist at the outset of the agreement for the lessee to acquire title to the asset at any time.
3. The lessee carries the risk of obsolescence and has the exclusive rights to use the asset, subject to the conditions of the lease, which includes a requirement for the asset to be maintained in good working order.
4. There is a main non-cancellable period of the lease during which the lessor expects to receive sufficient rentals to recover all, or substantially all, of the capital outlay and to make a profit margin after all costs.
5. At the end of the lease the lessee may continue the lease at a nominal rental or arrange, as agent for the lessor, for the equipment to be sold or scrapped.

The price at which the asset can be disposed of at the end of the lease will generally be influenced by:
(a) the amount, if any, that the lessor may need to achieve full pay-out and
(b) any requirements of the tax laws relative to the granting of deprecia-
    tion allowances and/or tax credits.

The deductibility in full of lease rentals for tax purposes by the lessee is of fundamental importance in tax-based leasing. Although lessee accounting for the asset has generally followed the payment pattern of the lease, the introduction of SSAP 21 in the UK has resulted in a radical departure with leased assets being capitalized and amortized over their useful life. The importance of 'cash flow' in leasing does, however, remain and, next to the conceptual benefits of 'use without ownership', is one of the most salient features of any lease and the key to its cost effectiveness.

Notwithstanding these changes, finance leasing is still regarded essentially as a means of financing the use of an asset without acquiring ownership. From this principal feature flows all the characteristics of a lease although, as will be seen from the following definitions, the distinction between one form of finance and another stems from the narrow difference in emphasis of the main features previously described.

Outright acquisition Purchase using own or borrowed funds.

Unsecured loan Purchase with borrowed funds but with no security for the lender.

Mortgage or charge Purchase with borrowed funds secured by the asset

Credit sale Purchase with extended credit provided by the supplier.

Conditional sale Purchase with title passing on payment of all instalments.

Hire purchase Legally, a hiring with option to purchase at a purely nominal sum at the end of the term (e.g. £1, not, for instance, 1 per cent).

Finance lease Tax-based lease with the lessor retaining some benefit from any residual value.

Lease purchase 'Lease purchase' with title and tax benefits passing to lessees.

Operating lease Any lease that meets the accounting definitions of SSAP 21 in the UK.

Short-term lease A short-term lease with cancellation and renewal option where title remains with the lessor.

Contract hire A form of operating lease (mainly for motor vehicles), often incorporating maintenance.

Rental Another form of operating lease often shorter in duration than contract hire.

Plant hire Hire for relatively short periods, usually to a number of users, of plant and machinery.

As will be seen from the facilities described above, there is no clear dividing line between use and ownership and different distinguishing features apply for different purposes. Under a hire-purchase contract, for example, legal ownership does not pass to the hirer until the option to purchase is exercised after the last instalment has been paid, whereas economic ownership has been enjoyed from the outset.

The spread of leasing has resulted in the term being applied to many forms of instalment finance even though upon close examination they will be found to be more akin to hire purchase. In the UK, at the end of a lease, lessors generally give a rebate to the lessee of between 95 and 99 per cent of the net sale proceeds, although the inconvenience of arranging an arm's length sale to an unconnected third party frequently leads to lessees continuing into a secondary period and paying a 'peppercorn' annual rental until the equipment is finally scrapped.

Types of leasing activity

Finance leasing is by far the most common form of leasing, having become an important item in the product range of most banks. It is, however, also used by a wide range of manufacturers and distributors of capital equipment. The most common types of leasing activity in the UK are as follows:

SMALL-TICKET LEASING (see Chapter 24)

Activity in this sector of the market is concentrated on catering, shop and office equipment such as refrigeration, cash register, word processors, photocopying machines, telecommunications equipment, etc.

Given the small unit size (£1,000–15,000) and the consumer credit implications (see Chapter 22) the number of active lessors in this market has tended to be small; however, the larger lessors have recently re-examined the considerable opportunities in this sector following a number of years in which the demand for leasing enabled them to concentrate their limited resources on the larger scale transactions — indeed several major lessors have already moved into this market. Leasing companies operating in this sector generally rely heavily on equipment dealers for new business introductions.

Documentation, and acceptance procedures tend to be simplified and a certain level of bad debt is anticipated in the pricing, with profit margins of around 10 per cent being considered quite normal.

Established lessors in this market include a number of small companies operating exclusively in this sector and often funding themselves on a back-to-back basis with keenly priced tax-based leasing facilities from major lessors.

RETAIL LEASING

This term is often used to denote the small- to medium-sized leasing activities of banks or leasing companies and frequently indicates a standard form of transaction, marketed to a wide base of customers often through a branch network.

The types of asset financed typically include industrial plant and machinery, office equipment, cars and commercial vehicles. Lease periods will generally be shorter than the useful life of the asset and rentals will very often be fixed except for any material changes in the tax assumptions.

In the UK, despite the phasing out of first-year allowances in the 1984 Finance Act, subsequent provisions for the de-pooling of short-life assets for tax purposes (see Chapter 13) provides some continued scope for tax efficient pricing.

Although lessors will place some reliance on the recoverable value of the asset, especially in the case of motor vehicles, credit decisions will generally be based on the financial standing and covenant of the lessee. The type of lessee and size of transaction vary considerably but at the top end may easily extend into the range of values more commonly associated with the 'medium ticket' sector.

SALES-AID LEASING

This form of leasing activity covers much the same markets as the previous two, but is based on schemes specifically designed to assist manufacturers and distributors increase the sales of their products. This area requires special branding of the leasing product, flexibility in dealing with discounts, trade-ins, up-grades, terminations, etc., and a skilful balancing of the conflicting interests of the supplier, whose main aim is to sell equipment, and of the lessor, who seeks to finance only credit-worthy purchasers (see Chapter 24).

LARGE-TICKET LEASING

This term embraces a wide range of leasing activities which, due to the type of asset, are not only large in value but, more importantly, require extremely complex lease documentation. Such assets typically include aircraft, ships, oil and chemical equipment and integral production lines often including immovable plant and buildings.

The main lessors operating in these markets are subsidiaries of the commercial banks, and UK merchant or American investment banks will often play a prominent role in 'arranging' or advising on the leasing facility. Such facilities have generally been tax based and cover periods of around 15–20 years. In view of the size of exposure, the credit risk is often spread by syndication among a number of lessors in partnership or, when feasible, by each party leasing separately identifiable parts of a plant.

Tax benefits, coupled with very long-term financing, have been the main factors behind the success of leasing in this sector of the market. Lessees have typically been companies in highly capital-intensive industries, e.g. airlines, shipping, oil and chemicals, and thereby very often unable to take immediate advantage of the fiscal incentives.

Leverage leasing (described in Chapter 25) has so far not developed in the UK due to the absence of willing non-recourse lenders and rigidity of the tax law governing the deductibility of loan interest in situations where the loans could be construed as being 'quasi-capital'.

Commercial aircraft leasing (see Chapter 24) has, for a number of years, been a major activity and grew in the USA on the back of investment tax credits until, as in the UK, restrictions were introduced preventing the effective transfer of fiscal benefits abroad. Despite the very small number of domestic operators, high aircraft values coupled with the ready availability of syndicated bank guarantees and the decline in US dollar-based leases, have resulted in a significant increase in aircraft leasing in the UK. A number of such transactions are now being structured as operating leases in line with the SSAP 21 requirements and banks have assumed a degree of asset risk behind the manufacturers.

Although now in decline, ship leasing or 'demise charter', as it is more properly described, was an active market in the 1970s and included cable-laying and support vessels in the off-shore oil industry in addition to the more standard bulk and crude oil carriers. In the UK, the concept of ownership of vessels being divisible into sixty-fourths and registerable provided a ready means of perfecting joint title and it was common for single-purpose leasing companies to be used to avoid the risk of a sister ship being arrested in the event of a lessee default.

In the chemical and oil and manufacturing sectors there have been a number of major leasing projects including entire refineries and production plants where the lease has been preceded by a construction period of two or three years. With such large transactions, lessors have tended to avoid taking any true project risk although the transactions have often been structured to accommodate repayment from the associated cash flow.

CONTRACT HIRE AND CAR LEASING

Because of its size, this sector merits special mention and is described in greater detail in Chapter 24. The market is centred on the vast number of motor dealerships that exist and require a high level of financial support coupled with service to their customers.

This support is provided from a number of very specialized sources, including the captive finance areas of the motor manufacturers such as General Motors Acceptance Corporation and Ford Motor Credit whose operations are globally based and rival any of the more broadly based finance companies who compete for business in this sector.

The type of finance provided is typically a mixture of stocking finance for new and used cars, which is very often granted on favourable terms in return for first refusal of retail business, i.e. the opportunity to finance the sale of cars to the consumer.

However, for most motor dealers, it is their increasing involvement as financiers that supplements the profit from their distribution activities. For the most part these financial activities take the form of contract hire of fleets of vehicles for use by companies in the commercial sector. Contract hire is in essence a form of true operating lease where maintenance and residual value assumptions are included in the rental. Such contracts normally cover periods of 2–5 years and there will often be provisions in the agreement for additional rental to be payable if certain mileage levels are exceeded or excessive repair costs result from misuse of the vehicle.

A large number of other specialist vehicle contract hire companies have grown up in recent years and in the UK these have tended to be substantially owned by banks or finance companies.

OPERATING LEASING

With the introduction of SSAP 21 and the requirement for capitalization of finance leases by lessees (see Chapter 15) operating leasing in the UK has taken on new connotations. This product, more commonly referred to as 'rental', had traditionally been geared towards relatively low value assets in volume markets such as television, video, photocopiers and to some extent computers. Such equipment is normally leased for a minimum period of one year and there is a heavy reliance on the customer's inertia for the continuation of the lease and consequent improvement in the lessor's pay-back.

This form of finance has been developed into a highly profitable business by a number of manufacturers such as Xerox and, in general, financial institutions have been unable to find a means of directly engaging in these activities in the way they have penetrated contract hire in the motor market.

There are, however, a number of specialist computer lessors who provide mainly IBM equipment on an operating lease basis. Unlike the traditional short-term rental market, these agreements tend to be carefully structured to meet SSAP 21 classification as an operating lease, and owing to the relatively long committed term (up to five years) they generally provide the opportunity for the specialist lessor to finance the transaction with a third party lessor often through a head lease, in such a way that reliance on future residual values is reduced to a minimum. Invariably, because of their ability to re-market the equipment, a second profit opportunity exists for the specialist lessor.

Generally speaking, owing to obsolescence factors, computer manufacturers are less than willing to provide rental facilities, although occasionally the majors, such as IBM, find it necessary in order to market their products when a new range of machine is announced.

In the aircraft sector, Guinness Peat Aviation, which is based in Shannon, Eire, stands out as a true operating lessor of aircraft, with a fleet of aircraft and trained flight deck crew which it deploys in short/medium-term hire agreements with various airlines around the world.

On a slightly different basis, there is an increasing trend for aircraft leases to be structured as operating leases within the meaning of SSAP 21. It is usual in such cases for a full pay-out head lease to be made to a special-purpose company which then subleases to the aircraft operator on an operating lease basis. Such arrangements usually rely on a combination of bank guarantee and manufacturer re-marketing support to achieve required termination sums at given points in the leases, at which time the aircraft operator has the option to continue or terminate the lease.

Procedure for obtaining a leasing facility

It is important for a company contemplating the acquisition of capital equipment and considering leasing to do so at the outset rather than leave it until the moment of delivery. This is the case because such matters as the passing of title to the lessor can be complicated if the lessee first acquires the asset.

Agency arrangements

It is common for a company regularly using leasing to enter into formal agencies with a number of lessors in order to facilitate the order process. In any event, the lessee selects the equipment to be leased and negotiates the purchase terms with the supplier. Where an agency agreement is used it may be a general one incorporating authority for the lessee not only to order, but also to make payments on behalf of the lessor for a number of related purchases. Where only a single item of equipment is involved, it is more normal for the agency to cover the placing of the order with the supplier, who is requested to send an invoice to the lessor for direct payment.

In some instances the order will be placed directly in the lessor's own name, although this requires the lease agreement to be signed in advance or for some other form of indemnity to be given by the lessee to protect the lessor against the risk of the transaction not proceeding.

The practice in the past led to a relatively extensive use of unwritten and often undisclosed agency relationships between lessors and lessees, but there was concern that, if challenged, some might not be able to be evidenced to the satisfaction of auditors or such bodies as the tax and other authorities responsible for the granting of capital incentives. Accordingly, many lessors now insist on written agencies for a defined term, stating:

- a description of the goods to be ordered
- a limitation on the cost
- the anticipated delivery date

- an obligation on the lessee to accept and advise when delivery takes place
- the party responsible for making payment to the supplier and the method of reimbursement of the lessee, where applicable
- the date when the lease will be incepted.

If the lessee has already placed an order for the item when the decision to lease is taken, the lessor may acquire title to the equipment in the following manner.

1. *Novation*   A tripartite agreement between the supplier, the lessee and the lessor, who enter into a novation of the original contract where-under the rights and obligations are transferred from the lessee to the lessor. These agreements are quite frequently used, especially where it is the standard practice to place orders well in advance of delivery owing to long manufacturing periods.
2. *Sale and leaseback*   Where title has passed to the intended lessee it is normal for this to be transferred to a lessor by means of a sale and leaseback agreement. Such agreements are usually timed to take effect after delivery of the asset but before it is brought into use in order to avoid the possibility of its being considered second hand. In the UK this is less important now than previously as the standard rate of depreciation for all assets, excluding property, is the same as that laid down in Schedule 8 of the Finance Act 1971 for sale and leaseback and no distinction is now made between new and used equipment.

In order to carry out a preliminary assessment of the cost benefits of leasing, the prospective lessee will often seek an indication of rental terms either direct from a lessor, from a broker, or from an investment/merchant bank if there is a need for independent advice on some of the more complex matters. The fees payable to an 'arranger' of leasing facilities are generally paid by the lessee or passed on by inclusion of the fee in the amount financed.

Having selected the desired method of approach, the following details are normally sent to a selected number of lessors, inviting them to quote terms on which they would be prepared to write the business:

- the type of equipment, proposed date of delivery and location
- the estimated cost and timing of payment
- the required period of lease, rental pattern and fixed or variable basis
- financial details of the lessee.

On receipt of this information a lessor will be in a position to assess the credit worthiness of the lessee and to decide whether the proposal will stand on its own merits or whether some additional support is necessary, such as a parent company's guarantee of its subsidiary or a bank guarantee.

This decision made, it is then possible for the lessor to decide what profit margin is appropriate relative to the risk involved. Rentals are calculated using present value analysis techniques of the projected after-tax cash flow of the proposed transaction and are formally submitted to the lessee for consideration.

In the large-ticket transactions it is not uncommon for lessors to reveal their cash flows and profit margin in order to help lessees compare competitive quotations and to assess more easily the true underlying interest cost in the lease.

A full statement will be provided of the other assumptions made by the lessor such as the funding and taxation parameters as well as the timing of any grant receivable, etc. Following the change to a reducing balance basis of capital allowance for tax purposes in the UK and the special provisions for de-pooling short-life assets (see Chapter 13), the treatment of the unclaimed balance of allowances at the end of the primary period can be a critical element of the pricing and needs to be clearly established.

The lessee normally evaluates the competitiveness of the various quotations by calculating the respective implicit rate of interest represented by the lease rentals as well as the absolute amount of rental payable. The chosen lessor is then advised but there is generally no firm commitment by either party until such time as the lease or agreement to lease is actually signed.

Risks involved in leasing

A leasing company entering into a finance lease looks to the lessee for the recovery of the full, or at least a major part of, the outlay on a leased asset. The lessor needs to be assured that the user of the equipment is in a position to meet the rentals payable during the primary lease periods as they fall due.

In the event of premature termination of the lease before the end of the primary period — through default by the lessee or in other circumstances such as a total loss of the equipment — the lessor will require the outstanding capital cost of the equipment to be paid as a lump sum. In the absence of insurance proceeds, the lump sum terminal payment has to be found by the lessee. The terminal payment is usually calculated by discounting future rentals from their due dates to the date of measurement at a rate specified in the lease and, except in the case of total loss of the leased equipment, by deducting therefrom an amount related to its then market value. For most types of equipment, it is unlikely that the second-hand value at the date of termination will be high enough to eliminate the outstanding capital cost, in which case any unrecovered balance will remain to be paid by the lessee; from time to time there are assets which are exceptions (such as aircraft and ships in a period of rapid inflation and other items of equipment in limited supply) and which retain a sufficiently high market value. The legal implications of a default and the calculation of the lump sum terminal payment are considered in Chapters 19 and 9, respectively.

From a credit-worthiness viewpoint, a finance lease is akin to a medium-term loan secured on the equipment. Leasing companies need to make the same enquiries and obtain the same information regarding the credit standing of prospective lessees as banks and other financial institutions do for loan applications.

A credit appraisal is necessarily a subjective assessment of the solvency of a potential lessee. Although the past cannot be ignored, leasing companies also place particular emphasis on a lessee's future viability. The following list presents some of the criteria taken into account by lessors.

1. The nature of the lessee's business.
2. The quality of management.
3. Future prospects, particularly the adequacy of the forecast of future cash flow to meet rentals and other outgoings.
4. The financial position shown by the latest accounts.
5. The likely value over the primary lease period of the equipment to be leased.

Although, in certain circumstances, financial institutions may regard one form of medium-term finance as more risky than another, a finance lease, a secured loan for the full cost of equipment, and a hire-purchase facility (without an initial deposit) have much the same degree of credit risk. Groups providing a range of financial services usually assess the credit-worthiness of a prospective customer on the same basis, whatever type of equipment finance is required. If a bank or finance house decided that it could not lend or provide hire purchase to a company for the purchase of equipment, then an associated leasing company would be likely to be equally unwilling to provide a leasing facility for the same equipment.

For marginal propositions, leasing companies can improve the credit position in the same way as other financial institutions. They can take additional security, such as guarantees, floating charges and cash deposits. They can require a higher initial rental to be paid.

There are several specific factors that may make the overall risk in leasing different for the lessor from that in other forms of finance. For example:

1. *The inherent risks of ownership* As owner of the equipment, a lessor may be liable for claims from third parties for losses arising out of the use of the leased asset. In some situations, considered in Chapter 20,

both the owner and the user are legally responsible. In other cases the law is uncertain, and a lessor could possibly be involved in expense in defending an action for damages; injured parties may prefer to institute proceedings directly against a leasing company, as part of a large financial group, rather than a lessee. Although a lessor is normally indemnified by the lessee against any such claims, and may be entitled to the proceeds of insurance covering the equipment against third-party liabilities, there will be occasions when the lessee has insufficient resources to meet the indemnity and there is inadequate insurance cover.

2. *Default claims*   The law applying to a claim for repayment of a loan following a default by a borrower is more certain and tested than the corresponding claim by a financial lessor for recovery of the unamortized cost of equipment.

3. *Collateral*   A lessor is financing the acquisition of an individual item of equipment and may be unable to enjoy the benefit of additional security in the same way as a lender who also provides a comprehensive banking service to a customer and who may have previously arranged collateral security such as a floating charge.

4. *Interest and tax assumptions*   For leases without variation clauses, there is a risk that an adverse change in interest rate or taxation is more detrimental to the lessor's return than the element, if any, included in the rental to compensate the lessor for assuming these risks. In particular, a lessor's cash flow is more sensitive to a change in the rate of corporation tax or in the general basis of taxation than that of an equivalent medium-term loan. For leases with interest or tax variation clauses, a change may result in higher rentals, which increase the lessor's overall exposure.

There is also the danger for a leasing company that there will be insufficient taxable capacity within its group to obtain immediate benefit of the capital allowances, which have been assumed for rental calculation purposes.

On the other hand, leasing may reduce the level of risk.

1. *Asset recovery*   It may be easier and cheaper for a lessor as owner to repossess leased equipment following a default by the lessee than it would be for a mortgagee or chargee.

2. *Productive investment*   A lessor may often be leasing income-producing or expense-saving equipment and not just augmenting a firm's general body of assets.

3. *Value of investment incentive*   A lessee unable to take immediate advantage of any capital allowance that would be available if the

equipment was purchased receives a benefit to the extent that the capital allowance claimed by the lessor is reflected in the rentals. The lessor's risk is thus less than that of a lender providing an equivalent medium-term loan because of the actual reduction in rentals and the improvement in the lessee's overall financial position as a consequence of paying less for the use of the equipment concerned.

The essential feature

Throughout the commercial world, businesspeople and governments are continuously concerned with the rights and obligations of property owner-ship. Economic, legal and fiscal measures are necessarily complex and anomalies frequently arise in the treatment of specific items. The differ-ences between the risks of lessors and lenders and, for equipment users, between leasing and buying equipment arise principally as a result of financing the long-term use rather than the ownership of an asset, the essential feature of finance leasing.

9. Financial terms

The basic commercial term in a finance lease is the rental payable during the primary lease period.

The nature of rental

In a short-term hiring agreement, rental represents simply the amount charged by the owner for the use of the equipment during a specified period of hire. However, in the case of a finance lease, rental, although nominally related to a period of use (the primary period), is usually calculated as being the amount which over the primary lease period will recover for the owner the capital cost of the equipment together with his or her outgoings, principally interest, and profit margin, taking into account any tax charges and allowances that may apply.

On occasions rental is likened to an annuity or equalized mortgage repayment made to a building society or other lender. From this perspective, the rentals or loan repayments comprise a capital element and an interest element and the early instalments comprise a smaller amount of principal and a larger proportion of interest than later repayments, because of the reducing amount of outstanding capital on which the interest is computed. A lender's rate of recovery of capital cost is illustrated graphically in Figure 9.1 and in tabular form in Table 9.1.

This 'loan' analogy may be useful in understanding the general nature of lease rentals under a 'full payout' finance lease, but it can be misleading

Table 9.1 Lender's rate of recovery of capital cost

Half year	Opening balance £	Rental £	Capital elements £	Interest element £	Closing balance £
0 (Start date)	100,000	12,795	12,795	–	87,205
1	87,205	12,795	7,603	5,192	79,602
2	79,602	12,795	8,056	4,739	71,546
3	71,546	12,795	8,536	4,259	63,010
4	63,010	12,795	9,044	3,751	53,966
5	53,966	12,795	9,582	3,213	44,384
6	44,384	12,795	10,153	2,642	34,231
7	34,231	12,795	10,757	2,038	23,474
8	23,474	12,795	11,398	1,397	12,076
9	12,076	12,795	12,076	719	–

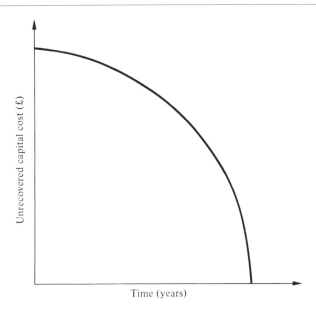

Figure 9.1 Lender's rate of recovery of capital cost

when lease quotations are being evaluated. In a loan quotation the main considerations are simply interest rates and repayment provisions, but with a lease many additional factors influence the evaluation, several of which arise from the impact of taxation on a lease transaction. Unlike a loan, where only the interest element of the repayments is subject to tax, the whole of a lease rental is treated as income in the books of the lessor, and the rental is allowable in full against the lessee's taxable profits.

Although these additional factors tend to complicate the lease evaluation, they can enable leasing companies to provide terms that are designed to fit the needs of a particular customer and the circumstance of a particular transaction. The remainder of this chapter considers these additional factors and illustrates them by showing the effect on a typical lease rental of varying each factor. The rental for our representative facility is based on fiscal and monetary conditions prevailing in 1988. Although lease rentals are most often payable at quarterly intervals, a semi-annual frequency has been chosen here to reduce the number of figures shown in each table. The typical lease agreement has been taken as:

Capital cost of equipment: £100,000
Primary lease period: 5 years
Rentals: £12,795 payable semi-annually in advance

Lease rentals are usually quoted as a rate per £1,000 of equipment cost, in this case £127.95 per £1,000. Occasionally the nominal interest rate (11.9 per cent in this example) may be given. It would not be usual practice to quote compounded rates, but, for the record, our typical lease would give a compound annual rate of 12.26 per cent.

Full-payout finance leases

In the calculation and evaluation of finance lease rates, any secondary period rentals or renewal rentals that may be payable are normally ignored. The equipment is regarded as being fully paid for over the primary lease period. After the end of the primary period the lease is usually terminable by the lessee at any time, and hence it would be imprudent for a lessor to rely on any secondary period income in evaluating the overall return.

In evaluating a 'full payout' or finance lease, a leasing company in the UK seeks to recover out of the rentals payable during the primary lease period the whole of the capital cost of leased equipment plus a margin. However, in certain cases, a lessor may place a residual value on the equipment and, thereby, reduce the amount of each rental. This situation can arise if, for example:

(a) the lessor has agreed to sell, or has an option to sell, the equipment to a third party, perhaps the manufacturer or distributor of the equipment, at the end of the primary period at a prearranged price; or

(b) the lease provides for a period or periods of compulsory extension, or extension at the lessor's (rather than, normally, the lessee's) option, which effectively extends the primary lease period to include some or all of the secondary period.

In both cases, the action contemplated to recover the unamortized cost at the end of the primary period prevents the lessor from granting the lessee an option to extend the lease at a much reduced secondary period rental, which is a commercial term commonplace in financial leasing in the UK.

Any under-recovery of capital cost which is acceptable to the lessor will, naturally, significantly reduce the primary period rentals payable. The variations to the illustrated rental necessary to maintain the lessor's rate of return for changes in the extent of capital cost recovered are shown in Table 9.2. (The figures are not simply reduced proportionately and take into account the effect of 25 per cent writing-down allowances on the full amount of the expenditure.)

Table 9.2 Recovery of less than 100 per cent of capital cost

Recovery of capital cost during primary period %	Rental payable semi-annually in advance £	Nominal rate %
100	12,795	11.91
95	12,407	11.79
90	12,023	11.70
85	11,643	11.63
80	11,263	11.57
75	10,883	11.50

Primary lease period

The length of the primary period is an important factor in evaluating a leasing proposal. A lessee's choice of the most suitable available period will depend on a number of factors, including the anticipated period of use of the asset and the possible need to match cash inflows (earning capacity of the assets) with outflows (lease rentals).

The length of the primary lease period is normally related to the useful life of the equipment. A primary period of around 75 per cent of the useful life may be regarded as typical, although both the percentage and individual estimates of the length of the useful life of the equipment vary widely. A general pattern of primary periods, ranging from three years upwards, has emerged for most types of equipment. Five years is the most common period for many types of equipment, including plant, machinery and agricultural and transportation items.

For larger items of plant and assets, such as aircraft and ships, longer periods are appropriate and leases of 10 years and more are not uncommon. There is no recognized maximum primary period. Railway rolling stock has a long useful life and has in the past been regarded as suitable for a 20-year period, although it is unlikely that a leasing company would be willing to consider a lease of that length under current economic conditions. Aircraft and ships have been leased for periods of 15 years or more.

It is important to determine the length of the period over which the primary period rentals are payable. An extension of only three months in the primary period results in an appreciable reduction in each primary period rental but increases the total rentals payable during the primary lease period. This is illustrated in Table 9.3 which shows the semi-annual rentals required to achieve the same nominal rate (11.9 per cent) as our typical five-year lease over varying primary lease periods.

Table 9.3 Varying the period of a lease

Length of period (years)	Semi-annual repayments £	Total repayments £	Nominal rate £
3	19,165	114,990	11.9
4	15,171	121,368	11.9
4.5	13,848	124,632	11.9
5	12,795	127,950	11.9
5.5	11,938	131,318	11.9
6	11,229	134,748	11.9
7	10,125	141,750	11.9

However, a loan at a rate of 11.9 per cent would produce exactly the same effect, since Table 9.3 fails to take into account the after tax return of the lease transaction over varying periods. Table 9.4 shows the semi-annual rentals required to achieve the same after-tax return to the lessor over varying primary lease periods; and, by taking into account the tax effects on a lease, the rentals show a more marked variation with changes in the primary lease period.

In most financial leases, there will be an opportunity to extend the term of the lease beyond the agreed primary period. This and other options normally open to a lessee are discussed later.

Rental payment patterns

The variety of rental payment patterns is an area where financial leasing shows its natural flexibility. There are several sets of possibilities.

Table 9.4 Varying the primary period of a lease

Length of primary lease period (years)	Semi-annual rentals £	Total primary lease period rentals £	Nominal rate %
3	19,750	118,500	14.65
4	15,391	123,128	12.86
4.5	13,934	125,406	12.26
5	12,795	127,950	11.90
5.5	11,846	130,306	11.53
6	11,076	132,912	11.30
7	9,857	137,998	10.89

ADVANCE OR ARREARS

Since 1958, when the stamp duty on leasing agreements — which had previously acted as a deterrent to the payment of rentals in advance — was rationalized, leasing companies have gradually moved towards requiring rentals in advance, principally for security reasons. This trend has also been reflected in the procedure — used by government in the past to control consumer spending — of specifying the number of monthly rentals to be paid in advance of supply on certain types of consumer equipment. Currently, rentals are often payable in advance, although there is no longer a statutory requirement.

The basic difference between the cash flow for a lease with rentals payable in advance and one requiring payment in arrears is six months' interest on the initial capital cost. The effect of paying rentals in arrears is to increase the illustrated rental from £12,795 to £13,557. (Strictly speaking the rental should increase further to £13,582 in order to maintain the lessor's after tax rate of return, rather than simply maintaining the nominal rate of the lease rentals.)

FREQUENCY

Prior to the 1970s, most rentals were payable monthly. Over the years there has been a gradual move towards less frequent payments, partly to reduce the lessor's administration costs and partly to increase the amount paid in advance without an initial requirement for more than one rental to be paid.

Quarterly rentals are the most common today (although monthly rentals remain the most appropriate for smaller leases). Semi-annual and annual payments are also in general use for large facilities.

The total primary lease period rentals payable for different rental frequencies reflect the reduced or additional interest, depending on whether rentals are payable in advance or in arrears, respectively, arising from the lengthening of the payment interval. The effect of changing the frequencies of rental payments while maintaining the effective (or compounded) rate is illustrated in Table 9.5.

'TAILORED' RENTALS

In addition to the various payment patterns with level or equal rentals, there are a variety of ways in which rentals can be structured to meet the special requirements, usually based on anticipated cash flows, of individual lessees. Schemes can be designed to meet most sets of circumstances provided the final terms are both commercial and credit-worthy from the lessor's point of view. The most common are described below.

61

Table 9.5 Rental payment frequency, advance and arrears

Frequency	Amount of each rental £	No. of rentals	Total primary period rentals £
Rentals in advance			
Monthly	2,184	60	131,040
Quarterly	6,490	20	129,800
Semi-annually	12,795	10	127,950
Annually	24,871	5	124,355
Rentals in arrears			
Monthly	2,205	60	132,300
Quarterly	6,680	20	133,600
Semi-annually	13,557	10	135,570
Annually	27,921	5	139,605

1. *Seasonal* Inclusive tour airlines and hotels may have leased aircraft, catering and other equipment with higher rentals payable in the summer months and lower rentals in the winter. Examples of seasonal rentals, with an assumed two to one ratio, are shown in Table 9.6.
2. *Stepped* The leasing arrangement may recognize the likely revenue increase, for inflationary or other reasons, expected to be generated by the equipment over the primary period. This is accomplished by stepping rentals so that each rental, or the rentals for each year, are either the same percentage or the same actual amount over the previous level (or occasionally below). Increases of 5 and 10 per cent per annum would result in the rentals given in Table 9.7 (for simplicity of illustration, the nominal interest rate is maintained at 11.9 per cent).

Reference has already been made to the practice of including a compulsory renewal period, which has the effect of extending the primary lease period. This is simply an example of a downward stepped payment pattern. If a two-year compulsory renewal at an annual rental, payable in advance, of 1 per cent of the cost were taken into account, each primary period rental would need to be reduced to £12,659 to

Table 9.6 Seasonal rentals

Lease commencing	Rental payable each		Average semi-annual rental £	Nominal rate %
	summer £	winter £		
In summer	16,896	8,448	12,672	11.9
In winter	17,224	8,612	12,918	11.9

Table 9.7 Stepped rentals

Year	Level £	5% increase £	10% increase £
1	12,795	11,706	10,710
2	12,795	12,291	11,781
3	12,795	12,906	12,959
4	12,795	13,551	14,255
5	12,795	14,229	15,681

produce the same nominal interest rate as 10 semi-annual payments of
£12,795.

3. *Deferred*   Certain types of equipment do not generate revenue until
some time after they are installed, or may not produce immediate cost
savings. In such cases, a lessee may wish to have the cash flow benefit of
a rent free period until such time as the equipment is fully integrated
into the company's operations. A rental moratorium significantly
increases the total interest payable during the primary lease period. The
rentals payable with moratoria of up to 18 months are shown in Table
9.8 (for simplicity of illustration, the nominal interest rate is again
maintained at 11.9 per cent).

4. *Ballooned*   On occasions, one of the parties may wish to limit the
length of the primary lease period to less than might be regarded as
usual, taking into account the useful life of the equipment; but it is
considered acceptable for rentals payable during the primary period to
be based on the recovery of less than the whole capital cost. In these
circumstances, it is possible to have a lump sum balloon rental payable
on the expiry of the primary period; there is an opportunity to review
the arrangements at that time with a view to the possible rephasing of
the lump sum rental over a secondary period. The primary period
rentals payable under a ballooned scheme would be similar to those
shown in Table 9.2 above.

Table 9.8 Rental moratorium

Length of moratorium (months)	Amount of each rental £	Number of rentals	Total primary period rentals £
0	12,795	10	127,950
6	14,672	9	132,048
12	17,031	8	136,248
18	20,076	7	140,532

COMMITMENT FEES

A lessor, in entering into a lease, agrees to provide lease finance for a specific item of equipment or a group of items, selected by the lessee. There will be occasions when a lessee decides not to proceed with the acquisition of an item of equipment (because, for example, of an unforeseen reduction in demand for the goods produced by the equipment concerned) and wishes to cancel the arrangements rather than proceed with the lease. Alternatively, a lessee may have arranged a 'shopping basket' facility to be utilized by a set date for an agreed total value of equipment but because of delivery delays, may no longer need the full amount of the facility.

In these circumstances the lessor will have allocated certain resources, funds and taxable capacity or capital to support a committed facility for the lessee's use and may require compensation for the cancellation of the facility particularly if it is not possible to redeploy the resources elsewhere. There are two main ways of providing for such compensation.

Firstly, the leasing terms can include a commitment fee payable at the time of setting up the facility, which is non-refundable. In this case the lessor receives just the same cash return if the facility is drawn down in full, and if it is not drawn down, he retains the initial fee in compensation. The amount of the commitment fee may be reflected either in a corresponding reduction in the amount of the first rental or treated simply as an additional payment, the subsequent rentals being reduced accordingly. Comparable rentals with and without a commitment fee of 2 per cent of the capital cost, payable six months before the start date of the lease, are shown in Table 9.9.

Alternatively, a fixed commitment fee may be payable either at the time of cancellation or on expiry of the facility, in addition to the normal rentals payable. Thus, in Table 9.9, the lessor receiving a 2 per cent commitment fee would receive an additional £2,000 in consideration for holding cash and tax capacity resources available for the lessee.

Table 9.9 Commitment fees

Half year	2% commitment fee		No commitment fee
	Reduction in first rental £	Level rentals £	£
−1	2,000	2,000	–
0	10,780	12,524	12,795
1–9	12,780	12,524	12,795

Renewal options

As explained in Chapter 1, finance leasing agreements in the UK do not include an option for the lessee to acquire title to the leased equipment either at a nominal price or at an agreed reduced purchase price although such options are a normal feature of financing arrangements referred to as leases in several other countries.

In most UK finance leases, a lessee has an option to extend the lease beyond the end of the agreed primary lease period at a much reduced rental, which is fixed at the time of the original negotiations on the lease agreement. Currently, secondary period rentals are mainly in the range 0.25–1 per cent of the cost of the equipment and are payable annually in advance. In certain cases, the renewal rental may be expressed as a percentage of the primary period rental or of the estimated market value of the equipment.

The secondary period is usually an agreed number of years, although it may be an indefinite period. There may be an option providing for the extension of the lease for a given secondary period or the secondary period may run on a year-by-year basis, or indefinitely until the giving of three months' notice by the lessee. In large-ticket leases, there may be more than one renewal period, the secondary period being followed by a tertiary period with yet lower rentals, and so on.

If a lessee no longer wishes to continue to use the leased asset in his or her business on or after the expiry of the primary period, the equipment may be returned to the lessor to be sold, re-leased, or scrapped. Alternatively, it may be sold by the lessee, acting as the selling agent of the lessor, without the equipment physically passing into the possession of the lessor. There is unlikely to be any additional rent payable when a lease is terminated during a secondary period; however, on the other hand, it is unusual for there to be a specific refund of rent paid in advance for a year's renewal when a lease is terminated during the course of a year.

Provided that a lessee has fulfilled all the obligations under a leasing agreement, the majority of leasing companies will pass on to the lessee the major part of any sale proceeds in the form of either a rebate of rentals or, less commonly, a commission for handling the disposal of the equipment. The normal practice among leasing companies is to pass 95 per cent or 97.5 per cent of the net sale proceeds to the lessee. In other cases, lessees receive the excess of the net sale proceeds over an amount fixed at the inception of the lease or obtain a preferential rental on the lease of a new asset.

Where the lessor is prepared to renew the lease at a less than economic rent and/or rebate a proportion of the sale proceeds, he or she is forgoing the opportunity to use a major part of the value of the equipment as a source of profit after the end of the primary period. The initial leasing arrangement is being regarded as a financing activity which is expected to last the whole or most of the useful life of the equipment. The leasing company sees its reward as principally the excess of primary period rentals over the capital cost of the equipment, interest and expenses (taking into account tax allowances and charges). Renewal rentals and the lessor's share of the residual value may be considered as the additional consideration necessary for the lessor to provide finance by way of a leasing facility and to take on the inherent risks of ownership for the whole of the lease period.

If a lessor is prepared to grant one of these favourable options, there is no particular reason why a lessee should not enjoy residual value benefits, provided that there are no adverse tax consequences.

These renewal terms give the lessee economic, as opposed to legal, ownership of the equipment; the lessee has the opportunity to use the equipment for most of its useful life, and can share substantially in its residual value. This is important to lessors as well as to lessees. The lessee has a much greater incentive to maintain equipment in good repair if he or she is to receive a share of the proceeds, thereby enhancing the lessor's security interest in the equipment during the primary period, and perhaps, reducing any risk arising through the use of the equipment while defective.

Timing differences

So far we have illustrated the flexibility of lease periods, and primary rental payment patterns with reference to the inherent rate of a typical five-year semi-annual lease. Tables 9.3 and 9.6 to 9.9 all illustrate the variation in lease rentals required to achieve a similar nominal rate. These examples serve the purpose well enough, but it is necessary now to take account of the factors which relate to the tax influences on lease evaluation. In considering the effect of varying these factors we must recognize that, strictly speaking, it is the maintenance of the lessor's 'after-tax rate of return' on the transaction, rather than the nominal interest rate, which is essential to the lessor's evaluation. In a number of cases the difference (between rentals required to maintain the nominal rate and to maintain the after-tax return) will be insignificant, and for simplicity's sake, therefore, reference will continue to be made to the maintenance of the nominal rate where the difference is immaterial.

The date of acquisition of equipment, or, more precisely, the date the expenditure on the equipment is incurred, may influence the rental a lessor is prepared to quote. Leasing companies will quote different rentals for expenditure taking place at different times during their financial year. A lessor with a 31 December financial year-end may have a series of monthly standard rentals ranging from a highest figure for January to a lowest figure for facilities for equipment to be acquired during December. Some leasing companies have quarterly bands, while others choose to quote level rentals throughout their financial year, notwithstanding the fact that their return may vary with the timing of the expenditure on the leased equipment.

The reason for the timing difference is the variation in the length of time before a lessor obtains tax relief on the expenditure. The period between a company's year-end and the due date for payment of corporation tax will generally be 9 months. For a leasing company with a 31 March year-end and a liability to pay tax 9 months after the end of its accounting year, the interval can vary between 9 months and 21 months, as follows:

1. Equipment acquired by incurring expenditure on 31 March 1987 qualifies for a 25 per cent writing-down allowance in the company's accounting period ending on that day, and tax relief will be obtained on 1 January of the following year — a delay of 9 months.
2. Equipment acquired by incurring expenditure on 1 April 1986 also qualifies for 25 per cent writing-down allowance in the company's accounting period ending 31 March 1987, and tax relief will be obtained on 1 January 1988 — a delay of 21 months.

The difference can be significant to a lessor's return. Figure 9.2 shows that a lessor maintaining the after-tax rate of return at the same level throughout the year could charge semi-annual rentals varying from £13,123 for a lease starting on 1 April to £12,747 for a lease starting on 31 March. It will be seen from this that our typical £12,795 semi-annual rental lease assumes that expenditure is incurred on 1 March. It has been assumed throughout that the lease is completed and the primary period begins on the same day that the expenditure is incurred.

This timing difference can be seen more clearly by looking at the lease rental figures that would have applied prior to the 1984 Finance Act, i.e. when first-year allowances were 100 per cent of equipment cost and the corporation tax rate was 52 per cent. In this case the 31 March lease would have required a semi-annual rental of £11,196 as compared with a rental of £11,904 for the 1 April lease, to maintain the lessor's after-tax rate at the same level. This difference of £708 is much greater than the £376 range under the 25 per cent writing-down allowance tax system as illustrated in Figure 9.2. The reason for this more extreme difference is illustrated in Figure 9.3 which compares the lessor's net cash investment in a 100 per cent first-year allowance lease commencing on 31 March and a 100 per cent first-year allowance lease commencing on 1 April 1977.

Comparing the lease cash flows for 31 March and 1 April in Figure 9.3, we can see how the lessor's cash investment in the lease reduces sharply after 9 months and 21 months respectively, illustrating the substantial tax

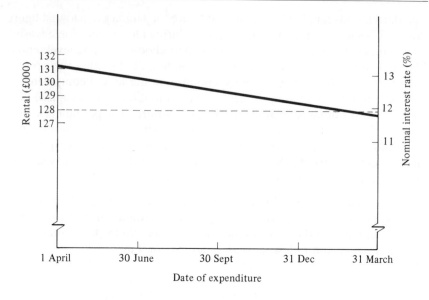

Figure 9.2 Timing differences

credit arising as a result of 100 per cent first-year allowances which were then available at a 52 per cent corporation tax rate. The larger amount of cash invested for longer in the 1 April start lease requires the lessor to charge a higher rental in order to maintain an equivalent rate of return on the (higher level of) cash invested.

The cash invested reduces, reflecting semi-annual rental repayments and annual tax credits, but later in the lease the graph shows the negative investment or surplus cash required in order to pay the tax charge arising in later years. Interest accrues throughout, both increasing the cash invested in years 1–3, and increasing the surplus in years 4–7 (the reinvestment rate is more prudently assumed to be, usually, about two-thirds or half of the assumed funding cost rate).

Although rental payments cease after year 5, the lessor's cash flow shows that the effect of the lease transaction continues for a further two years.

Returning to the 25 per cent writing-down allowance tax position, the timing difference is similar in principle to that illustrated above, but, as indicated in Figure 9.2, the effect on lease rentals is much less significant.

It is often difficult to forecast the timing of future expenditure accurately; however, the consequences of any changes should be recognized. A delay within a leasing company's financial year is likely to be beneficial (to either the lessee or the lessor), but a deferment to the subsequent financial

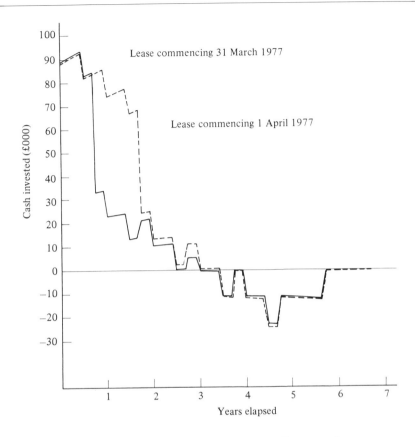

Lease commencing 31 March 1977

Lease commencing 1 April 1977

Figure 9.3 A 100 per cent first-year allowance lease

year may have adverse financial consequences because of the postpone-
ment of the date of receipt of tax relief by one year.

Any manufacturing or service company acquiring equipment is in the
same position. The timing phenomenon may indicate a mixed financial
strategy. A business may be able to optimize sources of finance by buying
(using its own funds or borrowed money) or by taking on hire purchase the
equipment that is to be delivered close to its own year-end, and leasing that
equipment which is to be acquired early in its own but towards the end of a
leasing company's financial year.

The development of quotations based on the timing of expenditure has
created something of a seasonal pattern in rental rates. Lower rates have
been in evidence in September and December, when leasing subsidiaries of
the majority of the clearing bank groups have year-ends. There are,

however, some leasing groups with a number of different year-end subsidiaries throughout the calendar year; this is designed to keep the group competitive. Some lessees exploit this situation by arranging a series of facilities with different lessors in each case for expenditure close to that lessor company's year-end; others prefer the certainty, the administrative simplicity, and the continuity of dealing with one leasing company through-out a financial year.

Variation clauses

Up to this stage, the comments on the various payment patterns described are equally applicable to rentals fixed at the commencement of the lease for the whole of the primary period and to floating rentals, i.e. those that are subject to variation during the lease period. No statistics have been published on the proportions of fixed and floating rentals, but it is likely that the majority by number of finance leases executed are on fixed rentals, although large ticket leases are more likely to be on a variable basis.

Rentals vary most frequently for corporation tax rate and interest rate changes but leasing agreements may also provide for adjustment to the amount of the rental for several other factors, including the following:

ENTITLEMENT TO WRITING-DOWN ALLOWANCES

Rentals are normally arrived at on the assumption that the lessor is entitled to writing-down allowances on any expenditure on leased equipment beginning in the accounting period in which the lessor incurs the expenditure. This assumption may prove to be invalid because of a change in the system of allowances, or because the expenditure is regarded as ineligible for such allowances; for example, expenditure may have been incurred on plant, some or all of which should have been classified for tax purposes as expenditure on industrial buildings.

Some leasing agreements have been known to go further and to require that rentals be increased if the lessor does not receive (whether or not entitled to do so) the benefit of the writing-down allowances. This could depend on the lessor having sufficient taxable profits to offset all capital and other allowances and also on the tax position of other companies within the lessor's group. Lessees should be cautious of the inclusion of this condition in a leasing agreement. Case study 9.2 at the end of this chapter gives details of a case where there was a challenge to a claim for allowances.

WRITING-DOWN ALLOWANCE ASSUMPTIONS

For the purposes of most lease evaluation calculations, it is generally assumed that tax allowances are granted on the basis that each leased asset

70

constituted a separate 'pool', notwithstanding that in fact most of the lessor's assets (excluding, for example, exported assets covered by the 10 per cent allowance provisions of S. 70, Finance Act 1982, and higher value cars) will be aggregated together in one pool.

Unlike the 100 per cent first-year allowance lease illustrated in Figure 9.3, leases calculated under the current writing-down allowance rules can continue to give the lessor writing-down allowances for many years after the end of the primary period of the lease. Since the allowances are calculated on a reducing balance basis, the tax effect of the lease continues in the lessor's books indefinitely, as shown in Table 9.10.

If the leased asset continues to be used after a five-year primary period for, say, a 10- or 15-year secondary period, then a lessor would continue to claim writing-down allowances for 15 or 20 years in total, by which time the residual written-down value at 0.3 per cent of original cost is relatively immaterial. However, at the end of the five-year primary period the lessee may not want to take up the option to continue to lease the equipment for a secondary period, and at this stage arrangements may be made for the sale of the asset to a third party.

Table 9.10 Annual 25 per cent writing-down allowances

Year	Cost/Written-down value brought forward £	Writing-down allowance at 25% £
1	100,000	25,000
2	75,000	18,750
3	56,250	14,063
4	42,187	10,547
5	31,640	7,910
6	23,730	5,932
7	17,798	4,449
8	13,349	3,337
9	10,011	2,503
10	7,508	1,877
11	5,631	1,408
12	4,223	1,056
13	3,167	792
14	2,375	594
15	1,781	445
16	1,336	334
17	1,002	250
18	752	188
19	564	141
20	423	106
21	317	
22	etc.	

The sale proceeds realized will be deducted from the leased asset 'pool' and will determine how much (if any) is available to be carried forward. Referring to Table 9.10, if the asset is sold after the end of year 5 for the then tax written-down value (£23,730), the lessor will receive no further writing-down allowances in future years, and will write off the 95 per cent rental rebate against profits for the year.

If, however, the leased asset realized, say, only £10,000 — less than its then written-down value — the lessor would have less future writing-down allowances available and would also suffer corporation tax on a higher profit figure in the year of sale.

Table 9.11 presents the effect on the lessor's taxable profits in the year of sale, and the balance carried forward in the 'pool' assuming (1) a sale at the then tax written-down value (£23,730), (2) a sale for £10,000 and (3) the continuing of the leasing into a secondary period. Clearly the lessor's position can differ appreciably depending on the action taken at the end of the primary period, and the assumptions made regarding this issue when calculating the original lease rental.

Most lessors will evaluate their small- and medium-ticket lease rates to cover the 'most pessimistic' assumption (i.e. continuing indefinite secondary period as illustrated in Table 9.11(3). However, competitive pressure and market conditions have led to lessors including variation clauses in some of their large-value leases which state that the lease rate has been calculated on the assumption that the equipment will be sold to a third party at the end of the primary period for a sale price equal to its then tax written-down value. If this does not happen, the lessee is required by the

Table 9.11 Tax effects of the sale of equipment

	(1) Sale at tax written-down value £	(2) Sale for £10,000 £	(3) Continuing secondary period £
Other business profits	100,000	100,000	100,000
Secondary period rental	–	–	1,000
Rental rebate (95% of sale proceeds)	(22,544)	(9,500)	–
Writing-down allowances	–	(3,433)	(5,932)
Taxable profits, year 6	77,456	87,067	95,068
WDV carried forward (assuming separate leased asset 'pool')	nil	10,297	17,798

variation clause to pay an adjustment rental at that time, calculated to maintain the lessor's return at the level it would have been, had the assumed sale occurred.

The effect of such a clause is complex to calculate and administer for a portfolio of small leases, and the uncertainty involved would be commercially unacceptable both for lessor and lessee. With a large lease, however, a variation clause of this type is not unusual.

TAXATION SYSTEM

A change in the basis of taxation may materially affect a leasing company's return. A provision in a lease agreement requiring an adjustment to rentals for any such change may be included by a lessor in contemplation of a change in the whole structure of the corporation tax system, for example, to a system based on some form of inflation accounting. A lessor may also wish to limit the risk of a loss arising from other, less extensive, taxation changes, such as changes in the due dates for payment of tax. A lessor's cash flow would be adversely affected if, for example, due dates of payment were brought forward after the benefit of the first year's 25 per cent writing-down allowance had been received but before tax was due to be paid on the corresponding proportion of the rentals receivable under the lease.

NON-RECEIPT OF GRANTS

Lease rentals are normally subject to variation if expenditure on leased equipment by a lessor fails to qualify for any regional development or other grants that were assumed to be receivable by the lessor as owner, when calculating the original lease rentals payable (see Chapter 18). The effect of a variation clause relating to any non-taxable grants such as the regional development grants applying in the UK prior to 1988 can be significant, because:

(a) a grant received by the lessor free of tax will not be allowed as a charge against taxable profits if it is reclaimed (or disallowed), and

(b) the payments between the lessee and the lessor are 'rentals' or 'rental adjustments', and as such are taxable, whether or not they arose as a result of a tax-free grant.

As a result, the lessee's rental adjustment arising under a variation clause of this type will be the grossed-up equivalent of any grant reclaim made. This is illustrated below, although strictly speaking the grossing-up calculation is more complex, taking into account the timing differences between receipt of the rental adjustment and payment of tax.

Grant	Lessor	Lessee
£10,000	Grant (tax free)	Low rental lease
	Grant reclaim £4,000	Rental adjustment $4,000 \times \dfrac{100}{65} = £6,154$

Similarly any receipt of grant by the lessor not taken into account when calculating the original lease rental should result in a rental reduction under such a variation clause. Following the introduction of Regional Enterprise Grants in the UK in 1988, grants became payable to the lessee, largely eliminating the need for any grant variation provisions in the lease.

EXCHANGE RATES

A lease may include an arrangement for the rental to be adjusted to reflect any gain or loss on exchange in cases where a lessor intends to finance the acquisition of a specific, normally large-valued item of equipment by way of borrowing in a foreign currency.

CASH FLOW PROFILE

For large-value leases, rentals are frequently calculated on a provisional basis by reference to a preliminary set of assumptions agreed by the lessor and lessee. Once the actual figures are known, an adjustment is made (either on a lump sum basis or to future rentals) for any of the assumptions that are not fulfilled. The range of assumptions will vary between individual leasing facilities, but may include the dates of progress payments, the maximum expenditure in any one financial year (for the purpose of limiting the lessor's taxable capacity allocation), the amount of interest incurred in the pre-delivery period, the start date of the lease, and the date of receipt of any regional development or other grants.

In making an adjustment to rentals for a change in any of the assumptions initially used in their computation, a lessor is effectively putting a lessee in the position of being the purchaser of the equipment when the consequences of a change in taxation or other factor would fall directly on the lessee. It is not possible to specify in a leasing agreement the amount by which rentals would vary for any general change in the basis of taxation or for changes in some of the other assumptions described above. In such circumstances, the lease terms will generally require that the rentals are increased, or reduced, by such amount as is appropriate in order to maintain the rate of return on the lessor's investment at the same level as it would have been, had the change not occurred. The difficulty for lessees lies in the number of possible methods by which a lessor can measure the rate of return on an individual lease. Many leasing companies are not prepared to divulge the details of the basis of their calculation, but some leases include a provision whereby the accuracy of any rental adjustment is certified by a firm of chartered accountants, usually the lessor's auditors. Methods of evaluating a lessor's return are considered in Chapter 12.

Case study 9.1 on page 10 gives an example of a recent case involving the adjustment of rentals.

INTEREST VARIATION

Leasing companies use several bases for calculating interest adjustments, apart from the broad approach of maintaining the rate of return.

1. Rentals may be fixed in relation to a specified lending rate at the date of expenditure on the leased equipment. Once determined, rentals would remain at the same level throughout the lease period. Lending rates prescribed include Finance House Base Rate, London Inter-Bank Offered Rate (related to a specific loan period for funds such as one year) and the base rate of a bank specified by the lessor. A lease including provisions of this type is generally described as 'variable up to drawdown'.

2. The facility may provide for a specifically calculated periodic adjustment for the difference between the actual lending rate and the rate of interest initially assumed for the purpose of calculating rentals. Such adjustments are usually made quarterly, semi-annually or annually in arrears either by applying:

   (a) the average difference in interest rates over that period, or
   (b) the difference in interest rates on the first day of each quarterly, six-monthly or annual period (depending usually on rental frequency)

   to the amount of the lessor's cash investment in the lease from time to time.

3. There may be a formula setting out the amount by which the rentals are to vary for each 1 per cent change in the average lending rate over the primary lease period. In some cases, the amount of the percentage adjustment is fixed throughout the term; in most cases, however, it varies year by year, reflecting the lessor's reducing cash investment over the primary period of the lease.

In conjunction with any of these methods, the lease may stipulate either a range of interest rates inside which there is to be no rental adjustment or a maximum and/or minimum lending rate above or below which rentals are not to be adjusted. The possible permutations demonstrate the different ways in which both lessors and lessees appraise leasing arrangements, and the different funding arrangements available to the lessor.

Ignoring taxation allowances and a lessor's overheads, an interest variation at the start date of the lease would increase or decrease, as the case may be, the effective interest rate of a rental by the same amount as the change in the prescribed lending rate. Subsequent changes would have a proportionately smaller impact. However, to the extent that tax timing differences (allowances claimed and rentals charged) are taken into account in calculating the lease rentals, the effect of interest variation clauses will not necessarily alter the nominal interest rate of the lease by 1 per cent for every 1 per cent change in interest costs.

Once the lessor's cash investment has been reduced to nil at some point during the primary lease period (see Figure 9.3), the cost of money is no longer directly relevant and interest variation clauses based on maintaining the lessor's return cease to be operative. In theory, the adjustment during the remainder of the lease period, the reinvestment or cash surplus stage, should be in reverse. Any increase in interest rates in this period over that assumed for the purpose of calculating the rentals increases a lessor's earnings from a lease — the leasing company receives more interest on its cash surplus. Similarly, a reduction in interest rates decreases a lessor's earnings.

TAX VARIATION

To take account of changes in the rate of corporation tax, lease agreements provide for rentals to be adjusted either by stating that the lessor's rate of return is to be maintained, or by reference to a formula. The formula shows the amount of increase or decrease for each 1 per cent change in the rate of corporation tax applicable to each fiscal year, part or all of which falls within the primary lease period. Some leasing companies make the adjustment by applying a specified factor to a notional taxable income figure which is set out for each rental period in an appendix to the lease.

The rate of corporation tax has historically been announced during the budget speech at the end of each fiscal year. In March 1984 the Chancellor of the Exchequer took the unusual step of announcing the corporation tax rates for the year ended 31 March 1984 and the proposed rates for the subsequent three years. The reason for this unusual step was that the stepped reductions in the corporation tax rate over these years was part of an overall tax strategy, and linked to the reduction and phasing out over the same period of first-year allowances in favour of 25 per cent writing down allowances. Since then, the corporation tax rate for the coming year has been announced in the budget, but the rate could still be altered in retrospect, should the Chancellor so decide. Rental adjustments in respect of changes in the corporation tax rate would thus often have to be made retrospectively, some time after the relevant fiscal year. For this reason the ELA has made representations to the Inland Revenue in favour of the announcement of corporation tax rates in advance, thus reducing the number and scale of retrospective tax variation adjustments which lessees may have to suffer.

The policy of making an advance announcement would also help to ensure that the lessee has the benefit of any rental reduction in the year that the corporation tax rate has been reduced, and suffers any increase in the same year in which the tax rate is increased, thus keeping the lessee's after-tax profit (after charging lease rentals) as level as possible.

Tax variation clauses normally appear only in leasing arrangements that also reflect the benefit of capital allowances. When there is no significant difference between the rentals received by a lessor (net of interest costs) in each accounting period and the depreciation allowed for tax purposes (i.e. the writing-down allowances), the only effect of a change in the rate of corporation tax is to increase or reduce the after-tax earnings of the leasing company in the same proportion as the change in earnings of any other manufacturing or service company. A lessor's return is, however, more sensitive to a change in the rate of corporation tax when the timing of writing-down allowances claimed in each year of the lease differs significantly from the timing of receipt of net rental income.

The greatest variation generally occurs when a change in the corporation tax rate takes place in the year following the acquisition of the equipment, especially if the lease commences towards the lessor's year-end. When this happens, the first writing-down allowance benefit is obtained at one rate of corporation tax and tax is payable on comparable rental income at a different rate; it is not simply the lessor's net rental income after depreciation that is affected. Assume, for example, an increase from 35 to 45 per cent in the rate of corporation tax in year 2 of a lease. A lessor company with a 31 March year-end will have a corporation tax rate of 35 per cent in year 1 and 45 per cent in year 2 and subsequent years. Table 9.12 shows the taxation implications for a leasing company of equipment costing £100,000 purchased on 1 March for a five-year primary lease period at a semi-annual rental, payable in advance, of £12,795.

It has been assumed, for simplicity, that the equipment is sold at the end of the five-year primary period at its then tax written-down value (see Table 9.11) and the lessee receives a 100 per cent rental rebate. The net taxable profit column shows, clearly, that the timing of any tax change can significantly alter the lessor's after-tax return, and in this case the timing of the tax rate change in year 2 means that the large loss in year 1 will produce tax relief at only 35 per cent, whereas in later years when a taxable profit results the tax charge will be at 45 per cent, resulting in an average rate

77

Table 9.12 Effect of a corporation tax rate increase in year 2

Year	Rentals/ (rebate) £	Writing- down allowances £	Lessor's interest cost £	Net taxable profit £	Tax charge/ (relief) £
1	2,133	25,000	727	(23,594)	(8,258)
2	25,590	18,750	8,231	(1,391)	(626)
3	25,590	14,063	5,901	5,626	2,532
4	25,590	10,547	3,961	11,082	4,987
5	25,590	7,910	2,021	15,659	7,046
6	23,457	–	204	(477)	(215)
	(23,730)	–	9	(9)	(4)
Rentals	127,950				
Rebate	(23,730)	76,270	21,054	6,896	5,462

Average tax rate 5,462/6,896 = 79 per cent

over seven years of 79 per cent. In order to maintain an after-tax rate of return the lessor will require each of the 10 rental payments to be increased from £12,795 to £l3,231.

Figure 9.4 shows the changes required (to maintain the lessor's after-tax rate of return) to our typical lease rental of £12,795, assuming a corporation tax rate change in any of the first seven years after inception of the lease.

A lessee's view of the relative attractions of fixed and floating rentals depends on an assessment of future interest and tax rates. Variation clauses seem more desirable when money costs are high or the rate of corporation tax is expected to fall. However, for some lessees, the possible benefit of reduced rentals is outweighed by the elimination of the risk of an increase in rentals and the certainty of the cash flow when rentals are fixed, with the consequent advantages for cost budgeting and cash flow forecasting.

INDEX LINKING
One form of rental variation that has not yet appeared in finance leases is index linking. It is found in several types of operating leasing, such as computers, with rentals being fixed annually either directly or implicitly by reference to a suitable index, such as the replacement cost of the type of equipment being leased. For finance leasing, the introduction of index linking of rentals may depend on developments in the indexing of interest rates.

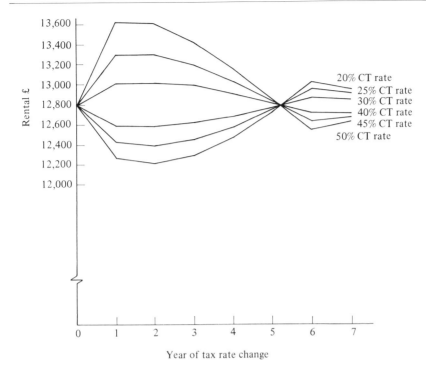

Figure 9.4 Year of tax rate change

Other factors

PROGRESS PAYMENTS

The acquisition of equipment can involve progress payments to the manufacturer or supplier. In some cases, the pre-delivery period is a few months, but in others, particularly for large-valued items such as ships and aircraft, the construction period of the asset may stretch over several financial years. There are a number of possible methods of arranging progress payments:

1. *Sale and lease-back before use* The prospective lessee places the order for the equipment, makes the progress payments, and sells his or her interest in the equipment to the lessor immediately before the asset is brought into use.
2. *Pre-delivery rentals* The lessor places the order and makes the progress payments. The lessee pays periodic pre-delivery rentals related to the interest incurred by the lessor during the pre-delivery period. The

79

primary period rentals, commencing on the date of delivery of the equipment, are calculated in relation to the capital cost of the equipment.

3. *Capitalizing interest*   The pre-delivery interest is 'rolled-up' or capitalized by the lessor. (This is sometimes described as 'rentalized'). As in 'Pre-delivery rentals', the lessor makes the progress payments, and a sum equal to the total interest incurred by the lessor on the progress payments up to the date of delivery of the equipment is added to the cost of the equipment for the purpose of calculating primary period rentals.

There is normally a difference between the treatment of capital allowances for method 1 and methods 2 and 3. In cases 2 and 3, the allowance may be claimed by the lessor in the financial years in which the progress payments are made, subject to the anti-avoidance provisions in the Finance Act 1985 which prevent artificial acceleration of allowances. In case 1, the lessor can only claim an allowance in the year in which the expenditure is incurred and, hence, unless progress payments are made to the lessee the lessor is not entitled to allowances until expenditure is incurred immediately prior to the commencement of the lease.

LESSOR'S OUTGOINGS

A leasing company often incurs out-of-pocket expenses in setting up a leasing facility, particularly in relation to large-value leases. Such costs may include fees for legal, taxation, and accountancy advice, insurance premiums, survey and valuation charges, and commitment fees and other expenses in connection with any loan being arranged by the lessor, such as under the ship mortgage or export finance schemes. A lessor may also pay a commission to a broker for the introduction of business, although often an introductory or consultancy fee is settled directly between the lessee and the broker or adviser.

There are three ways in which a lessor generally recovers outgoings:

1. The lessee makes a separate payment to the lessor for any expenses incurred.
2. The lessor 'capitalizes' the expenses for rental purposes by adding them to the cost of the equipment to arrive at the principal amount on which the rentals are to be calculated.
3. The lessor quotes rentals which include an element for any outgoings. Under this arrangement any over- or underestimate of expenses is for the lessor's account.

VALUE ADDED TAX

Rentals, excluding VAT, are normally quoted as a rate per £1,000 of the cost of leased equipment, which also excludes the VAT element. VAT at the applicable rate is then added to the amount determined by applying the quoted rate, to arrive at the total rental instalment payable by the lessee. For private cars, where the VAT payable on the acquisition of the equipment is non-recoverable, the cost of the asset for the purpose of calculating rentals includes the non-recoverable VAT.

For most commercial lessees, VAT payable on rentals is deductible or recoverable in the same way as for any other input tax, without giving rise to any problem. However, if a significant part of a lessee's activities are exempt for VAT purposes, so that only a proportion of its input tax is recoverable, there is a disadvantage in leasing compared with borrowing which needs to be taken into account in conjunction with other advantages and disadvantages. For lessees with exempt activities, part of the non-recoverable VAT relates to the interest element in rentals (since the rental on which VAT is payable covers both the cost of the equipment and the inherent interest), whereas if equipment is purchased, the interest payable on funds borrowed to finance the acquisition is exempt for VAT purposes.

EARLY TERMINATION

Lessors and lessees enter into finance lease agreements with the intention of continuing the leasing of the equipment for the whole of the primary lease period. A finance lease is normally unlikely to be attractive to a lessee contemplating termination soon after the start date, and leases do not generally contain specific provisions for voluntary early termination, although provision is made for termination due to a total loss of the goods or following default by a lessee. However, leasing companies are normally prepared to agree to a voluntary early termination during the course of the primary period.

There are various ways of calculating the amount of the terminal payment to be made by the lessee on a voluntary termination, or following a total loss of the equipment. In some cases, the basis is the same as that stipulated in the lease for a termination following a default by the lessee. Although there is no necessity for the provisions to be similar, it is unusual for prescribed voluntary termination arrangements to be significantly more favourable to a lessee because of the possible implication that the payments required to be made on default constitute a penalty in law.

The most common method of calculating the termination payment is to discount future rentals from their due dates back to the proposed date of payment. The rate at which rentals are to be discounted for calculating the terminal payment varies, but is frequently around 4–5 per cent per annum.

An alternative, more often found in facilities for large-valued items, is for the leasing company to compute a series of termination payments for each month or quarter of the primary lease period using a computer program and taking into account the main lease terms, the required rate of return and the assumed sale proceeds of the leased equipment. These amounts, expressed as a percentage of the cost of the equipment and sometimes called 'stipulated loss values', are then set out in an appendix to the lease agreement. If the lease includes a rental variation clause, the amounts of the termination payments are normally also subject to adjustment for the same factors as the rentals. The appendix may also be subject to variation depending on the actual sale proceeds realized on disposal of the equipment.

THE PACKAGE

The lessee's choice of the most suitable of the various terms described in the previous sections depends on their availability, cash flow and other requirements. A leasing company is not necessarily prepared to offer prospective customers all the various alternatives and may insist on adhering to its standard terms.

It is not difficult to separate a lessor's leasing quotation into its component parts – rate of primary period rental, length of primary period, renewal options, variation clauses, etc. Individual lessees will assess the relative importance of the various financial terms differently on the basis of their own requirements, and the equipment or project concerned. Although in certain cases one or more of the terms may be crucial, it is generally the acceptability to both lessor and lessee of the combination of all the terms as a package that matters for the conclusion of a satisfactory transaction.

Case studies

CASE STUDY 9.1

In 1980, two leasing subsidiaries of the Forward Trust Group entered into similar leases with Tyne and Wear Passenger Transport Executive in respect of metro cars. A basic feature of these leases was the assumption that if the normal rate of corporation tax payable by the lessors at any time during the primary period was other than 52 per cent and such change in the rate affected the lessors' after-tax return on the capital expenditure incurred by the lessors in the provision and leasing of the equipment, then the rentals payable would be adjusted by such amount as the auditors of the lessors, acting as experts and not as arbitrators, conclusively certified in writing to the lessors and the lessees so as to leave the lessors with the same after-tax return as the lessors would have obtained if no such change had occurred.

Initially, following the changes in corporation tax rates introduced by the Finance Act 1984, the rentals of both leases were re-evaluated by simply re-running the original evaluations, inserting the new tax rates and assuming the rate of 35 per cent applied to all remaining years; thereby calculating the future revised rentals.

The Chancery Division of the High Court heard evidence of a dispute between the parties as to the method to be used by the lessors' auditors to calculate the adjustment of rentals and the two methods proposed were:

1. For the lessors; the Actuarial After Tax Margin (AATM) method which calculates an after-tax return on funds from time to time invested in the lease over and above the interest cost of such funds.
2. For the lessee; the 'cash method' which calculates, excluding interest, reinvestment income and timing, the 'after-tax' return as equal to the gross rentals less tax less capital cost plus the value of capital allowances.

The Court considered the meaning of the word 'return' and held it to be capable of more than one use but that it had to be related within the commercial context of a tax-based equipment lease. The fact that the leases, on the insistence of the lessee, contained no provision for interest rate variation and the evidence given by the parties regarding their awareness of the effect of this on profitability, was held to show the importance attached to borrowing costs. It was held, also, that the use of a prospective rate of corporation tax for the remaining years was in accordance with the intention of the parties. The evidence given was held to show conclusively that the original method of evaluation, and therefore the method to be used for the re-evaluation, was the AAMT method.

In the certificate provided, the isssue of which was itself the subject of dispute, the auditors stated *inter alia* that the Owner will receive 'the same after-tax return, expressed as a percentage of funds invested, from the amended rental stream'. It was held that the words 'expressed as a percentage of funds invested', which had been added, served to protect the lessee and the certificate was conclusive for the purpose of the rental variation clause.

CASE STUDY 9.2
In 1984, Barclays Mercantile Industrial Finance Ltd (BMI) — now Barclays Mercantile Business Finance Ltd — entered into an agreement

with Warner Bros Inc. (WBI) to purchase a film produced by a wholly owned UK subsidiary of WBI, for the purpose of leasing the film to Warner Bros Distributors Ltd (WBDL), another UK subsidiary of WBI. The film in question was a box-office success.

A similar type of agreement had been entered into between BMI and Columbia Pictures Industries Inc. (CPII) for the purchase of another film. This film was not a success at the box-office.

Both films received certificates from the Secretary of State for Trade confirming they were British films and therefore qualifying films for the purpose of Section 72, Finance Act 1982.

The appeal by BMI against the refusal to grant 100 per cent first-year allowances was heard by the Special Commissioners of Inland Revenue who held that the films were not used for the purposes of the trade of the lessees within the meaning of Section 64(2)(a) of the Finance Act 1980. BMI appealed this decision to the Chancery Division of the High Court and the Inland Revenue cross-appealed on the grounds that the sole or main benefit of the capital expenditure was the obtaining of an allowance (Section 75(1)(c) of the Capital Allowances Act 1990 — formerly, paragraph 3(1)(c) of Schedule 8, Finance Act 1971).

It was conceded at both appeals that the equipment purchased was plant and that the plant was leased to WBDL. In the High Court, the Inland Revenue contended that the distribution agreements between the lessees, WBDL and CPII, constituted a use for the purpose of leasing and were transactions outwith the trades of the lessees, thereby precluding the granting of an allowance. It was held by the Court that even partial use of the equipment for a purpose other than leasing is sufficient to satisfy the requirement and the granting of distribution rights did not amount to the disposal of the rights of the lessees, only to a restriction on the exercise of such rights. It was held, also, that the transactions were within the trades of the lessees.

With regard to 'sole or main benefit', it was held that the plant acquired by BMI had not previously been used by WBI or any company in the WBI group and that the price paid did not exceed the cost to the vendors. The purpose of BMI was to make a profit on the purchase and lease of the plant.

10. *Leasing and investment decisions*

An item of equipment can be obtained either by purchase from the supplier or by hire (in its most general sense) from the owner for a period that meets the user's requirements. Each of these methods of procurement offers choices as to the form of finance. The purchase option can be for immediate unfettered ownership from the purchaser's cash resources or unsecured borrowings, or through a secured loan or deferred acquisition under a hire-purchase or conditional sale agreement. The leasing option can similarly take the form of a finance lease over a period equivalent to the useful life of the asset, or an operating lease or short-term hire agreement.

When contemplating the use of an asset, a company needs to make a series of related decisions, including the following:

1. Is the physical use of the asset justified, taking into account the company's objectives and constraints (including the availability of finance) and the costs of the various alternative courses of action?
2. The most suitable period of use taking into account projected cash flows and the expected useful life of the asset (obsolescence, etc.).
3. The method of financing.
4. The earliest date the asset is required.
5. The proposed location of the asset.
6. Selection of the particular asset and supplier.

It may not always be possible to choose the desired period of use. Many types of asset are not available for hire on a short-term basis and, in such a circumstance, an intending user has no alternative but to purchase the asset or to pay the equivalent of the purchase price under a financial leasing arrangement. For equipment that can be hired or acquired by way of an operating lease, such as construction plant or computers, the most suitable period of use will depend on several factors, including the relative costs of purchasing and hiring, the purpose for which the asset is required, and the rate of technological change (the possibility of more advanced equipment becoming available before the cost has been fully amortized).

When examining the role to be played by financial leasing as a source of equipment finance, two decisions are of major importance. It is necessary, firstly, to establish that the use of the equipment, and hence its acquisition, is desirable in the long term — the investment decision; and, secondly, to select the method of finance — the financing decision. Other aspects of the decision-making process, such as any government financial assistance, may affect the cash flows and require evaluation, but should not alter the basis on which the investment and financing decisions are approached.

The investment decision

The investment decision can take a number of forms. There may be no alternative, as in the case of replacing an essential part of a production line or a new legal requirement for safety equipment. It may be an 'accept or reject' decision, where the equipment is to be an integral part of a new production process to be set up provided that it meets the company's investment criteria. Where a lack of resources limits the total number of projects that can be selected, it may be a ranking decision either between mutually exclusive projects or in determining in which of several projects a company should engage.

The theory of investment appraisal is outside the scope of this book. However, it is important to note the interrelationship between investment and financing decisions. In order to reach an equipment investment decision, it is necessary to have regard to the cost of the funds to be used for the acquisition of the equipment. If a company's overall investment policy is being appraised, its average cost of capital is relevant. If one additional project is under review, it may be appropriate to take into account only the marginal cost of borrowing the necessary additional funds (itself a component of the average cost of capital). Frequently, both measures of the cost of funds are used. The method of financing therefore needs to be considered to determine the cheapest form of finance for the purpose of evaluating the investment decision, and to derive the 'hurdle' rate of return above which projects should, at least in theory, be accepted.

There has been extensive academic debate concerning whether the investment and financing decisions should be separated or combined — a debate that even a Chancellor of the Exchequer entered when, during the 1984 Budget speech, it was argued that investment decisions should be taken on a pre-tax, not a post-tax, basis. However, in a narrow leasing context, the debate has become simplified and enshrined in the phrases 'lease or borrow' and 'lease or buy'. Should companies be deciding between leasing and borrowing (a purely financial decision) or between leasing and buying (a combination of the investment and financing decisions)?

From a practical viewpoint, it is necessary to simplify the decision-making process as far as possible. For most equipment procurement decisions, the investment decision should be made independently of the method of finance to be used. The implications of leasing should be excluded at the investment decision stage, subject to the proviso that, where a company has arranged or expects to arrange a significant amount of lease finance, its average and marginal cost of funds should reflect the costs of leasing as well as the costs of equity and borrowed funds. This will ensure that companies do not reject investment opportunities by failing to take account of the possible availability of lease finance at a lower cost or in a more flexible form than traditional forms of borrowing.

Apart from the question of how to approach the decisions, there are semantic dangers lurking in the use of the phrases 'lease or buy' and 'lease or borrow'. Companies either lease or buy equipment, but in so doing they select a method for financing the procurement, which is usually a choice between leasing and borrowing. The term 'lease or buy' tends to blur the distinction between investment and financing decisions, and implies a link with operating leasing. 'Lease or borrow' seems to be a more apposite description of the choice facing a company when deciding whether or not to enter into a finance lease. However, it should be borne in mind that there will be circumstances when a company with a cash surplus and no intention of borrowing will, for tax or other reasons, find it advantageous to lease. The financing decision is between buying, using either internal or external funds, and leasing.

The various stages are shown in the form of a decision tree in Figure 10.1.

The financing decision

There are various ways open to finance the acquisition of capital equipment. The main categories are as follows:

1. Retained earnings (cash resources)
2. New capital from rights issues to shareholders
3. Long-term debt including bonds and debentures
4. Short-term debt (overdrafts, bills, commercial paper, etc.)
5. Secured loan
6. Hire purchase/conditional sale
7. Leasing.

The process of choosing the most appropriate method in any particular circumstances may be divided into distinct steps. Firstly, an examination of the non-financial factors involved and, secondly, a comparison of the costs of each type of finance. Sometimes, the non-financial factors are of critical importance, eliminating the need for any cost comparison; usually, however, these factors need only be weighted against any cost differences. The review of the non-financial factors is also of assistance in the task of identifying the assumptions that need to be made when comparing the costs of the various alternative sources of finance.

The INVESTMENT decision | The FINANCING decision

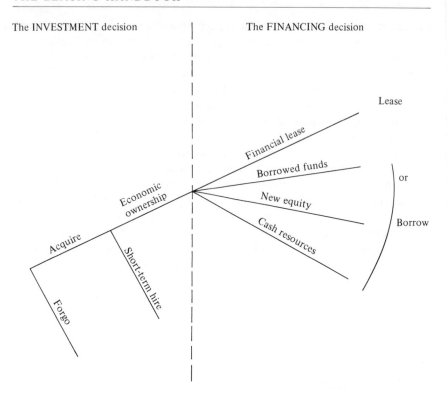

Figure 10.1 Capital expenditure decisions

A checklist should be prepared of factors to be examined by a company's management before commencing the financial evaluation. Matters frequently requiring consideration include:

1. *Capital adequacy* It is important that a company has adequate shareholders' equity for its planned level of trading. Where capital levels are inadequate, the problem should be addressed either by issuing new capital, or by retaining a greater proportion of earnings at the expense of dividend distributions, rather than by taking on further debt obligations (assuming further loan or lease finance is available).

2. *Financing strategy* The method of finance to be selected for a new project should be compatible with a company's overall financing strategy. It may be appropriate to provide for a mix of financial facilities in order to reduce risk. Companies may wish to structure debt payments so as to avoid loan maturities coinciding and to arrange sources of finance so as not to be unduly dependent on particular types of debt. The part to be played by leasing in a company's overall financing strategy may well depend on its management's view of the extent to

which leasing may enable the company to increase its overall debt-raising capacity.

3. *Liquidity* A company needs to retain sufficient liquidity to meet any sudden unexpected shortfall in cash inflows or additional operating or capital expenditure.

4. *Availability* The initial availability of the various types of finance should be ascertained. Fixed rate finance for the period required might, for example, only be available by leasing equipment rather than through loan arrangements. Companies should also assess the importance of the guaranteed continuing availability of the finance, as in the case of a financial lease, rather than the possibility of repayment on demand as normally stipulated in overdraft and certain other types of loan arrangements.

5. *Marshalling of security* There may be ways of arranging finance secured on the assets of a company, which increase its overall debt capacity. In addition to leasing, fixed and floating charges fall in this category.

6. *Benefit eligibility* Although most types of investment incentives are equally available for purchased and leased equipment, it is important that the method of finance does not adversely affect a company's eligibility for government grants and other benefits.

7. *Restrictions* The chosen method of finance needs to comply with all restrictive covenants and governmental regulations. There may be borrowing restrictions in a company's Memorandum or Articles of Association, in a debenture trust deed or long-term debt agreement.

8. *Administrative convenience* Companies may be attracted to those methods of finance, including leasing, which simplify bookkeeping procedures and assist expense budgeting and cash flow forecasting.

The second stage in the financing decision is the comparison of the costs of the various available sources of finance. To simplify the financial evaluation, it is necessary to make certain assumptions concerning the characteristics of the leasing and borrowing cash flows.

The principal assumptions made (usually on an implicit basis) when comparing the costs of leasing and borrowing are:

1. The decision to acquire the equipment has already been taken by the company carrying out the evaluation.

2. Lease finance is equivalent to borrowing and does not increase debt capacity.

3. The company has sufficient other borrowing requirements to remain in a debt situation: there are no periods of overall cash surplus.

4. Rentals and interest rates equally reflect the company's credit-worthiness.

5. Lease finance and the available forms of borrowing have similar risk characteristics, i.e. there are no differences in the types of security interest in the equipment afforded to the providers of the finance or in other terms such as a lender's right to require repayment on demand.
6. Inflation may be disregarded. All of the cash flows are money rather than real cash flows.
7. Any uncertainty about future corporation tax rates is ignored, so that tax cash flows may be discounted at the same rate as other cash flows.
8. There are no economies of scale achievable by leasing, for example, as a consequence of the lessor negotiating with the supplier a reduction in the cost of the equipment or of being able to obtain a higher selling price for the equipment at the end of the lease period.
9. Leasing provides the best means of a company taking advantage of any available capital allowances from which the company cannot itself most effectively benefit either because of a lack of taxable capacity or for timing reasons.

The methods of evaluation are described in Chapter 11, together with illustrations of the calculations and comments on how the evaluation techniques may be extended to relax certain of the assumptions set out above. The remainder of this chapter surveys the growth of leasing and the relevance of this growth to existing preconceptions regarding the cost of leasing, and reviews the impact of leasing on a company having a lack of taxable capacity, on the timing of the investment decision and on the extent to which leasing as an alternative source of finance may increase a company's debt capacity.

PRECONCEPTIONS
As leasing has grown over the past few years, misconceptions have arisen of the advantages and disadvantages of leasing compared to other sources of finance. Prejudices have appeared both in favour of and against leasing. The confusion is explained partly by the historical development — leasing being regarded as 'last resort lending' and off-balance sheet finance; partly by the lack of clear understanding of the main characteristics of finance leasing; and partly by insufficient distinction being drawn between different lease market sectors.

The most commonly held preconception is that leasing is a purely tax driven form of finance and that following the changes to the system of corporate taxation announced in the Finance Act 1984, is no longer of relevance in serious financial decision making. However, although the growth of the leasing market was greatly promoted by tax factors, this view does not appear to be wholly supported by the available empirical research, nor necessarily by a detailed 'lease buy' analysis.

The historic influence of the corporate tax system on leasing has been discussed in Chapter 5 . There is little doubt that without the underlying tax advantage to lessor and lessee in the 1970s, the leasing industry would not have grown so quickly. However, to relate the total growth of leasing to tax advantage alone is a severe oversimplification.

To study this assertion, it is first necessary to distinguish between finance and operating leasing. The operating lease sector, particularly at the smaller, sales aid end of the market, has grown significantly, largely independently of tax advantage. Here lessees have been attracted by the advantages of service and convenience rather than cost. Tax considerations have been most important at the larger end of the market where decisions are often made on the grounds of cost alone.

A study made in 1979 of the financial leasing industry in the UK, concluded that there was a dominant distinction between big-ticket and small-ticket leasing, with tax capacity playing a major part in most big-ticket but not such an important factor in smaller-ticket leasing. It went on to qualify the conclusion further by reporting that there was also evidence of non tax-based leasing even in big deals. These findings were supported by a series of interviews carried out in 1976 with major leasing companies where it was found that not all lessors regard leasing as a tax-sheltering device but simply meeting a demand for asset-based financing, provided as part of an integrated range of financial services.

Evidence from the lessee end of the market unfortunately does not differentiate between the various market sectors. However, this seems also to indicate that tax advantage has not necessarily been regarded by lessees as an important reason to lease. In an early study, Fawthrop and Terry[1] found that almost two-thirds of companies surveyed found tax advantages to be irrelevant in the leasing decision; a conclusion supported by a further study by Sykes.[2] A study that included an analysis of the significance of leasing to small firms, found little evidence of tax matters being considered.

It was reported in 1980 that 48 per cent of sampled companies that had been taxable over the previous two years had in fact leased, whereas the corresponding figure for leasing by non-tax-paying companies was only (by comparison) 59 per cent. It was further found that for 54 per cent of companies studied, conservation of cash flow was an important reason to lease.

Further research is perhaps required in this area, but there is certainly a basis of evidence in these studies to suggest that growth of leasing in the UK is not entirely tax based: the flexibility of leasing; budgetary accuracy; on occasion, off-balance sheet characteristics; leasing as an additional line of credit; and provision, in some cases, of 100 per cent financing, are also extremely important in a lessee's decision-making process. In many cases leasing provides one, if not the only, source of fixed-rate finance available — a feature of lease development more dependent on treasury management than tax benefits.

DEBT CAPACITY

There continues to be much debate in business and academic journals on the impact of leasing on a company, but there is most controversy concerning the extent to which leasing may increase a company's overall debt-raising capability.

When evaluating the 'lease or borrow' decision, it is a convenient assumption that lease finance displaces an equal amount of debt. The position in practice may well be different. Even since the introduction of the SSAP 21 requirement to capitalize finance leases (see Chapter 15), there is general agreement among British commentators that the use of leasing will, at least marginally, increase the overall borrowing capability of companies. Credit analysts in most financial institutions will now always take lease obligations into account in reviewing credit lines. It is thus no longer imperfect knowledge on the part of lenders, but rather the less quantifiable results of two financing markets adding up to a figure greater than the constituent parts, that leads to greater debt availability. More precisely, some financial institutions may find the risks lower through leasing (as a result of security, sharing in residual values, etc.); and its fixed term nature gives greater security and comfort to other financiers than would be the case if the borrower's funds were all repayable immediately on demand, as in the case of an overdraft.

Opinions on the extent to which companies may increase their debt capacity by leasing are necessarily subjective. The views taken by individual companies and the attitudes of different financial institutions vary considerably. It is not feasible to quantify the effects of leasing on debt capacity in any particular circumstances.

Taxable capacity

However, this is not the case when a company has insufficient taxable capacity. It is possible to calculate precisely, for any particular set of assumptions, the effect of leasing on a company having no, or an inadequate level of, taxable profits against which to offset the capital allowances available on the purchase of equipment.

Reference has already been made to the impact on the growth of leasing in the UK of the combined effects of the introduction of accelerated first-year capital allowance and the general scarcity of taxable capacity that resulted among the manufacturing and trading sector. Indeed, the massive increase in the volume of leasing in 1984 and 1985 demonstrated the awareness in industry of the tax advantages of leasing as lessees sought to take final advantage of available first-year allowances by bringing forward projects that might otherwise not have been sanctioned until later in the year. However, now that we have moved through the transitional phase to a period of more stable tax rates and writing-down allowances, there is a danger that many businessmen will again seriously undervalue the benefit of being able to defer tax by taking immediate advantage of those capital allowances still available.

The value of taxable capacity when assessing leasing depends on the following external factors, apart from the absolute value of capital allowances:

- the tax regime, including the method of taxing company profits and dividend payments, the treatment of foreign taxes, and the period of delay, if any, between earning profits and paying tax thereon
- the standard rate of corporation tax — the higher the rate, the more valuable becomes the taxable capacity
- the level of interest rates — again, the higher the rate, the more valuable becomes the ability to defer tax
- whether there are other means, apart from leasing, of taking advantage of unused capital allowances
- the level of any unused relief against a company's 'mainstream' tax liability for advance corporation tax (ACT) paid on dividend distributions, in the case of the so-called 'marginal taxpayer', and the likely run-off of this unused relief in future.

For individual companies with a shortage of taxable capacity, the advantage of leasing compared to other forms of finance is obviously greater the longer the tax horizon — i.e. the later the date on which the company first expects to pay mainstream corporation tax. Even the timing during the lessee's tax year when the lease or purchase would have taken place is relevant where a lessor with a more tax-efficient year-end can take advantage of the writing-down allowances earlier than can the lessee. Forecasts of a company's taxable income and dividend payments, etc., will show the date on which it is anticipated that sufficient tax will become payable against which to offset the capital allowances. Calculations can be made of the relative costs of leasing and borrowing for various tax payment assumptions.

The value of taxable capacity may be illustrated by looking at the cash flows associated with a typical equipment purchase. The example is equally relevant to an industrial or commercial company buying equipment for use in its business and to a leasing company acquiring equipment for leasing to customers. In the former case, the periodic revenue represents the income generated by the equipment or the expense savings; in the latter, it represents rental receipts.

The assumed lease terms are set out in Table 10.1. To simplify the example, it is additionally assumed that the equipment is the only asset owned by the company and that it is wholly financed by borrowings. (In the case of the leasing company, the equivalent assumption is that the lease is the only transaction carried on by the company, but on the basis of a continuing trade for tax purposes.) The principal consequence of this assumption, as will be seen from the cash flows, is that the acquisition of equipment qualifying for 25 per cent annual writing-down allowances generally involves a period of borrowing (referred to as the investment period) followed by a period when the purchaser has surplus funds, i.e. the amount of tax deferred exceeds the unrecovered cash cost of the equipment. In practice, the purchase of equipment is normally only one of many transactions undertaken by a company and the cash surplus is in fact used to offset other borrowing requirements (in which case assumption 11 in Table 10.1 becomes the cost of borrowing during the surplus period). The

Table 10.1 Terms assumed for taxable capacity illustration

Equipment acquired by industrial user	Equipment acquired by lessor	Assumptions
1. Cost of equipment	Cost of equipment	£10,000
2. Date of acquisition	Date of acquisition	1 April
3. Useful life	Primary lease period	5 years
4. Income generated or expense saved	Rentals receivable	£650 each quarter commencing on the date of acquisition
5. Cost of money borrowed to finance the acquisition of the equipment	Cost of money borrowed to finance the acquisition of the equipment	2.5% per quarter
6. Capital allowance	Capital allowance	25% writing-down allowance
7. Corporation tax rate	Corporation tax rate	35%
8. Company year-end	Company year-end	30 June
9. Tax payment date	Tax payment date	9 months after year-end
10. Scrap value	Renewal rentals and residual value	Nil
11. Earnings rate on cash surplus	Reinvestment rate	1.75% per quarter
12. Other costs	Overheads	Nil

choice of reinvestment rate for evaluation purposes is considered further in Chapter 12.

Table 10.2 shows the cash flow on the basis that the purchaser has sufficient taxable capacity to utilize the whole of the 25 per cent annual writing-down allowances in the year in which they arise. Figure 10.2

Table 10.2 Cash flow with adequate taxable capacity

Financial year	Qtr end	Cost[1] £	Revenue/ rental £	Tax[2] £	Average net cash investment £	Interest paid (rec'd)[3] £	Profit taken out[4] £
1	30.06	10,000	(650)		9,350	234	47
2	30.09		(650)		8,981	225	45
	31.12		(650)		8,601	215	43
	31.03		(650)		8,209	205	41
	30.06		(650)	(729)	7,076	177	36
3	30.09		(650)		6,639	166	33
	31.12		(650)		6,188	155	31
	31.03		(650)		5,724	143	29
	30.06		(650)	(34)	5,212	130	26
4	30.09		(650)		4,718	118	24
	31.12		(650)		4,210	105	21
	31.03		(650)		3,686	92	19
	30.06		(650)	210	3,357	84	17
5	30.09		(650)		2,808	70	14
	31.12		(650)		2,242	56	11
	31.03		(650)		1,659	41	8
	30.06		(650)	401	1,459	36	7
6	30.09		(650)		852	21	5
	31.12		(650)		228	6	1
	31.03		(650)		(415)	(7)	0
	30.06			562	140	4	1
7	30.09				145	4	1
	31.12				150	4	1
	31.03				155	4	1
	30.06			(156)	4	0	0
8	30.06			(4)	0	0	0
		(10,000)	(13,000)	250		2,288	462

1. The lessor's initial investment in the lease is the cost of the leased asset (£10,000).
2. Tax is payable/receivable on 1 April each year, based on rentals, interest paid, interest received, and capital allowances in the previous accounting year, as shown in the table below.

Year to 30 June	Rental £	Capital allowances £	Interest £	Total £	Tax rate %	Tax payable (receivable) £
1	650	(2,500)	(234)	(2,084)	35.00	(729)
2	2,600	(1,875)	(822)	(97)	35.00	(34)
3	2,600	(1,406)	(594)	600	35.00	210
4	2,600	(1,055)	(399)	1,146	35.00	401
5	2,600	(791)	(203)	1,606	35.00	562
6	1,950	(2,373)	(24)	(447)	35.00	(156)
7	0	0	(12)	(12)	35.00	(4)
	13,000	10,000	(2,288)	712		£250

In order to simplify the calculations of the tax cash flows, it has been assumed that the amount of expenditure unrelieved after five years' writing-down allowances is received in the computation for the year ending 30 June in the sixth year. In practice, this will apply only if the lessor sells the asset at the end of the lease term for an amount equal to the tax written-down value of the asset, and also if the proceeds of the sale are passed to the lessee. Otherwise, the tax written-down value of the asset will remain as part of the pool of unrelieved expenditure, and the lessor will continue to receive writing-down allowances on a reducing balance basis into the future. Where the remaining unrelieved expenditure is not recovered by the end of the lease term, it may be appropriate for the lessor to delay the recognition of some of his or her gross earnings.

3. Interest paid is calculated at 2.5 per cent per quarter on the average net cash investment in each quarter. Interest received is calculated at a conservative rate of 1.75 per cent per quarter on the average cash surplus in each quarter.

4. Profit is assumed to be removed from the lease at a constant rate of return on the average net cash investment during the investment period. (This rate is referred to as the profit take-out — or the actuarial rate.) To calculate this rate, the lessor needs to use an 'iterative' process that involves making a succession of trial-and-error estimates of the rate. Each estimate of the rate will change the net cash investment in each period, the interest paid and received, tax, and the total profit taken out of the lease. The overall position on the transaction is:

	£
Revenue	13,000
Less: Cost of equipment	10,000
	3,000
Interest payable (net)	2,288
	712
Tax thereon (35%)	250
Profit after tax	£462

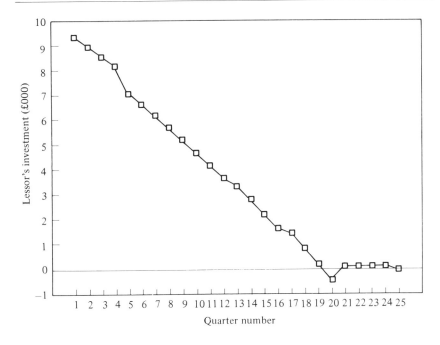

Figure 10.2 Cash flow with adequate taxable capacity

portrays graphically the cash flow profile of Table 10.2 at the beginning of each quarter.

Figure 10.3 shows the effect on the purchaser's cash flow of a two-year delay in the receipt of the benefit of the writing-down allowances, which have been carried forward as a trading loss and used in full on the first available day (to the extent the delay in utilization is greater than this, then so will be the benefits of leasing). The shaded area above the line in the figure shows the additional borrowing that the purchaser would need to arrange during the investment period if he or she did not lease.

Summary

The lessee's decision to enter into a finance lease is primarily a financing decision. Managers should first make the investment decision — i.e. determine what specific investment projects the company should under-take within a planned capital budget — and then select the methods by which the investments should be financed.

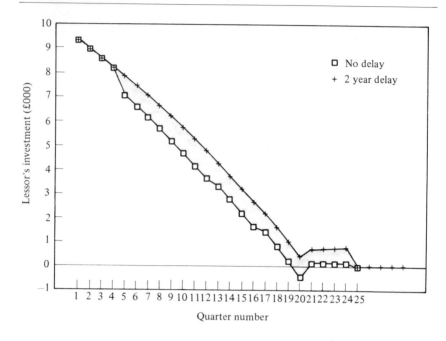

Figure 10.3 Two-year delay in receipt of allowances

The method of finance should be decided by identifying and weighing the non-financial factors and then comparing the costs of the various alternative methods. In some circumstances further equity capital may be needed, because additional debt may not be obtainable or a company may not wish to increase its overall borrowing to what might be regarded as an excessive level. Where a company's debt capacity has not been reached, the leasing and borrowing alternatives should be examined. When making any capital expenditure decision, instinctive guesswork is no substitute for a precise evaluation of the alternatives using the discounted cash flow techniques, as described in Chapter 11.

NOTES

1. Fawthrop and Terry, 'Debt management and the use of leasing finance in UK corporate financing strategies,' *Journal of Business Finance and Accounting*, **2** (3) (1975), 313.
2. Sykes, 'The lease–buy decision', *Management Survey Report No 29*, British Institute of Management, London 1976, pp. 19–20.

11. *Lease v buy consideration*

Various tables have been published which purport to assist in the comparison of the true cost of leasing with the cost of alternative methods of finance. These tables show the effective before-tax interest rates of rentals, normally payable in advance, over a range of primary periods and with different payment frequencies. The difference between the effective rate of a rental and the rate of interest payable on an equivalent loan (provided both rates are compounded at the same intervals) is a suitable measure for non-taxable bodies, such as local authorities, of the cost advantage of leasing over borrowing, or vice versa. However, this sort of comparison is usually misleading for taxable companies since it takes no account of the after-tax cash flows, including, particularly, the eligibility for capital allowances.

The cash flows associated with one source of finance are likely to be of different methods, occur at different levels, and be spread over a different number of years to those of an alternative source. To evaluate financing decisions, a method is needed for comparing in a consistent manner these different sets of cash flows. It is necessary to take account of the 'time value' of cash flows; £1 today is worth more than £1 in a year's time. Discounted cash flow (DCF) methods of investment appraisal take into account the time value of money by discounting future cash flows to the present time at a given or derived rate.

Discounted cash flow methods

There are three main discounting methods: net present value, internal rate of return (or yield), and annual capital charge. The annual capital charge method, also known as the annuity or sinking-fund method, is used by some nationalized industries and others who charge depreciation on a sinking-fund basis. This method (which compares the average annual charges for depreciation and interest with annual net cash flows, adjusted if necessary to give a constant flow) is not generally used in leasing evaluations and is not considered further.

The net present value method discounts future cash flows back to the start date of a project using a predetermined discount rate. This discounted value is then compared with the initial cash outlay giving rise to the cash flows. The internal rate of return method derives the return or discount rate which discounts the future cash flows to the same amount as the initial cash outlay. This rate is then compared with the chosen discount rate to assess the attractiveness of the project. Both methods may be used for evaluating financial leases.

It is essential that a thorough knowledge of the basics of DCF should be obtained before trying to apply the technique. There are several excellent introductory textbooks which compare the relative strengths and weaknesses of the net present value and internal rate of return methods and identify the particular circumstances when one or other method may be more suitable.

There are pitfalls for the unwary. Take, for example, the following cash flows[1]:

$$
\begin{array}{ll}
\text{Year 0} & -\ 4,000 \\
\text{Year 1} & +13,200 \\
\text{Year 2} & -14,510 \\
\text{Year 3} & +\ 5,313 \\
\hline
& +\quad 3
\end{array}
$$

The overall return on an initial investment of £4,000 is £3. However, as shown in Table 11.1, the cash flows have an internal rate of return of 5, 10 and 15 per cent.

Multiple internal rate solutions appear when the net cash flow changes from positive to negative, or vice versa. Each change gives rise to an additional solution. This difficulty can be overcome by using the dual rate of return or extended yield method. To apply this method, it is first necessary to identify the period or periods during which the cumulative cash flows, discounted at the internal rate, produce a cash surplus. For any such periods, the cash flows are discounted at a predetermined rate so as to enable the internal or yield rate to be calculated for the remainder of the cash flows.

This refinement to the internal rate of return method is important when evaluating a project that has surplus cash generated at some stage in its life.

Table 11.1 A DCF pitfall

Year	Cash flows	Discounted at 5%	Discounted at 10%	Discounted at 15%
1	13,200	12,572	12,000	11,478
2	(14,510)	(13,161)	(11,992)	(10,971)
3	5,313	4,589	3,992	3,493
	4,003	4,000	4,000	4,000

This may well happen in the case of financing decisions for equipment acquisition, as shown by the cash flows illustrated in Chapter 12. Implicit in the net present value method is the assumption that, during such a period, funds can be reinvested at the same rate of interest as that used to discount the flows. (This is satisfactory if the rate of discount is a company's capital market borrowing rate, unless the surplus cash flows of the project results in the company's overall financial position changing from a net borrowing position to a temporary cash surplus.) The unmodified internal rate of return method makes the different and unsatisfactory assumption that these funds can earn a return equal to the project's internal rate of return.

The net present value method provides a simple and convenient way of solving lease or borrow problems and is recommended in preference to the internal rate of return method. The net present value method is generally acknowledged to be the less complicated of the two bases, it avoids the problems of multiple solutions and discounting surplus funds at a fixed rate and, unlike the internal rate of return method, it is able to cope with multiple discount rates over time.

Merrett and Sykes[2] quote three advantages of internal rate of return over net present value, of which two — firstly, that the internal rate is a more useful measure of profitability when assessing risk projects, and, secondly, that it obviates the need to determine a firm's cost of capital — apply exclusively to investment decisions. The third advantage cited, that businesspeople more easily understand the method, may be applicable to financing decisions (as well as investment decisions where the internal rate is the return on capital), but this virtue is offset by the scope afforded by the internal rate of return basis for error and misinterpretation of the results. However, the three factors are pertinent for investment appraisals undertaken by lessors (see Chapter 12).

There are certain fundamental principles that should be followed in using DCF methods:

1. Estimates of cash flows form the basis of every evaluation and should be made as accurately as possible.
2. Assessments should be made on an individual basis, taking account of a company's own financial structure and taxation position.
3. All taxation receipts and payments should be included in the cash flows and the evaluation carried out on a net of tax basis to ensure that any timing differences on tax receipts and payments are incorporated in the analysis.
4. Simplifying assumptions should be made whenever possible. DCF calculations can later be extended to assess the sensitivity of individual factors.

5. Particular care should be taken over the selection of the discount rate (see below). A small difference in the rate may make a significant difference to the present value.

The procedure adopted is to compare the present value of the lease cash flows with the purchase cost of the equipment less the present value of the tax relief. When a firm is in a net borrowing position, the discount rate used to discount both leasing cash flows and the tax relief on an equivalent purchase should be the company's marginal cost of borrowing. If the interest rate selected is that which the company would pay on loan finance of a comparable amount and term, there is no need to evaluate the borrowing cash flows (except to compare alternative borrowing arrangements at different interest rates), as discounting at the inherent interest rate only has the effect of eliminating the interest element, so that the present value of the cash flows equals the principal amount of the loan, i.e. the cost of the equipment.

This approach is based on the Borrowing Opportunity Rate Method originally proposed by Vancil in 1961,[3] but incorporating a number of the changes which have since been made to the techniques, most notably those by Myers *et al.*[4] and by Franks and Hodges.[5]

The discount rate

Choosing the right discount rate is one of the most difficult aspects of DCF. By treating a lease evaluation as a separate financing decision, the need to calculate and use a discount rate based on a company's weighted average cost of capital is eliminated. However, there are also problems associated with determining the appropriate borrowing discount rate, albeit not as great as those involved in arriving at the cost of capital for the purpose of making investment decisions. The main areas of difficulty are as follows:

1. *Equivalent amount of borrowing*   The borrowing profile equivalent to the leasing cash flows is irregular because of the impact of tax relief on the payments.
2. *Equivalent borrowing cost*   The marginal cost of the equivalent borrowing is not necessarily the same for each year of the lease. The yields on government securities vary according to their maturity, and loans for which the interest rate increases over the loan period are now appearing more frequently. Different discount rates may be avoided by using a middle rate, although this will distort the calculations when the borrowing yield curve is steep.
3. *Frequency of interest payments*   The annual borrowing cost will depend on the frequency of interest payments. The discount rate should be

adjusted to the equivalent annual cost or, alternatively, calculations should be made on the basis of compounding at the same intervals as interest payments are assumed to be made.

4. *Overall cash surplus* In some cases, a company will be deciding not between leasing and borrowing but between leasing and using surplus cash. In these circumstances, the appropriate rate is the earnings opportunity rate for the surplus funds and not the marginal cost of borrowing. The rate should be based on the proposed alternative use for the excess funds; a suitable rate might be the average yield on government securities maturing over the lease period or the rate receivable on an equivalent deposit in the inter-bank market. Where the cash position is only temporary, the earnings opportunity rate and the borrowing rate should each be used for the relevant period.

5. *Tax position* When estimating the cost of borrowing, an adjustment may have to be made for tax relief on interest payments.

For bodies not subject to tax, the net-of-tax and before-tax cost of borrowing are the same and no adjustment to the discount rate is required.

For taxable companies, the discount rate needs to reflect the fact that the amount of interest paid is deducted from income in computing the liability for corporation tax. Ignoring any delay in the payment of tax and receipt of tax relief, the net-of-tax cost of borrowing is $r(1 - T)$ per cent if r per cent is the cost of borrowing and T the rate of corporation tax. Assuming a 10 per cent cost of borrowing and a 35 per cent rate of corporation tax, the net-of-tax cost is $10(1 - 0.35) = 6.5$ per cent.

However, for UK companies, there is normally a significant delay between the date of earning income and the due date for payment of tax thereon. In the case of companies that were trading before April 1965, tax used to be payable between 9 months (by companies with March year-ends) and 21 months (by companies with early April year-ends) after the end of their accounting period. For all companies not trading in April 1965, the due date has always been 9 months after the year-end.

In the Finance Act 1987, the due date was standardized at 9 months after the year-end for all companies and tax is payable on average 15 months after the date of receipt in respect of income arising on and after 1 January 1990.

The relationship between the net-of-tax cost of borrowing r^* and the before-tax cost r, taking into account the delay in payment of tax, where T is the rate of corporation tax and where n is the period of delay, is:

$$r^* = r - \frac{rT}{(1 + r^*)^n}$$

103

Therefore,

$$r = \frac{r^*}{1 - T(1 + r^*)^n}$$

There is no exact expression for r^* as a function of r; an approximate formula that may be used for n is

$$r^* = r - \frac{rT}{(1 + r - rT)^n}$$

Table 11.2 shows before-tax and corresponding net-of-tax borrowing costs calculated from this formula, assuming a 15-month tax delay and a 35 per cent rate of corporation tax (with quarterly compounding).

As a result of a company being temporarily in a non-tax-paying position, the period of delay in payment of tax may be significantly longer. Instead of computing a different net-of-tax discount rate for each year (the period of delay reduces by 12 months for each successive financial year), a before-tax discount rate may be used during the period when no tax is payable and an after-tax rate thereafter. When using a before-tax discount rate, it is necessary to adjust the derived present value for the notional tax on the interest carried forward to the first tax payment date. This procedure may be most easily understood by working through the examples given later in this chapter.

The period of tax delay is one of the most important elements in any lease or borrowing evaluation. Present values should be computed and compared using different tax delay assumptions (which affect both the net-of-tax discount rate and the timing of the cash flows). The effect of incorrectly estimating the first tax payment date may be seen in Table 11.3, which shows the net-of-tax borrowing costs for various periods of tax delay (assuming a 35 per cent rate of corporation tax).

Table 11.2 Before-tax and net-of-tax borrowing costs; 15-month tax delay

Before tax %	Net of tax %
6	4.0
8	5.4
10	6.8
12	8.2
14	9.7

Table 11.3 Net-of-tax borrowing costs

Before-tax rate %	Period of delay in months				
	0 %	15 %	27 %	39 %	51 %
6	3.9	4.0	4.1	4.2	4.3
8	5.2	5.4	5.5	5.7	5.8
10	6.5	6.8	7.0	7.2	7.4
12	7.8	8.2	8.5	8.8	9.1
14	9.1	9.7	10.1	10.5	10.9

Worked example 11.1

The initial assumptions for the example showing how to evaluate the lease or borrow decision are set out in Table 11.4.

Interest on the equivalent borrowing is assumed to be payable quarterly. Ten per cent per annum, payable quarterly, represents a true annual rate of 10.4 per cent. All discounting has been done on a quarterly compounding basis, although it would be equally correct to discount on an annual compounding basis at the higher rate of 10.4 per cent, or the net-of-tax equivalent as appropriate. For simplicity of presentation and calculation, a 7 per cent net-of-tax rate has been used, although, as shown in Table 11.3, the correct equivalent rate to a 10 per cent before-tax rate in the case of an average 15-month tax delay is approximately 6.8 per cent.

If the company has sufficient taxable capacity to utilize the 25 per cent writing-down allowance each year, the purchase and lease cash flows will be as shown in Table 11.5

The approach now adopted in the illustration is to show, first, the erroneous and misleading results arising from the use of unsuitable rates to

Table 11.4 Assumptions for worked example 11.1

Cost of equipment	£100,000
Date of acquisition	1 July 1988
Primary lease period	4 years
Rental	£75 per £1,000 payable quarterly in advance
Marginal borrowing rate	10% before tax (payable quarterly)
Corporation tax rate	35%
Capital allowance	25% p.a. on the declining balance
Company year-end	31 December
Tax payment date	9 months after year-end
Useful life of equipment	4 years (so renewal rentals and residual writing-down allowances may be ignored)

Table 11.5 Purchase and lease cash flow

PURCHASE

Date	Description	Amount £
July 1988	Purchase price	100,000
October 1989	Tax relief	(8,750) = 25% of £100,000 @ 35%
October 1990	Tax relief	(6,563) = 25% of £ 75,000 @ 35%
October 1991	Tax relief	(4,922) = 25% of £ 56,250 @ 35%
October 1992	Tax relief	(3,691) = 25% of £ 42,187 @ 35%
October 1993	Tax relief	(11,074) £ 31,640 @ 35%
	Net cash flow	£65,000

LEASE

Date	Rentals £	Tax relief £	Net cash flow £
July 1988	7,500		7,500
October	7,500		7,500
January 1989	7,500		7,500
April	7,500		7,500
July	7,500		7,500
October	7,500	(5,250)	2,250
January 1990	7,500		7,500
April	7,500		7,500
July	7,500		7,500
October	7,500	(10,500)	(3,000)
January 1991	7,500		7,500
April	7,500		7,500
July	7,500		7,500
October	7,500	(10,500)	(3,000)
January 1992	7,500		7,500
April	7,500		7,500
October		(10,500)	(10,500)
October 1993		(5,250)	(5,250)
	120,000	(42,000)	78,000

discount the purchase and leasing cash flows and then the recommended basis for carrying out the evaluation from which the decision whether to lease or borrow may readily be made (in conjunction with various non-financial factors referred to in Chapter 10).

BEFORE-TAX DISCOUNTING

Using a 10 per cent before-tax rate to discount the cash flows in Table 11.5 to their values at July 1988, the present values of the purchase and lease alternatives are shown in Table 11.6.

Table 11.6 Cash flows in Table 11.5 discounted at 10 per cent

PURCHASE

Date	Cash flow £	PV factor	Present value £
July 1988	100,000	1.0000	100,000
October 1989	(8,750)	0.8838	(7,733)
October 1990	(6,563)	0.8007	(5,255)
October 1991	(4,922)	0.7254	(3,570)
October 1992	(3,691)	0.6572	(2,426)
October 1993	(11,074)	0.5954	(6,593)
	65,000		74,423

LEASE

Date	Cash flow £	PV factor	Present value £
July 1988	7,500	1.0000	7,500
October	7,500	0.9756	7,317
January 1989	7,500	0.9518	7,139
April	7,500	0.9286	6,965
July	7,500	0.9060	6,795
October	2,250	0.8838	1,989
January 1990	7,500	0.8623	6,467
April	7,500	0.8413	6,310
July	7,500	0.8208	6,156
October	(3,000)	0.8007	(2,402)
January 1991	7,500	0.7812	5,859
April	7,500	0.7621	5,716
July	7,500	0.7436	5,577
October	(3,000)	0.7254	(2,176)
January 1992	7,500	0.7077	5,308
April	7,500	0.6905	5,179
October	(10,500)	0.6572	(6,901)
October 1993	(5,250)	0.5954	(3,126)
	78,000		69,672

NET-OF-TAX DISCOUNTING

However, this approach is inappropriate since, as explained, no account is taken of the tax effect on the amount of the discount. (Although the rate of discounting is suitable for non-tax paying bodies, the cash flows in Table 11.5 require to be adjusted to exclude the tax relief on rentals and the corresponding capital allowance benefit on purchase.) Using a 7 per cent net-of-tax discount rate, the present values become those shown in Table 11.7.

Table 11.7 Cash flows in Table 11.5 discounted at 7 per cent

PURCHASE

Date	Cash flow £	PV factor	Present value £
July 1988	100,000	1.0000	100,000
October 1989	(8,750)	0.9169	(8,023)
October 1990	(6,563)	0.8554	(5,614)
October 1991	(4,922)	0.7981	(3,928)
October 1992	(3,691)	0.7446	(2,748)
October 1993	(11,074)	0.6947	(7,693)
	65,000		71,994

LEASE

Date	Cash flow £	PV factor	Present value £
July 1988	7,500	1.0000	7,500
October	7,500	0.9828	7,371
January 1989	7,500	0.9659	7,244
April	7,500	0.9493	7,120
July	7,500	0.9330	6,998
October	2,250	0.9169	2,063
January 1990	7,500	0.9011	6,758
April	7,500	0.8856	6,642
July	7,500	0.8704	6,528
October	(3,000)	0.8554	(2,566)
January 1991	7,500	0.8407	6,305
April	7,500	0.8263	6,197
July	7,500	0.8121	6,091
October	(3,000)	0.7981	(2,394)
January 1992	7,500	0.7844	5,883
April	7,500	0.7709	5,782
October	(10,500)	0.7446	(7,818)
October 1993	(5,250)	0.6947	(3,647)
	78,000		72,057

Based on the assumptions set out in Table 11.4 and the additional assumption that the company has sufficient taxable capacity to obtain immediate benefit of the 25 per cent writing-down allowances, borrowing is seen, in Table 11.7, to be cheaper than leasing, albeit narrowly. It should be noted from comparing Tables 11.6 and 11.7 that the higher the discount rate the more advantageous leasing appears. Thus, discounting the purchase and lease cash flows in Table 11.5 at the net-of-tax cost of capital rather than at the marginal cost of borrowing usually gives an answer unjustifiably biased towards leasing.

TEMPORARY SHORTAGE OF TAXABLE CAPACITY

If the company is expected to have no mainstream tax liability until its 1990 financial year, the purchase and lease cash flow profiles are no longer those shown in Table 11.5. The revised cash flows are shown in Table 11.8, reflecting the fact that no tax is payable until 1 October 1991, 9 months after the end of the company's 1990 financial year.

Discounting the cash flows in Table 11.8 at 7 per cent net-of-tax rate, the present values of purchasing and leasing are shown in Table 11.9, where leasing is shown to be cheaper than borrowing.

However, as pointed out, it is not strictly correct to discount, as shown in Table 11.9 at a net-of-tax rate in respect of a year in which a company is not

Table 11.8 Cash flows with temporary shortage of taxable capacity

PURCHASE

Date	Description	Amount £
July 1988	Purchase price	100,000
October 1991	Tax relief	(20,235)
October 1992	Tax relief	(3,691)
October 1993	Tax relief	(11,074)
		65,000

LEASE

Date	Rentals £	Tax relief £	Net cash flow £
July 1988	7,500		7,500
October	7,500		7,500
January 1989	7,500		7,500
April	7,500		7,500
July	7,500		7,500
October	7,500		7,500
January 1990	7,500		7,500
April	7,500		7,500
July	7,500		7,500
October	7,500		7,500
January 1991	7,500		7,500
April	7,500		7,500
July	7,500		7,500
October	7,500	(26,250)	(18,750)
January 1992	7,500		7,500
April	7,500		7,500
October	–	(10,500)	(10,500)
October 1993	–	(5,250)	(5,250)
	120,000	(42,000)	78,000

Table 11.9 Cash flows in Table 11.8 discounted at 7 per cent

PURCHASE

Date	Cash flow £	PV factor	Present value £
July 1988	100,000	1.0000	100,000
October 1991	(20,235)	0.7981	(16,150)
October 1992	(3,691)	0.7446	(2,748)
October 1993	(11,074)	0.6947	(7,693)
	65,000		73,409

LEASE

Date	Cash flow £	PV factor	Present value £
July 1988	7,500	1.0000	7,500
October	7,500	0.9828	7,371
January 1989	7,500	0.9659	7,244
April	7,500	0.9493	7,120
July	7,500	0.9330	6,998
October	7,500	0.9169	6,877
January 1990	7,500	0.9011	6,758
April	7,500	0.8856	6,642
July	7,500	0.8704	6,528
October	7,500	0.8554	6,416
January 1991	7,500	0.8407	6,305
April	7,500	0.8263	6,197
July	7,500	0.8121	6,091
October	(18,750)	0.7981	(14,964)
January 1992	7,500	0.7844	5,883
April	7,500	0.7709	5,782
October	(10,500)	0.7446	(7,818)
October 1993	(5,250)	0.6947	(3,647)
	78,000		73,283

in a tax-paying position. This basis has the opposite effect to discounting at a before-tax rather than at a net-of-tax rate — this time there is an unfair bias towards borrowing and against leasing. In the example in Table 11.9, the advantage of leasing would have been increased by £766.

DIFFERENTIAL DISCOUNTING APPROACH

A before-tax discount rate should be used for the period up to December 1989 and a net-of-tax rate thereafter. The present values of the purchase and lease cash flows in Table 11.8 discounted on this basis are calculated in Tables 11.10 and 11.11 respectively.

Table 11.10 Purchase values — differential discounting

Date	Cash flow £	PV factor		Present value £
July 1988	100,000	1.0000		100,000
		To Jan. '90	To July '88	
October 1991	(20,235)	0.8856	0.8623	(15,452)
October 1992	(3,691)	0.8263	0.8623	(2,630)
October 1993	(11,074)	0.7709	0.8623	(7,361)
				(25,443)
	65,000			74,557

Table 11.11 Lease values — differential discounting

Date	Cash flow £	PV factor		Present value £
July 1988	7,500	1.0000		7,500
October	7,500	0.9756		7,317
January 1989	7,500	0.9518		7,317
April	7,500	0.9286		6,964
July	7,500	0.9060		6,795
October	7,500	0.8839		6,629
	45,000			42,344
		To Jan. '90	To July '88	
January 1990	7,500	1.0000	0.8623	6,467
April	7,500	0.9828	0.8623	6,356
January 1989	7,500	0.9659	0.8623	6,247
October	7,500	0.9493	0.8623	6,139
January 1991	7,500	0.9330	0.8623	6,034
April	7,500	0.9170	0.8623	5,930
July	7,500	0.9011	0.8623	5,828
October	(18,750)	0.8856	0.8623	(14,318)
January 1992	7,500	0.8704	0.8623	5,629
April	7,500	0.8554	0.8623	5,532
October 1992	(10,500)	0.8263	0.8623	(7,481)
October 1993	(5,250)	0.7709	0.8623	(3,490)
	33,000			28,873
		Notional tax charge		2,291
	78,000			73,508

The value of the post-December 1989 cash flows totalling a negative amount of £35,000 at January 1990 is the negative amount of £29,506 (£25,443 divided by 0.8623).

Accordingly, the notional interest for the period from July 1988 to December 1989 is £4,063 (£29,506 − £25,443). The notional tax relief is thus £1,422 (35 per cent of £4,063) and its present value at July 1988 amounts to £1,281 (£1,422 × 0.9011) the 7 per cent net-of-tax discount rate for the six periods between July 1988 and January 1990.

The notional tax charge in Table 11.11 is calculated in a similar way to the notional tax relief and the purchase cash flows in Table 11.10. The value of the post-December 1989 cash flows totalling £33,000 at January 1990 is £33,484 (£28,873 divided by 0.8623). Accordingly, the notional interest for the period from July 1988 to December 1989 is £7,267 (£45,000 − £42,344 + £33,484 − £28,873). The notional tax charge is thus £2,543 (35 per cent of £7,267) and its present value at July 1988 amounts to £2,291 (£2,543 × 0.9011).

EXTENSION OF EVALUATION

This method of comparing leasing and purchasing cash flows can readily be extended to include items such as progress payments, regional development grants, renewal rentals, and residual values. The same form of analysis may also be used to determine the sensitivity of variables such as the assumed cost of borrowing (by discounting at different rates), the rentals, and the rate of corporation tax (although the basis of calculation will vary depending on whether the rental is subject to adjustment for tax rate changes).

From a comparison of cash flows, it will be seen that the value of leasing for companies unable to take immediate advantage of writing-down allowances increases as the length of the primary lease period increases and the more that rentals are deferred or ballooned.

EFFECT OF INFLATION

The effect of inflation may also be incorporated. Most of the cash flows associated with leasing and borrowing are money rather than real cash flows, so that money discount rates are applied to the actual cash flows (after adjusting for any real cash flows, normally only the residual value of the equipment). If the lease rentals are fixed in relation to changes in the cost of money, and the rate of inflation is expected to vary during the period of the cash flows, it is necessary to use different discount rates for different periods. If, for example, the rate of inflation was expected to increase after two years, the higher discount rate derived from the increased cost of borrowing (assuming that there was likely to be no change in the general level of supply and demand for money) should be used to discount the leasing cash flows occurring after two years to their value at the two-year point, and then the lower discount rate applied to determine their present value.

Worked example 11.2

The assumptions for the second example of the recommended method of lease evaluation, with additional variables, are set out in Table 11.12.

Assuming that leasing does displace an equivalent amount of borrowing, the net-of-tax discount rates are approximately 7 per cent up to December 1993 and 7.5 per cent thereafter (when the marginal borrowing rate and the corporation tax rate are assumed to be 12 per cent and 40 per cent per annum respectively. The purchase and lease cash flows are shown in Tables 11.13 and 11.15 respectively, and Table 11.14 lists the calculated tax relief on purchase.

Tables 11.16 and 11.17 show the differential discounting approach applied to the purchase and lease cash flows of Tables 11.13 and 11.15 respectively. A comparison of the present values of the purchase and lease cash flows (£68,610 vs £66,815) shows that, for worked example 11.2 with the assumptions set out in Table 11.12, leasing is cheaper than borrowing.

Table 11.12 Assumptions for worked example 11.2

Cost of equipment	£100,000
Payment schedule	£30,000 on 1 January 1988
	£60,000 on 1 July 1988
	£10,000 on 1 October 1988
Date of delivery and start date of lease	1 July 1988
Date of disposal	1 July 1997
Sale proceeds	15% of cost
Primary lease period	7 years
Primary rental	£48 per £1,000 payable quarterly in advance from delivery
Renewal rental	1% of cost per annum
Residual value treatment	95% of proceeds as rental rebate
Marginal borrowing rate	10% before tax until December 1993; 12% before tax thereafter (payable quarterly)
Corporation tax rate	35% until December 1993; 40% thereafter
Capital allowance	25% per annum on the declining balance
Company year-end	31 December
Tax payment date	9 months after year-end
Taxable capacity	No tax payable until 1992 financial year

113

Table 11.13 Worked example 11.2: purchase cash flows

Date	Description	Amount
1 January 1988	Progress payment	30,000
1 July 1988	Delivery payment	60,000
1 October 1988	Retention payment	10,000
1 October 1993	Tax relief	(26,695)
1 October 1994	Tax relief	(2,077)
1 October 1995	Tax relief	(1,780)
1 October 1996	Tax relief	(1,335)
1 July 1997	Sales proceeds	(15,000)
1 October 1997	Tax relief	(1,001)
1 October 1998	Tax balancing charge	2,996
		55,108

Table 11.14 Calculation of tax relief on purchase

Year to 31 December	Tax relief					£
1988	25% of	£100,000	=	£25,000	@ 35%	8,750
1989	25% of	£75,000	=	£18,750	@ 35%	6,563
1990	25% of	£56,250	=	£14,062	@ 35%	4,922
1991	25% of	£42,188	=	£10,547	@ 35%	3,691
1992	25% of	£31,641	=	£7,910	@ 35%	2,769
	Receivable 1 October 1993					26,695
1993	25% of	£23,731	=	£5,933	@ 35%	2,077
1994	25% of	£17,798	=	£4,449	@ 40%	1,780
1995	25% of	£13,349	=	£3,337	@ 40%	1,335
1996	25% of	£10,011	=	£2,503	@ 40%	1,001
1997	Proceeds	£15,000	=	(£7,492)	@ 40%	(2,996)

Summary

The steps to be taken to evaluate a lease or borrow decision are as follows:

1. Identify and assess the non-financial factors.
2. Draw up cash flows for the purchase and lease alternatives.
3. Select a suitable before-tax discount rate based on the company's marginal cost of borrowing.
4. Except for non-taxable bodies, which would use the before-tax discount rate, calculate the corresponding net-of-tax discount rate, taking into

Table 11.15 Worked example11.2: lease cash flows

Date	Rentals £	Tax payable (relief) £	Net cash flow £
July 1988	4,800		4,800
October	4,800		4,800
January 1989	4,800		4,800
April	4,800		4,800
July	4,800		4,800
October	4,800		4,800
January 1990	4,800		4,800
April	4,800		4,800
July	4,800		4,800
October	4,800		4,800
January 1991	4,800		4,800
April	4,800		4,800
July	4,800		4,800
October	4,800		4,800
January 1992	4,800		4,800
April	4,800		4,800
July	4,800		4,800
October	4,800		4,800
January 1993	4,800		4,800
April	4,800		4,800
July	4,800		4,800
October	4,800	(30,240)	(25,440)
January 1994	4,800		4,800
April	4,800		4,800
July	4,800		4,800
October	4,800	(6,720)	(1,920)
January 1995	4,800		4,800
April	4,800		4,800
July	1,000		1,000
October		(7,680)	(7,680)
July 1996	1,000		1,000
October		(4,240)	(4,240)
July 1997	(14,250)		(14,250)
October 1997		(400)	(400)
October 1998		5,700	5,700
	122,150	43,580	78,570

account the rate of corporation tax, the period of delay in payment of tax (and, if required, the proportion of borrowing capacity displaced by lease finance).

5. Calculate and compare the present values of the purchase and lease cash flows applying a net-of-tax discount rate unless the company is in a

Table 11.16 Purchase cash flows in Table 11.13 discounted

Date	Cash flow £			PV factor			Present value £
1 January 1988	30,000			1.0000			30,000
1 July 1988	60,000			0.9518			57,108
1 October 1988	10,000			0.9286			9,286
	100,000						96,394
		To Oct. '93	To July '94	To Jan. '88			
1 October 1993	(26,695)	0.8856	0.9635	0.6736			(15,925)
1 October 1994	(2,077)	0.8704	0.9458	0.6736			(1,152)
1 October 1995	(1,780)	0.8704	0.8781	0.6736			(916)
1 October 1996	(1,335)	0.8704	0.8152	0.6736			(638)
1 July 1997	(15,000)	0.8704	0.7710	0.6736			(6,780)
1 October 1997	(1,001)	0.8704	0.7568	0.6736			(444)
1 October 1998	2,996	0.8704	0.7026	0.6736			1,234
	(44,892)						(24,621)
						Notional tax relief	(3,163)
	55,108						68,610

The value of the post-January 1992 cash flows is £24,621 divided by 0.6736, i.e. £36,551. The notional interest is therefore £36,551 − £24,621, i.e. £11,930. (The notional tax relief is 35 per cent of £11,930 (£4,176) and the present value is £3,163 (£4,176 discounted at the 7 per cent post-tax rates for eight periods).)

temporary non-tax-paying position, in which case differential discount rates should be used in the manner described in this chapter.

NOTES AND REFERENCES

1. The pitfall illustration is taken from P.K. Karmal, 'The marginal efficiency of capital', *Economic Record*, **35** (1959), 430 (quoted in J.W. Bennett, J.McB. Grant and R.H. Parker, *Topics in Business Finance and Accountancy*, Cheshire, Melbourne, 1964, p.57).
2. A.J. Merrett and Allen Sykes, *The Finance and Analysis of Capital Projects* (2nd edn), Longman, London 1973, p.123.
3. R.F. Vancil, 'Lease or borrow — new method of analysis', *Harvard Business Review*, **39** (5) (1961), 122–136.
4. S.C. Myers, D.A. Dill and A. J. Bautista, 'Valuation of financial lease contracts', *The Journal of Finance*, **31** (3) (1976), 799–819. The authors derive a mathematical formula for lease evaluation on the basis of the theoretical assumption that a company has the objective of maximizing its market value.

Table 11.17 Lease cash flows in Table 11.15 discounted

Date	Cash flow £	PV factor			Present value £
July 1988	4,800	0.9518			4,569
October	4,800	0.9286			4,457
January 1989	4,800	0.9060			4,349
April	4,800	0.8839			4,243
July	4,800	0.8623			4,139
October	4,800	0.8413			4,038
January 1990	4,800	0.8207			3,939
April	4,800	0.8007			3,843
July	4,800	0.7812			3,750
October	4,800	0.7621			3,658
January 1991	4,800	0.7436			3,569
April	4,800	0.7254			3,482
July	4,800	0.7077			3,397
October	4,800	0.6905			3,314
	67,200				54,747
		To Jan. '92	To Jan. '94	To Jan. '88	
January 1992	4,800	1.0000		0.6736	3,233
April	4,800	0.9828		0.6736	3,178
July	4,800	0.9659		0.6736	3,123
October	4,800	0.9493		0.6736	3,069
January 1993	4,800	0.9330		0.6736	3,017
April	4,800	0.9169		0.6736	2,965
July	4,800	0.9011		0.6736	2,914
October	2,400	0.8856		0.6736	(15,176)
	From Jan. '94				
January 1994	4,800	0.8704	1.0000	0.6736	2,814
April	4,800	0.8704	0.9816	0.6736	2,762
July	4,800	0.8704	0.9635	0.6736	2,712
October	(1,920)	0.8704	0.9458	0.6736	(1,065)
January 1995	4,800	0.8704	0.9284	0.6736	2,613
April	4,800	0.8704	0.9113	0.6736	2,565
July	1,000	0.8704	0.8945	0.6736	524
October	(7,680)	0.8704	0.8781	0.6736	(3,954)
July 1996	1,000	0.8704	0.8305	0.6736	487
October	(4,240)	0.8704	0.8152	0.6736	(2,026)
July 1997	(14,250)	0.8704	0.8152	0.6736	(6,442)
October	(400)	0.8704	0.7568	0.6736	(177)
October 1998	5,700	0.8704	0.7026	0.6736	2,348
	11,370				9,484
				Notional tax charge	2,584
	78,570				66,815

The value of the post-December 1991 cash flows is £14,080 (£9,484 divided by 0.6736). The notional interest for the period from January 1988 to December 1991 is £9,743 (£67,200 − £54,747 + £11,370 − £14,080). The notional tax charge is therefore £3,410 (35% of £9,743) and its present value at January 1988 is £2,584 (£3,410 × 0.7576).

5. J.R. Franks and S.D. Hodges, 'Valuation of financial lease contracts: a note', *The Journal of Finance*, **33** (2)(1978), 657–669. The authors present a simplified derivation of the Myers' valuation formula and extend it to include the case of a company that is in a temporary non-tax-paying position.

12. *Lessor Evaluation*

Under a financial lease, the primary period rental is the amount that, over the primary lease period, recovers the full capital cost of the equipment (unless any residual value has been placed on the equipment), together with related fees, interest, and other expenses and which provides the lessor with the required profit in respect of the primary period. A financial lease usually also provides an opportunity for a financial institution to receive or share in the value of the equipment financed at the end of the primary period; the lessor is entitled to receive renewal rentals for any secondary period (some, or all, of which may be profit) and to receive some or all of the proceeds of sale of the equipment at the end of the lease. These additional sources of profit, which, among other features, distinguish leasing from lending, may be regarded as either negligible or a factor that should be taken into account in the lessor's cash flows and financial evaluation. The overall profit rewards the lessor company for the risks undertaken and the resources employed.

Sources of profit

The main risks usually borne by lessors are as follows:

1. Credit:
   (a) the non-payment of rentals;
   (b) claims from third parties arising from the ownership of equipment not being recoverable from the lessee owing to insufficient resources being available.
2. Funding:
   (a) increase in the cost of funds over the investment period of the lease (unless the rental is variable for interest charges);
   (b) lack of funds for the initial purchase of the equipment or later in the investment period of the lease.
3. (a) Corporation tax or other taxation changes (unless the lease contains a tax variation clause).
   (b) Insufficient taxable capacity.
4. Losses arising from the ownership of equipment which are not recoverable from the lessee through the operation of the law.

Other risks with which a lessor may be involved include:

5. The realization of any value placed on the equipment at the end of the primary period by the lessor in the lease evaluation.

6. Losses arising on loans in foreign currencies.
7. The ability to earn the anticipated return on any surplus funds that may be generated by the lease.
8. Adverse changes in the timing of expenditure.
9. Non-recovery of legal and other costs incurred on uncompleted facilities.

The following resources are employed:

1. Funds
2. Taxable capacity
3. Professional expertise.

It is difficult to assess and value the third factor, the contribution of management skills and professional expertise. Certainly, some reward is appropriate for the management time spent in designing, marketing and negotiating a complex and specialized financial leasing package. In some leases of large-valued items, the lessor treats this factor as a separate component of the overall profit by charging an initial negotiation fee; in other cases, it is regarded as an unspecified element of the rental. For general facilities, where standard documentation is used, it is not normal to include in the rental calculation any separate profit contribution for 'packaging'. For evaluation purposes, it may be assumed that there is no shortage of management skill and, accordingly, this factor does not require special treatment as a scarce resource.

The principal sources of profits for equipment leasing companies may therefore be regarded as follows:

1. Assumption of credit risk.
2. Use of funds (and assumption of risks associated therewith).
3. Use of taxable capacity (and assumption of risks associated therewith).

CREDIT RISK

Credit risks are frequently ignored in the evaluation of leases, except that a facility will not be extended if the risk is considered to be unacceptably high. However, there are degrees of credit-worthiness; leasing companies can rank lessees in order of potential risk in the same way as bankers classify borrowers and charge interest at different levels above a base rate.

In theory, the adjustment for credit risks should be related to the amount of risk from time to time, i.e. the present value of outstanding rentals less the value of the leased equipment (and any collateral security that may be held by the lessor). In practice, this amount is difficult to calculate and is dependent on subjective judgements concerning the value of the equipment over the primary lease period.

If the value of the equipment is ignored, the risk becomes proportional to the present value of outstanding rentals. However, this is not the same as the lessor's outstanding investment in the lease, because of the impact of tax relief arising from the lessor's entitlement to claim capital allowances. In the first three years of a typical five-year lease, the present value of outstanding rentals exceeds the lessor's outstanding investment by approximately 8 per cent of cost. Accordingly, it is not appropriate to allow for credit risks by increasing for riskier investments the rate at which the net-of-tax cash flows are discounted. Instead, the effective interest rate of the rentals should be increased by an amount corresponding to the increase that would be made to the rate of interest charged on an equivalent loan. For effective rates of interest between 5 and 15 per cent, there is an almost linear relationship between interest rates and rentals for five-year leases, so that the same result may be achieved by increasing rentals by a fixed amount.

For example, if potential lessees were classified into four bands, the additions for credit risk would be as shown in Table 12.1 for the typical leasing arrangement illustrated in Chapter 11.

The importance of this approach for the lessor's evaluation is that credit risks may be excluded from the project analysis. All calculations may be carried out on a minimum risk basis and the adjustment for risk made separately.

USE OF RESOURCES

Financial leasing is, above all, a type of finance available to industry and commerce. Profits are earned by lessors through the use of funds for the acquisition of capital equipment. A subsidiary factor currently relevant to much of the leasing activity in the UK is the use of taxable capacity.

The limit on a leasing company's ability to undertake additional profitable business is set by the availability of funds and demand for its facilities.

Table 12.1 Assumption of credit risks

risk classification	Charge over base rate on equivalent loan %	Additional effective interest rate lease %	Quarterly rental £ per £1,000	Effective interest rate %
A	1.0	–	75.00	10.5
B	1.5	0.5	75.55	11.0
C	2.0	1.0	76.11	11.5
D	3.0	2.0	77.22	12.5

Additionally, the amount of available taxable capacity is relevant if there are no opportunities to undertake leasing business other than tax-based arrangements whereby the lessor claims the capital allowance and reflects the benefit in the rentals quoted. Different rental profiles result in different rates of regeneration of funds and taxable capacity for use in other leasing facilities. As examples, a typical three-year lease will use up taxable capacity in the first year equivalent to approximately 20 per cent of the asset's cost, but will regenerate taxable capacity in the second year, equivalent to approximately 12 per cent of the asset's cost. A typical seven-year lease, however, will also use up taxable capacity in the second year (equivalent to perhaps 10 per cent of cost) and possibly a small amount in the third year. Thus, the longer the primary period of the lease, the less funds and taxable capacity that will become available in the early years of the facility to enable the company to undertake additional leasing business in those years. A lease of equipment located in a development area would require a larger allocation of taxable capacity than similar equipment that does not qualify for a regional development grant, because of the reduction in rentals reflecting the benefit to the lessor of the receipt of the non-taxable grant.

Profit maximization for a leasing company thus involves the optimal use of its two scarce resources: funds and taxable capacity. The problem is one of determining the most profitable type or mix of financial leasing business, given assumptions concerning both the amount of new funds and taxable capacity likely to be available to the leasing company each year and the market rates of rentals (and, hence, achievable profits) for different rental profiles and primary lease periods.

Alternatively, looking at the problem the other way round, a method is required for calculating rental terms that are consistent and provide acceptable profits for different rental profiles, primary lease periods, and types of facilities, including those eligible for regional development grants.

These may be viewed as mathematical programming problems and linear or non-linear programming techniques applied to obtain optimal solutions. (There are, of course, also unquantifiable aspects, such as a lessor's specialist knowledge of a certain area of the market.) Programming is an important computational tool for dealing with situations where more than one resource is rationed. Moreover, programming models produce opportunity costs (the dual values of linear programming) for the scarce resources. The use of this technique to maximize the profits of different types of financial leasing business is outside the scope of this book. The remainder of this chapter examines methods of evaluation that are appropriate for determining and comparing rates of return for financial leases where there are no constraints on new business or where there is a shortage of taxable capacity for financial leases.

Comparison of methods

The evaluation of loans is a routine activity for financial institutions, but lease evaluations may be less familiar. Unlike the 'lease or borrow' financial decision faced by a lessee, a leasing company is required to make investment decisions on whether to purchase equipment for leasing to customers and what lease terms should apply.

There are several conventional methods of appraising investment projects. Two of the most common are the pay-back and the accounting or average rate of return methods. These and other approaches which are not based on discounted cash flow techniques are of only limited value in the analysis of capital projects with irregular cash flows, and should not normally be used by lessors for lease evaluation. The pay-back method neglects the exact timing of cash flows and only takes account of cash flows up to the point when they equal the initial outlay. It is more a measure of the liquidity than of the profitability of a project, but serves a useful purpose in appraising investments under risk conditions; for example, for an export lease where rental payments may be restricted by the action of a foreign government.

The accounting rate of return method also ignores the timing of cash flows and tends to confuse reported profits and the net cash flow of a project.

DCF methods of evaluation make it possible to calculate and compare present values or rates of return for transactions having irregular cash flows, such as the after-tax cash flows of a financial lease. The same present value approach used in Chapter 11 to evaluate the lessee's decision may also be used by lessors. Subject to any differences in tax timing, the purchase cash flows remain the same and the lease cash flows are also identical, but with the signs reversed. Discounting at the lessor's assumed net-of-tax cost of borrowing, the present value of the lease cash flows may be compared with the cost of the investment. Thus, looking at the worked examples in Chapter 11, the disadvantage of £63 (£72,057 lease present value − £71,994 purchase present value) from the point of view of the lessee, revealed in Table 11.7, corresponds to a present value gain of the same amount for the lessor, if he or she purchases the equipment for leasing on the quoted terms.

Although the present value approach is regarded as the most suitable for use by lessees when deciding on the cheapest method of financing the acquisition of capital equipment, a rate of return basis is preferred for the lessor's evaluation. Managements of financial institutions can more easily interpret a rate of return on capital than a single present value figure. Present values also lack the advantage of measuring return over time in a manner that allows managers to assess the return in relation to the cost of capital and to identify the margin allowed for risk.

As illustrated in Chapter 9, a financial lease normally involves a leasing company in a period of borrowing (the investment period), followed by a period during which it has temporary surplus funds, since the amount of tax deferred exceeds the outstanding rentals. Because of the existence of periods of both positive and negative net cash flows, the internal rate of return method produces misleading results. As explained, this method (unmodified) makes the unsatisfactory assumption that, during the surplus period, the surplus funds can earn a return equal to the project's internal rate of return (so that in effect the profit earned through the utilization of these funds in a new lease has already been taken into account).

Accordingly, it is necessary to adopt the dual rate of return (or extended yield) method, whereby the cash flows are assumed to earn a predetermined reinvestment rate of interest during any period when the cumulative cash flows are in surplus. The reinvestment rate to be used will, in principle, be either the rate the surplus funds are expected to earn during the surplus period or, in the more usual situation of the lessor continuing to be in an overall borrowing position during the surplus period, the rate the lessor is expected to be paying on borrowed funds during this period and which the surplus funds will effectively be reducing. It is prudent for a lessor to assume that interest rates will fall and, accordingly, the reinvestment rate for the surplus period is normally set at a lower level than the borrowing rate assumed for the investment period. (This is a kind of negative risk premium.) With the reinvestment rate specified, the dual rate is the rate of return to be earned on capital outstanding in the lease during the investment period.

This dual rate may be calculated for the anticipated cash flows of a proposed lease as a rate of return (as if the cost of acquiring the equipment were financed wholly by equity) and then compared to the leasing company's assumed cost of capital to assess the attractiveness of the proposition in conjunction with the related risks. When this 'equity rate of return' approach is adopted, the assumed cost of capital for the purpose of this comparison is sometimes taken as the lessor's net-of-tax borrowing opportunity cost, on the basis that each new lease can be wholly financed by borrowing. However, in practice, the amount of leasing business undertaken has a direct effect on the gearing of the leasing company, or at least of the group of which the lessor is a member, so that the weighted average cost of capital will be greater than the pure borrowing cost.

An alternative approach, which avoids the need to arrive at a weighted average cost of capital, is to include in the cash flows the cost of financing the investment in the equipment. This 'net return' approach is described after the next section, which illustrates the different answers that arise from the use of the internal and dual rate of return methods.

INTERNAL V DUAL RATE OF RETURN

The distortion of a lessor's evaluation using the internal rate of return basis rather than a dual rate is illustrated by reference to a simple leasing arrangement with a three-year primary period commencing in July 1988 of equipment costing £100,000 at a rental of £37,500 payable annually in advance. The tax assumptions are the same as for the examples in Chapter 11; interest has been ignored, i.e. it is assumed that the lease is wholly financed by equity. The cash flows are shown in Table 12.2.

These cash flows are equivalent to an internal rate of return of 9.25 per cent (net of tax), as shown in Table 12.3.

When using the dual rate of return approach, it is necessary to select a suitable reinvestment rate. If it is assumed that the surplus funds during the period July 1990–September 1991 will earn 3 per cent net of tax (or, on a portfolio basis, will reduce the lessor's borrowing, which is expected to cost 3 per cent net of tax in the surplus period of the lease), the dual rate of return on the lease is 8.75 per cent net of tax, 0.5 per cent less than the internal rate of 9.25 per cent net of tax (which assumes a 9.25 per cent net-of-tax reinvestment rate). The calculation of the 8.75 per cent dual rate is shown in Table 12.4 .

It could be argued that the difference of 0.5 per cent between the two methods of evaluation is so small that the dual rate method can be ignored. The technique is, however, covered at some length in this chapter because circumstances can change; alteration to the basis of UK corporate taxation could cause the lessor's surplus funds to have a greater impact on this evaluation.

Table 12.2 Three-year lease cash flows

Date	Purchase cost £	Rental £	Tax payable/ (relief) £	Net cash flow £	Balance of investment/ (surplus funds) £
July 1988	100,000	(37,500)	–	62,500	62,500
July 1989	–	(37,500)	–	(37,500)	25,000
Oct. 1989	–	–	(6,562)	(6,562)	(18,438)
July 1990	–	(37,500)	–	(37,500)	(19,062)
Oct. 1990	–	–	6,562	6,562	(12,500)
Oct. 1991	–	–	8,203	8,203	(4,297)
Oct. 1992	–	–	(3,828)	3,828	(8,125)
	100,000	(112,500)	4,375	(8,125) =	profit before interest

125

Table 12.3 Internal rate of return approach

Period	Opening capital invested £	Earnings at 9.25% £	Reinvestment at 9.25% £	Net cash flow £	Closing capital invested £
July 1988–June 1989	62,500	5,985		(37,500)	30,985
July 1989–Sept. 1989	30,985	717		(6,562)	25,140
Oct. 1989–June 1990	25,140	1,784		(37,500)	(10,576)
July 1990–Sept. 1990	(10,576)		(245)	6,562	(4,259)
Oct. 1990–Sept. 1991	(4,259)		(407)	8,203	3,537
Oct. 1991–Sept. 1992	3,537	348		(3,828)	57
		8,834	(652)		
		(652)			
		8,182			
Rounding of discount rate		57			
Net earnings		8,125			

Table 12.4 Dual rate of return approach

Period	Opening capital invested £	Earnings at 8.75% £	Reinvestment at 3% £	Net cash flow £	Closing capital invested £
July 1988–June 1989	62,500	5,651		(37,500)	30,651
July 1989–Sept. 1989	30,651	670		(6,562)	24,759
Oct. 1989–June 1990	24,759	1,661		(37,500)	(11,080)
July 1990–Sept. 1990	(11,080)		(83)	6,562	(4,601)
Oct. 1990–Sept. 1991	(4,601)		(139)	8,203	3,462
Oct. 1991–Sept. 1992	3,462	313		(3,828)	(52)
		8,295	(222)		
		222			
		8,073			
Rounding of discount rate		52			
Net earnings		8,125			

When lessors were able to claim 100 per cent first-year allowances and surplus funds could arise very early in a lease, the difference between the two methods of evaluation could be as much as 6 per cent.

Evaluation with associated funding

The illustration of the dual rate of return method in the previous section ignores the method used by the lessor to finance the purchase of the equipment and the cost of this financing. Most leasing companies in the UK are members of larger financial or commercial groups and obtain most or all of the funds required through loans or overdraft arrangements with parent or associated companies. In these circumstances, individual leases may be evaluated assuming that the equipment is wholly financed on an overdraft basis and taking into account interest payments in the project cash flows. The dual rate of return is then net of tax and financing costs and shows the return earned by the leasing company from the employment of the funds in the lease. One major advantage of this 'net return' basis over the 'equity rate of return' basis of applying the dual rate of return method is that it is relatively simple to incorporate into the calculations different interest cost assumptions for different parts of the investment period.

The net return method is a useful but complicated procedure because of the treatment required for the surplus period. Interest earned on the 'cash' surplus during this period is credited in the cash flows to be discounted. As in the case of the reinvestment rate of return selected in the above example, it is prudent to assume that this earning rate is lower than the assumed borrowing rate for the earlier investment period. As the lease is now being evaluated with its associated funding, and the interest earnings in the surplus period have already been taken into account, a nil reinvestment rate should be used for the surplus period in the calculation of the dual rate of return. The method of employing the various interest and earnings rates to arrive at the net return is best understood by working through the example. In practice, it is only feasible to calculate net returns using a suitable computer program.

A leasing company would, in practice, be unable to finance the whole of its equipment acquisitions using borrowed funds or, alternatively, to obtain the necessary funds from another member of the same group without affecting the group's overall availability of funds and, hence, gearing. However, this factor can be taken into account in the interest rate assumed to be charged by the lender of the funds.

In a similar way to the net return method, evaluations may be carried out on the basis of part of the finance being obtained by way of outside loans, such as ship mortgage finance, and part by way of overdraft or equity finance. Care is needed to ensure that the rate of return derived is properly identified. In some circumstances, there may be virtually no equity requirement, so that a high rate of earnings (applied to the small equity) represents only a small lump sum profit in relation to the cost of the equipment and the risks involved. To avoid this difficulty, rates of return should normally be calculated on the total funds employed rather than on only the equity element.

Illustration of net return method

The recommended method of evaluating the lessor's investment decision — the net return basis (the dual rate of return method with the assumption that the investment is financed wholly on an overdraft basis) — is illustrated using the same assumptions as for the main examples in the previous chapter (see Table 11.4), except that the lessor's year-end is assumed to be 30 September and an allowance is incorporated for the lessor's overhead costs. Estimated expenses may either be shown separately in the cash flows or added to the assumed borrowing cost. For this illustration, there are assumed to be additional administrative expenses at a level requiring a 1 per cent adjustment to a 9 per cent before-tax cost of borrowing during the investment period and a 7 per cent reinvestment rate in the surplus period (i.e. 9 per cent + 1 per cent = 10 per cent in the investment period and 7 per cent − 1 per cent = 6 per cent in the surplus period). A 9 per cent borrowing rate may be regarded as comparable to the 10 per cent rate assumed for the purpose of the lessee's evaluation in Chapter 11, the additional 1 per cent representing the margin over the lender's base rate.

The assumptions are restated in Table 12.5 and the lessor's cash flow is shown in Table 12.6.

The lessor's cash flow in Table 12.6 represents a net return (i.e. rate of profit) on funds invested of approximately 0.75 per cent (compounded quarterly). Table 12.7 demonstrates how, when this earnings rate is applied to the cash flows, there is a nil profit at the end of the cash flow period. However, it is emphasized that this calculation is proving rather

Table 12.5 Lessor's evaluation assumptions

Cost of equipment	£100,000
Date of acquisition	1 July 1988
Primary lease period	4 years
Rental	£7,500 payable quarterly in advance
Cost of money	10% per annum payable quarterly (or 9%, see text)
Reinvestment rate	6% (or 7%, see text)
Capital allowance	25% p.a. on the declining balance
Corporation tax rate	35%
Company year-end	30 September
Tax payment date	9 months after year-end
Renewal rentals and residual value	Nil
Basis of taxation	Accruals basis

Table 12.6 Lessor's cash flow

Date	Purchase cost £	Rental £	Interest payable/ (receivable) £	Tax payable/ (relief) £	Net cash flow £	Closing capital invested/ (surplus funds) £
July 1988	100,000	(7,500)			92,500	92,500
October		(7,500)	2,312		(5,188)	87,312
January 1988		(7,500)	2,183		(5,317)	81,995
April		(7,500)	2,050		(5,450)	76,545
July		(7,500)	1,914	(6,934)	(12,520)	64,025
October		(7,500)	1,601		(5,899)	58,126
January 1990		(7,500)	1,453		(6,047)	52,079
April		(7,500)	1,302		(6,198)	45,881
July		(7,500)	1,147	1,226	(5,127)	40,754
October		(7,500)	1,019		(6,418)	34,273
January 1991		(7,500)	857		(6,643)	27,630
April		(7,500)	691		(6,809)	20,821
July		(7,500)	520	3,856	(3,124)	17,697
October		(7,500)	442		(7,058)	10,639
January 1992		(7,500)	226		(7,234)	3,405
April		(7,500)	85		(7,415)	(4,010)
July			(60)	5,930	5,870	1,860
October			46		46	1,906
January 1993			48		48	1,954
April			49		49	2,003
July			50	(3,317)	(3,267)	(1,264)
	100,000	(120,000)	17,975	761	(1,264)	

than arriving at the answer. Calculations to ascertain the evaluation assumptions that will produce a specified rate of profit are only feasibly obtainable using a computer.

The net return may be grossed up using the formula in Chapter 11 (p.103–104), which takes account of the average delay in payment of tax. It should be noted that the net return and the overdraft interest are calculated on different capital investment balances, so that it is not correct to add the grossed-up net return and the overdraft interest rate together to obtain an overall before-tax earnings rate for the investment.

EXTENSION OF EVALUATION
The lessor's cash flow may also incorporate items such as renewal rentals, residual value benefits, value added tax, and regional development grants.

Table 12.7 Net return calculation

Period	Opening capital invested £	Earnings at 0.75% £	Reinvestment at 0% £	Net cash flow £	Closing capital invested £
July 1988–Sept. 1988	92,500	173		(5,188)	87,485
Oct. 1988–Dec. 1988	87,485	164		(5,317)	82,332
Jan. 1989–Mar. 1989	82,332	155		(5,450)	77,037
Apr. 1989–June 1989	77,037	144		(12,520)	64,661
July 1989–Sept. 1989	64,661	121		(5,899)	58,883
Oct. 1989–Dec. 1989	58,883	111		(6,047)	52,947
Jan. 1990–Mar. 1990	52,947	99		(6,198)	46,848
Apr. 1990–June 1990	46,848	88		(5,127)	41,809
July 1990–Sept. 1990	41,809	78		(6,481)	35,406
Oct. 1990–Dec. 1990	35,406	67		(6,643)	28,830
Jan. 1991–Mar. 1991	28,830	54		(6,809)	22,075
Apr. 1991–June 1991	22,075	41		(3,124)	18,992
July 1991–Sept. 1991	18,992	36		(7,058)	11,970
Oct. 1991–Dec. 1991	11,970	22		(7,234)	4,758
Jan. 1992–Mar. 1992	4,758	9		(7,415)	(2,648)
Apr. 1992–June 1992	(2,648)	–	0	5,870	3,222
July 1992–Sept. 1992	3,222	6		46	3,274
Oct. 1992–Dec. 1992	3,274	6		48	3,328
Jan. 1993–Mar. 1993	3,328	6		49	3,383
Apr. 1993–June 1993	3,383	7		(3,267)	123
		1,387			
Rounding of discount rate		123			
Net earnings		1,264			

The net return method of evaluating a lessor's cash flow may be used to calculate the termination rental payable for an early termination of a lease during the primary period (maintaining the rate of return for the period up to termination) and, for leases containing interest and/or tax variation clauses, also the adjustment required to a quoted rental for any change in interest rates or in the rate of corporation tax.

For leasing facilities without variation clauses, calculations may be made to show the sensitivity of the rate of return to changes in the assumptions used in the evaluation and to determine break-even positions. In this way, lessors may assess the degree of risk involved in undertaking financial leasing business at fixed rates. Assumptions, which may be varied, include the following:

1. Date of acquisition of equipment — to see how the rate of return varies when expenditure takes place earlier or later in the lessor's financial

year than forecast, particularly the reduction when expenditure is delayed from just before to just after the year-end (see Chapter 9).

2. Availability of taxable capacity — to determine the consequences of not having sufficient taxable capacity available in the year of acquisition of the equipment.
3. Cost of money (at various stages during the investment period).
4. Reinvestment rate.
5. The rate of corporation tax (at various stages during the primary lease period).
6. Exchange rates — to determine the effect of a change in the rate of exchange where rentals are receivable and/or loans are arranged in foreign currency.

RENEWAL RENTALS

The correct evaluation of renewal rentals is particularly important where the primary period is sufficiently short to encourage 'de-pooling' treatment (see Chapter 13) or where the lessor has assumed a residual value benefit at the end of the primary period. In these circumstances, the renewal rentals should be more than 'nominal'.

The calculation of the primary period rental of £7,500 in Table 12.6 assumes that the asset will be sold within the time scale laid down for short-life assets. If the lessee elects to renew the lease for a further year, the lessor loses the benefit of a 'de-pooling' provision and should reflect this in the calculation of the renewal rental.

Table 12.8 illustrates the effect on the lessor's capital invested of the extra period, and Table 12.9 shows that the annual renewal rental should be £2,400 to maintain the lessor's earnings.

Actuarial approach

The net return method described previously makes the implicit assumption that the lessor's profit is reinvested in the lease rather than being taken out either in the form of dividend payments or on a notional distribution basis. Alternatively, a lease may be evaluated using an actuarial approach, whereby, in calculating the net-of-tax rate of return, it is assumed that the profit earned is removed at periodic intervals (normally monthly) from the lessor's investment account during the investment period on the basis of a fixed proportion of the balance outstanding. The rate of release of profit, which represents the net-of-tax rate of return, is such that immediately the final taxation payment has been made there is a nil balance on the investment account.

131

Table 12.8 Lessor's cash flow with a one-year secondary period

Date	Rental £	Interest payable/ (receivable) £	Tax payable/ (relief) £	Net cash flow £	Closing capital invested/ (surplus funds) £
January 1992	(7,500)	266	–	(7,234)	3,405
April 1992	(7,500)	85	–	(7,415)	(4,010)
July 1992	(2,400)	(60)	5,930	3,470	(540)
October 1992	–	(8)	–	(8)	(548)
January 1993	–	(8)	–	(8)	(564)
July 1993	–	(8)	5,212	5,204	4,640
October 1993	–	116	–	116	4,756
January 1994	–	110	–	119	4,875
April 1994	–	122	–	122	4,997
July 1994	–	125	(6,406)	(6,281)	(1,284)

Table 12.9 Net return calculations with a one-year secondary period

Date	Opening capital invested £	Earnings at 0.75% £	Reinvestment at 0% £	Net cash flow £	Closing capital invested £
Jan. 1992–Mar. 1992	4,758	9		(7,415)	(2,648)
Apr. 1992–June 1992	(2,648)	–	0	3,470	822
July 1992–Sept. 1992	822	2		(8)	816
Oct. 1992–Dec. 1992	816	2		(8)	810
Jan. 1993–Mar. 1993	810	2		(8)	804
Apr. 1993–June 1993	804	2		5,204	6,010
July 1993–Sept. 1993	6,010	11		116	6,137
Oct. 1993–Dec. 1993	6,137	12		119	6,268
Jan. 1994–Mar. 1994	6,268	12		122	6,402
Apr. 1994–June 1994	6,402	12		(6,281)	133
			Rounding of discount rate		(133)

The cash flows using the actuarial approach are similar to those shown in Table 12.7 except that, because the earnings are assumed to be actually taken out, the overall interest cost is higher and the rate of return slightly lower. The difference between the two rates increases as the primary lease period lengthens.

13. *Taxation*

Taxation factors have been critical to the development of the UK leasing industry. It is, therefore, appropriate to look at the general way in which leasing companies are taxed in the UK. The rules relating to capital allowances are first examined and then there is a review of leasing company strategy which indicates how practical effect is given to the relief afforded by capital allowances.

Although this chapter is concerned with the lessor's tax position it should be noted that normally rentals wholly and exclusively paid out by a lessee as a business expense are fully deductible in the period to which they relate. The exceptions are in a sale and leaseback situation where the deduction is limited to a commercial rent (Income and Corporation Taxes Act 1988, S. 782) and where motor cars costing over £12,000 are leased (see below).

Capital allowances

There can be no doubt that the availability of capital allowances has been a large influence in establishing leasing as a major source of capital investment in the UK.

The role of the capital allowance system is to provide a means for companies to write off a capital expense against revenue — the fiscal equivalent of depreciation. The statutory basis of the current system is the Capital Allowances Act 1968, subsequently amended by the Finance Act 1971, and (in the case of leasing in particular) the Finance Act 1986. Legislation since then has aimed primarily at the closing of loopholes. The Finance Act 1984 saw the most radical amendment to the then generally accepted principle of using tax incentives to encourage investment. It was felt by the government of the day that uneconomic investments were being made financially viable only through the tax deferral afforded by capital allowances. The thrust of the Finance Act 1984 was to reduce capital allowances progressively from 100 per cent to 25 per cent p.a. for 1984 to 1986, while at the same time reducing the corporation tax rate from 52 to 35 per cent which, it was argued, would increase the net of tax returns from investments and still make capital investment attractive. Corporation tax rates were reduced further to 33 per cent in 1991.

Thus the system of capital allowances has moved from one concentrating upon incentives for capital investment to one that merely provides some allowance for wear and tear on the capital asset. Figure 13.1 illustrates the comparison of writing-down allowances against accounting depreciation

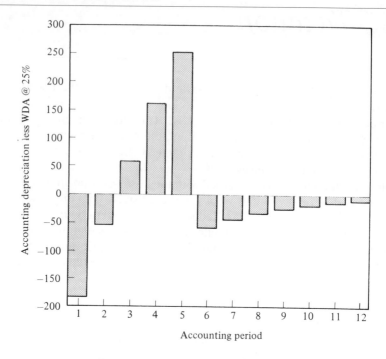

Figure 13.1 Graph of the annual depreciation charge less the annual writing-down allowance at 25 per cent

for a typical lease period of five years considered over a twelve-year period. This indicates the extent of mismatch of tax to accounting measures even in a relatively simple situation.

The effective present value of the difference between tax and accounting depreciation, assuming 33 per cent tax rates and a post-tax interest rate of, say, 7 per cent is a deficit of 1.14 per cent of the original cost to the Inland Revenue's advantage. This, however, reverses for leases of assets with a useful life in excess of seven years.

The value of using a residual sales value to eliminate the unused tax written-down value can be illustrated by Figure 13.2 where, as will be seen later, the proceeds will eliminate the tax writing-down allowance. The optimum tax residual value, as shown in Table 13.1, will be that which equates to the tax written-down value, but this must of course be realistic.

BROAD TYPES OF CAPITAL ALLOWANCES
The system of capital allowances has provided for relief to be given in one or more of three stages:

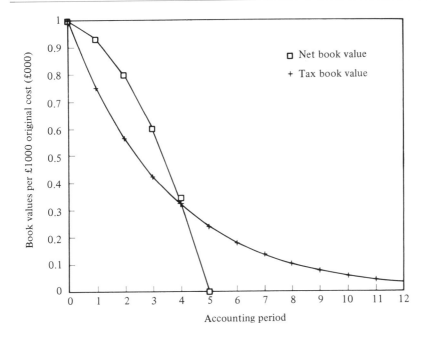

Figure 13.2 Graph to illustrate the different book values between tax and accounting on a typical five-year lease

1. An 'initial' or first year allowance (FYA) — available in the year of acquisition.
2. An annual writing-down allowance (WDA) — which writes down the remaining value of the asset over its period of use by the taxpayer.
3. A final balancing allowance or balancing charge given by relating the sales proceeds of the asset against its tax written-down value (although this is modified in the pooling system discussed later).

Table 13.1 Optimum residual values

After years	Original cost %	Annual depreciation rate %
3	31.6	22.8
4	23.7	19.1
5	17.8	16.4
6	13.3	14.4
7	10.0	12.8
8	7.5	11.6

For expenditure incurred after 13 March 1986, the rates of allowances over the main allowance categories are shown in Table 13.2.

For equipment leasing, the rules relating to plant and machinery are by far the most important, and in the remainder of this chapter all references will be to those unless otherwise stated.

Capital allowances are given where:
(a) a person carrying on a trade had incurred capital expenditure on the provision of machinery and plant wholly and exclusively for the purposes of the trade, and
(b) in consequence of incurring the expenditure, this machinery and plant belongs (or has belonged (S.44(1) FA 1971)) to that person.

Table 13.2 Rates of allowances for expenditure incurred after 13 March 1986

Category	FYA	Initial	WDA
Plant and machinery	—	—	25% p.a. on balance
Industrial buildings	—	—	4% p.a. on cost
Hotels	—	—	4% p.a. on cost
Industrial buildings in Enterprise Zones	—	100%	25% p.a. on cost
Scientific research	100%	—	—
Patents	—	—	25% p.a. on balance
Know-how	—	—	25% p.a. on balance
Ships	—	—	Free depreciation

For plant and machinery, WDAs are generally given at the rate, currently, of 25 per cent on the 'reducing balance' basis: i.e. 25 per cent of the cost of the asset is allowed against taxable income in the year in which the asset is acquired; in the second year, $18\frac{3}{4}$ per cent (i.e. 25 per cent of the remaining 75 per cent of cost); and in each subsequent year, 25 per cent of the tax written-down value at the start of the year.

In the period when leasing activity grew most strongly, between 1972 and 1984, 100 per cent FYAs were granted in the year of acquisition — though taxpayers had the alternative of disclaiming the FYAs and opting instead for WDAs if their need for allowances was likely to be greater in years following the period of acquisition. As a way of reducing the burden of administration on the taxpayer and the Inland Revenue, instead of giving allowances individually to separate classes of assets (as had been the case pre-1970), the residual of cost less FYAs claimed on all plant was added to a 'pool' of unclaimed allowances, which was subject each year to the 25 per cent writing-down allowances.

First-year allowances were phased out over two years in 1984–86. The FYA rates in force during the transition were as follows:

Assets acquired in the period	FYA rates
21.3.72–13.3.84	100 per cent
14.3.84–31.3.85	75 per cent
1.4.85–31.3.86	50 per cent
1.4.86 to date	0 per cent

Since 1 April 1986, as no FYAs are available, the entire expenditure is added to the pool of expenditure brought forward, and then the 25 per cent WDA is applied to the new and residual balances.

Capital allowances are given by means of a deduction against the taxable income of the company, thereby reducing the taxable profit, increasing taxable losses, or moving from taxable profits to taxable losses.

While taxable profits give rise to a tax charge, taxable losses can be used in a number of ways:

1. They can be set against the total UK profits subject to corporation tax of the chargeable period, from all sources.
2. They may be transferred to or from other members of a group or consortium of companies.
3. They can be carried back to set off against profits of a previous period, except to the extent that losses attributable to capital allowances may be carried back three years. For accounting periods ending on or after 1 April 1991 all trading losses may be carried back three years.
4. To the extent that losses cannot be otherwise used, taxable losses may be carried forward to offset taxable profits arising in the same trade.

CAPITAL ALLOWANCES APPLIED TO LEASING

Prior to April 1980, any person could establish a leasing trade and claim capital allowances. This benefit could be passed on, through reduced rentals, to the lessee irrespective of the latter's underlying tax position. Even if the lessee were a non-taxable entity, tax benefits could be effectively obtained. In its study of the taxation of banks in 1979 the Institute of Fiscal Studies estimated that approximately 80 per cent of the benefit was transferred to lessees.

Tax-based leasing in that period was not restricted to incorporated lessors. To an extent leasing was used as a vehicle to shelter income tax liabilities through various personal tax schemes.

In view of these developments there have been a number of amendments to the capital allowance legislation with specific reference to leasing. The Finance Act 1980 introduced the most fundamental changes, namely that

FYAs on leased assets, whether used in the course of trade or not, were to be excluded unless it was certified by the lessor that the plant and machinery would be used for a qualifying purpose and for a requisite period (S. 64(1) FA 1980).

Plant and machinery was used for a qualifying purpose if:

(a) it was leased to a lessee who used it for a trade, other than leasing, and could have claimed first-year allowances if he had incurred the expenditure himself (i.e. this excluded leases to all non-trading entities, mainly, local authorities and government agencies);

(b) it was used for short-term leasing in the UK (thus avoiding the administrative problems of lessors having to determine the tax status of lessees whose hire period might be very short (generally less than 30 days));

(c) it was used for a purpose other than leasing — i.e. it formed part of the leasing company's own fixed assets.

The 'requisite period' was set at four years, or shorter if the asset ceased to belong to the lessor. If a lease failed these tests, then only WDAs were available. Following the withdrawal of FYAs, the Finance Act 1986 has removed the basic regulation (S. 64(1), FA 1980), but has left all the definitions on the statute book. One reason for this is that when the Finance Act 1985 introduced short-life asset 'de-pooling' arrangements, the qualifying user test was retained.

For all claims for FYAs on leased assets in the chargeable periods from 1980 to 1986, the lessor is obliged to sign and submit with the annual tax computations a certificate stating that the assets on which FYAs are claimed form part of leases that comply with the requirements of qualifying purpose and requisite period (S. 67, FA 1980).

The Finance Act 1980 also introduced legislation to allow losses arising from the trade of leasing to be set off against other income only when the lessor carries on a trade of leasing for at least six months in a year, and devotes a substantial amount of time to that trade. The onus is upon the taxpayer to prove this devotion. This requirement has effectively ended the individual income-tax-based leasing transactions.

A further provision to restrict allowances to leasing companies was introduced in Section 70, Finance Act 1982, when the level of WDAs was reduced from 25 per cent to 10 per cent per annum for assets leased outside the UK. This was to prevent the export of capital allowances, which at that time were valued at 52 per cent (i.e. the corporation tax saving to the leasing companies). Section 70 is also restrictive in the case of export leasing rentals by preventing effectively contract variations for interest rate and tax changes which are common in domestic UK leasing and thus increasing the risk on the lessor. Effectively this legislation has precluded direct UK-to-foreign leasing since 1982; and UK leasing companies are now involved in overseas leasing activity only through their corporate links with international leasing groups, with the assets being owned by a foreign leasing company within the group. The ELA has pressed strongly for changes in the 1982 legislation, particularly in view of the moves by the European Community towards a single market by the end of 1992 — by which time the European legislation may well call into question the distinction in the UK tax code between leasing to UK customers and leasing to those elsewhere in the Community.

In recent years the focus of legal attention has been redirected at the essential requirements as to the ability of taxpayers to be able to claim capital allowances — particularly in the areas of incurring expenditure and the concept of 'belonging' as referred to earlier (S. 44, FA 1971).

CLAIMING CAPITAL ALLOWANCES

Incurring expenditure

In 1984, when the Chancellor announced phased changes in capital allowances in advance over the next two years, it became necessary to review the legislation determining the precise dates when expenditure is deemed to be incurred for the purposes of capital allowances. Previously accepted principles were challenged by the Inland Revenue's assertion, against the strength of commercial and accounting practice, that expenditure is incurred when cash is actually paid out for the asset, rather than on the invoice date or on the date of sale. Under the Capital Allowances Act 1968, it had generally been accepted that expenditure is incurred when it becomes payable. Under Section 57, Finance Act 1985, expenditure is now defined as incurred, for accounting periods ending after 17 December 1984, on the date on which an obligation to pay an amount becomes unconditional and before that on which the asset becomes the property of the lessor. A month's grace is given at the end of an accounting period between the obligation being established and the obligation becoming unconditional, to allow the earlier date to be taken for the purpose of claiming capital allowances in that accounting period. Also the maximum period of credit brought forward between the obligation becoming unconditional and actual payment has been set at four months, i.e. if payment is made beyond that cut-off point then the date of payment will become the date on which expenditure is incurred.

Belonging

Also, in 1984 the law of property was found to conflict with the intentions of giving allowances. This related to plant and machinery which, when installed in a building, became a fixture of that structure (and thus the property of the owner of the interest in the land) and as a result incapable of 'belonging' to the equipment lessor. In Stokes v Costain Property Investments Ltd ((1984) STC 204, (1984)1 All ER 849 CA), a case which centred on the affixing of lift equipment, it was held that neither party could claim capital allowances because each failed to meet both of the basic rules. The company that had incurred the expenditure did not have an interest in the property and so the asset could not 'belong' to it, and the company actually owning the property in which the assets had become a fixture had not incurred the expenditure. The inadequacy of this rule led to the introduction in the Finance Act 1985 of special rules for plant that becomes a fixture (S. 59 and Sch. 17, FA 1985). This is a highly complex piece of legislation, with special sections relating to the leasing of equipment (see Chapter 21).

Essentially, however, it allows the lessor and the lessee to elect, for the purposes of taxation that the relevant Section 59 will apply, so that for all material purposes the equipment will be treated as belonging to the equipment lessor in consequence of the incurring of expenditure, and the lessor may claim the capital allowances.

Capital allowances relating to specific assets

Plant and machinery

The criteria in this chapter cover the points in respect of capital allowances for plant and machinery. However, what actually constitutes 'plant' is a complex subject and, unfortunately, there is no definition of plant in any of the taxes Acts. A basic description of plant was propounded by Lindsay LJ in Yarmouth v France (1887):

> In its ordinary sense it includes whatever apparatus is used by a businessman for carrying on his business, not his stock in trade which he buys or makes for sale, but all goods and chattels, fixed and moveable, live or dead, which he keeps for permanent employment in his business. (1887, 19 QBD 647)

In the 1970s, when the rate of FYAs for plant exceeded the rate of initial allowances for industrial buildings, the definition of plant was further explored in the courts. Generally, the judgments have related to whether the item performs a function in the taxpayer's trade or is merely the setting in which the trade takes place. For example, a dry dock has been held to be plant (IRC v Barclay, Curle & Co. Ltd) (1969 All ER 732, 4 STC 221). Even more recently, items that help to create an atmosphere in which the trade takes place have been held to be plant (e.g. lights, decorations — IRC v Scottish & Newcastle Breweries Ltd (1982 STC 296); and glass partitions, with the company's logo etched on them – Leeds Permanent Building Society v Proctor (1982 STC 82); although general shop lighting and electrical fittings have been disallowed — Cole Bros Ltd. v Philips (1982 STC 307 HL).

Where an asset is held not to be plant, it will not be subject to 25 per cent WDAs. If deemed part of an industrial building, it will qualify only for industrial buildings allowances (see below) at a lower rate. Where a 'non-plant' asset is deemed to be part of a commercial building, such as shops and offices, no capital allowances can be claimed on the expenditure. Commercial buildings do not qualify for capital allowances, on the grounds that they do not depreciate in value over time.

Ships

In view of the nature and size of expenditure on ships there have been a number of special rules for capital allowances thereon. Shipowners are able to elect to postpone the whole or a part of the 100 per cent FYA on expenditure on the acquisition of a ship and then claim the amount postponed in such future period or periods as they wish. This allowance for ships was known as 'free depreciation', in contrast to the system for plant described above.

The principal benefit of free depreciation arises in relation to the surrender of losses by way of group relief. Ordinarily, tax losses may be surrendered in the year in which they arise or they may be carried forward against the profits from the same trade of the individual company concerned; it is not permissible to carry forward losses and then group relieve them in a subsequent year. The flexibility of the allowance system for ships enabled companies to maximize the group relief potential. In the current circumstances, with fewer tax-exhausted companies, this effect is diminished but retains some importance.

Until 1985 the system for free depreciation applied only to 'new' ships, but under Section 58, Finance Act 1985, it was made available for all ships.

Motor cars

Capital allowances for motor cars, excluding commercial vehicles, have been restricted to an annual writing-down allowance (FA 1971). Cars with an original market cost of less than £12,000 are restricted to annual allowances of £3,000 or 25 per cent of the tax written-down value, whichever is the lower. The reference to original market value allows expensive vintage cars to obtain greater allowances than equally 'high cost' new cars. The so-called expensive (i.e. over £12,000 if acquired after 10 March 1992 or £8,000 if acquired before 11 March 1992) cars are dealt with as separate trades in the capital allowance calculations, in so far as sales proceeds can only be set against the car to which it related; thus generating separate balancing charges or allowances for each car. As will be seen later, this ironically provides a 'de-pooling' arrangement for expensive cars which is not available for cars less than £12,000 (£8,000 if acquired before 11 March 1992).

Where 'high cost' cars are leased, the effect of the restriction on the lessor's capital allowance is compounded by a parallel restriction on the deductibility of lease rentals as revenue expenditure of the lessee (Sch. 12(8), FA 1971). This discriminates against leasing, since the lessee is in any event affected by the impact on lease rentals of the lessor's capital allowance restriction. The ELA has made strong representations for a review of the relevant legislation.

Companies in the business of short-term car hire, as opposed to lessors or companies acquiring cars for their own employees' use, have been able to treat such cars as 'plant and machinery' rather than being affected by the restrictions on capital allowances for cars. The car-hire firms thus continued to obtain FYAs up to 1 April 1986.

Industrial buildings

Industrial building allowances (IBAs) are given when expenditure is incurred in the construction of an industrial building which is to be occupied for the purpose of a trade. Only costs of construction are allowed, and costs relating to the acquisition of the interest in the land are specifically excluded.

The rate of IBAs is 4 per cent in 'straightline' terms, as distinct from the 'reducing balance' basis for WDAs on plant: i.e. the full cost of buildings can be written off over 25 years in equal amounts each year. As the description suggests, the buildings must be used for industrial purposes. As with the definition of plant there are numerous cases that have set out the boundaries of classification. If a building is partly used for industrial purposes and partly for other (e.g. offices, shops, showrooms, and repair shops), the non-qualifying element will be specifically excluded (S. 7(3), CAA 1968). This is done through an apportionment of costs — though this rule is relaxed under Section 7(4), CAA 1968, where the element of non-qualifying expenditure fails to exceed 25 per cent of the total capital expenditure of the building and if this is the case, then the whole building will be regarded as qualifying in full.

For the purpose of granting IBAs for buildings in enterprise zones, the only non-qualifying building is a dwelling house, so that hotels, shops, leisure complexes, hypermarkets, etc., are all capable of attracting 100 per cent FYAs and this explains the move of major retailing chains to build out-of-town stores in enterprise zones.

In order to claim the IBAs the taxpayer must hold a 'relevant interest' in the land, except in the case of long leases (i.e. one that exceeds 50 years,

S.38, ICTA 1988), where, by means of an election between the lessor and lessee, the lessee may be able to claim IBAs on expenditure incurred (S. 37, FA 1978).

If the owner buys the building new and unused from the developer then the IBAs will be based upon the original cost. If, within 25 years, the building is sold or the relevant interest in the land sold, then a balancing charge or allowance will arise. The new purchaser will be entitled to IBAs based upon the residue of expenditure (i.e. the unrelieved expenditure of the vendor) plus or minus the balancing charge or allowance suffered by the vendor. However, this value is then spread evenly over the remainder of the 25-year period from when the building originally came into use.

Example 13.1
An industrial building is sold for £1,500,000 after six years of continuous use (original cost £1,200,000). The new owner will be entitled to IBAs of:

			£
Stage I:	Cost		1,200,000
	Annual IBA @ 4 per cent	£48,000	
	Allowances given over six years		288,000
	Tax written-down value		912,000
	Sales proceeds		(1,500,000)
	Balancing charge		588,000

Stage II: Purchaser's IBAs:

$$\frac{£912,000 + £588,000}{(25 - 6)} = £78,947 \text{ p.a.}$$

Films, tapes and discs
Originally, 100 per cent FYAs were available for expenditure incurred on master copies of films, etc., whether or not the films were actually made in the UK. Under Section 82, Finance Act 1983, the use of FYAs was limited to films that qualified for the 'Eady levy' (i.e. films that were substantially produced in the UK). The Eady levy was superseded by the Films Act 1985, which also sets down requirements for UK production, and remains the determinant as to whether capital allowances are available.

Recent legislation however, enables film production companies — as an alternative to claiming capital allowances — to write off expenditure against revenue over the expected useful life of the film. This has meant that capital allowances are not claimed on films as frequently as before.

THE POOLING SYSTEM

In a number of overseas countries, the system for capital allowances, or their equivalent, requires each asset to be depreciated separately for tax purposes. In fact, even in the UK, within a company's fixed asset register it is possible that each asset will have its own depreciation calculated. However, it was decided that, in order to ease the administration of the taxpayer and the Inland Revenue, the capital allowances system would run on the pooling system. A form of pooling system has run for a number of years, although the current system was introduced in the Finance Act 1971.

The basic concept is that the company maintains a pool of the residue of expenditure incurred (after deducting previous allowances available, e.g. FYAs and WDAs), and against this overall total an annual WDA is calculated. This removes the need to calculate tax allowances for each individual asset. The WDA is an annual allowance and if the accounting period is less than 12 months, then the allowance is reduced in proportion to the accounting period.

The usual operation of the allowance structure is illustrated in Table 13.3 (i.e. as a single asset), which the pooling system is of course designed to avoid. In addition, this simplification hides some important elements of the

Table 13.3 The capital allowance computation

			£
Pool brought forward at the start of the accounting period			100,000
Deduct:	Lower of sales proceeds or original cost of assets disposed		(20,000)
Add:	Expenditure incurred on assets for which first-year allowances are not available		40,000
			120,000
Deduct:	Annual writing-down allowance (at the rate of 25% per annum)		(30,000)
			90,000
Add:	Expenditure incurred on assets for which first-year allowances are available	50,000	
	Less: FYA claimed (say 50%)	(25,000)	
			25,000
Leaving:	Pool of residue of expenditure to carry forward to next accounting period		115,000

system. Table 13.4 shows the effect on three assets with different FYAs. From this one can see that potential balancing charges and balancing allowances, if related to individual assets, are actually spread over the duration of the pool at the rate of 25 per cent per annum. This is an important feature for companies where there is a large asset base where 100 per cent FYAs have been given. For such mature leasing books the sales proceeds are being protected by the increasing pool of expenditure from assets acquired under the 25 per cent regime. When considered in the context where rental rebates of the sales proceeds are given, lessors are benefiting from additional deferrals of corporation tax, providing additional profits (see Table 13.5).

Table 13.5 considers the excess of sales proceeds over the tax written-down value of the asset, and rental rebates of 95 per cent of sales proceeds treated as immediate revenue deductions. The table assumes a tax written-down value of £100,000, and so with a tax rate of 33 per cent, the tax benefits arising from the various sales proceeds will be as shown. If the lease in this example was priced on the assumption that a sale would occur at not less than tax written-down value, then the lessor would generate additional cash inflow of £3,350; that is, a sale at tax written-down value of £100,000 produces a net present value of £31,350 which, together with the actual net cash received of £5,000, exceeds the required tax value of £33,000 by £3,350.

Recently formed leasing companies will not have the same level of advantage. One other problem is that instead of the single pool we have been considering so far, in reality in a leasing company there will be a number of separate leasing pools that do not allow balancing charges and allowances to be spread against other pools. These have arisen as a result of legislation specifically concerned with leasing. Until 1986 the separate pools potentially required by a leasing company (subject to the range of business) would have been:

1. *General pool*   Own fixed assets used in his trade, and leased assets for which no special rules applied.
2. *Motor car pool*   Cars of original market value less than £8,000 (£12,000 if acquired after 10 March 1992).
3. *Non-qualifying leases*   Leases to non-qualifying users, e.g. local authorities.
4. *Foreign leases*   Leases to non-UK residents where the WDA is only 10 per cent p.a.
5. *Cars with original market value in excess of £8,000 (£12,000 if acquired after 10 March 1992)*   Each car will form its own individual pool.

In the Finance Act 1986, this has been amended to allow assets, subject to leasing agreements, which have been purchased after 1 April 1986 to be

145

Table 13.4 Example of capital allowance computation

Asset	Date of purchase	Cost £	FYA claimed %	Date of sale	Sale proceeds £
A	1.4.83	100,000	100	1.4.87	50,000
B	1.4.84	100,000	50	1.4.88	45,000
C	1.4.85	100,000	0	1.4.89	40,000

The company's accounting period ends on 30 June

	Actual Pool £	Allowance claimed £	Splitting the pool notionally between		
			Asset A £	Asset B £	Asset C £
The opening pool at 1 July 1985 will comprise:					
Original cost	200,000		100,000	100,000	
FYAs claimed	(150,000)	(150,000)	(100,000)	(50,000)	
Pool at 1.7.85	50,000		0	50,000	0
Additions	100,000				100,000
Sales proceeds					
	150,000		0	50,000	100,000
Writing-down allowance	(37,500)	(37,500)	0	(12,500)	(25,000)
Pool at 1.7.86	112,500		0	37,500	75,000
Additions					
Sales proceeds	(50,000)		(50,000)		
	62,500		(50,000)	37,500	75,000
Writing-down allowance	(15,625)	(15,625)	12,500	(9,375)	(18,750)
Pool at 1.7.87	46,875		(37,500)	28,125	56,250
Additions					
Sales proceeds	(45,000)			(45,000)	
	1,875		(37,500)	(16,875)	56,250
Writing-down allowance	(469)	(469)	9,375	4,219	(14,063)
Pool at 30.6.88	1,406		(28,125)	(12,656)	42,188
Additions					
Sales proceeds	(40,000)				(40,000)
	(38,594)		(28,125)	(12,656)	2,188
Balancing charge	38,594	38,594	28,125	12,656	(2,188)
Pool at 30.6.89	0	(165,000)	0	0	0

Table 13.5 The tax value of rebated rentals against sales proceeds in the pool of expenditure

Sales proceeds £	Rental rebate @ 95% £	Net present value of the tax value of rebate versus pool value at 7% £
150,000	142,500	34,138
145,000	137,750	33,859
140,000	133,000	33,580
135,000	128,250	33,302
130,000	123,500	33,023
125,000	118,750	32,744
120,000	114,000	32,465
115,000	109,250	32,186
110,000	104,500	31,908
105,000	99,750	31,629
100,000	95,000	31,350
95,000	90,250	31,071
90,000	85,500	30,792
85,000	80,750	30,514
80,000	76,000	30,235
75,000	71,250	29,956
70,000	66,500	29,677
65,000	61,750	29,398
60,000	57,000	29,120
55,000	52,250	28,841

amalgamated into a single pool, although the restrictions in respect of expensive cars will remain and the existing pools will be retained.

A pooling system was particularly advantageous for leasing companies in the transitional period of the tax changes in 1984–86, with assets on which 75 per cent and 50 per cent FYAs had been allowed and in periods of inflation where the general level of second-hand values has tended to increase. In the future this benefit will reverse, and the pooling system will become disadvantageous, particularly when applied to assets subject to higher levels of obsolescence (e.g. 'high-tech' equipment).

DE-POOLING

The tax life of an asset could spread to infinity, if never sold, but in reality 95 per cent of the cost will be taken in the first 10 years. With assets of an estimated short useful life this will be a distinct disadvantage. As a direct result of this, an option to 'de-pool' selected assets was introduced in the Finance Act 1985 (S. 57 and Sch. 15, FA 1985 — further explained in an

Inland Revenue Statement of Practice, SP1/1986 — Short Life Assets). This provision relates to assets acquired after 1 April 1986 (excluding cars, and for the purposes of leasing, non-qualifying assets (S. 64(2), FA 1980), and leases to non-UK residents), and requires the taxpayer to elect within two years after the end of the chargeable period in which the expenditure was incurred.

Once an election has been made, the asset will be treated as if it is within a separate trade, so that if the asset is disposed of within a certain period then a balancing charge or allowance will be available. Obviously, if the sale is within the two-year period then the taxpayer will be aware of the most efficient route, otherwise he or she will have to take a view on the most effective course of action. If the asset is not disposed of within a chargeable period ending on or before the fourth anniversary of the end of the chargeable period related to the incurring of the expenditure, then the balance of expenditure remaining will be transferred back to the overall pool and dealt with in the normal way. The effect of relating the life to the chargeable period, in the normal course of leasing, will restrict the maximum lease period to three years.

The major beneficiary of this treatment is meant to be 'high-tech' assets with little or no value at the end of their useful life. The election must specify the asset, the capital expenditure, and the date of incurring the expenditure. The statement of practice makes clear that Inspectors of Taxes will allow assets of similar type and size to be treated as single units, if satisfied about the underlying accuracy of the records of the assets. In those cases where the asset is scrapped or has little value, then a balancing allowance will be allowed to be taken if details of the disposals are submitted. Also, as an additional concession the Inland Revenue will allow special treatment in disposals where assets are held in large numbers, and where it is possible, but impractical, to identify individual sales proceeds. The Inland Revenue cite the example of scientific instruments; however, it may well apply to all types of leased equipment. The basis of the concession is that the sales proceeds are applied to a pro-rated tax written-down value to arrive at the balancing charge or allowance, in each year of disposal.

The trade of leasing

Leasing is regarded by the Inland Revenue as a trade for tax purposes. Accordingly the profits that a leasing company make are taxable according to the principles of Schedule D, Case I. There is no specific set of rules as to what amounts to the carrying on of a trade and it is necessary to examine the facts of each case to determine whether there is an intention to trade and whether the pattern of transactions is indicative of the fulfilment of that intention.

While a series of transactions with a view to profit will establish a trade for tax purposes, one single transaction on its own might well not be considered a trade. If a trade is not established, any tax losses arising from a capital allowance claim may be 'stranded' — i.e. not available for surrender to another group company and not available to be carried forward or backward to be set off against the profits of other trades in the same company.

It should be noted that the pre-tax profit reported in a company's accounts is usually a very different figure from the profit to be taxed under Schedule D, Case I. Taxable profits are arrived at by adjusting reported book profits according to statutory rules. For example, certain expenditure charges in the profit and loss account are not allowable for tax purposes. The expense of entertaining UK customers is one such item. Depreciation is a more important item that is not deductible from income for tax purposes in the same way as for accounting purposes; though it is addressed by a capital allowance (see above). Equally, certain income may not be taxable, e.g. regional development grants and dividends from UK companies.

Deferred taxation
Accountants draw a distinction between items of income and expense that are permanently non-taxable or non-allowable and those items where the income or expense is merely dealt with in a different accounting period for tax purposes from that in which they appear in the accounts. For the non-permanent or timing differences a provision for deferred taxation is often established in the balance sheet. The contra entry will be a component in the tax charge and has the effect of smoothing the charge so as to equate more closely with the rate of taxation as applied to the published pre-tax profits.[1]

In a leasing company the principal timing difference for which a deferred tax provision will be appropriate is the difference between the depreciation charge and the capital allowance claim. To arrive at the level of provision required, the tax written-down value of assets is compared with their book written-down value. Where the tax written-down value is smaller, a deferred tax provision will normally be established.

Proforma accounts and tax computation
The profit and loss account of a typical leasing company will look much as that shown in Table 13.6, and although the examples are simplified, the format of many leasing companies accounts and computations are actually quite straightforward.

149

Table 13.6 Profit and loss account of a typical leasing company

		£000
Turnover	Leasing income earned	5,500
Comprising		
	Accounting profit/(loss) on sale	300
		5,800
Cost of sales	Commonly includes interest charged	(4,000)
		1,800
Administrative costs		(500)
Pre-tax profit		1,300
Tax charge	Tax at 33%	(1,320)
	Deferred tax (full provision)	990
		(330)
Post-tax profit		970

Assuming a capital allowance claim of £10m then this would generate the following tax computation:

Pre-tax profit		1,300
Add back	Capital repayments of leases	13,000
	(i.e. rentals less income earned)	
	Accounting (loss) on sales	–
		14,300
Less	Capital allowances	10,000
	Accounting profit on sales	300
Taxable profit		4,000

Rental income

Rental income is worth exploring in a little more detail because practice can vary from one leasing company to another.

Lease rentals are normally earned over the period of the lease. Actual payment by the lessee to the lessor may be made on a variety of bases, however. Payment intervals can be monthly, quarterly, half-yearly or annually, and rents can be in advance or in arrears.

Some leasing companies may initially credit rental receipts to suspense, releasing them to profit and loss account on a time-apportioned basis. Other leasing companies credit rental income to profit and loss as it arises. They then achieve apportioned earnings within published turnover by adjusting the capital repayment charge. Capital repayments are, of course, added back in the tax computation so that, unless a further adjustment is made for tax purposes, lease rentals would be taxed on a receipts basis. In such cases adjustments are usually made in the tax computation to reconvert the rental income to a time-apportioned basis. For rentals in advance the Inland Revenue are normally content with this approach. It is worth noting here that capital repayment charges are flexed additionally in order to implement income recognition policies, e.g. investment period method, actuarial method etc.

Tax payable

Assuming that the result in Table 13.6 shows a taxable profit and that no other reliefs are available to the company, then corporation tax (currently 33 per cent)[2] will be payable nine months[3] after the year-end involved.

If, prior to the year-end, the leasing company can forecast a taxable profit on the basis of no new business, then the company could write incremental leasing business to absorb some of those profits. In evaluating the rentals to be charged to lessees the company will assume the relative tax saving (deriving from any surplus of capital allowance and interest costs over rental income) to fall in nine months after the year-end.

Leasing company strategy

This section is concerned with the manner in which the industry uses the tax reliefs generated by capital allowances and, in turn, how those strategies may impact upon rentals that are charged to lessee customers.

TAXABLE CAPACITY

The most important strategic requirement for a leasing company is to have available a source of taxable profit against which to utilize the relief afforded by capital allowances. The industry has over the years termed taxable profit as 'taxable capacity', although the term 'tax shelter' is often used.

Tax capacity may be available to a leasing company in two ways. Firstly, the leasing company itself may have taxable profit. This may arise, particularly in an established leasing company, when taxable rentals exceed the interest costs borne by the leasing company and the capital allowances claimed. The second source of tax capacity is the taxable profits arising in a leasing company's parent company, its subsidiary companies or its fellow subsidiaries. Access to the tax capacity of other members of the leasing company's group is given by the mechanism of Group Relief, which is dealt with below.

THE GROUP STRUCTURE OF LEASING COMPANIES

As noted above, if a leasing company has a taxable profit, in normal circumstances tax will be payable nine months after the end of the accounting period. Rentals in respect of incremental leasing business which utilize tax capacity will be evaluated on that basis. In other words, the mathematical model used for evaluation will take account of the delay between the date upon which expenditure is incurred and the date upon which tax is saved. Expenditure incurred on the last day of an accounting period will naturally be only nine months before the relative tax is saved. If expenditure is incurred at the start of an accounting period the delay before receipt of tax benefits will be one year and nine months and, other things being equal, rental will therefore be more expensive.

To smooth out the effect of incurring expenditure at different times of the year, a leasing group may arrange to have leasing companies with different year-ends. A frequent practice is to have four companies with year-ends in March, June, September and December. Having established such a series of companies, leasing business will be written in the company with the next occurring year-end and seasonal fluctuations in rental quotes can be minimal.

The other main reason for multiple leasing companies in a group is to maximize the benefits arising from surrendering tax losses under group relief rules. Before turning to group relief loss surrender, it is worth making the point that, in order to surrender a tax loss, the leasing company must first of all have tax losses. Since 1984 the reduction in the level of capital allowances has resulted in most leasing companies operating in 1984 becoming 'mature'; this is to say, that rental income in these companies now exceeds capital allowances and 'cost of money' interest charges.

In order to take full advantage of group relief rules, leasing groups have incorporated many more companies and have begun to trade through those new companies. In effect the new business so written generates tax losses, at least for the first year or so, without having first to utilize in-built tax capacity as in a mature leasing company. Tax losses thus generated can hence be surrendered more efficiently under group relief rules.

GROUP RELIEF

Tax law, while normally concerned with the separate taxation of companies, is prepared to recognize the existence of groups of companies. Various special reliefs are available:

- freedom from payment of advance corporation tax (ACT) on inter-company dividends
- ability to surrender ACT from a parent to a subsidiary
- freedom from tax on chargeable capital gains on intra-group asset transfers
- ability to surrender a trading loss to offset taxable profits of other companies in a group or consortium.

The last of these, group relief, is the subject of this section.

Group relief is available between a parent company and its 75 per cent owned subsidiaries, and the losses can flow in either direction. There are various technical restrictions as to which companies may enjoy the relief and the extent to which they may do so.

While discussion of many of these restrictions is outside the scope of a work of this nature, it should be noted that temporary grouping of a company will usually severely restrict any available relief. Furthermore, the companies involved in a group relief claim must all be UK resident, and no relief will be available if a profit on the sale of shares in the subsidiary is to be treated as a trading receipt on the grounds that the shares are not a permanent investment.

Typically the leasing company will have trading losses which it will surrender to other members of its group, those other members having taxable profits. The claimant company (the company with taxable profits) will normally pay for those tax losses. Payment is tax neutral providing it is no more than 100 per cent of the loss surrendered (Section 402(6), Income and Corporation Taxes Act 1988). Equally, no payment for group relief is actually necessary, although normally the payment is equal to the tax saved by the claimant company. For complete neutrality the claimant company will pay for the losses surrendered to it on the date when it would otherwise have paid corporation tax to the Inland Revenue.

Corresponding accounting periods

There are important rules that govern the position where the accounting periods of surrendering and claimant companies do not coincide. In one sense the rules are restrictive but, in another, they present an opportunity. Leasing companies regard the corresponding accounting period rules rather as the latter.

Generally where there are differing year-ends in a group it is necessary to time-apportion the trading losses and taxable profits of the companies involved to show the maximum amounts that can be dealt with under group relief rules for each period. The loss surrendered is related to the time-apportioned profit or loss (whichever is the smaller), attributable to the 'overlap' common to the accounting periods of the two companies.

Example 13.2
A Bank Ltd has a 31 December year-end
L Lessor Ltd has a 30 June year-end

Results		£
A Bank Ltd	31 December 1988 tax profit	10,000
	31 December 1989 tax profit	40,000
L Lessor Ltd	30 June 1989 tax losses	(20,000)

Losses of L Lessor Ltd can be surrendered as follows:

31.12.88	6/12ths of smaller of:	£		
	A Bank Ltd	10,000		
	Lessor Ltd	20,000		
	= 6/12ths of	10,000	=	5,000
31.12.89	6/12ths of smaller of:			
	A Bank Ltd	40,000		
	Lessor Ltd	20,000		
	= 6/12ths of	20,000	=	10,000

A total of £15,000 of L Lessor's June 1989 loss may be surrendered to A Bank Ltd.

In Example 13.2, £5,000 of L Lessor's loss remained unrelieved but group relief allows more than one claimant company to claim relief providing a corresponding (time apportionment) period rule is followed and that no more than the total loss of L Lessor is claimed.

Example 13.3
Assume the same basic facts as in Example 13.2 but, in addition, there are two fellow subsidiaries each with tax profits of £20,000 in the year to 31 December 1988.

Losses of L Lessor Ltd can now be surrendered as follows:

31.12.88	6/12ths of smaller of:	£		£
	A Bank Ltd	10,000		
	L Lessor Ltd	20,000	=	5,000
	6/12ths of smaller of:			
	No. 1 Subsidiary Ltd	20,000		
	L Lessor Ltd	20,000	=	10,000

6/12ths of smaller of:

No. 2 Subsidiary Ltd	20,000	
L Lessor Ltd	20,000	
= £10,000 but restricted to		5,000
since L Lessor Ltd has only		
£20,000 of loss in total		
		20,000

Example 13.3 is particularly important to a leasing company. While the corresponding accounting period rule (S. 408, ICTA 1988) is essentially a restriction on the losses available for surrender, it applies on a company-by-company basis as indicated. Providing a leasing company is a member of a group of companies such as in the examples, it could write leasing business in its year to 30 June 1989 but surrender tax losses 'back' wholly to 31 December 1988. Lease rental evaluation can therefore assume that receipt of tax benefits will arise on 1 October 1989, this being the date when the claimant companies would otherwise pay tax. The tax credit delay, as it is often called, has, in Example 13.3, been shortened from the notional nine months from L Lessor's year-end to an actual delay of three months from its year-end.

It would be possible, if desired, to maximize fully the benefit described above. Consider there being 12 companies with a December 1988 year-end, each of which have at least £12,000 of taxable profit upon which tax is payable on 1 October 1989. If a leasing company with a November 1989 year-end has a tax loss of £12,000 then, providing all the companies are members of the same group throughout the periods involved, each of the 12 can claim £1,000 of the loss of the leasing company.

Suppose, for example, that the leasing company wrote the incremental business to achieve the £12,000 loss on, say, 30 November 1989 it could evaluate the rentals so as to assume the receipt of tax benefits on 1 October 1989 — i.e. almost two months before incurring the relative expenditure.

This example serves to underscore a trend that is currently discernible in the leasing industry where highly competitive rentals for large-value transactions are common.

BALANCING CHARGES AS A SOURCE OF CAPACITY

It may be that a leasing company has a very small general pool of unallowed expenditure. This may well be the case for a company that wrote more leasing business before 1 April 1985, with 100 or 75 per cent FYAs, than subsequently. An opportunity may arise if a large leasing transaction is prematurely terminated, giving rise to substantial sales proceeds from the asset.

Providing the level of the potential balancing charge can be forecast with some accuracy, the leasing company may incur expenditure prior to its year-end and shelter the potential balancing charge with the new expenditure, thus effectively claiming 100 per cent allowances on that new expenditure. This route will, of course, only be beneficial where the de-pooling election (see above) is not made; and will only be viable if the termination rental on the asset sold is calculated to assume a balancing charge on that asset.

Although not usually keen to have early termination of leases, some lessors are willing to consider the effect a major asset sale may have on their pool of unallowed expenditure. The effect is to accelerate the relief on the pool so that rather than calculate termination rentals to assume an immediate balancing charge on the sale proceeds, they will recognize the benefits of accelerating some of the pool expenditure. However, to the extent that benefit is given to the terminating lessee it cannot also be reflected in rentals to be charged on the new expenditure.

JOINT ACTIVITIES

For the very largest transactions an individual leasing company, or indeed individual groups of companies, may not wish to take the entire credit risk. Furthermore, tax capacity constraints may mean that a single group is unable effectively to use the tax losses involved. In such a case leasing groups may join together to form a consortium.

A consortium-owned company will be formed to engage in the leasing activity and the ownership of that company will be vested in anything between 2 and 20 other companies. The definition of a consortium is satisfied where not less than 75 per cent of the ordinary share capital is held by two or more companies, each of which owns not less than 5 per cent.

The tax losses of the leasing company owned by a consortium may be surrendered to the members subject to the corresponding accounting period rules noted above and subject to the additional restriction that the share of loss claimed by each member is limited to the percentage of ordinary share capital which it owns.

Alternatively, leasing can be carried on by two or more partners. In this case no surrender of tax losses is involved. A company that is a member of a partnership merely brings into its own tax computation the appropriate share of the partnership loss or profit for tax purposes as if that share had been derived from a trade carried on by that company in its corresponding accounting period.

SUB-LEASING

Following the reductions in and demise of first-year allowances some leasing companies have sought to develop their business by offering leasing where they themselves are not the head lessor. For such a transaction, no capital allowances are claimed by the leasing company in its role as intermediate lessee/lessor.

Instead of capital allowances the intermediate lessee/lessor company claims as a trading expense the rentals paid to the head lessor. In some cases the rentals paid as head lease rentals have been accelerated *vis-à-vis* the rentals paid by the end lessee on the basis that there is some extra benefit as compared with a conventional 25 per cent writing-down allowance lease.

The intermediate lessee/lessor must be careful not to compress its head lease rental into too short a period in case, in so doing, the quality of the payments are changed. The head lessor may or may not also claim capital allowances depending on whether it is resident in the UK or not. If it is UK resident then whether or not it evaluates its rental to assume allowances will depend on whether it has capacity.

Value added tax

In addition to the corporation tax features described above, lessors are also involved in the operation of value added tax (VAT). In economic terms, the burden of VAT is designed to fall on the personal sector as final consumers. The tax is, however, collected by businesses as 'VAT-registered traders'; and because of the nature of VAT as a multi-stage tax, intermediate business-to-business transactions such as leasing are effected.

For VAT purposes, most business transactions of VAT-registered traders fall clearly into one of the following categories:

- *Standard rated*   Here VAT at the standard rate (currently $17\frac{1}{2}$ per cent) is charged on the trader's output or sales, and the trader recovers the VAT that has been paid to suppliers on his or her 'inputs', i.e. purchases carrying VAT. The net effect is that tax is charged on the trader's value added (broadly equating with his or her internal labour costs plus profit margins), where both output and/or inputs are standard rated.
- *Zero rating*   This gives full relief from VAT to the final consumer. A nil tax rate is charged on the trader's 'output', but the trader still recovers VAT paid on any standard-rated inputs.
- *Exemption*   This gives less than full relief to the final consumer. No VAT is charged on an exempt sale, but the trader cannot recover associated input VAT and so must pass on to the customer the latter

cost. Where a VAT-registered trader's total output comprises a mixture of exempt and standard-rated (or zero-rated) items, some of the trader's input VAT may have to be apportioned between the exempt output (where the relevant input VAT is irrecoverable) and the standard or zero-rated outputs (with recoverable input VAT). In that case the trader is part-exempt.

• *'Outside the scope'* These transactions are ignored for VAT purposes. The effect is the same as exemption except that 'outside the scope' items are not counted in calculating the recovery ratios of partially exempt traders.

VAT is applied to both goods and services, but there are significant operational differences in the treatment of goods as compared with services. Supplies of goods are generally either standard or zero rated, but supplies of services may fall into any one of the above categories.

Equipment leasing constitutes a supply of services for VAT purposes. In this respect it differs from hire purchase and conditional sale arrangements — which are treated as supplies of goods, but with the finance charges representing a VAT-exempt service.

Lessors of assets which, in law, are landlord's or tenant's fixtures may on occasion need to acquire a land interest in order to perfect a claim to capital allowances (see above). In this event the plant lease will assume the VAT status appropriate to the lease of the land to which it is affixed. Under Chapter 2, Section 18, Finance Act 1989, landlords may elect to treat property lease rents either as VAT-exempt or standard rated. The most appropriate option from the tenants' standpoint will depend upon that person's own VAT position. If the tenant is fully taxable, he or she will prefer to pay VAT on rents which can be recovered against output tax: where rents are VAT-exempt, they will have to contain an element to recover VAT on the landlord's construction costs and overheads, which will not then be recoverable by the tenant. A VAT-exempt or partially exempt property lessee will, however, often prefer to pay VAT-exempt rents, since this irrecoverable element may be lower than the irrecoverable proportion of VAT on the gross rent.

Supplies of services that are paid for periodically give rise to tax points (the time at which supplies are treated as taking place) at the earlier of date of payment or issue of tax invoice. VAT charged on lease rentals must be accounted for by the lessor (as output tax payable to HM Customs and Excise) and by the lessee (as input tax recoverable from Customs) at the end of the VAT accounting period in which the tax point falls. To simplify administration and avoid having to issue a separate tax invoice for each rental due, lessors may issue a single tax invoice annually which details every rental payable in the ensuing year and the rate and amount of VAT chargeable on each (SI 1985, No. 886, para. 23(2)). A change in the rate of VAT invalidates the annual tax invoice from that time, and the lessor must issue a new tax invoice for rentals due after the change.

VAT on equipment lease rentals is normally charged at standard rate, but some exceptions are laid down under Schedules 5 and 6, Value Added Tax Act 1983. Apart from landlords' and tenants' fixtures discussed above, the most important of these are:

1. Ships of 15 tonnes gross tonnage or more and aircraft of 8,000 kilogrammes or more, which are zero rated under Schedule 5, Group 10, Items 1 and 2.
2. Medical, scientific, computer, etc., equipment leased to charities and hospitals, which are zero rated under Schedule 5, Group 16, Item 5.
3. Means of transport leased for use in a place outside the European Community, which are zero rated under Schedule 5, Group 9, Item 2.
4. Goods, other than transport, leased to a business within the EC for use outside the UK, which are zero rated under Schedule 5, Group 9, Item 5.
5. Goods, other than transport, leased to a private person outside the EC for use outside the UK, which are zero rated under Schedule 5, Group 9, Item 6.

Termination payments from lessee to lessor have caused problems in the past, particularly where they are outside the terms of the lease contract. Customs acknowledge that VAT status depends on the legal nature of the supply, which is not always easy to determine, and have stated that where lessor and lessee agree, the supply may be treated as standard rated. Where lessor and lessee do not agree, it becomes necessary to determine the exact nature of the payment, which may be either outside the scope of VAT because it is not regarded as consideration for any supply, or standard rated as consideration for the lessor's surrender of his or her right to pursue further legal action against the lessee (S. 3(2)(6), VAT Act 1983). Payments which are made expressly at the order of a Court are deemed to be for nil consideration and outside the scope of tax.

Rebates of rental from lessor to lessee have also given rise to disputes as to VAT status. Where rebates are made out of sale proceeds, Customs have agreed that the payment may be made exclusive of VAT where the parties so agree. Where the parties do not agree the lessor must issue a credit note and apply VAT thereto. Customs' view is that since the rebate applies rateably to all rentals paid throughout the lease term, the VAT thereon must recognize any change in VAT rates that have occurred within that period. It is probable that VAT inclusive rebates will be demanded by partially exempt lessees in order to mitigate the cost of irrecoverable input tax. Lessors, in turn, may prefer to give VAT inclusive rebates (provided there have been no VAT rate changes) where the lessee, entitled to full rebate of sales proceeds, is holding those proceeds together with associated VAT and is disinclined to remit the tax element to the lessor.

The features described above are set out in two statements of practice issued by HM Customs and Excise 1984 ('Lease termination payment' and 'Rebates of rentals'), following a special agreement reached with the ELA.

Lessors will normally be able to recover from Customs, in full, the input tax paid on equipment purchased for leasing. This is because the goods are supplied to the lessee in the same state as that in which they were purchased, and applies equally to items acquired for onward supply by way of hire purchase or conditional sale.

Special rules apply, however, to motor cars (VAT (Cars) Order, SI Act 1980, No. 442). VAT paid on cars acquired for use in the purchaser's business (which includes use for leasing and contract hire) cannot be reclaimed from Customs, forms part of acquisition cost for capital allowance purposes, and must be taken into account when calculating lease rentals. Cars acquired for hire purchase or conditional sale are not used in the finance company's business, and VAT paid on new cars is therefore available for input tax credit. Special rules apply also to sales of cars on termination of leases. Along with certain other goods, used cars in respect of which input tax credit has not been claimed may be sold under a VAT Second Hand Goods Scheme, in which case VAT is charged only on the mark-up, if any, obtained by the vendor. Normally, the selling price will be less than the cost, to the lessor, of the vehicle and therefore no VAT will be chargeable.

Lessors are likely to be partially exempt for VAT purposes because their business also encompasses hire-purchase and/or loan activities. As far as possible input tax is first to be directly attributed to taxable supplies on the one hand and to exempt supplies on the other. The balance of input tax not capable of direct attribution may be allocated in the same ratio as above, or in some other manner that equitably measures the taxable as opposed to non-taxable use to which the items in question are put. Alternatively, Customs may allow the ratio of taxable supplies to total supplies to be applied to the balance of input tax to find the recoverable proportion thereof.

A special partial exemption method agreed between the Customs and the Finance Houses Association in 1984 provides detailed rules for the partial recovery of input VAT on hire-purchase transactions. Many lessors who write both types of business (i.e. leasing and hire purchase) apply the special FHA agreements to their hire-purchase transactions, while recovering in full the input VAT on equipment used for leasing with its associated overheads. Others apply special methods negotiated individually with Customs, where these can best address their circumstances.

Special partial exemption methods are governed by two statutory instruments, SI 1985, No. 886 and SI 1987, No. 510.

The burden of VAT on partially exempt businesses can be very severe. The tax is complex and requires constant attention from the taxpayer as a result of changes both in legislation and in the nature and mix of the taxpayer's business. Mistakes as to VAT status may lead to demand for output tax which has not been charged to customers and to denial of input tax recovery even though VAT has been paid to suppliers. The lessor can structure exempt and taxable business into separate companies individually registered for VAT where this will minimize irrecoverable input tax, but must be careful also to combine companies into a single VAT group where the partial exemption arithmetic shows a saving to be made thereby. Customs, for their part, are concerned to minimize loss of revenue and have weapons to deploy against artificial schemes of tax avoidance. Taxpayers may of course document their transactions and structure their businesses with the legitimate intent to maximize recoverable and minimize irrecoverable input tax. They would be unwise, however, to adopt uncommercial or artificial devices to achieve these ends.

NOTES
1. Readers are referred to Statement of Standard Accounting Practice No. 15 for detailed explanations.
2. The 'small companies rate' (Section 95, Finance Act 1982) is ignored.
3. Transitional relief for long established companies under Section 36, Finance Act 1987, is here ignored.

14. *Lease funding*

Introduction

The last decade has seen increasingly volatile and unpredictable behaviour in UK interest and currency rates, and in many other aspects of the financial environment.

The financial management of companies involved in the provision of asset finance has rapidly become more sophisticated in line with growing competition and the volatile environment. Whereas until only recently the finance director, controller or company accountant would monitor the cash and bank relationships within the lessor company as part of his or her overall duties, this is now beginning to be replaced by specific treasury expertise provided either by employing permanent staff or by 'ad hoc' outside consultancy.

With regard to a lessor's liquidity management, the aim is to ensure that adequate funds are available when required to finance both day-to-day working capital and, of course, the underlying leasing and asset finance transactions.

Regularly updated cash flow forecasting is particularly important. This may often extend to as far as 10 years and beyond in the case of companies involved in medium- and long-term financing. With interest rate exposure management in mind, this may also involve some form of 'bank type' gap management reporting, to aid identification and help develop strategies to manage the risks associated with asset/liability mismatches. The importance of the forecasting time horizon cannot be overemphasized — too short a time frame and significant funding requirements may be missed with possibly severe refunding cost consequences.

The rapid advancement in recent years of information technology has greatly aided these types of analyses both in terms of accuracy and also in the continuous timely production of management data.

Currently the emphasis within leasing organizations is generally towards passive management of balance sheet asset/liability mismatches. Development is in its early stages, particularly with regard to the large number of cash flows (individually often small in size) which are a characteristic of the industry. However, the development of more sophisticated information systems is allowing more effective balance sheet planning and control and, in future, lessors will increasingly view their funding operations as an integral part of their attempts to achieve competitive advantage alongside issues such as product development and marketing skills.

Among larger leasing organizations there has been a steady trend towards an increased centralized treasury function. The more progressive operations are becoming more accustomed to using a wider variety of market instruments and systems and these changes will undoubtedly be reflected in their attitudes to treasury risk and the opportunities to develop consolidated risk management functions, making full use of both internal and external resources.

As with other forms of risk, lessors need to develop a strategy to ensure they are protected. This involves defining the risks associated with balance sheet and funding policy; monitoring the various risks and, where possible, predicting them in advance; developing a policy to reduce risk; and informing operational management of this policy.

A lessor's funding and risk management controls, in their simplest form, may be viewed as a netting operation whereby all revenues (rentals) and loans (intra-group flows) are channelled through the treasury or finance department often located at the group or company head office. The principle behind netting is that company or group exposures are controlled and minimized by the netting centre before residual exposures are hedged in the external markets. This results in all risks being transferred to the centre and handled as a net group or company exposure.

One of the major advantages of centralizing funding and risk management operations are the economies of scale derived from netting effects, thus reducing the number of external hedging transactions required to manage the lessor's business. The costs associated with hedging, using both on- and off-balance sheet instruments, can be markedly reduced by identifying opportunities for matching both cash flows and assets and liabilities.

Any centralized risk management function must have the ability to identify future exposures and recognize matching opportunities. The fundamental tool for the construction of an internal risk management function is an effective cash and exposure forecasting system based on a forward date ladder. This is the prerequisite of effective planning, risk evaluation and management. For a company wishing to establish a centralized risk management function this will involve developing a detailed forecasting system that identifies all cash flows and exposures by expected timing and likely amount. This means that adequate systems must be in place for operating departments to report their present expected future funding requirements.

Reporting requirements should lay down the levels of risk that must be reported and the timing of the report. The priority given to certain risk reporting will depend on the company's own definition of its risk management decision as to what exposure it is prepared to tolerate at the operating level.

Interest rate exposure: the lessor's perspective

Because of the nature of many asset finance products and industry conventions the lessor may well be faced with a number of interest rate exposure risks which require identification monitoring and controlling. These may include any or all of the following:

1. *Position or mismatch risk* This arises because of the potential losses that may be incurred due to both size (implied capital) and maturity mismatches with regard to leasing assets and funding liabilities.
2. *Reinvestment risk* This arises in cases where assets (leases, hire-purchase contracts, etc.) and funding (liabilities) are mismatched with regard to interest-compounding periods. An example of this would be a hire-purchase agreement paying monthly rentals (monthly interest compounding) funded by loan finance requiring interest payment on an annual basis (annual compounding).
3. *Basis risk* This arises in cases where the reference interest basis differs between assets and liabilities (e.g. FHBR, LIBOR, Base Rate, CP, etc.).
4. *Termination risk* Where assets (lease, hire-purchase, etc.) maturities vary from that originally envisaged, losses may arise where termination sums reinvested will not generate enough income to immunize the associated funding liabilities. A lessor faces greatest risk of losses from this type of exposure where periods of rapidly falling interest rates coincide with significant lease terminations, particularly where no provision is available within customer documentation under which breakage cost can be recovered.

Part I: Funding

The sources of funds that are potentially available to a lessor may be summarized as follows:

1. Bank overdrafts
2. Money market loans: (a) term loans; (b) structured
3. Sales and/or purchases of cash flows
4. Acceptance credits
5. Securitized lease receivable backed paper
6. Commercial paper
7. Lease finance.

BANK OVERDRAFTS
This source of funds is important particularly with regard to day-to-day management of bank current accounts and possible very short term liquidity problems due to rental collection or other value date shortfalls.

It is an extremely risky method of funding a fixed lease because of the risk of (a) the overdraft facility being withdrawn and (b) losses due to unhedged upward movements in term interest rates.

Funding fixed rate leasing in this way is tantamount to deciding to back falling period interest rates in the short term, e.g. in expectation of base rate cuts, etc.

Money market loans

Term loans

This is probably the most common source of funds for the lessor. Here, lessors are able to draw on capital for fixed periods from banks who will charge lessors cost of funds based on the London Interbank Offered Rate (LIBOR). This is a reasonably flexible source of funds since the funding period can be anything from overnight money to two years. Beyond two years, swap financing (see below) is probably more reliable and efficient with regard to price, although longer term loans are not unknown.

Structured funding

Leasing and asset finance transactions characteristically involve complex implied capital repayment profiles. Amortizing structures, balloon payments and complex cash flows are common.

The problem of portfolio asset liability mismatches with regard to capital and interest payment profiles can sometimes be minimized via structured funding.

Certain specialist funders will provide tailored loan funding which closely mirrors the lessor's exposure with regard to a particular leasing transaction.

The cost of funds is derived from a blend of rates weighted depending on the capital repayment profile and the appropriate interest rate term structure.

Sales and/or purchases of cash flows

In a similar manner to structured funding, some specialist funders will buy or sell lessors' cash flows — effectively the net present value of an income or payment stream based on the appropriate interest rate term structure. This can prove useful not only for individual transactions but also for net cash flows generated by a portfolio of leases, thus crystallizing their value.

Acceptance credits

An acceptance facility normally takes the form of a written agreement between a bank and its lessor customer which allows the lessor to draw bills

165

of exchange on the bank up to an agreed total figure. These bills, which would be payable at the maturity date, would be 'accepted' by the bank and usually sold on the lessor's behalf in the London discount market in order to provide cash for the lessor. Only bills which finance 'eligible' trade can be bought by the Bank of England. A strict definition of trade is not given by the bank, but as a general guide it is understood that the underlying transaction for which this form of finance is being arranged should be 'short term and self-liquidating.'

For extended periods during the last few years, circumstances have arisen where, particularly in the 30–90 day bank acceptance market, credit lines have effectively been cheaper than LIBOR loans. The reasons for the existence of this apparent arbitrage stems from government monetary policies, particularly with respect to overfunding the PSBR (i.e. issuing more debt than was needed to finance the PSBR). Excess gilt sales created potential shortages in the money markets which were alleviated by the aggressive purchase of commercial bills driving down interest rates, and bill yields in particular.

SECURITIZED LEASE RECEIVABLE BACKED PAPER

The concept of asset securitization is slowly beginning to take root in Europe, following on from the very successful mortgage-backed security (MBS) market in the US. When the market in MBSs in the UK was initiated two and a half years ago, investors were originally concerned by the lack of liquidity; now average life is also a key issue.

The vast majority of asset-backed issues tend to be floating rate notes (FRN) with numerous possible and actual maturities.

Securitization of lease receivables is not new. The first US non-mortgage asset-backed securities were backed by computer leases, with credit card and auto loan receivables coming later. In the US computer leases account for some US$1 billion of publicly traded bonds and US$ 700 million of privately placed issues rated by Standard and Poors.

The attraction to the investor of such asset-backed securities depends to a large extent on the reliability of the lease receivables.

The attraction to the lessor of securitization lies in (a) the crystallization with regard to the value of future cash flow associated with the leased assets and (b) the removal from the lessor's balance sheet of both assets and liabilities associated with the leased portfolio.

The UK market with regard to these instruments is still relatively underdeveloped although MBS issues comprise one-third of the FRN market. Still untapped is a vast reserve of fixed-rate investors who could be looking for alternatives to a shrinking gilts market, including pension and insurance funds wanting to match their long-term liabilities with long-term assets.

In the case of lease-backed bond/note issues principally in the US, the cash flows (aggregate rentals) reimburse the principal and pay interest. The issues are usually achieved via a trust structure or separate entity with the appropriate credit rating. The former case may well rely on the underlying asset quality with respect to security and in these cases credit-rating agencies may be crucial.

Asset-backed transactions frequently require additional comfort to service any liquidity shortfalls, for example, through letters of credit.

COMMERCIAL PAPER

Commercial paper is an unsecured promissory note with a fixed maturity. The lessor promises to pay the investor a fixed amount on some future date but pledges no assets, only his or her liquidity status and established earning power, to guarantee the promise.

Typically rates on commercial paper, like those on bills, are quoted on a discount basis. However, commercial paper in interest-bearing form is known, simplifying calculations for the investor.

The majority of investors in commercial paper are large institutions such as pension and insurance funds, etc.

The largest and most developed market for this type of security is in the US where commercial paper is a much used alternative to short-term bank borrowing. Being securitized debt as opposed to, say, non-transferable bank loans, commercial paper can be bought and sold by investors.

The UK market for these instruments is considerably smaller than the one that has developed in the US. Only since 1976 has it been possible to issue, under one-year maturity, sterling-denominated negotiable notes within the UK market because of regulatory constraints. There are several restrictions on the issue of sterling commercial paper; issuing companies or guarantors owning 100 per cent of the share capital of the issuing companies must have net assets of over £50 million and must be quoted on the Stock Exchange; issue sizes must be in tranches of £500,000 with a minimum tranche of £500,000. Generally, therefore, issuers must be large companies with very high credit status.

However, issues of this type in the past resulted in an effective and competitive source of funding for many companies. Larger lessors might well, in certain circumstances, find this type of security appropriate with respect to part of their overall funding requirements.

LEASE FINANCE

Lessors can obtain funding for specific leases by means of head-lease or 'back to back' lease funding. This may be an exactly matched structure or may, in certain situations, be mismatched because of particular circumstances.

167

Part II: Managing interest rate exposure

Unmanaged interest rate volatility, as experienced over the last decade, can undoubtedly result in unacceptable swings in financing costs with respect to its impact on the lessor's balance sheet and profit and loss reporting. Together with the ever-increasing complexity of financial products, this has forced many lessors to become increasingly sophisticated about interest rate exposure measurement and management techniques.

Initially, before considering hedging techniques, it is very important that the lessor has a firm view as to its objectives with regard to risk exposure. The control and management of funding costs will have not only major implications with regard to the company's equity exposure, composed of the market value of assets (leases) and liabilities (funding), but also may impact directly on the lessor's ability to use funding and treasury management as a source of competitive advantage. This will be particularly true of those companies who take a portfolio view of their funding and cash management activity.

The four primary methods for measuring interest rate risk exposure are gap management, duration analysis, sensitivity analysis and simulation analysis.

From an individual lessor's view point, any one of these techniques may be more or less appropriate, depending on circumstances and the level of sophistication with regard to funding management.

GAP MANAGEMENT

This is often also referred to as gap analysis or cash matching. It is frequently used by banks to provide information on asset/liability mismatches and is one of the more established tools available to risk managers. The concept is to monitor the net difference in the total par value of assets less total par value of liabilities repricing or maturing during a specified time period. If, for each time period, the par value of assets exceeds the par value of liabilities, then a positive gap exists; if assets equal liabilities, then the period is gap neutral; if assets are less than liabilities, then a negative gap exists. Gap analysis was originally designed to monitor cash flow needs and to identify interest rate exposure. It is fairly successful in the case of the former, but relies to some extent on subjective judgement with regard to the latter.

Gap analysis does not account for the time value of money. For example, gap analysis assumes that a five-year asset (lease) is neutralized by a five-year liability even if one generates monthly interest payments (asset rental) and the other generates annual interest payments (e.g. money market loan). As long as rates are stable and, thus, prices do not change, relative price sensitivities can be ignored. They cannot, however, be ignored in an unstable rate environment.

Gap management cannot also effectively measure the interest rate exposure associated with such contingent agreements as option-based products.

An effective exposure measurement system must identify the relative price sensitivities of the financial constitutents both 'on' and 'off' the lessor's balance sheet. Gap management, therefore, forms a crude basis for initial risk evaluation and short-term cash management. Used in conjunction with other interest rate exposure techniques, particularly those based on 'time value of money' criteria, it represents a useful and important starting point.

DURATION ANALYSIS

Duration analysis was originally developed and applied to bond portfolios where, for many years, investment portfolio managers have measured the price movement of a bond for a given change in yield. Its use in other areas of interest rate risk exposure management is more recent but it has rapidly become a standard risk measurement tool. The pace of acceptance is due to several factors, including its ease of use and the relevance of its output. It has one major shortcoming, known as convexity, which is associated with the technique's non-static nature in periods of interest rate volatility and changing yield curve shape.

The purpose of duration is to identify the magnitude of a company's interest rate exposure, and this is expressed in terms of the maturity of a zero coupon bond that would result in the same percentage price exposure as the instrument being measured.

Duration is a price exposure scale against which all interest sensitive instruments can be measured. The more price sensitive an instrument, the longer its duration.

Duration can be thought of as the weighted average number of years over which an instrument's total cash flows occur, the essential element being the weighting based on the term structure of interest rates appropriate to the products cash flows timing. This approach may be contrasted with the average life of the product as described by the instrument's par value (i.e. disregarding the time value of money considerations) which will tend to overstate the life of the product.

The duration of a money market loan, for example, can be calculated as follows:

$$\text{Duration} \quad \dfrac{\displaystyle\sum_{t=0}^{n} C_t \times (1/(1 + r)) \times t}{\displaystyle\sum_{t=0}^{n} C_t \times (1/(1 + r))}$$

169

where C_t = Cash flow occurring at time t
   r = one period yield curve rate appropriate to maturity t
   n = final cash flow period
   t = time.

One of the most useful aspects of duration is its additivity property. This property enables the risk manager to take incremental steps in controlling exposure and to search for relative value among all maturities of assets and liabilities. This has particular application within leasing portfolios due to their characteristic cash flow complexity. The additivity property of duration states that the price times the duration of one instrument plus the price times the duration of a second instrument divided by the combined price of both instruments equals the total portfolio duration.

This additivity principle enables an exposure manager to take incremental actions in adjusting the risk profile of the company's assets and liabilities. To adjust duration, the manager chooses the most advantageous spot on the yield curve to buy or sell the appropriate market value of assets or liabilities.

Duration is not a static analysis. As interest rates change, duration will also change. A portfolio that is duration neutral when rates are at one level may well not be duration neutral at another level. This phenomenon is know as convexity. Essentially, the price or value relationship to yield is not linear in nature but has varying rates of change with the associated change in interest rate exposure. Portfolio management using duration is thus an interactive process requiring adjustments as and when rates move.

Duration analysis is, therefore, a very flexible tool that can measure accurately complex exposures as are commonly found in leasing portfolios. It requires a little more quantitative skill to develop than some of the other management tools, but in return generates useful information.

Duration does, however, provide very little useful information with regard to the actual physical timings of specific cash flows.

SENSITIVITY ANALYSIS
Sensitivity analysis, based on the term structure of interest rates, is one of the more sophisticated methods of interest rate exposure management, particularly when applied to the lessor's overall portfolio. It involves constructing a forward ladder of net cash flows associated with both assets and liabilities, on a specific period basis. Greatest accuracy is achieved using daily netting periods. This does, however, require extensive system processing, particularly in the case of the lessor engaged in small/medium-value funding where large numbers of cash flows are common (e.g. motor industry funding, contract hire, etc.). Longer netting time periods may in these cases be more appropriate.

Once all net future cash flows associated with assets (leases) and liabilities (loans) have been consolidated by date, the resulting cash flows can be time valued by discounting each net position by the appropriate zero coupon rate (market-determined zero coupon rate, i.e. the rate associated with a notional zero coupon bond maturing at the appropriate date). The overall result is thus the present value of the asset/liability portfolio.

Appropriate note must be taken of any relevant cash flows such as those associated with tax payments or receipts — which is particularly relevant in tax-based leasing. The technique effectively allows the financial assets and liabilities on and off the balance sheet to be revalued on an ongoing basis.

This technique allows the risk manager to evaluate the portfolio overall value sensitivity to changes in interest rates. Mismatched asset and liability risk profiles can be closely monitored with respect to the overall value change associated with particular rate movements or yield curve shifts. Appropriate hedging techniques and/or possible additions to the portfolio can be evaluated for changes in the overall portfolio risk profile. This technique, being a 'time value of money' based approach, has many common features with duration type techniques. One drawback, particularly in the case of large portfolios, where the number of implied capital and interest movements is large, relates to the requirement for more sophisticated database-processing systems to deal with the greater numbers and complexity of cash flows.

This technique is particularly useful in cases where a lessor has made a strategic decision to manage its funding on a portfolio basis with all the advantages with regard to the natural hedging opportunities this implies.

SIMULATION ANALYSIS

Simulation analysis involves the construction and testing of a model of the lessor's business, often closely related to the company's budget. The model's integrity is tested against a variety of assumptions about future market conditions. This type of analysis can be used to project best, worst and most likely interest rate scenarios. Monte Carlo type randomly-generated rates and variables can also be included within the methodology.

The technique attempts to evaluate the consequences of differing interest rate environments upon the lessor's balance sheet and profit and loss statement. However, the technique often requires extensive collection of data input to be effective and, as such, can be expensive in terms of time and resources. The analysis can, however, provide useful information with regard to the company's risk management decision-making process.

Risk reduction techniques and products

A number of quantitative or semi-quantitative measurement techniques have been discussed above which provide the lessor's risk manager with interest rate exposure and risk information with regard to the company's asset/liability mismatches. Implicit within many of these analyses is the portfolio approach to funding. The assumption is that all internal company exposures are netted, resulting in one external risk exposure. This may be managed by a centralized treasury or netting centre. An obvious advantage of this approach is the reduction in funding, hedging and transaction costs that result from the consolidation of offsetting exposures.

The alternative is to match exactly each individual exposure, as it arises, with suitable funding or derivative products — in effect, passing all risk to the funder or provider of derivatives who may well be better placed and more willing to manage these types of exposure.

Any treasurer of a medium-sized or large lessor is unlikely to be short of information on various instruments available; in addition to becoming more active in the area of treasury products, many banks have put greater emphasis on marketing them as the return on risk with regard to the traditional lending areas have continued to decline.

The major problems facing the treasurer are whether, firstly, the identified exposure requires action in respect of hedging potential adverse rate movements, and if so, which product represents the most effective and appropriate solution. Obviously these decisions must be considered within the framework of the lessor's strategic view with regard to the total interest rate exposure and risk. After all, should the lessor be running unnecessary and possibly unmanaged risks which endanger the otherwise healthy profitability of its core business?

A major consideration will, of course, be the materiality of the exposure in respect of the impact of adverse rate movements. The treasurer may very well decide that, because of size constraints, the cost of hedging outweighs its advantages. If, however, the exposure is of sufficient size, and the risk is perceived to be such that action must be taken to avoid the consequences of adverse interest rate movements, the treasurer has a number of treasury products from which to choose. Derivative interest rate instruments broadly fall into one of two groups:

1. Fixed future interest rate cost instruments (fixing the funding cost), e.g. exchange-traded futures contracts, forward rate agreements, interest rate swaps, fixed rate borrowings.
2. Fixed maximum cost through the purchase of option-based products (interest rate insurance), e.g. interest rate caps, interest rate guarantees, swaptions, exchange-traded options.

Other than spot funding and facilities as described above, the lessor in general has two sources of interest rate derivative products for risk managment:

(a) Exchange-traded financial futures contracts.
(b) Over-the-counter (OTC) products, as marketed by banks.

One way derivative products can be defined and distinguished from the underlying product is by their off-balance sheet and contingent liability nature. Derivative products (financial futures) contracts have been traded most successfully for a number of years in a number of key centres around the world. The first financial futures exchange, the International Monetary Market (IMM), which is a subsidiary of the Chicago Mercantile Exchange, opened in 1972 for the trading of foreign exchange futures. The first traded interest rate future began trading on the Chicago Board of Trade (CBOT) in 1975. Since then trading in interest rate futures contracts has grown rapidly and in 1982 the London International Financial Futures Exchange introduced to Europe the world of financial futures trading.

A characteristic of all exchange-traded contracts is their standardized nature, daily mark to market (valuation) by the exchange, and regular margin call (settlement with the exchange of the net change in value of the contract). Exchange-traded contracts are generally bought and sold through a brokerage house who charge a small commission per contract and manage the position on a daily basis on behalf of their customers. These products have tended to attract the sophisticated professional user. However, to the larger lessor with a centralized treasury function these products may well represent a very important source of risk reduction instruments.

Many lessors, however, find it more convenient to obtain a tailored service directly from a bank to match its specific exposure requirements with regard to nominal principal and hedge period. Administration costs are reduced as there are no margin or valuation calls as compared with exchange-traded products.

FIXING THE FUNDING COST

There are three main types of derivative instruments available which will in effect guarantee a future cost of funds for a specific period. These are:

1. Exchange-traded futures contracts
2. Forward rate agreements
3. Interest rate swaps.

Exchange-traded futures contracts

A financial futures contract is simply a binding agreement to buy or sell a financial instrument during a specified month or day in the future for the traded price agreed by the parties when entering the contract.

Futures contracts cover one interest period only (although in some cases futures strips can be executed, i.e. covering consecutive time periods). Appendix 14.1 contains details of some important interest rate futures. In the case of deposit/loan rate contracts (e.g. LIFFE three-month sterling contract) there is no movement with respect to principal and all cash is settled on the notional delivery date of the contract.

Appendix 14.2 gives a simple example of hedging techniques using the three-month sterling contract traded on the London International Financial Futures Exchange.

Forward rate agreements

The forward rate agreement (FRA) is a simple and flexible contract between two parties under which an interest rate is agreed for a period commencing at a future date. The difference between the FRA rate and the actual market rate for that period is discounted and settled as a cash payment.

These instruments are very similar to the three-month exchange-traded futures deposit/loan contracts. However, these products are marketed by banks directly to customers (over-the-counter or 'OTC'). The main advantages of these products are the tailored nature of the agreement that the lessor can negotiate with the bank, and the lack of margin and valuation calls — characteristic of exchange-traded futures.

There is no cash movement of the principal amount. An FRA covers one interest period only, although of course a whole strip of FRAs covering a number of successive interest periods can be executed at the same time.

Appendix 14.3 presents an example of the use of FRAs for simple hedging purposes. The example assumes sterling-denominated lessor liabilities, although FRAs are available in many other currencies including US dollars, Deutschemarks, Swiss francs, Yen and Dutch guilders.

Interest rate swaps

An interest rate swap is a transaction in which two parties agree to make periodic payments to each other, calculated on the basis of specified interest rates and a specified principal amount. For example, a lessor may enter into an agreement with a bank whereby it makes payments based on a fixed agreed rate of interest for the life of the swap, while it receives payments based on some floating rate basis (LIBOR, commercial paper rate, etc.) for the life of the swap.

An interest rate swap may therefore be used by the lessor to transform one type of asset or liability/interest obligation into another. The swap represents a very powerful risk management and funding tool enabling a swap participant to tailor its asset and liability position with respect to a given interest rate structure, costs of borrowing, risk profile and exposure.

Closely related to the FRA product, interest rate swaps are available generally for periods varying from 1 to 10 years but transactions up to 25 years are not unknown. The International Swap Dealers Association currently believes the size of the global swap market to be some US$1,300 billion. Swaps are currently available in a very large number of currencies.

Whereas an FRA covers one interest period only, a swap covers a series of interest periods typically at semi-annual intervals over a number of years.

The settlement procedure is normally different — FRA interest equalization payments are typically discounted and payable at the beginning of an interest period, while swap payments are not discounted and are payable at the end of an interest period — the end result is effectively the same.

A number of banks will provide tailored swap products to suit non-bullet profiles, e.g. amortizing notional capital profiles, etc. This can prove particularly useful in the leasing industry where such risk structures are the norm.

Although swap agreements are off-balance sheet items with no principal involved, banks will treat a swap as a credit risk and this may therefore reduce its ability to conclude other transactions with the borrower.

Appendix 14.4 contains an example of a simple sterling swap transaction.

INTEREST RATE INSURANCE

The principal interest rate option products available to a borrower are:

- Interest rate caps (and derivative products).
- Interest rate guarantees (option on individual FRAs).
- Swaptions (also known as swap options).
- Exchange-traded options (on interest rate futures).

Interest rate caps

An interest rate cap (also known as a ceiling) is an arrangement whereby in return for a premium normally payable on the deal date, the seller (writer) of the cap undertakes over an agreed period to compensate the buyer of the cap whenever a reference interest rate (e.g. three-month LIBOR) exceeds a pre-agreed maximum interest rate (the 'cap rate').

An interest rate cap can be thought of as a one-sided interest rate swap. The method of rate fixing and calculating interest equalization payments is identical for swaps and caps whenever the reference rate is above the cap rate. The difference arises when the reference rate is fixed below the cap rate. In this case, for a swap the borrower (the fixed rate payer) would have to pay the difference between the short-term rate and the swap rate; however, the buyer of the cap is not required to make any payment. Obviously, as for any option, the seller of the cap has to be compensated for this one-sided arrangement and this is achieved through the initial payment to the seller by the buyer of a premium. The premium depends, rather like insurance, on the level of cover and the period for which cover is required. Obviously the lower the interest rate above which the buyer wishes to be compensated, the more expensive the cap premium will be.

The appeal of a cap is when the floating reference rate is below the cap rate. At such times, because the buyer of the cap is not locked into fixed rates he or she may enjoy the lower rates offered by the floating reference rate.

As with other types of OTC derivative product, some banks will provide amortizing and structured cap products tailored to match a lessor's exposure. One advantage of the cap structure is its lack of credit risk implications — i.e. selling a cap does not use up a bank's credit lines. There is therefore no need for differential pricing for a cap between weak and strong borrowers.

Appendix 14.5 outlines a simple cap product example.

The overall cost of the initial premium must be weighed up by the lessor against the expected interest saving through being able to fund at the short-term rate rather than locking into medium-term fixed rate, as with a swap.

A further point that should be borne in mind for any Treasury product is taxation. For example, if, under the borrower's country's tax laws, cap premiums are fully deductible against the current year's income, it may be additionally beneficial to buy a cap because of the resultant deferment of tax. However, if a cap premium is not deductible for tax purposes at all, and if swap or interest payments are deductible, then a cap would not be as attractive after taxation is taken into account.

Interest rate guarantees

An interest rate guarantee (IRG) is an option to enter into a forward rate agreement (FRA) and as such can be viewed as one period cap agreement. The product has similar characteristics to the LIFFE exchange-traded option on the three-month sterling future agreement. As with the other OTC products, the exact details of the guarantee can be tailored to the lessor's requirements.

An interest rate option is a contract giving the buyer the right, but not the obligation, to fix the rate of interest on a notional loan or deposit for an agreed period on a specific forward date. On the expiry date, the bank will make a payment to the lessor to compensate for the extent (if any) to which the strike (IRG) rate is more advantageous to the lessor than current LIBOR.

The original work on pricing and valuation of options was first published by Fisher Black and Myron Scholes in 1973. These ideas have been further developed in the 1970s and 1980s by both academic researchers and practitioners.

The amount a lessor must pay to buy an interest rate option is determined by four factors, which are the strike rate, maturity, expected market volatility and market conditions.

Strike rate   This is referred to as: (a) 'at the money' — the strike is equal to the current market rate; or (b) 'in the money' — the strike rate is more favourable to the lessor than the current market rate (for which the premium is thus higher than for an 'at the money' option); or (c) 'out of the money' — the strike rate is less favourable to the lessor than the current market rate (for which the premium is thus lower than for an 'at the money' option).

Maturity   The longer the maturity (time to expire) of the option the higher the probability of larger interest rate movements and hence of profitable exercise by the buyer. The option is thus more valuable to the lessor, and as the risk to the bank is greater, the premium is larger.

Expected market volatility   The higher the volatility the greater the probability of profitable exercise of the option by the lessor. The option is more valuable to the lessor, the risk to the bank is greater, and hence the premium is larger.

Market conditions   Various market factors may lead to an increase in the option premium, including: events such as government intervention, the possibility of the imposition of withholding taxes/exchange controls or illiquidity in the markets.

Swaptions

A swaption (also known as a swap option) is an option to enter into an interest rate swap. In return for a premium payable in advance, the borrower has the right, but not the obligation, to enter into a swap at a pre-agreed level.

A swaption is a valuable tool when a lessor may require a swap, but is uncertain with regard to timing, etc. The typical structure would be for a borrower to buy a six-month or one-year option to conclude an interest rate swap at near current market levels. This type of product can be particularly useful in situations where the lessor is quoting on new business which involves a considerable or material exposure but where the company is uncertain as to the outcome of the tender. The maximum loss the lessor faces is thus the premium amount.

A swaption is not directly comparable to a cap, since the period of protection is very different. For example, a one-year option to enter into a four-year swap gives the right to exercise within one year; after one year the borrower has either exercised the swaption, in which case he or she is locked into a swap, or has allowed the swaption to expire, in which case no protection is in place for the next four years. The swaption is a valuable product, however, and has a useful role in liability management — particularly where a borrower prefers the certainty of paying fixed rate through a swap.

Exchange-traded options

Within many of the exchange-traded interest rate futures markets, options contracts on these products have also developed. For example, the London International Financial Futures Exchange trades an options contract on the three-month sterling futures contract.

In an exchange-traded options contract, in similar manner to a cap, the buyer pays the seller (or 'writer') a premium for the right to purchase or sell a product (e.g. three-month sterling futures contract) at a given price (strike or exercise price). Rights to purchase are termed 'calls', rights to sell are termed 'puts'. The life of most exchange traded options is usually from a few days to about one year. Exchange-traded interest rate options of futures such as the three-month sterling futures option have very similar characteristics to caps and short-term OTC interest rate option products.

Conclusion

From relatively small beginnings, interest-rate-based derivative products have grown to represent an invaluable toolbox to the asset and liability managers of leasing companies.

Instruments such as swaps and options neatly complement one another — a swap provides for certainty while an option allows a manager to control uncertain events and the associated exposure. Very active markets already exist for many of the options described in this chapter, and the depth and innovation is growing exponentially. Some of the myriad of products now being offered have been outlined. No attempt, however, has been made to provide an exhaustive list of available instruments and it is very important that individual treasurers of lessors work closely with their bankers and funders so that their particular requirements are adequately satisfied.

Appendix 14.1: Interest rate futures contracts

Exchange	Futures contract	Contract size	Option on future
LIFFE	3-Month Sterling	£500,000	Yes
LIFFE	Long Gilt	£50,000	Yes
CBOT	US Treasury Bond	US$ 100,000	Yes
IMM	3-Month Eurodollar	US$ 1,000,000	Yes
LIFFE	German Bund	DM 250,000	Yes
LIFFE currently	3-Month Euromark	DM 1,000,000	No
LIFFE currently	Japanese Government Bond	Y 100,000,000	No
MATIF	French Treasury Bond	Ffr 500,000	Yes
	3-Month Eurofranc	Ffr 5,000,000	Yes
LIFFE currently	3-Month Euroecu	ecu 1,000,000	No

LIFFE London International Financial Futures Exchange
CBOT Chicago Board of Trade
IMM International Monetary Market
MATIF Marché à Term International de France

Appendix 14.2: Three-month sterling hedging example

A sterling futures contract fixes the effective interest rate for borrowing or lending three-month sterling funds at a specific date in the future. On that date, unless the contract has previously been closed out, there is a cash settlement with final 'profit' or 'losses' being credited based on a final exchange delivery settlement price determined from current interest rates in the cash market. It is this final convergence of the futures implied interest rate and cash market interest rates which enables the hedger to fix the sterling interest rate in advance.

Example
On 12 February 1990 a lessor sells a June three-month sterling futures contract at a price of 85.29.

The lessor has fixed an effective LIBOR rate for the third Wednesday in June of 14.71 per cent (i.e. 100.00 minus 85.29 futures price = 14.71 per cent).

Suppose that the three-month LIBOR on Wednesday 20 June 1990 is 15.125. The June futures contract will stand at 84.88 (100.00 minus 15.125). The 41 basis point 'profit' (i.e. 85.29 minus 84.88) will compensate the lessor for continued high short-term interest rates for the period of the future. The future will obviously also provide protection against further

179

interest rate rises over the period 12 February 1990 to 20 June 1990 with regard to a funding or refunding liability as described by the contract specification.

LIFFE *three-month sterling future contract specification*

Unit of trading	£500,000
Delivery months	March, June, September, December
Delivery day	First business day after last trading day
Last trading day	11.00 am, third Wednesday of delivery month
Quotation	100.00 minus interest rate
Minimum price movement (tick size and value)	0.01 (12.50)
Trading hours	8.20 am–16.02 pm

Appendix 14.3: Forward rate agreement hedging example

The forward rate agreement (FRA) is an off-balance sheet interest rate product which may be used for covering short-term interest rate exposures. The FRA is an interest equalization contract which, conceptionally, is very similar to one interest period of an interest rate swap agreement or an OTC (over the counter) interest rate futures contract. No exchange of principal is involved. As with interest rate swap, FRA contracts are for notional amounts. A lessor with floating rate liabilities and wishing to hedge against a rise in short-term interest rates might purchase one or more FRAs covering one or more future interest periods.

Example

Value 12 February 1990. The lessor borrows sterling floating rate funds based on six months LIBOR and requires funding for a period of two years. The lessor's sterling denominated assets are fixed rate, and of an amortizing repayment (capital) profile as follows:

Date	Asset £000	Repayment £000	Floating rate funding £000
12.02.90	20,000	–	(20,000)
13.08.90	15,000	5,000	(15,000)
12.02.91	10,000	5,000	(10,000)
12.08.91	5,000	5,000	(5,000)
12.02.92	–	5,000	–

The lessor borrows at an interest rate for the first six months of six-month LIBOR flat and the lessor is confident of being able to borrow at LIBOR flat for the next three interest periods, which will start on 13 August 1990, 12 February 1991 and 12 August 1991 respectively.

LIBOR for the period 12 February 1990 to 13 August 1990 is 15.1875 per cent p.a.

The lessor has a fixed rate interest income asset and a floating rate interest liability. The lessor is thus exposed to any upward movement in short-term interest rates that have not been reflected in the fixed rate asset pricing.

One solution to this exposure problem, is to enter into FRAs on 12 February 1990, for the appropriate periods with reference to reducing capital structure as follows:

Rate (Loan)	Rate (FRA)	Rate (FRA)	Rate (FRA)
15.1875	14.23	13.16	12.74
12.02.90 . . . 13.08.90	. . . 12.02.91	. . . 12.08.91	. 12.02.92
Notional Nominal:	15,000,000	10,000,000	5,000,000

The difference between LIBOR (on the rate-fixing day) and the FRA rate will be paid to/from the lessor such that the lessor's net interest cost is always the appropriate FRA rate.

In the swap market, it is usual to settle interest amounts in arrears. However, in the FRA market it is common (though not mandatory) to discount the net interest amount and settle at the beginning of an interest period.

Reflecting the time value of money, the FRA interest settlement formula calculates a discounted interest amount using the prevailing LIBOR rate as the discount rate.

Interest settlement formula (advance) =

$$\frac{\textit{Interest amount due in arrears}}{1 + \dfrac{\text{LIBOR}}{100} \times \dfrac{\text{Tenor of FRA}}{365}}$$

Appendix 14.4: Hedging interest rate exposure using swaps

Swaps are the major interest rate risk exposure management tool in the 2 to 10-year maturity range. The example given below represents only one simple application of swap techniques.

In their simplest form interest rate swaps enable borrowers to fix floating rate debt (or float fixed rate debt) through counterparty transactions.

Swaps represent a major pricing and risk management tool for lessors involved in medium- to long-term funding.

Example

A lessor wishes to hedge its substantial fixed rate assets but is funded on a floating rate basis. To immunize partly its exposure to higher interest rates it wishes to convert some of its floating rate liabilities to fixed rate liabilities without the use of further funding. The lessor therefore enters into an agreement to pay the swap counterparty (bank) fixed rate interest and in return receive floating rate interest.

Interest flows

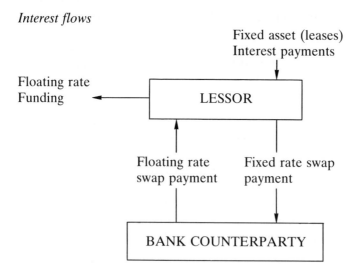

This is the simplest situation, often known as a vanilla swap. Many market participants offer a tailored approach to the lessor's risk management problems which can lead to more complex structures. However, as with all derivative products, the lessor should appreciate that the more complex and difficult to manage is the risk problem, the more expensive is the solution likely to be relative to simpler vanilla structures.

Appendix 14.5: Hedging interest rate exposure using caps

A lessor is able to raise three-year, floating rate sterling funding at nil spread over a three-month sterling LIBOR (this assumes that the lessor will simply roll-over short-term funding rather than lock-in three-year committed fixed rate funding for which a spread may be required).

Concurrently, the lessor purchases from a bank a three-year cap on three-month sterling LIBOR with a cap rate of 15 per cent at a premium of

0.85 per cent flat. The lessor's costs might be as set out as below, where column D shows the cost excluding the initial premium. Column E includes a figure of 0.37 per cent p.a., being the premium amortized over three years at an appropriate discount rate.

The table assumes a series of LIBOR rates that might apply throughout the three-year period.

In this example, the lessor's three-month LIBOR base is capped at 15 per cent p.a. to give an all-in rate of never more than 15.37 per cent p.a., including the amortized premium. Additionally, the lessor enjoys the benefits when LIBOR is below the cap rate. The level of premium depends, rather like insurance, on the period for which cover is required and on the level of cover required. Obviously, the lower the interest rate above which the lessor wishes to be compensated, the more expensive the cap premium will be.

Cost analysis: Funding at sterling LIBOR flat + 15% p.a interest rate cap at premium of 0.85%

A	B	C	D	E
		Payment from	*Lessor's*	*Lessor's*
Assumed	*Lessor's*	*bank to lessor*	*funding cost*	*maximum*
average	*funding*	*under cap*	*ignoring*	*funding cost*
sterling	*cost*	*contract*	*premium*	*LIBOR*
	(=A)	*(A−15% p.a.)*	*(B−C)*	*(B−C+0.37)*
15.0	15.0	–	15	15.37
15.5	15.5	0.5	15	15.37
16.0	16.0	1.0	15	15.37
15.0	15.0	–	15	15.37
14.0	14.0	–	14	14.37
13.0	13.0	–	13	13.37
12.0	12.0	–	12	12.37
11.0	11.0	–	11	11.37

15. *Lessee accounting*

Background

In August 1984, after almost a decade of debate within the accounting profession on how lessees and lessors should account for leases, the member bodies of the Consultative Committee of Accountancy Bodies (CCAB), which at that time approved standards drafted by the Accounting Standards Committee (ASC), finally approved SSAP 21 (Statement of Standard Accounting Practice — accounting for leases and hire-purchase contracts) for publication. This standard, which sets out the basic lease accounting requirements for both lessees and lessors in the UK, became effective for accounting periods commencing on or after 1 July 1984 with the full impact of the standard being felt from 1988. The work of the ASC was taken over by the Accounting Standards Board (ASB) in July 1990.

The accounting profession's reason for introducing SSAP 21 was to redress the growing distortion in lessees' balance sheets created by the use of finance leasing as a source of 'off-balance sheet finance'. Prior to SSAP 21, most companies in the UK simply dealt with lease rental payments as a revenue charge in their profit and loss accounts. In this way the rights in the leased asset and the related liabilities for future rentals were not reflected on the lessee's balance sheet. The tremendous growth in leasing activity from the mid-1970s and the collapse of Court Line highlighted the hidden dangers of excessive use of off-balance sheet financing and led to criticism of the then existing accounting practices.

The accounting profession's response to this criticism was to propose that lessees should show their leased assets and lease liabilities on the face of their balance sheets in much the same way as if they had acquired the assets by using any other source of finance. In this way the balance sheets would reflect a 'true and fair' view of the financial gearing and level of business operations. This approach had already been adopted in the US and Canada and was later endorsed in the international accounting standard on leasing (IAS 17) published in March 1982.

However, the approach was not without its critics in the UK. In 1981, when the ASC first published, in the form of Exposure Draft 29 (ED 29), its proposals to show the effect of finance leases on the face of the lessee's balance sheet, it was met with considerable opposition. In particular, the leasing industry expressed considerable concern, maintaining that it would be misleading and incorrect to show as assets on a lessee's balance sheet items of plant and equipment to which there was no legal title or ownership.

The ASC took note of the criticisms made of its original proposals and incorporated a number of important changes into SSAP 21. Nevertheless, on the central issue of accounting for finance leases the ASC remained convinced that, in order to show a true and fair view, leased assets and lease liabilities should be reflected on the face of lessees' balance sheets. In September 1982 the ASC announced its plans to publish a standard on leasing along the broad lines of ED 29, but with somewhat different transitional arrangements and simpler lessee disclosure requirements. However, it was not until August 1984 that all the member bodies of the CCAB finally approved SSAP 21 for publication.

The introduction of SSAP 21 coincided with the stimulus provided by tax rate reductions in the years 1984–86, thereby making it difficult to measure the real impact. However, there has been a continuing buoyancy in the demand for leasing of all types. One of the changes that the leasing industry anticipated as a result of SSAP 21 was that industrial companies would switch from finance leasing to operating leasing. There is evidence to suggest that this has been happening, although it is unclear whether the trend towards operating leasing is motivated by the accounting treatment of operating leases or by other factors.

Main provisions of SSAP 21

ACCOUNTING CONCEPTS

SSAP 21 is based on a very simple concept: namely, that the accounting treatment of a lease should depend on the substance of the arrangement between the parties. Thus a finance lease, which in substance passes over to the lessee substantially all the risks and rewards normally associated with the ownership of the asset (other than ownership itself), is treated by the standard as creating both an asset and a liability in the lessee's balance sheet. The asset reflects the lessee's rights in the asset; the liability reflects the lessee's future obligations under the lease. In contrast, an operating lease gives the lessee the limited use of an asset for a short period of time having, therefore, the nature of a contract to supply services rather than finance and is accordingly treated simply as an operating expense.

Much of the earlier debate about lease accounting concentrated on the conceptual issue of substance over legal form. Many argued that the inclusion of leased assets in the lessee's balance sheet was misleading because the lessee had no legal title and no right to acquire title to those assets. Others argued that to leave the related liabilities off-balance sheet was equally wrong since they represented a contractual obligation. When drafting SSAP 21 the ASC reached a compromise between these views by making the fine distinction that the asset capitalized is not the leased asset itself, but the lessee's rights to use the asset. Thus, conceptually, it could be argued that lease capitalization does not create a theoretical conflict between substance and legal form.

LEASE CLASSIFICATION

Under SSAP 21, the accounting treatment adopted for a lease will depend on whether the lease is a finance lease or an operating lease. Consequently, the first practical difficulty a lessee will encounter will be to classify leases correctly. The definition of a finance lease under SSAP 21 is quite subjective. It is defined as a lease that transfers to the lessee substantially all the risks and rewards of owning an asset (other than the legal right of ownership). All other leases are defined as operating leases. In practice, all leases transfer some risks and rewards of ownership to the lessee and, therefore, the distinction is one of degree. Consequently, the standard sets a present value test under which it will normally be presumed that the risks and rewards of ownership have passed to the lessee. Only in those exceptional circumstances where it can be clearly demonstrated that the risks and rewards have not been transferred to the lessee should the present value test be overridden.

The present value test

Under SSAP 21 it is normally presumed that a lease transfers substantially all the risks and rewards of ownership to the lessee:

> . . if at the inception of a lease the present value of the minimum lease payments, including any initial payments, amounts to substantially all (normally 90% or more) of the fair value of the leased asset.

The rate used to perform the present value test should be the interest rate implicit in the lease, or if this rate is unknown, a rate the lessee would expect to pay on a similar lease.

In practice, the results of the present value test can often be determined very quickly by estimating the present value of the lessor's residual investment in the leased asset, and determining whether this is less than 10 per cent of the asset's fair value. For example, in a full-payout lease the lessor usually has no interest at all in the residual value of the asset and often passes back the benefits of any sales proceeds to the lessee through the medium of a rental rebate. In these circumstances it is pointless carrying out the present value test as the present value of the minimum lease payments must be equal to the fair value of the leased asset. Similarly, certain short-term leases with high residual values are unlikely to satisfy the 90 per cent test if the present value of the residual conservatively calculated at a high interest rate is significantly greater than 10 per cent of the asset cost. Consequently, most leases are relatively easy to classify. Only in those circumstances where the present value test is likely to be marginal is it necessary to perform all the detailed calculations.

Before discussing the present value test further it is necessary to explain some of the terms used in the test. This is because these terms have a precise meaning within the standard which are, in some instances, different from their accepted commercial meanings.

LEASE TERM

The lease term has an effect both on the calculation of the minimum lease payments and on the depreciable life of the leased assets. It follows that its precise meaning should be clearly understood. Contrary to the normal commercial meaning of the lease term, which includes only the primary period of the lease, SSAP 21 defines the lease term as both:

(a) the period for which the lessee has a contractual obligation to lease the asset (the 'primary period'); and

(b) further periods for which the lessee has the option to continue to lease the asset (with or without payment), provided that it is reasonably certain at the inception of the lease that the lessee will exercise that option.

The lessee must, therefore, look closely at those terms of the lease relating to the period of the lease, cancellation, and options to extend, before determining the lease term for accounting purposes.

THE MINIMUM LEASE PAYMENTS

These are the minimum payments that the lessee is committed to make during the lease term, plus the full amount of any guarantees that the lessee has made to the lessor concerning the realization of the asset at the end of the lease term. In determining the minimum lease payments, any element of the rental charge in respect of services or taxes borne by the lessor should be excluded from the calculation. For example, many operating leases include a rental element in respect of maintenance provided by the lessor. Unless this maintenance element is removed from the calculation of minimum lease payments, the calculation will not reflect the correct gross liability for the asset.

There are also a number of other practical difficulties that the lessee may encounter in determining the minimum lease payments. There are three key areas that may cause difficulty: contingent rentals, rental rebates, and guarantees. Many finance leases in the UK contain contingent rental variation clauses that protect the lessor from interest rate changes or tax changes that could affect the yield. These clauses can be ignored for the purpose of determining the minimum lease payments. This is because the present value test is performed at the date of the inception of the lease based on the information known at that date. If subsequent changes in rentals occur as a result of the effect of these contingencies they should be accounted for in the periods to which they relate. For similar reasons, rental rebates should not be anticipated in the calculation of the minimum lease payments unless they are known with certainty. For example, a rebate in respect of an anticipated receipt of a regional development grant could be included in the minimum lease payments calculation, but a rebate conditional on the amount of sales proceeds from the ultimate sale of the residual should be ignored.

Another area of practical difficulty is the treatment of residual guarantees. If the lessee undertakes to guarantee the eventual proceeds from sale of the asset, then the amount included in the minimum lease payments should be the full amount of the guarantee and not just the net amount the lessee ultimately expects to pay. For example, if the lessee guarantees that the sale of a car at the end of the lease term will realize £2,000 then this is the sum that should be included in the minimum lease payments even though the likelihood of the vehicle realizing less than, say, £1,000 may be remote. It also follows that if the lessee guarantees the full amount of the lessor's expected residual value, the lease must be a finance lease. In these circumstances, the present value of the minimum lease payments must be equal to 100 per cent of the fair value of the asset. Thus even very short-term leases can be finance leases if they include such guarantees.

THE IMPLICIT RATE IN THE LEASE

This is the rate of discount (or internal rate of return) that, when applied at the inception of the lease to the amounts that the lessor expects to receive and retain from his or her investment in the lease, produces a present value equal to the fair value of the lease asset. The amounts that the lessor expects to receive and retain will include:

1. The lessee's minimum lease payments as above plus any further guarantees by third parties concerning the residual value of the asset.
2. Any part of the anticipated residual value of the asset at the end of the lease which is not guaranteed and therefore excluded from 1. above.
3. Less: Any amount of 1. or 2. above for which the lessor is accountable to the lessee (for example, a rental rebate based on the proceeds of sale of the asset).

In practical terms, if the interest rate implicit in the lease is unknown the lessee will need to estimate it. Where the lease is a full payout lease, the amount of the residual can be assumed to be zero and the implicit rate will be simply calculated using the relationship between rentals and the cost of the asset. This can be calculated quite easily either by using a programmed calculator or by using an iterative process of trial and error estimates of the rate. Where, however, the residual is expected to be significant the lessee will need either to calculate the implicit rate using an estimate of the residual, or to use a reasonable estimate of the rate based on a similar lease.

THE INCEPTION DATE OF THE LEASE

This is the earlier of the rental start date and the date on which the asset is brought into use by the lessee. Thus, if a lease provides for a rental-free period at the start of the lease, the lessee would treat the inception date as the date from which he started to use the asset.

THE PRESENT VALUE OF THE MINIMUM LEASE PAYMENTS

The present value of the minimum lease payments should be calculated using the interest rate implicit in the lease. This is illustrated in Table 15.1.

In this simple illustration the present value of the minimum lease payments amounts to 89.9 per cent of the fair value and the lease would normally be classified as an operating lease. If, however, the guarantee had been increased by only £1, the present value of the minimum lease payments would have been 90.0 per cent of the fair value and the lease would have satisfied the test. This marginal effect has led some to criticize the present value test on the grounds that it will lead to a trend to structure leases just below the 90 per cent threshold so that lessees can still keep their leased assets and liabilities off-balance sheet. Such critics point to the US experience where certain artificial lease structures have evolved merely to retain the accounting classification of operating leases.

However, it must be remembered that the UK definition of a finance lease is based on a pragmatic view of whether substantially all the risks and rewards of ownership of the asset have been passed to the lessee. The 90 per cent test is generally a good yardstick for measuring risk, because it measures the amount of residual asset risk retained by the lessor. However, if a lease is clearly structured in such a way that the lessee gains residual benefits and takes substantially all the residual risks, then the lease should be classified as a finance lease irrespective of the results of the present value test.

Table 15.1 Example of calculation of present value of a minimum lease payments

Cost of asset	£1,000	
Lease term	5 years	
Rentals quarterly in advance	£60	
Maintenance borne by lessor per quarter	£10	
Anticipated residual value	£250	
Lessee's guarantee	£100	

The implicit rate calculates at 2.02% per quarter

The present value test is as follows:

	Gross amount £	Present value £	% of fair value
Rentals (£60 − £10 × 20	1,000	832.44	
Guarantee	100	67.03	
Minimum lease payments	1,100	899.47	89.9
Unguaranteed residual	150	100.53	10.1
	1,250	1,000.00	100.0

Accounting treatment of finance leases

Under SSAP 21 a finance lease should be recorded in the lessee's balance sheet as an asset and a liability. At the inception of a lease both the asset and the liability will be recorded at the present value of the minimum lease payments. In practice, the fair value of the asset will usually approximate quite closely to the present value of the minimum lease payments and, therefore, the standard permits its use as a practical substitute.

During the lease term, each rental is allocated between a reduction of the liability and interest expense so as to produce a constant periodic rate of interest payable on the remaining sum outstanding. This means that the interest charges will decline during the lease term as capital is gradually repaid, in much the same way as if the asset had been funded by borrowings.

The asset capitalized will be depreciated over the shorter of the lease term and the economic life of the asset using the lessee's normal depreciation policy for such assets. As explained above, the lease term could include secondary rental periods if, at the inception of the lease, it is reasonable to expect the lessee to exercise his or her option to such periods. Thus, a five-year lease term with a nominal secondary rental period of a further two years would mean that the lessee could depreciate his or her leased assets over seven years provided that this was not longer than the normal economic life for such assets.

190

Prior to the publication of SSAP 21, very little attention was given to the income effects of lease capitalization — the debate centred upon the effects on the lessee's balance sheet. Yet lease capitalization can have a very significant effect on a lessee's profit and loss account where the leases are of significant long-life capital assets such as aircraft or ships. The overall effect of lease capitalization on a lessee's profit and loss account will obviously vary from company to company depending upon the size of the interest and depreciation effects discussed above. The interest effect will have an unfavourable effect on the earlier periods of a lease, particularly where the lease has a long term, but the depreciation effect may well have a favourable effect by spreading the overall leasing charges over a longer period than the primary period of the lease.

Methods of allocating finance charges

Under SSAP 21, the total finance charges arising under the lease will represent the difference between the minimum lease payments and the amount at which the lease is capitalized at the inception of the lease (the present value of the minimum lease payments or an approximation thereof). The lessee will need to apportion these total finance charges to each period during the lease term in such a way that the charge for each period represents a constant rate on the balance of principal outstanding. There are three methods of achieving this: the actuarial method, the sum-of-the-digits method, and the straight-line method.

The actuarial method produces an exact constant rate of charge and, as such, is the most accurate. However, the sum-of-the-digits method will normally provide a reasonable approximation to the actuarial method and is, therefore, equally acceptable. These two methods are illustrated using the five-year finance lease shown in Table 15.2.

THE ACTUARIAL METHOD
The rental payments are deducted from this balance and interest is applied at the periodic rate of 2.952 per cent. The results of these calculations are

Table 15.2 Example of a five-year lease

Cost of leased asset	£10,000
Primary period	5 years
Rentals — quarterly in advance	£650
Secondary period — free	2 years
Economic life	7 years
Residual value	Nil
Inception date	1 April 1987
Lessee's year-end	30 June

Table 15.3 Allocation of finance charges of lease in Table 15.2, using actuarial method

Period ending	Capital sum £	Rentals £	Capital during period £	Finance charge £
30 June 1987	10,000	650	9,350	276
30 September 1987	9,626	650	8,976	265
31 December 1987	9,241	650	8,591	254
31 March 1988	8,845	650	8,195	242
30 June 1988	8,437	650	7,787	230
30 September 1988	8,017	650	7,367	217
31 December 1988	7,584	650	6,934	205
31 March 1989	7,139	650	6,489	192
30 June 1989	6,681	650	6,031	178
30 September 1989	6,209	650	5,559	164
31 December 1989	5,723	650	5,073	150
31 March 1990	5,223	650	4,573	135
30 June 1990	4,708	650	4,058	120
30 September 1990	4,178	650	3,528	104
31 December 1990	3,632	650	2,982	88
31 March 1991	3,070	650	2,420	71
30 June 1991	2,491	650	1,841	53
30 September 1991	1,894	650	1,244	37
31 December 1991	1,281	650	631	19
31 March 1992	650	650	–	–
		13,000		3,000

summarized in Table 15.3 to show the allocation of interest and capital for each period.

Under the actuarial method the leased asset will be capitalized at the inception of the lease at the same amount as that of the liability: namely, the present value of the minimum lease payments. In Table 15.4, the present value of the minimum lease payments is the same as the cost of the asset, £10,000, although this need not necessarily be the case. The leased asset will then be depreciated over the shorter of the lease term and the economic life. In Table 15.2 the lease term is seven years — the primary period of the lease (five years) plus the free secondary rental period (two years). Assuming the lessee has a straight-line depreciation policy, the annual depreciation charge would be £1,429. The overall effect on the lessee's balance sheet and profit and loss account can be summarized as shown in Table 15.5.

This summary illustrates quite clearly the effects that lease capitalization can have on the profit and loss account. If the lease had been treated as an

Table 15.4 Summary of allocations of lease in Table 15.2 (actuarial method)

Year ending	Rental £	Finance charge £	Capital repayment £	Liability outstanding £
Start	–	–	–	10,000
30 June 1987	650	276	374	9,626
30 June 1988	2,600	991	1,609	8,017
30 June 1989	2,600	792	1,808	6,209
30 June 1990	2,600	569	2,031	4,178
30 June 1991	2,600	316	2,284	1,894
30 June 1992	1,950	56	1,894	–
	13,000	3,000	10,000	

Table 15.5 Effect on lessee's accounts of lease in Table 15.2

Year	Balance sheet		Profit and loss account		
	Net book value £	Lease liability £	Depreciation charge £	Interest charge £	Total charge £
Start	10,000	10,000			
30 June 1987	9,644	9,626	356	276	632
30 June 1988	8,215	8,017	1,429	991	2,420
30 June 1989	6,786	6,209	1,429	792	2,221
30 June 1990	5,357	4,178	1,429	569	1,998
30 June 1991	3,928	1,894	1,429	316	1,745
30 June 1992	2,499	–	1,429	56	1,485
30 June 1993	1,070	–	1,429	–	1,429
30 June 1994	–	–	1,070	–	1,070
			10,000	3,000	13,000

operating lease, the lease rentals would simply be charged to profit and loss over the years 1987–92 at an annual charge of £2,600. It also means that significant differences can arise between the amounts charged to the profit and loss account and those amounts allowed for tax (usually the actual rentals accrued). These tax effects will be discussed later.

THE SUM-OF-THE-DIGITS METHOD (OR RULE OF 78)
This is a practical method that normally produces a reasonable approximation to the more accurate actuarial method. Under the sum-of-the-digits method the total finance charges are apportioned over the lease term in

proportion to the balance of outstanding rentals. The main advantage of the method is that it is simple to use. This can be illustrated by a straightforward example of a one-year lease with 12 monthly instalments. The finance charges are apportioned into 78 parts (78 being the sum of the digits $1 + 2 + 3 + \ldots + 12$). In the first month 12/78ths of the finance charge is recognized, in the second 11/78ths, in the third 10/78ths, and so on.

In the actuarial example shown in Table 15.3, the lease is a five-year lease with 20 quarterly payments. However, as the rentals are in advance no interest will accrue over the last quarter. The sum of the digits can be calculated for any number of equal payments (n) by the formula:

$$\text{Sum of digits} = \frac{n(n + 1)}{2}$$

If the interest charges are spread over 19 periods, the sum of the digits is 190. Thus the first quarter will bear 19/190ths, the second, 18/190ths, etc. Using the sum-of-the-digits method, this can be summarized for each year, as shown in Table 15.6. From this table we can summarize the effects of the sum-of-the-digits method as shown in Table 15.7.

THE STRAIGHT-LINE METHOD

Although the straight-line method of recognizing finance charges does not produce a constant rate of charge on the outstanding liability, SSAP 21 recognizes that there may well be practical circumstances that make it appropriate. Generally, its application will be restricted to those circumstances where the overall impact of using the straight-line method compared with that of using an accurate method has an immaterial effect

Table 15.6 Allocation of finance charges of lease in Table 15.2, using the sum-of-the-digits method

Year		Allocation of finance charge £
30 June 1987	$(19)/190 \times £3,000$	300
30 June 1988	$(18 + 17 + 16 + 15)/190 \times £3,000$	1,042
30 June 1989	$(14 + 13 + 12 + 11)/190 \times £3,000$	789
30 June 1990	$(10 + 9 + 8 + 7)/190 \times £3,000$	538
30 June 1991	$(6 + 5 + 4 + 3)/190 \times £3,000$	284
30 June 1992	$(2 + 1 + 0)/190 \times £3,000$	47
		3,000

Table 15.7 Summary of allocations of lease in Table 15.2 (sum-of-the-digits method)

Year	Rental £	Finance charge £	Capital repayment £	Liability outstanding £
Start				10,000
30 June 1987	650	300	350	9,650
30 June 1988	2,600	1,042	1,558	8,092
30 June 1989	2,600	789	1,811	6,281
30 June 1990	2,600	538	2,062	4,219
30 June 1991	2,600	284	2,316	1,903
30 June 1992	1,950	47	1,903	–
	13,000	3,000	10,000	

on the profit and loss account for the period and of future periods. Thus, a large company may wish to use an accurate method, such as the actuarial method, for determining the finance charges on its large leases, but use the simpler straight-line method on its insignificant leases.

CHOICE OF METHODS
The method a lessee adopts will depend on the overall impact that finance leasing has on financial statements, and on practical factors such as the volume of leases and the methods of computation available. The impact of the three methods outlined above on the finance charges for each period are compared in Table 15.8 for the above example.

Deferred taxation

As explained above, the charge to the profit and loss account in each period for finance charges and depreciation on leased assets will differ from the actual rental charges allowed for tax purposes. These differences represent timing differences and will need to be accounted for in accordance with SSAP 15 ('Accounting for deferred taxation'). Using the above example of finance charges under the actuarial method, the timing differences and their tax effects (assuming a 35 per cent tax rate) will be as shown in Table 15.9.

SSAP 15 requires companies to account for deferred tax to the extent that it is probable that a liability or asset will crystallize in the foreseeable future, and not to carry forward a net deferred tax asset except to the extent that it is recoverable without replacement by an equivalent debit balance. Timing differences arising from the treatment of finance leases

Table 15.8 Comparison of methods used for allocating finance charges of lease in Table 15.2

	Actuarial £	Sum of the digits £	Straight line £
1987	276	300	150
1988	991	1,042	600
1989	792	789	600
1990	569	538	600
1991	316	284	600
1992	56	47	450
	3,000	3,000	3,000

Table 15.9 Timing differences and tax effect of lease in Table 15.2 (using actuarial method)

Year	Depreciation charge £	Finance charge £	Total charge £	Rental £	Timing difference £	Tax effect (35%) £
Start						
1986/87	356	276	632	650	18	6
1987/88	1,429	991	2,420	2,600	180	63
1988/89	1,429	792	2,221	2,600	379	133
1989/90	1,429	569	1,998	2,600	602	211
1990/91	1,429	316	1,745	2,600	855	299
1991/92	1,429	56	1,485	1,950	465	163
1992/93	1,429	–	1,429	–	(1,429)	(500)
1993/94	1,070	–	1,070	–	(1,070)	(375)
	10,000	3,000	13,000	13,000		

are only one element of a company's total timing differences and will, therefore, have to be considered in the overall context of the company's tax position.

Finance lease accounting disclosure

SSAP 21 sets out certain minimum disclosure requirements that apply to finance leases and hire-purchase contracts. These requirements relate to the disclosure of leased assets, lease obligations and the charges to profit and loss for depreciation and interest. The standard permits a range of different ways in which this information may be disclosed so that the lessee has a number of choices to make.

DISCLOSURE OF LEASED ASSETS

The lessee has the choice of either showing the gross amount, related accumulated depreciation and the depreciation charge for the period for each class of leased asset separately, or including this information within totals shown for each class of owned asset. Where the lessee chooses to include the information in the analysis of owned assets, it will also be necessary to disclose separately both the aggregate net book value and the depreciation charge in respect of assets held under finance leases.

Generally, the approach adopted will depend on the materiality of the leased assets. Where the amount of leased assets is not a significant part of the total fixed assets then aggregation of information with owned assets will avoid unnecessarily complex fixed asset notes. Where, however, leased assets form a substantial part of the operating capacity of the company then separate disclosure is desirable. Tables 15.10 and 15.11, illustrate the two different methods adopted by S. W. Berisford and Turner & Newall.

DISCLOSURE OF FINANCE LEASE OBLIGATIONS

The lessee must disclose the net liability for obligations under finance leases separately from other liabilities. This may be entered on the face of the balance sheet or in the notes to the financial statements.

The lessee must also give a maturity analysis of the finance lease obligations in the notes to the financial statements. This can be done in one of three different ways:

1. The lessee can show separately the net obligations under finance leases (net of future finance charges) analysed between amounts payable in the next year, amounts payable in the second to fifth years inclusive from the balance sheet date, and aggregate amounts payable after the fifth year. Listed companies will need to give one year's extra detail because the Stock Exchange's listing agreement imposes a more detailed maturity analysis than that of SSAP 21. The additional requirement is to disclose amounts payable in the second year. Thus the analysis becomes amounts payable in the next year, amounts payable in the second year, amounts payable in the third to fifth years inclusive from the balance sheet date, and aggregate amounts payable thereafter.

2. If the lessee includes the net obligations under finance leases within the totals of other liabilities on the face of the balance sheet (for example, 'Bank loans and obligations under finance leases') then he or she may

197

Table 15.10 Disclosure of leased assets (courtesy of S. W. Berisford plc)

		Tangible fixed assets				
		Plant and equipment		Assets under	1987	1986
Group	Land and buildings £000	Owned £000	Leased £000	construction £000	total £000	total £000
Cost or valuation						
At 1 October	266,586	358,379	15,500	12,348	652,813	610,948
Currency realignment	(1,717)	(1,379)	–	(68)	(3,164)	8,360
Acquisitions (disposals) of subsidiaries	(11,528)	(21,631)	(145)	(449)	(33,753)	143
Additions	8,621	18,950	381	20,786	48,738	58,545
Disposals	(5,297)	(7,776)	(14)	–	(13,087)	(21,033)
Reclassifications	849	9,208	(20)	(10,616)	(579)	(3,172)
Revaluation adjustments	16,781	–	–	–	16,781	(978)
At 30 September	274,295	355,751	15,702	22,001	667,749	652,813
At cost	27,446	355,165	15,702	22,001	420,314	426,006
At valuation in 1980	–	586	–	–	586	605
1981	167	–	–	–	167	1,045
1985	350	–	–	–	350	350
1986	1,624	–	–	–	1,624	224,807
1987[1]	244,708	–	–	–	244,708	–
	274,295	355,751	15,702	22,001	667,749	652,813

Depreciation

At 1 October	12,289	134,920	1,530	–	148,739	128,968
Currency realignment	(672)	(793)	–	–	(1,465)	4,601
Acquisitions (disposals) of subsidiaries	(2,352)	(6,816)	(66)	–	(9,234)	54
Provided during the year	7,543	22,446	1,195	–	31,184	32,567
Disposals	(750)	(8,000)	(9)	–	(8,759)	(9,889)
Reclassifications	(120)	173	(2)	–	51	(1,597)
Revaluation adjustments	(6,034)	–	–	–	(6,034)	(5,965)
At 30 September	9,904	141,930	2,648	–	154,482	148,739
Net book value at 30 September[2]	264,391	213,821	13,054	22,001	513,267	504,074

1. At 30 September 1987 a valuation of the Group's above freehold and leasehold land and buildings was carried out by Chartered Surveyors in the UK and their equivalent overseas. The basis of the valuation was either open market with existing use or depreciated replacement cost where more appropriate. The resulting valuations have been incorporated in the accounts at 30 September 1987.
2. The net book value of land and buildings comprises:

	1987	1986
	£000	£000
Freehold	256,219	242,480
Long leasehold	1,367	3,442
Short leasehold	1,902	2,586
Oil and gas properties	4,903	5,789
	264,391	254,297

199

Table 15.11 Disclosure of leased assets (courtesy of Turner & Newall plc)

	Tangible fixed assets						
	Mining assets	Land and buildings		Plant and machinery		Total	
	Group £m	Group £m	Company £m	Group £m	Company £m	Group £m	Company £m
Cost or valuation							
At 1 January 1986	104.7	56.2	33.6	150.0	86.7	310.9	120.3
Valuation adjustments		1.5				1.5	
Capital expenditure	0.8	1.0	0.2	24.6	10.9	26.4	11.1
Acquisitions: AE Group		47.9		198.5		246.4	
Other		0.8	0.1	6.4	2.4	7.2	2.5
Disposals	(1.1)			(4.1)	(2.9)	(5.2)	(2.9)
Divestments		(4.0)	(3.6)	(14.0)	(12.4)	(18.0)	(16.0)
Currency translation	(3.8)	(0.3)		(1.2)		(5.3)	
At 31 December 1986	100.6	103.1	30.3	360.2	84.7	563.9	115.0
Comprising							
Cost	100.6	65.2	3.7	349.3	83.2	515.1	86.9
Valuation in 1986		4.7				4.7	
1985		1.2		1.3		2.5	
1984		0.5		0.3		0.8	
1982				4.9		4.9	
1981				1.9		1.9	
1980		24.3	21.7			24.3	21.7
Other years		7.2	4.9	2.5	1.5	9.7	6.4
	100.6	103.1	30.3	360.2	84.7	563.9	115.0

Depreciation							
At 1 January 1986	73.1	7.3	4.2	75.7	47.2	156.1	51.4
Valuation adjustments		(0.3)		0.5		0.2	
Charge for the year	2.3	1.3	0.7	12.1	5.3	15.7	6.0
Acquisitions: AE Group		4.6		104.2		108.8	
Other		0.1		0.8		0.9	
Disposals	(1.1)			(3.6)	(2.7)	(4.7)	(2.7)
Divestments		(0.8)	(0.7)	(7.6)	(6.8)	(8.4)	(7.5)
Currency translation	(2.7)	(0.3)		(0.8)		(3.8)	
At 31 December 1986	76.1	11.9	4.2	181.3	43.0	264.8	47.2
Net book value at 31 December 1986	29.0	91.2	26.1	178.9	41.7	299.1	67.8
at 31 December 1985	31.6	48.9	29.4	74.3	39.5	154.8	68.9

	Group		Company	
	1986 £m	1985 £m	1986 £m	1985 £m
Net book value of land and buildings				
Freehold	86.2	45.6	26.0	29.3
Long leasehold (over 50 years unexpired)	4.6	2.3	0.1	0.1
Short leaseholds	0.4	1.0		
	91.2	48.9	26.1	29.4

Included in plant and machinery at 31 December 1986 are capitalized leases at £30.9m (1985 £7.0m) comprising cost of £45.9m (1985 £10.3m) and depreciation thereon of £15.0m (1985 £3.3m). Certain overseas tangible fixed assets were valued by the directors on a market value for existing use basis during 1986 and £1.8m surplus arising has been credited to reserves.

give an equivalent analysis of the combined balance sheet amount as an alternative to separate disclosure of the above analysis. However, the lessee will still need to disclose the total net liability in respect of finance leases that has been included in the analysis.

3. If the lessee discloses the net obligations under finance leases separately, he or she may, as an alternative to analysing the net obligations, analyse the gross obligations, and show future finance charges as a separate deduction from the total. This is the form of disclosure adopted by the US accounting standard FAS 13, although the US standard requires a more detailed maturity analysis. This approach may therefore appeal to those UK companies with US parent companies who need to produce accounts both for UK and US purposes. An example of this form of disclosure is set out in Table 15.12, which shows the disclosure adopted by S. W. Berisford.

PROFIT AND LOSS DISCLOSURE

The standard requires the separate disclosure of finance charges. These are usually disclosed in the notes to the financial statements either as part of a separate note showing the analysis of interest charges, or as part of the statutory disclosure note of items charged in arriving at the trading profit for the year. Either approach is equally acceptable.

In addition to the above, the Companies Act 1985 imposes a requirement to disclose the amount charged to revenue in respect of hire of plant and machinery. For a finance lease this amount will usually comprise the depreciation and interest charges on such assets.

OTHER DISCLOSURE REQUIREMENTS FOR FINANCE LEASES

It is quite possible that, at the balance sheet date, a lessee could have entered into a finance lease arrangement where the asset has not been brought into use and the rentals have not started to accrue. Such leases would, for accounting purposes, have an inception date after the year-end and would not be shown in the lessee's balance sheet. However, such leases represent future financial commitments and both SSAP 21 and Schedule 4 of the Companies Act 1985 require such financial commitments to be disclosed separately in the notes to the financial statements.

SSAP 21 also requires the lessee to disclose the accounting policy adopted for finance leases.

In addition, it is important to remember that Statements of Standard Accounting Practice set out the minimum disclosure requirements. There is an overriding requirement in company law to show a true and fair view and there may well be circumstances where additional disclosure is required in order to do so.

Table 15.12 Maturity analysis disclosure (courtesy of S. W. Berisford plc)

Borrowings and lease obligations	Group			Company		
	Banks £000	Other £000	Total £000	Banks £000	Other £000	Total £000
Bank and other loans are repayable:						
Within one year	393,851	13,048	406,899	261,699	9,948	271,647
Between one and two years	–	29,459	29,459	–	–	–
Between two and five years	200,000	18,894	218,894	200,000	–	200,000
Thereafter, by instalments	–	1,200	1,200	–	–	–
	593,851	62,601	656,452	461,699	9,948	471,647
Less: due within one year	(393,851)	(13,048)	(406,899)	(261,699)	(9,948)	(271,647)

The future minimum lease payments to which the Group is committed under finance leases are as follows:

	1987 £000	1986 £000
Within one year	3,296	3,542
Between one and five years	3,168	5,364
Thereafter	29	54
	6,493	8,960
Deduct: Finance charges allocated to future periods	640	807
	5,853	8,153
Disclosed in the accounts as:		
Creditors due within one year	2,980	3,217
Creditors due after more than one year	2,873	4,936
	5,853	8,153

Disclosure of operating leases

The accounting treatment of operating leases is unlikely to pose too many problems for the lessee. Under SSAP 21, unless a more rational or systematic basis is appropriate, operating lease rentals should be charged to the profit and loss account on a straight-line basis over the lease term. Any difference between amounts paid and amounts charged would therefore be reflected as a prepayment or accrual.

For the vast number of operating leases that are on a fixed rental basis, rentals are simply charged to revenue in the usual way. However, where the lease is structured with a rental-free period or an uneven rental structure that is not representative of the service provided, the lessee will need to adjust the charges to the profit and loss account to reflect a 'normal' basis. In most circumstances the straight-line approach, which allocates charges on the basis of time, will be the most appropriate way of determining a normal charge for each period. However, the standard recognizes that in some circumstances other rational and systematic bases might be appropriate. For example, if the varying charges during the lease term reflect different levels of usage then an activity basis of allocating charges might be more appropriate than the straight-line pattern. Similarly, it might be inappropriate to use a straight-line basis where the rental structure reflects the lessor's true anticipated cost of providing the service in each period. In practice, the approach a lessee adopts will depend not only on the nature of the operating lease charges, but also on the significance of those charges within the context of the lessee's profit and loss account.

DISCLOSURE OF OPERATING LEASE CHARGES

SSAP 21 requires the lessee to disclose the total operating lease rentals charged to the profit and loss account, analysed between amounts payable in respect of hire of plant and machinery and in respect of other operating leases. Thus the disclosure requirements for SSAP 21 go somewhat further than those of the Companies Act, which simply requires the disclosure of amounts charged to revenue in respect of hire of plant and machinery.

DISCLOSURE OF OPERATING LEASE COMMITMENTS

The Companies Act requires disclosure of future financial commitments. SSAP 21 goes further in that it requires an analysis of the operating lease payments which the lessee is committed to pay in the year following the balance sheet date, analysed according to the period in which that annual commitment expires. The analysis should give the annual payments under agreements expiring next year, those expiring within the second to fifth years inclusive, and those expiring over five years from the balance sheet date. The analysis should also show annual commitments in respect of land and buildings separately from those of other operating leases.

Although at first glance this analysis looks very similar to that of finance lease obligations, it is important to stress that it is an analysis of annual charges according to the time scale in which they expire. It is, therefore, quite different from the disclosures required for finance leases, which analyse the total liability according to the periods in which it is to be repaid.

This form of disclosure is also quite different from that adopted under US accounting standard FAS 13, which requires an analysis of the total commitment. UK subsidiaries of US parent companies will therefore have to produce different information for their US parent company to that which they publish in their own financial statements.

An example of SSAP 21 operating lease commitment disclosure is given in Table 15.13, which shows the disclosure adopted by British Airways.

OTHER DISCLOSURE REQUIREMENTS
As with finance leases, the lessee will need to disclose his or her accounting policy in respect of operating leases. The lessee will also need to consider whether any additional matters need to be disclosed in order to show a true and fair view; for example, if future rentals were material and contingent on profits or performance, the nature of the arrangements may need to be disclosed.

Comparisons with international accounting practice

In the UK, compliance with SSAP 21 will ensure compliance in all material respects with International Accounting Standard 17, 'Accounting for leases'. Indeed, in principle SSAP 21 closely resembles the equivalent accounting standards produced by all of the major English-speaking nations. All such standards distinguish between finance and operating leases, and they all prescribe that finance leases should be capitalized by the lessee, and rentals under operating leases should be written off on a systematic basis. There are, however, a number of minor differences in the definitions offered, the range of acceptable accounting methods permitted, and the nature and extent of disclosure required. These differences are discussed below with reference to the two most representative of the other standards, IAS 17 and the US accounting standard FAS 13.

205

Table 15.13 Disclosure of operating lease commitment (courtesy of British Airways plc)

Leasing commitments	Group 1987 £m	Group 1986 £m	Company 1987 £m	Company 1986 £m
The aggregate payments, for which there are commitments as at 31 March 1987 under operating leases, fall due as follows:				
Fleet				
Within one year	113	79	113	79
Between one and four years	105	96	105	96
	218	175	218	175
Amounts payable within one year relate to commitments expiring as follows:				
Within one year	30		30	
Between one and four years	83	79	83	79
	113	79	113	79
Property and equipment				
Within one year	34	31	33	30
Between one and five years	52	61	50	59
Over five years, ranging up to year 2075	138	114	132	106
	224	206	215	195
Amounts payable within one year relate to commitments expiring as follows:				
Within one year	1			
Between one and five years	27	27	27	27
Over five years	6	4	6	3
	34	31	33	30

The fleet leasing commitments include the minimum three-year rental obligations assumed under the operating leases for 16 Boeing 737, 3 Boeing 747 and 9 Boeing 757 aircraft. On completion of the three years the Company has a yearly option to renew the operating leases up to the sixth year or it has the option, at any time after three years, to convert the operating leases to finance leases for the period to 15 years from delivery of the aircraft.

If these options are not exercised, the Company may be required to meet a small share of any loss on re-sale.

INTERNATIONAL ACCOUNTING STANDARD: IAS 17

In comparison with SSAP 21 and FAS 13, the International Accounting Standard on the subject of accounting for leases is brief and general in its approach. As a result it avoids significant contradiction of any of the major national accounting standards. Like SSAP 21 and FAS 13, it defines a finance lease as one that transfers substantially all of the risks and rewards of ownership to the lessee. IAS 17 does not prescribe any criteria to be used in order to identify a finance lease other than to state that such a lease is normally non-cancellable and secures for the lessor the recovery of capital outlay plus a return for the funds invested.

IAS 17 is consistent with FAS 13 in requiring that finance leases be capitalized by the lessee at the inception of the lease at the lower of the present value of the minimum lease payments and the fair value of the leased asset. This is different from SSAP 21, which requires the present value of the minimum lease payments to be capitalized but recognizes that for practical purposes the fair value can be used as a reasonable approximation. In practice, these differences in the amount capitalized will usually be insignificant within the context of the lessee's financial statements. IAS 17 states that, where practicable, the interest rate implicit in the lease shall be used to arrive at the present value of the minimum lease payments. Where this is impracticable the lessee's incremental borrowing rate is to be used. This differs slightly from both SSAP 21, which requires the use of the former rate, and FAS 13, which requires that the lower of the two rates be used.

The disclosure requirements of IAS 17 for lessees are similar but less detailed than those in either SSAP 21 or FAS 13. The amount of assets acquired under finance leases and the amount of the related current and long-term liabilities should each be disclosed. The periods in which this long-term liability and commitments under non-cancellable operating leases of more than one year fall due should be disclosed.

UNITED STATES: FAS 13

The US was the first country to adopt a lease accounting standard and the concept of lease capitalization it adopted has been subsequently embodied both in International Accounting Standards and the national accounting standards of many countries, including the UK, Canada, Australia and New Zealand.

Predictably the US standard is the lengthiest and most prescriptive of the standards. Like SSAP 21, it defines a finance (or capital) lease as one that transfers substantially all of the risks and rewards of ownership to the lessee, and states that such leases should be capitalized by the lessee in order that the level of the enterprise's economic resources and financial obligations shall not be understated. However, FAS 13 is much more prescriptive than SSAP 21 in its definition of what shall constitute a finance lease. FAS 13 defines a capital lease as one that satisfies one or more of the following criteria at the start of the lease:

1. The lease transfers ownership of the asset to the lessee by the end of the lease period.
2. The lease contains a bargain purchase option.
3. The lease term is equal to at least 75 per cent of the estimated economic life of the asset.
4. The present value of the minimum lease payments is equal to at least 90 per cent of the fair value of the asset at the start of the lease period.

Consequently, it is possible for a lease to be classified as a finance lease under FAS 13, using criterion 3 for example, and as an operating lease under SSAP 21 because criterion 4 is not satisfied. The US rules are also more inflexible than those of the UK. For example, most commercial property leases in the UK would be classified as operating leases because they usually contain rent review clauses which mean the lessor retains significantly the economic benefits from the asset. The approach in the US, however, is to apply strict rules to leasehold properties and to classify according to those rules.

The initial amount capitalized under SSAP 21 and FAS 13 may also differ slightly. SSAP 21 states that at the inception of a finance lease the lessee should capitalize the asset and the obligation at the present value of the minimum lease payments, adding that the fair value of the asset may often be used as an approximation to this figure. FAS 13 is more restrictive and stipulates that the lower of the present value of the minimum lease payments and the fair value of the asset must be the figure used. Furthermore, whereas SSAP 21 provides that the lessee shall use the interest rate implicit in the lease to arrive at the present value of the minimum lease payments, FAS 13 states that the lessee must use the lower of the lessor's implicit rate (where this is known) and his or her own incremental borrowing rate. The latter is effectively the rate at which the lessee could borrow funds in the market to finance the outright acquisition of the asset to be leased.

In common with SSAP 21, the US standard defines operating leases by default as all leases other than finance leases. Similarly, both standards prescribe that lessees shall write off the rentals payable under such leases on a systematic (usually straight-line) basis over the lease term, whether or not payments are made on such a basis.

As already explained above, there are also differences between FAS 13 and SSAP 21 in the disclosure requirements for finance and operating leases. The principal differences can be summarized as follows:

1. FAS 13 requires that future minimum rental payments are disclosed gross and future finance charges deducted therefrom to arrive at the liability in the balance sheet. SSAP 21 permits the use of either this method or the disclosure of the net liability (net of finance charges).
2. FAS 13 requires future rental payments to be analysed for each of the five years after the balance sheet date, and then in total for subsequent years. SSAP 21 permits this analysis to be either gross or net of future interest charges and shows less detail by aggregating amounts payable between two and five years.
3. FAS 13 requires disclosure of all future minimum rentals payable under non-cancellable operating leases analysed for each of the five years following the balance sheet date, and then in total thereafter. SSAP 21 requires disclosure of the operating rentals payable in the year following the balance sheet date analysed between the periods in which the operating lease commitments expire.

16. *Lessor Accounting*

Introduction

In the UK, the accounts of lessors must comply with the requirements of the Companies Acts and the various Statements of Standard Accounting Practice (SSAPs). From the viewpoint of the lessor the most important of these is SSAP 21 ('Accounting for leases and hire-purchase contracts'), which was published in 1984. As explained in the previous chapter, SSAP 21 brought about a radical change in the way lessees accounted for finance leases. However, its effect on lessor accounting was less dramatic. Although the standard did bring about some changes to the way lessors disclosed leased assets in their balance sheets, it had remarkably few other effects on existing accounting practices.

Indeed, it might be argued that SSAP 21 avoided the more contentious accounting issues that were being debated within the industry at that time by failing to give more detailed guidance. However, it is important to remember that SSAP 21 is a lease accounting standard and not a standard for the leasing industry. Accounting standards are issued in the UK to set out basic accounting principles and minimum disclosure requirements for accounting problems that are generally applicable to all companies. Leasing transactions can, and do, affect all companies and are therefore governed by standard accounting practice. It is not generally the practice in the UK for the Accounting Standards Board to prescribe specific practices for specific industry problems. It is left to the industries concerned to establish appropriate accounting practices.

There are two principal issues involved in lessor accounting. First and foremost, income recognition — i.e. which method should lessors use to allocate income to accounting periods? Secondly, balance sheet presentation — i.e. should lessors show leased assets as physical tangible assets or as receivables? SSAP 21 deals with both of these issues but still leaves considerable scope for choice in the method of accounting that a lessor uses.

Income recognition

Finance leases and operating leases are fundamentally different and this is reflected in their very different methods of income recognition. This section therefore deals with each type of lease in turn.

Income recognition: finance leases

As its name implies, finance leasing is a financing activity. Not surprisingly, therefore, the methods of accounting adopted by lessors reflect the financing nature of this activity.

At the start of a finance lease, the lessor will know with reasonable certainty the total amount of 'gross earnings' that is expected to be earned from the investment in the lease. This amount represents the total rentals receivable over the primary lease term (and any other guaranteed receipts) less the net cost of the asset. The lessor will also know, from the evaluation of the lease, the anticipated costs of funding the lease and therefore also the expected pre-tax margin. The purpose of all methods of accounting for finance leases is to allocate the total gross earnings from the lease to each accounting period during the lease term in such a way that each period fairly reflects the amount of profits earned.

In simple terms, the profits earned from a lease should be proportional to the service that the lessor provides. In a finance-leasing transaction, the service that the lessor provides is the use of finance to fund the 'acquisition' of the asset by the lessee. Consequently, the profits that a lessor should recognize in an accounting period should be proportional to the total amount of finance provided during that period. In other words, the lessor should seek to allocate the total gross earnings from a lease in such a way that the profits in each period represent a constant rate of return on the outstanding funds invested in the lease.

This means that a greater proportion of the total gross earnings from a finance lease will be recognized in the earlier periods of the lease, when the funds invested in the lease are high, than in the later periods, when the lessor may have recovered a substantial proportion of the initial investment through rentals received. This is precisely the same pattern of anticipated borrowings that a lessor would need to fund the lease. Thus, where the lessor is funding the lease by borrowings, the gross earnings recognized in the profit and loss account will match the related finance costs giving the lessor a constant net return (after interest) on the investment.

In order to account for gross earnings in this way the leasing industry has evolved a number of different accounting methods. All are broadly based on this principle of achieving a constant rate of return and differ only in their definitions of investment and return. In order to understand the different merits of these alternative methods it is first necessary to explain some of the background to their evolution.

In the 1960s, when the UK finance-leasing industry was still in its initial stages, the accounting methods used by lessors were relatively unsophisticated. At that time most lease finance business was conducted by the finance houses whose traditional business was hire-purchase finance.

211

Finance leasing and hire-purchase have many similar characteristics and it was therefore not surprising that the finance houses chose to account for their leases in the same way as their hire-purchase contracts. In 1964 the Institute of Chartered Accountants of England and Wales recommended two methods of hire-purchase accounting: the actuarial method and the sum-of-the-digits method. Under the actuarial method, finance income is allocated over the life of the hire-purchase agreement in proportion to the reducing principal balance outstanding. The sum-of-the-digits method is a simpler approximation that uses the proportion of outstanding rentals. In the days before calculators and computers were common, the actuarial method was considered too complicated to apply, and a simpler approximation, in the form of the sum-of-the-digits method, was widely adopted. The Institute's recommendation gave no specific guidance on the allocation of income for leasing other than that depreciation should be 'computed on an appropriate basis applied consistently from year to year'.

The sum-of-the-digits method, which releases gross earnings to the profit and loss account in proportion to the lessor's outstanding rentals, was generally regarded as satisfactory until the early 1970s. Until then the investment by a lessor in a finance lease and by a finance house in a hire-purchase contract were similar. However, in 1972 first-year capital allowances were increased to 100 per cent for most types of capital equipment, and this had a dramatic effect both on the cash flows associated with leases and on lease rates. Firstly, the tax effects of the lease significantly reduced the level and pattern of finance that the lessor required to fund the lease. Secondly, lease rates fell because of the competitive pressures in the industry, which meant that most of the cash flow benefits from deferring tax were passed to the lessee in the form of lower rentals. In these circumstances, the application of the sum-of-the-digits method (which takes no account of the reduction in the lessor's investment from the entitlement to tax allowances) produced a mismatch between gross earnings and interest costs, resulting in losses being shown in the early years of leases that were profitable overall. Such results were clearly unrealistic because the pattern of profits that emerged did not match the pattern of funds invested in the lease.

To overcome this problem leasing companies and their auditors examined various methods of profit recognition that reflected the funding requirements of a lease. All of these methods were broadly based on the principle of achieving a constant periodic rate of return on the net cash investment in a lease (after taking account of all cash flows, including tax) and bore a close relationship to the way lessors evaluated their leasing transactions. Although there were a number of different variants, two different approaches evolved and are now widely used in the industry.

These are the actuarial method after-tax (AMAT) and the investment period method (IPM).

Prior to the publication of SSAP 21, there was considerable debate in the leasing industry as to which of the two methods was most appropriate. Both methods had their advocates, and both methods had advantages and disadvantages associated with their use, which will be explained later in this chapter. It might have been expected that SSAP 21 would have made a clear choice between the alternative methods. However, as explained earlier, this was not the approach adopted by the standard.

The standard simply requires the lessor to allocate the gross earnings to each period during the lease term in a manner that will produce a constant rate of return (or a reasonable approximation to it) on each period's net cash investment. Both AMAT and IPM follow the constant rate of return principle. The principal difference between the two methods centres on their definitions of 'return'. AMAT uses an after-tax profit definition of return; IPM uses gross earnings. Under the standard either method can be adopted and examples of both methods are illustrated in the guidance notes accompanying the standard.

However, AMAT and IPM are not the only methods permitted by the standard. The standard also permits alternative methods that seek to allocate gross earnings in such a way that net earnings (gross earnings less anticipated interest costs) are allocated on a systematic basis. Thus, for example, the gross earnings from a lease could be allocated on a basis that allows the net earnings to emerge in proportion to the sum of the digits — a method known as the net earnings sum-of-the-digits method. Lessors therefore have considerable choice in the methods they use to allocate their gross earnings, provided that their methods accord with the general principle of matching gross earnings and interest. Whichever method a lessor uses will need to be properly disclosed in the accounting policy notes to the financial statements, and will need to be applied on a consistent basis from year to year.

INVESTMENT PERIOD METHOD (IPM)

Unfortunately, the term IPM can be interpreted differently within the industry. At one extreme some accountants regard it as embracing all methods of allocating income in proportion to the cash invested in the lease, including AMAT, while others at the opposite extreme take the narrow view that it is merely one of many specific variants of AMAT. In this book neither of these views is taken. IPM is used to describe those practical methods that seek to produce a constant rate of gross earnings on the net cash investment in a lease. AMAT is used to describe those other methods that seek to produce a constant rate of return at the post-tax profit level. Both IPM and AMAT have their variants but each has its own distinct objective in terms of the return measure that it pursues.

Under IPM, the total gross earnings from a lease are allocated to each accounting period during the lease term in which the lessor has a positive net cash investment balance, in proportion to each period's balance. Consequently, the first stage is to calculate the anticipated net cash investment balances for each month (or other interval) during the period of the lease. These net cash investment balances are usually derived from the calculations used in the initial actuarial evaluation of the lease and take into account the funding and profit assumptions used in that evaluation.

Thus the net cash investment balance for each period will represent the original cost of the asset less the cumulative cash flow receipts to date (rental income and tax relieved through receipt of capital allowances and through payment of interest), plus the cumulative cash flow payments to date (interest payments and tax payable on rental income). Under SSAP 21 it should also include an adjustment in respect of the profit that the lessor takes out of the lease. The reason for this is that the rentals deducted in the net cash investment calculation include not only an interest element, but also a profit element. Both of these elements need to be removed from the rentals in order to arrive at the rental component that represents the capital repayment.

Although not so common nowadays, some types of leases have such significant tax deferral effects that during certain periods of the lease the cumulative cash flow receipts exceed the original cost of the asset plus the cumulative cash flow payments. This negative net cash investment represents surplus funds that can be reinvested by the lessor to earn interest or to reduce interest costs on other leases. The cash flows used in the computation of the net cash investment in the lease may therefore need to reflect the effects of anticipated reinvestment income and tax thereon.

IPM may be more readily understood by following an example of its application. Although, in practice, monthly balances are normally used to calculate net cash investment balances, it is possible to use quarterly intervals for the lease detailed in Table 16.1 because all cash flows take place at quarterly intervals. The lessor's cash flows are set out in Table 16.2, and the allocation of gross earnings is shown in Table 16.3.

Table 16.4 shows the lessor's forecast profit and loss account for 1987 to 1993 using IPM, and the estimates of tax and interest used in the cash flow assumptions. It also shows that the gross earnings represent a constant rate of return on the lessor's net cash investment over the positive investment period.

It is important to remember that the profit and loss account illustrated in Table 16.4 is only a forecast based on the cash flow estimates used to evaluate the lease. The only accounting entries arising from the use of IPM

214

Table 16.1 Example of five year lease

Example:	
Lease term	Five years from 1 April 1987
Rental payments	£650 payable quarterly in advance
Asset cost	£10,000
Lessor's year-end date	30 June
Lessor's tax payment date	Nine months after the year-end
Cost of money	2.5% per quarter
Reinvestment rate	1.75% per quarter
Tax rate	35%
Capital allowances	25% writing-down allowance

are those that split the rental between its gross earnings element and that element representing amortization. The actual profit and loss account of future periods will bear the actual charges for interest costs and tax, which may well differ from those used in the original cash flow forecast. Under IPM (and other methods), once the allocation of gross earnings has been determined at the start of the lease the allocation is not revised during the lease term to reflect normal differences in the cash flow estimates, but it may be necessary to make suitable provision against future losses. Only in the event of a fundamental change in cash flow assumptions would it be necessary to revise the gross earnings allocation: for example, in the event of a fundamental change in tax rates or a significant loss of tax capacity.

The crude version of the IPM
The version of IPM illustrated in Table 16.4 is the same method as that illustrated in the guidance notes to SSAP 21 in that it takes account of the fact that part of the rental receipts represent a return of profit. This profit is unconnected with the amount of capital recovered through rentals and therefore should be treated as a notional distribution in the net cash investment calculation. Some of the earlier versions of IPM ignored this profit removal adjustment. Although this meant that IPM calculations were easier to perform, it also meant that the net cash investment balances fell more rapidly than the true amount of funds required to fund the lease. Consequently, under the cruder version of IPM, gross earnings were recognized earlier than would otherwise have been the case. Because of this lack of conservatism the guidance notes to SSAP 21 argue strongly against the use of this particular version of IPM.

ACTUARIAL METHOD AFTER-TAX (AMAT)
AMAT bears an even closer relationship to the way lessors evaluate leases than does IPM. Under AMAT, gross earnings are allocated to each

Table 16.2 Lessor's cash flow of lease in Table 16.1

Quarter end	Investment at start of quarter £	Cost £	Rental £	Tax £	Average net cash investment £	Average		
						Interest paid/ (received) £	Profit taken out £	Net cash investment at end of quarter £
30.6.87	0	10,000			9,350	234	47	9,631
30.9.87	9,631		(650)		8,991	225	45	9,251
31.12.87	9,251		(650)		8,601	215	43	8,859
31.3.88	8,859		(650)		8,209	205	41	8,455
30.6.88	8,455		(650)	(729)	7,076	177	36	7,289
30.9.88	7,289		(650)		6,639	166	33	6,838
31.12.88	6,838		(650)		6,188	155	31	6,374
31.3.89	6,374		(650)		5,724	143	29	5,896
30.6.89	5,896		(650)	(34)	5,212	130	26	5,368
30.9.89	5,368		(650)		4,718	118	24	4,860
31.12.89	4,860		(650)		4,210	105	21	4,336
31.3.90	4,336		(650)		3,686	92	19	3,797
30.6.90	3,797		(650)	210	3,357	84	17	3,458
30.9.90	3,458		(650)		2,808	70	14	2,892
31.12.90	2,892		(650)		2,242	56	11	2,309
31.3.91	2,309		(650)		1,659	41	8	1,708
30.6.91	1,708		(650)	401	1,459	36	7	1,502
30.9.91	1,502		(650)		852	21	5	878
31.12.91	878		(650)		228	6	1	235
31.3.92	235		(650)		(415)	(7)	0	(422)
30.6.92	(422)			562	140	4	1	145
30.9.92	145				145	4	1	150
31.12.92	150				150	4	1	155
31.3.93	155				155	4	1	160
30.6.93	160			(156)	4	0	0	4
30.6.94	4			(4)	0	0	0	0

Notes:

1. The lessor's initial investment in the lease is the cost of the leased asset (£10,000).
2. Interest paid is calculated at 2.5 per cent per quarter on the average net cash investment in each quarter. Interest received is calculated at a conservative rate of 1.75 per cent per quarter on the average cash surplus in each quarter.
3. Tax is payable/receivable on 1 April each year, based on rentals, interest paid, interest received, and capital allowances in the previous accounting year, as follows:

Year to 30 June	Rental £	Capital allowances £	Interest £	Total £	Tax rate %	Tax payable (receivable) £
1987	650	(2,500)	(234)	(2,084)	35.00	(729)
1988	2,600	(1,875)	(822)	(97)	35.00	(34)
1989	2,600	(1,406)	(594)	600	35.00	210
1990	2,600	(1,055)	(399)	1,146	35.00	401
1991	2,600	(791)	(203)	1,606	35.00	562
1992	1,950	(2,373)	(24)	(447)	35.00	(156)
1993	0	0	(12)	(12)	35.00	(4)
	13,000	(10,000)	(2,288)	712		250

In order to simplify the calculations of the tax cash flows, it has been assumed that the amount of expenditure unrelieved after five years' writing-down allowances, is received in the computation for the year ending 30 June 1992. In practice, this will apply only if the lessor sells the asset at the end of the lease term for an amount equal to the tax written-down value of the asset, and also if he or she passes the proceeds of the sale to the lessee. Otherwise, the tax written-down value of the asset will remain as part of the pool of unrelieved expenditure, and the lessor will continue to receive writing-down allowances on a reducing balance basis into the future. Where the lessor does not recover the remaining unrelieved expenditure by the end of the lease term it may be appropriate for that person to delay the recognition of some of his or her gross earnings.

4. Profit is assumed to be removed from the lease at a constant rate of return on the average net cash investment during the investment period. (This rate is referred to as the profit-take-out rate — or the actuarial rate.) To calculate this rate, the lessor needs to use an iterative process that involves making a succession of trial-and-error estimates of the rate. Each estimate of the rate will change the net cash investment in each period, the interest paid and received, tax, and the total profit taken out of the lease. The profit-take-out rate in this example calculates at 0.504 per cent per quarter.

Table 16.3 Allocation of lessor's gross earnings of lease in Table 16.1 (using IPM) Gross earnings = (£650 × 20) − £10,000 = £3,000

Quarter end	Net cash investment fraction	Apportionment of gross earnings under the investment period method £	£
30.6.87	9,631/94,550	306	306
30.9.87	9,251/94,550	294	
31.12.87	8,859/94,550	281	
31.3.88	8,455/94,550	268	1,074
30.6.88	7,289/94,550	231	
30.9.88	6,838/94,550	217	
31.12.88	6,374/94,550	202	
31.3.89	5,896/94,550	187	776
30.6.89	5,368/94,550	170	
30.9.89	4,860/94,550	154	
31.12.89	4,336/94,550	138	
31.3.90	3,797/94,550	120	522
30.6.90	3,458/94,550	110	
30.9.90	2,892/94,550	92	
31.12.90	2,309/94,550	73	
31.3.91	1,708/94,550	54	267
30.6.91	1,502/94,550	48	
30.9.91	878/94,550	28	
31.12.91	235/94,550	7	
31.3.92	0/94,550	0	40
30.6.92	145/94,550	5	
30.9.92	150/94,550	5	
31.12.92	155/94,550	5	
31.3.93	160/94,550	5	15
30.6.93	4/94,550	0	
	94,550/94,550	3,000	3,000

Notes:
1. In this example the investment period is from 1 April 1987 to 31 December 1991 and from 1 April 1992 to 1 April 1994. The reinvestment period (1 Jan. 1992 to 31 March 1992) is very short. This is because the tax deferral effects of a lease that is subject to 25 per cent writing-down allowances is minimal.
2. The effect of allocating gross earnings in this way can be summarized as follows:

| Year to 30 June | Rentals | | | Balance sheet |
	Total £	Profit and loss (gross earnings) £	Reduction in net investment £	Finance lease receivables £
1987	650	306	344	9,656
1988	2,600	1,074	1,526	8,130
1989	2,600	776	1,824	6,306
1990	2,600	522	2,078	4,228
1991	2,600	267	2,333	1,895
1992	1,950	40	1,910	(15)
1993	–	15	(15)	–
	13,000	3,000	10,000	

Table 16.4 Lessor's profit and loss account of lease in Table 16.1 (using IPM)

Year to 30 June	1987 £	1988 £	1989 £	1990 £	1991 £	1992 £	1993 £	Total £
Rentals	650	2,600	2,600	2,600	2,600	1,950	–	13,000
Less: Capital repayments	(344)	(1,526)	(1,824)	(2,078)	(2,333)	(1,910)	15	(10,000)
Gross earnings	306	1,074	776	522	267	40	15	3,000
Interest	(234)	(822)	(594)	(399)	(203)	(24)	(12)	(2,288)
Profit before tax	72	252	182	123	64	16	3	712
Current tax	729	34	(210)	(401)	(562)	156	4	(250)
	801	286	(28)	(278)	(498)	172	7	462
Deferred tax	754	122	(146)	(358)	(539)	162	5	0
Net profit	47	164	118	80	41	10	2	462
Average net cash investment	9,631	8,463	6,119	4,112	2,103	315	117	
Gross earnings yield	12.71	12.69	12.68	12.69	12.70	12.70	12.82	

accounting period in such a way that the anticipated after-tax profit for each period represents a constant rate of return on the lessor's net cash investment in the lease. This is achieved by first deriving the anticipated after-tax profit for each period and then by 'working backwards' to gross earnings by adding back tax and interest. This is best illustrated by example using the same lease data as for IPM.

As with IPM, the first step is to forecast the lease cash flows that make up the lessor's net cash investment in the lease. These are illustrated in Table 16.2. The most difficult aspect of these calculations is the profit take-out rate shown in column 8 and explained in note 4. This is calculated from the actuarial rate at which the lessor can withdraw profit from the lease — a rate that is best calculated by a computer program using an iterative process of trial-and-error estimates of the rate. Once the after-tax profit for each period has been derived, it is a simple process to work backwards in order to derive the appropriate gross earnings allocation. Pre-tax profits are derived by grossing up after-tax profits by the tax rates applicable for the period; and gross earnings are then derived by adding back the anticipated interest costs shown in the cash flow summary (Table 16.5). The lessor's forecast profit and loss accounts for 1987/93 using AMAT is shown in Table 16.6.

If the results of the AMAT example (Table 16.6) are compared with those produced by the IPM example (Table 16.4) it can be seen that the differences are very small. This is because the example is based on a lease with no unusual cash flow tax effects. There are two ways in which tax can affect the methods.

Firstly, the AMAT seeks to produce a constant after-tax rate of return on the net cash investment in the lease. In comparison, IPM produces a constant rate of gross earnings on the net cash investment in the lease, which, after taking interest into account, will usually produce an effect that approximates quite closely to a constant pre-tax rate of return on the net cash investment in the lease. When tax rates are consistent throughout the lease term the pattern of after-tax profits will be proportional to the pattern of pre-tax profits and no significant differences in profit patterns will arise between the two methods. However, where tax rates are changing during the lease term, as was the situation in the period 1984–86, the methods will produce quite different results.

Secondly, where the tax deferral effects of a lease are so significant that one or more periods of cash surplus arise during the lease term, a substantial proportion of the lessor's after-tax profit may be derived from anticipated reinvestment income from the cash surpluses. AMAT and IPM treat reinvestment income quite differently. IPM allocates gross earnings directly in proportion to the net cash investment in the lease and therefore takes no account of interest received when allocating gross earnings.

220

Table 16.5 Allocation of earnings of lease in Table 16.1 (using AMAT)

Quarter end	Anticipated after-tax profit £	Derived pre-tax profit £	Anticipated interest £	Derived apportionment of gross earnings £	£
30.6.86	47	72	234	306	306
30.9.86	45	69	225	294	
31.12.86	43	66	215	281	
31.3.87	41	63	205	268	1,075
30.6.87	36	55	177	232	
30.9.87	33	51	166	217	
31.12.87	31	48	155	203	
31.3.88	29	45	143	188	778
30.6.88	26	40	130	170	
30.9.88	24	37	118	155	
31.12.88	21	32	105	137	
31.3.89	19	29	92	121	523
30.6.89	17	26	84	110	
30.9.89	14	22	70	92	
31.12.89	11	17	56	73	
31.3.90	8	12	41	53	265
30.6.90	7	11	36	47	
30.9.90	5	8	21	29	
31.12.90	1	2	6	8	
31.3.91	0	0	(7)	(7)	36
30.6.91	1	2	4	6	
30.9.91	1	2	4	6	
31.12.91	1	2	4	6	
31.3.92	1	1	4	5	17
30.6.92	0	0	0	0	
	462	712	2,288	3,000	3,000

Notes:
1. The anticipated after-tax profit is taken from the cash flow summary.
2. The pre-tax profit is derived by grossing-up the anticipated after-tax profit by the appropriate tax rate. The tax rate is 35 per cent, and so the factor by which the after-tax profit is grossed up to arrive at the pre-tax profit is $1/(1 - 0.35)$.
3. The anticipated interest is taken directly from the cash flow summary.
4. The derived apportionment of gross earnings is simply the sum of the derived pre-tax profit and anticipated interest.
5. The effect of allocating gross earnings in this way can be summarized as follows:

	Rentals			Balance sheet
Year to 30 June	Total £	Profit and loss (gross earnings) £	Reduction in net investment £	Finance lease receivables £
1986	650	306	344	9,656
1987	2,600	1,075	1,525	8,131
1988	2,600	778	1,822	6,309
1989	2,600	523	2,077	4,232
1990	2,600	265	2,335	1,897
1991	1,950	36	1,914	(17)
1992	–	17	(17)	
	13,000	3,000	10,000	

Table 16.6 Lessor's profit and loss account of lease in Table 16.1 (using AMAT)

Year to 30 June	1987 £	1988 £	1989 £	1990 £	1991 £	1992 £	1993 £	Total £
Rentals	650	2,600	2,600	2,600	2,600	1,950	–	13,000
Less: Capital repayments	344	1,525	1,822	2,077	2,335	1,914	(17)	(10,000)
Gross earnings	306	1,075	778	523	265	36	17	3,000
Interest	234	822	594	399	203	24	12	2,288
Profit before tax	72	253	184	124	62	12	5	712
Current tax	729	34	(210)	(401)	(562)	156	4	(250)
Deferred tax	801	287	(26)	(277)	(500)	168	9	462
	754	122	145	358	540	161	6	–
Net profit	47	165	119	81	40	7	3	462
Average net cash investment	9,631	8,463	6,119	4,112	2,103	315	117	
After-tax yield	1.95	1.95	1.94	1.97	1.90	2.22	2.56	

Consequently, under IPM, interest received is recognized in the profit and loss account only as and when it is received. In comparison, AMAT recognizes that interest received on reinvested funds is an integral part of the lessor's overall profit from the lease. Under AMAT the total after-tax profit (including interest received) is recognized over the investment period in proportion to the net cash investment outstanding. This means that AMAT recognizes a sum in excess of the total gross earnings during the investment period of the lease, and negative gross earnings during the reinvestment period. These negative gross earnings should then offset the actual interest received to give an overall neutral effect on the profit and loss account during the reinvestment period.

For some time the accounting debate within the industry centred around the treatment of reinvestment income. Advocates of IPM argued that accounting prudence dictated that reinvested earnings should only be recognized as and when received. Supporters of AMAT claimed that it bore a closer relationship to the way that lessors funded and evaluated their leases and that failure to recognize reinvestment earnings would, in some instances, lead to losses being recognized in the early periods of leases that were profitable overall. Since leases that generate sufficient tax deferral effects to create significant reinvestment earnings are now less common, the differences between AMAT and IPM are less pronounced.

PRACTICAL PROBLEMS OF APPLYING IPM AND AMAT
It is important to remember that the apportionment of gross earnings under either IPM or AMAT will only be as valid as the assumptions on which the lease cash flow forecast is based. Lessors should therefore review their cash flow assumptions regularly and provide against any potential losses or major uncertainties. The principal assumptions are as follows:

1. Tax rates will be as predicted.
2. The anticipated capital allowances will be available in respect of the leased asset.
3. Sufficient taxable capacity will exist to utilize capital allowances in the forecast periods.
4. Borrowing and reinvestment rates will be as predicted.
5. Bad debts from default will not occur.
6. Early settlements will not occur and no other major uncertainties will affect future rental cash flows.
7. Administrative costs after the investment periods will be negligible.

Tax risks
The first three assumptions above relate to tax uncertainties: the first two relate to factors outside the control of the lessor, and the third relates to

the ability to forecast accurately the lessor's tax position. In practice, the profitability of a leasing transaction may well depend on the tax effects of the lease. If the lessor does not obtain the benefit of capital allowances at the dates forecast, the interest costs will increase and may well exceed the expected gross earnings from the lease. Accordingly, many lessors impose tax variation clauses on the lessee that pass some or all of the tax risks to the lessee. Thus, for example, if a change in tax rates occurs, the rentals under the lease will be recalculated in order to protect the lessor's after-tax rate of return. Most of these clauses also work in both directions — that is, any benefits from tax rate reductions are passed on to the lessee through rental reductions.

Where the tax effects of a lease are fundamentally different from those forecast, and the lessor is not fully protected by a tax variation clause, then it will be necessary for the lessor to revise the lease cash flow forecasts and make adequate provision against any potential losses that arise from revised interest estimates.

Funding risks

Interest costs are usually conservatively estimated at the start of the lease, based on the commercial rate or rates which the lessor expects to pay over the lease term. Reinvestment rates on net cash surpluses, where they are included in the lease evaluation, are usually estimated at the projected minimum return. When preparing accounts the lessor will need to review the lease portfolio and determine whether it is necessary to provide against future losses on those leases where the revised future interest costs exceed the remaining gross earnings. Obviously, no such provision will be necessary on those leases where the lessor is protected by an interest rate variation clause, or the lessor has protected his or her interest rate position through the usage of treasury instruments.

Default risk

Lessors should consider the need to make both specific and general provisions for bad debts. Where specific exposures have been identified they should be provided for having regard to the anticipated net proceeds from the realization of the leased asset. Where there is an established pattern of bad debt history, or new circumstances that increase the risk of bad debts, the lessor will also need to make a general provision for anticipated future losses based on loss experience and on the nature of the lease portfolio.

Termination risks and other uncertainties

Both IPM and AMAT accelerate the recognition of gross earnings during the lease term in order that those gross earnings are properly matched against the related funding costs. It is therefore important that the lessor considers the risk that the cash flow forecast, which is used to allocate gross earnings, might prove inaccurate. The lessor will need to consider both those factors that affect the overall profitability and also those that affect the pattern of cash flows. For example, an early settlement exercised under a termination clause not only changes the total rental, tax and interest cash flows that the lessor originally anticipated, but also accelerates those cash flows. Where the effect of IPM or AMAT has been to accelerate the recognition of income, the settlement from the termination clause may not be sufficient to cover the book value of the leased asset. This is because the lessor's original income allocation may have anticipated tax deferrals that will no longer be realized. It is, therefore, important that lessors recognize the risks associated with early termination and provide against probable losses. The level of such provisions would normally be based on past experience and the level of security provided by the termination clauses.

Even where the lessor considers the risk of termination to be small there may, in some circumstances, be justification for restricting the total amount of gross earnings recognized from a lease. This is because under certain types of long leases that have significant tax deferral effects, the total amount of gross earnings recognized under IPM or AMAT in the early periods of the lease can actually exceed the rentals receivable to date — an effect known as 'negative depreciation'. Many lessors consider that they should not recognize a profit that is attributable to 'negative depreciation' because it would mean recognizing rentals before they were due. The profitability of long-term leases may well depend on a range of future uncertainties such as future interest rates, tax rates, the basis of taxation and factors that could affect default and termination risks such as a change in general economic conditions. Accordingly, under both AMAT and IPM, some lessors restrict the amount of gross earnings that they recognize to date to the amount of rentals receivable to date, or, if this creates an accounting loss, to an amount sufficient to cover their funding costs. This approach has the advantage of being both prudent and simple to apply. Other lessors take the view that there are no theoretical objections to negative depreciation provided that sufficient provisions are made against the possibility of future defaults and terminations.

The impact of 'negative depreciation' is perhaps less important today than it was in the period 1972–84 when the general availability of 100 per cent first-year allowances for plant and machinery had a dramatic effect on lessors' funding requirements and therefore on the pattern of income recognition. Nevertheless, negative depreciation can still arise today in certain circumstances and lessors therefore need to decide how they intend to deal with it. Whichever policy a lessor adopts towards negative depreciation it should be applied consistently from year to year.

ADMINISTRATION COSTS

Both IPM and AMAT are based on the assumption that administration costs after the investment period will be negligible. Where the tax deferral effects of a lease are significant, the investment period of a lease may well be considerably shorter than the lease term. In these circumstances, all the gross earnings, and in the case of AMAT reinvestment earnings as well, will be recognized during the investment period leaving no gross earnings from the lease to cover the administration costs of collecting rentals during the reinvestment period. Consequently, where administration costs during the reinvestment period are expected to be significant, sufficient income from the lease should be deferred to cover these costs.

Income recognition: operating leases

It is important to draw a distinction between the accounting definition of an operating lease and of the operating lessor. An operating lease is defined for accounting purposes in SSAP 21 as a lease other than a finance lease. The definition of an operating lease therefore covers a host of different types of leases where the lessee has not acquired substantially all of the risks and rewards of ownership of the leased asset. It also follows that if the lessee has not acquired substantially all the risks and rewards of ownership, then the lessor must have retained a significant proportion of these risks and rewards. The retention of these risks is usually quantifiable in terms of the present value test, which indirectly measures the lessor's residual investment not recoverable under the lease agreement.

The term 'operating lessor' is usually used in a more general sense within the leasing industry to describe those lessors who provide a specialist range of leasing services to customers. These lessors are specialists in the assets they lease and their profits depend as much on their buying and selling skills and on the additional services they provide as on their leasing activities. In particular, an operating lessor's profitability depends upon his or her ability to predict accurately future residual values and to re-lease or sell the asset at the end of the lease term. The amount of residual exposure the lessor takes will vary according to the nature of the industry and to the type of business written. Such residual exposure may also vary across a lease portfolio. For example, it is not uncommon in the computer leasing sector for such a lessor to write a mixture of both short and long leases with varying residual exposure. Some of these leases may well have little residual exposure and would be classified for accounting purposes as finance leases, whereas other leases with significant residual exposure would be classified as operating leases. Because the accounting treatment of operating leases is quite different from that of finance leases, it is very important that such lessors classify their leases correctly.

The methods of income recognition that SSAP 21 requires for operating leases are based on a very simple accounting principle. The service that the lessor provides to the lessee is the use of the asset for a limited period of time. The method of recognizing rental income should consequently reflect the amount of service provided. SSAP 21 therefore requires that rental income from an operating lease (excluding charges for services such as maintenance and insurance) should be recognized on a straight-line basis over the period of the lease, even if the payments are not made on such a basis. An exception is made, however, where another systematic basis is more representative of the time pattern in which the lessor receives the benefit of the leased asset. No examples of such alternative bases are given in the standard or guidance notes, but such a basis might be appropriate where the rental structure is non-linear and properly reflects the anticipated time pattern of depreciation charges. In these circumstances both the method of income recognition and the method of charging depreciation should be properly matched and should reflect the economic reality.

The guidance notes to SSAP 21 concentrate almost exclusively on the accounting aspects of full-payout finance leases. This is perhaps because the concepts involved in accounting for finance leases are more complex than those for operating leases, and apply across the whole leasing sector. In contrast, accounting for operating leases can create as many practical difficulties as finance leasing, but the problems are more specific to the industries concerned. A good example of these practical difficulties is the accounting treatment of residual interests and obligations by computer lessors.

RESIDUAL VALUES

Generally, in quoting a lease rate to a customer, an operating lessor will need to take into account the estimated costs and profit margin. Two of the key elements in the cost structure of the lease will be anticipated depreciation and costs of finance. The costs of finance can usually be determined reasonably accurately; the depreciation charge will depend on an estimate of the anticipated value of the leased asset at the end of the lease term — the residual value. Should the lessor's residual value estimate prove too optimistic, the lessor's anticipated profit will be reduced and, indeed, losses could be realized. Should the lessor's estimate prove excessively conservative, the resulting rentals may be so high that potential customers are lost.

The importance of residual values can best be illustrated by reference to the disastrous failure in 1979 of Itel, a US computer-leasing company, and more recently the failure of Atlantic Computers plc, to which more detailed reference is made in Chapter 24. These examples clearly illustrate

227

the risk and uncertainty of operating leasing and the need to take a conservative view in accounting for residual values.

Accounting for residuals under an operating lease

The accounting treatment for a normal operating lease is straightforward. Rentals are recognized on a straight-line basis over the lease term. The depreciable amount is calculated as the difference between the cost of the asset and a conservative estimate of residual value and is allocated over the lease term — usually on a straight-line basis. Interest costs are recognized as incurred. Thus, the residual value estimate has an important effect on the amount of profit that is recognized for accounting purposes during the lease term.

It could be argued that residual values in an industry such as the computer industry are uncertain and therefore should not be considered for accounting purposes. This attitude has the advantage of being prudent but does not necessarily present a fair view. Many short-term computer leases would show losses if residuals were totally ignored, yet residual values are more easy to predict over the short term than over the long term. Most of the major computer lessors therefore recognize residual values in their accounts, but adopt a prudent approach to their valuation. In addition, it is normal practice to review residual value estimates at periodic intervals (for example, on a quarterly or half yearly basis) and, where necessary, to adjust depreciation rates and to provide against future losses that arise as a result of a deterioration in residual values forecast since the original accounting estimates were made.

Accounting for residual interests

The accounting treatment for operating leases described above is suitable for most simple operating lease arrangements. However, many of the arrangements that computer lessors enter into are more complex. For example, it is quite common in the computer industry for the specialist lessor to arrange and manage a lease between a third-party financing institution and their customer. Normally the financing institution has no recourse to the lessor in the event of default by the customer, but the lessor retains an interest in the residual value of the leased asset at the end of the lease term. There are a variety of different legal structures for achieving this result. The lessor may sell the equipment to the financing institution with an irrevocable option or commitment to repurchase; or the lessor may enter into a back-to back leasing arrangement with the financing institution under which the payment of rentals to the financing institution is conditional on the receipt of the sub-lease rentals — a 'non-recourse' arrangement.

SSAP 21 itself provides no guidance on how to account for these types of transaction although it does allow a manufacturer/dealer to recognize a
228

normal 'sales profit' from a finance lease (but not an operating lease). Paragraph 45 of the standard states:

> A manufacturer or dealer lessor should not recognize a selling profit under an operating lease. The selling profit under a finance lease should be restricted to the excess of the fair value of the asset over the manufacturer's or dealer's cost . . .

Thus a manufacturer/dealer can recognize a sales profit from a selling activity and a leasing profit from a leasing activity. However, the sales profit arises from the transfer of risks and rewards of ownership to the lessee, as occurs under a finance lease. An operating lease does not transfer the risks and rewards of ownership to the lessee and consequently no sales profit may be recognized.

Some lessors, however, have sought to interpret this sales profit from their dealing activities in a wider sense to relate to their lease-broking activities. By substituting the sum of the present value of rentals and the present value of the residual (calculated using the funding rate for discounting the rentals) as a proxy for 'fair value' they calculate a sales profit from their dealing activities that may well exceed the normal retail sales margin from selling the computer. This method can best be described as aggressive in the way profit is recognized.

A feature of this method is to treat the monies received from sale of the equipment to the financing institution as the sale proceeds for the rentals rather than as finance secured on the sublease rentals. Consequently, the leased assets and head lease liabilities are therefore not reflected on the lessor's balance sheet. The present value of the residual is recognized as residual income at the start of the lease and the discount between the future residual value and the present value of the residual is recognized as income over the lease term by a process known as 'accretion'. The method is best illustrated by an example based on the following information given in Tables 16.7 and 16.8.

The first matter to note from this example is that if the present value of the rentals is calculated at the discount rate received on the sale of rentals

Table 16.7 Example of operating lease with a residual value

Term	3 years
Annual rentals in advance	£171,403
Cost of the asset	£500,000
Directors' estimate of residual	£115,403
Implicit rate in the lease	20% p.a.
Present value of rentals sold to bank	£450,000
Discount rate on bank financing	15% p.a.
Present value of residual at 15%	£75,879
Present value of residual at 20%	£66,784

Table 16.8 Example of method of taking sales profits of lease in Table 16.7

	Year 1 £	Year 2 £	Year 3 £
Sale proceeds	450,000		
Residual income	75,879		
	525,879		
Cost of sales	500,000		
Gross profit	25,879		
Accretion (straight-line)	13,175	13,175	13,174
Total profit	39,054	13,175	13,174
Book value of residual at year-end	89,054	102,229	115,403

Note: Accretion is simply the method of spreading the discount between the present value of the residual (£75,879) and the future value (£115,403) over the lease term. In this example, a straight-line approach has been adopted.

to the bank (15 per cent) they represent 90 per cent of the asset's cost. On this basis some lessors treat such a lease as a finance lease, although strictly if the implicit rate (20 per cent) was used for the present value calculation (as is required by SSAP 21) the present value would be less than 90 per cent. It is therefore debatable whether a financial lease treatment is appropriate and whether sales profit should be recognized at all.

There are also a variety of ways of applying the above approach, which range in the amount of conservatism that is applied to the recognition of front-end profit. For example, because the residual value is subject to a degree of uncertainty the amount of residual recognized in the calculation of residual income might be restricted to a safe or conservative estimate (say 80 per cent of the directors' expected value) which would give a lower amount of residual income (£60,703) at the start of the lease. The 20 per cent contingency built into the residual value could then either be allowed to emerge as a 'back end' profit at the end of the lease agreement, or be accreted over the lease term. Alternatively, a higher discount might be applied in calculating the present value of the residual, which reflects the risk in the residual value.

However, all these variations do not strictly accord with the requirements of SSAP 21 to restrict sales profit to the excess of fair value over cost, where fair value is defined in the standard as the price at which the asset could be exchanged in an arm's length transaction. It might be argued that the requirements of SSAP 21 do not deal with these types of complex arrangements and the method adopted reflects their economic substance. Some very broad guidance is given in the guidance notes on the treatment of back-to-back leases, which gives at least some support for such a view. The guidance notes state that back-to-back leases and other three-party arrangements should reflect the 'substance' of the arrangements:

> If the intermediate party (the lessor) is in substance that of a broker or agent for the transaction between the original lessor (the financial institution) and the ultimate lessee (the customer) such that there is no recourse to the intermediate party in the event of default, then the intermediate party should not include the asset or obligation in the balance sheet and should account for any income due to him on a systematic and rational basis.

There are, of course, differing interpretations of the commercial effect of such complex transactions. One view is that where the lessor retains an interest in the residual value of the leased asset, but has no credit risk or further interest in the rental stream, then the substance of the arrangement could be regarded as a part disposal of the leased asset to the financial institution. An initial gross profit is therefore recognized on the 'sale', representing the difference between the present value of the rentals (that is, the amount received from the financing institution for the rights to the rentals) and the proportion of the cost of the asset sold.

Under this basis the residual value will be reflected in the balance sheet at its present value less the proportion of the expected profit from the transaction which relates to the residual. The present value of the residual would be adjusted at the end of each period during the lease by releasing interest income to the profit and loss account on a constant yield basis. This income would offset any financing costs that were incurred to fund the lessor's residual interest, and would therefore have a broadly neutral effect on the profit and loss account during the lease term. At the end of the lease term the residual would effectively be reflected at cost and the remaining proportion of expected profit would be recognized on the sale of the asset.

The difficulty with this approach is in determining the split of the expected profit between the finance-broking transaction and the eventual sale of the residual. One method is simply to use the ratio of the present value of the rentals to the present value of the rentals plus the present value of the future residual, as illustrated in Table 16.9.

There are two criticisms of this method. The first is whether a non-recourse financing arrangement is indeed 'in substance' a part sale of the original asset or whether it is in reality a source of secured finance for the lessor. These very different alternative explanations give very different balance sheet and profit and loss treatments. This is by no means a simple issue to resolve. ED 49 'Reflecting the substance of transactions in assets and liabilities' provides some guidance on how to interpret complex transactions. ED 49 states that the absence of recourse is not by itself a reason for omitting assets and liabilities from the balance sheet if it is

Table 16.9 Method of taking profit on part sale

	Year 1 £	Year 2 £	Year 3 £
Sale proceeds	450,000		
Cost of sale[1]	427,855		
	22,145		
Accretion[2] (yield basis)	10,822	12,445	14,312
Total profit	32,967	12,445	14,312
Book value of residual at year-end	82,967	95,412	109,724

Notes:
1. The cost of sale is determined by the ratio of the present value of rentals to the deemed fair value (present value of rentals plus present value of residual):

$$\text{Cost of sale} = \frac{£500,000 \times £450,000}{£450,000 + £75,879} = £427,855$$

The book value of the residual at the start of the lease is £72,145 and represents the original cost (£500,000) less the cost of the rentals sold (£427,855).
2. Accretion represents a 15 per cent yield each year on the opening book value of the residual. Accretion in year 1 is £10,822 (representing a 15 per cent return on £75,145).

judged that such an asset exists. Thus, it is a question of whether the lessor's asset is in reality the equipment or simply the future right to the equipment. ED 49 gives a considerable amount of guidance in its application notes to factoring arrangements and subparticipation arrangements that have some similarities to these types of transactions. In particular, ED 49 highlights the need to determine who bears the 'slow paying' risk in order to determine whether the seller has a continuing interest in the receivables 'sold' to the financing institution. Where the lessor has a continuing interest in the rental stream the proceeds should be treated as a source of finance and not as a sale of the asset.

The second criticism of this approach is that a simple pro-rata apportionment of the total expected profit between the broking element and the residual element may well prove to be an unfair allocation of profit. In practice, because an operating lease involves residual risk the lessor's yield will reflect a premium for that risk over and above that required from a finance lease to the same lessee. Thus, while a lessor may eliminate the credit risk by selling the rental stream, the higher residual risk remains until the end of the lease term and the asset is realized. Perhaps a fairer way of determining the amount of broking profit that the lessor could reasonably recognize might be to consider the normal broking profit an intermediary might earn on broking pure receivables. For example, if the intermediary could raise finance at a 1.0 per cent lower margin than the
232

lessee, then the broking profit would be the difference in discounting the rentals by, say, 15 and 16 per cent — £4,510. On this basis, the 'broking' argument is unlikely to give justification to the recognition of substantial 'front end' profit recognition and the pro-rata method may well recognize profit too aggressively.

Both these methods are progressive in the way they recognize income in the first year of the lease and for this reason have attracted considerable controversy. There are obviously simpler ways of recognizing profit. For example, front-end profits on broking transactions could be restricted to 'cash' profit (the difference between the present value of the rentals as discounted by the bank and cost). This, however, would mean that the amount of broking profit would be dependent on the amount of funds provided by the bank against the rental stream and could lead to devices to increase artificially the amount such as inflated repurchase commitments or guarantees at the end of the lease term.

The wide range of different accounting practices that have been applied to these types of transactions are naturally disturbing, since it is the objective of accounting standards to bring about a degree of consistency and comparability of accounting. However, the wide range of different types of arrangements precludes a prescriptive and mechanical approach to determining the appropriate accounting treatment. The move towards a new standard on 'Reflecting the substance of transactions in assets and liabilities' as set out in the current exposure draft, ED 49, at least goes some way towards showing how the substance of a transaction might be analysed.

In recent years, as a result of adverse criticism of some of the more progressive methods of recognizing residual income, there has been a move to change to more conservative methods of recognizing income, even to the extent of ignoring residual values until realized.

Irrespective of the type of transaction or treatment of residual adopted, it is important that the directors value the future residuals conservatively, taking into account market trends, future uncertainties and remarketing costs. It is also important that they give adequate disclosure of their accounting policies and additional information on residual risk exposures. For example, some computer-leasing companies give a comparison of book values against published International Data Corporation (IDC) values. Some lessors go further by giving additional information on residuals by asset type and maturity, and such additional voluntary disclosure should be encouraged.

Residual liabilities

A further issue that arises in these type of transactions where the lease receivables are sold to a financial institution is the treatment of contingencies arising from the residual. For example, the lessor may sell the asset to

233

a financial institution at an amount in excess of the present value of the rentals and be liable to the bank for the residual value of the equipment under repurchase arrangements or residual guarantees. Alternatively, the lessor may have given an undertaking to the lessee to take over the lessee's remaining rentals payable to the financial institution under certain clauses or conditions of the lease. In these circumstances, although the lessor will have sold the asset subject to the rental stream to a financial institution, significant risks will still remain. This gives rise to a number of difficult accounting issues.

The first issue is whether the sale of the leased asset to a financial institution is indeed a genuine sale or simply a means of funding the receivables of the lessor. If the transaction is treated as a sale, profits will be recognized immediately, whereas if it is not treated as a sale, profits will be spread over the lease term.

The second issue is whether the commitments given under guarantees, exchange agreements and buy-back arrangements expose the lessor to the risk of potential future losses. Where there are significant risks the nature and amount of such contingencies should be disclosed in the lessor's financial statements. Where losses are probable, provision should obviously be made.

Disclosure requirements

Balance sheet disclosures

Prior to SSAP 21, most lessors treated leased assets as fixed assets for accounts purposes and showed them in the balance sheet at cost less accumulated depreciation. This treatment was based on the fact that the lessor had legal title to the assets, and that the basis was consistent with the tax treatment of the assets. Under SSAP 21, the balance sheet treatment of leased assets now depends on whether they are leased on finance or operating leases.

SSAP 21 requires that the lessor shows net investment in finance leases and hire-purchase contracts as receivables, and shows the amounts in respect of each separately. Unless the lessor is an authorized institution, it will also be necessary to comply with the requirements of Schedule 4 of the Companies Act 1985. This means that the lessor will need to include the amounts receivable in respect of finance leases and hire-purchase contracts in current assets under the heading 'Debtors', and these amounts will need to be analysed between amounts receivable within one year and those amounts receivable thereafter.

Unlike the US accounting standard FAS 13, SSAP 21 does not require an analysis of the net investment in finance leases. For example, FAS 13 requires disclosure of details of future minimum lease payments, amounts representing executory costs, bad debt provisions, unguaranteed residual values and unearned income. FAS 13 also requires an analysis of the minimum lease payments for each of five succeeding years after the balance sheet date and more profit and loss information concerning initial direct costs and contingent rentals. The disclosure requirements of SSAP 21 are therefore much simpler than those of its US counterpart. There is, however, an overriding requirement in the UK that accounts must show a true and fair view. This means that if additional information is of such relevance to the users of financial statements that it affects their overall understanding of the accounts, then such information should be disclosed.

The balance sheet disclosure of assets held for use in operating leases under SSAP 21 is similar to that required for other fixed assets. The standard requires that the gross amount (the original cost or valuation) and the accumulated depreciation of assets held under operating leases should be disclosed. This information could be contained in an additional column in the normal balance sheet note for fixed assets, or shown as a separate note. Banks, however, should not combine information about assets held for use under operating leases with other infrastructure assets (for example, own premises), as they are distinctly different for determining capital adequacy.

TURNOVER AND ACTIVITY

Lessors other than authorized institutions will need to comply with the disclosure requirements of Schedule 4 of the Companies Act 1985. This schedule requires *inter alia* that companies should disclose 'turnover'. The guidance notes to SSAP 21 explain how this provision should be interpreted in the context of a lessor.

In the case of operating leases, a lessor should disclose rentals receivable in the accounting period as turnover. For finance leases, a lessor will need to disclose 'gross earnings' as turnover. This is because the activity of a finance lessor is analogous to a lending activity, and a lessor's gross earnings is analogous to 'interest receivable'. Schedule 4 of the Companies Act 1985 also requires the directors to adapt the headings used in the accounting formats in any case where the special nature of the business requires such adaption. The term 'gross earnings' can therefore be substituted for 'turnover' in order to make the profit and loss account disclosure more meaningful.

Also, in respect of finance leases, SSAP 21 requires certain additional information about the lessor's activities. The lessor should disclose the amount of rentals receivable under finance leases and the cost of assets acquired for letting under such leases. Thus the accounts of a finance lessor must show not one but three different bases of activity: gross earnings, rentals receivable and new business acquired.

Accounting policies

Both SSAP 21 and SSAP 2 ('Disclosure of accounting policies') require lessors to disclose their policies in respect of finance and operating leases. In particular, the standards place emphasis on the detailed disclosure of the policy adopted for the recognition of income from finance leases. Thus, the policy might disclose not only the basic method of income recognition (such as IPM or AMAT), but also the treatment of other significant factors such as initial direct costs, residual values, government grants and tax rate changes.

ACCOUNTING FOR TAX

Deferred taxation

Significant timing differences will usually arise between a lessor's accounting profits and taxable profits due to the effects of capital allowances and depreciation. SSAP 15, 'Accounting for deferred tax', requires all companies to provide deferred tax on the liability method to the extent that a liability is expected to crystallize in the future. Most industrial companies can forecast their future capital allowances reasonably well, because their capital expenditure plans are within their control. However, the lessor's task is more difficult because it involves forecasting his or her future level of leasing activity. Lessors also face other risks. For example, future tax rate reductions might trigger rental rebate payments to lessees. For these reasons, lessors should adopt conservative assumptions in their forecast of deferred tax reversals and provide prudently.

Tax effects of regional development grants

Where the leased asset is eligible for a regional development grant, the grant will have a significant effect on the overall profitability of the transaction. The normal accounting treatment for regional development grants is to spread the benefit of the grant over the lease term as part of IPM or AMAT calculations. However, there can also be unusual tax effects.

One of the side effects of such leases is that they sometimes show a pre-tax loss although in after-tax terms they are profitable. This arises because the tax benefits from the lease are usually passed on to the lessee by way of reduced rentals, even to the extent that the aggregate rentals receivable are below the net cost of the asset. These tax benefits arise because the grant is tax free and the lessor obtains capital allowances on the full gross cost of the asset before deduction of the grant.

Many lessors consider that to show a pre-tax loss on a lease that is profitable at the after-tax level gives a distorted view of their performance. Accordingly, they adopt an accounting policy of grossing-up the regional development grant credited to income by an amount of notional tax, and include the notional tax in the tax charge for the year. In this way a normal pre-tax profit and normal tax charge are shown. SSAP 21 permits this practice of grossing-up, but where it is adopted the lessor is required to disclose the amount by which the profit before tax and the tax charge have been increased as a result of the treatment.

17. *Residual value insurance*

Residual value insurance (RVI) was first conceived and developed in the mid-1970s. However, it had an unfortunate start with the introduction of insurance directed towards the support of IBM mainframe computers and certain peripheral equipment. This type of insurance was widely used by lessors in Europe and in the United States. Substantial reductions in the second-hand value of IBM equipment, particularly the 360 range, caused a large number of claims. The underwriters lost many millions of dollars and the residual value insurance market lost credibility for a time. It should be said that most residual value insurance schemes so far designed have been aimed at achieving off-balance sheet accounting treatment either for lessee or lessor — thus the use of the word 'insurance' may be somewhat misleading. The insurance approach was originally taken because of its flexible structure in syndicating capacity through the reinsurance 'treaty' method where numerous reinsurers commit to a chosen share of all business underwritten by a primary underwriter, whose judgement is unconditionally accepted by treaty reinsurers.

Insurance coverage

The purpose of RVI (also known as asset value insurance) is to indemnify the owner or lessor of an asset against loss resulting from the difference between a pre-agreed minimum future value and the actual value at a specific future date, as determined by a professional appraisal of fair market value. A policy can offer claims settlements based on the net sale value of the asset after deduction of broker's commission. This 'sale proceeds' method can have several drawbacks; one problem being that the asset must be sold, whereas there are a number of reasons why a lessor might purchase the insurance for a future date which, in the event, could turn out to represent only the half-way stage in a lease. This would be the situation if, for example, a 'walkaway' option was not exercised by the lessee and which may have been built into the lease to give it an 'operating lease' flavour.

If the insurance is not called upon by way of claim on the specified future date, it lapses. There is normally no interim date on which a claim can be made and only the elimination of the asset, such as a total loss in an accident, can otherwise void the insurance cover.

The aim of the insurance is usually to take residual risk and not credit risk. Providing cover at only one point in time is one way in which an insurer can minimize the risk. Certain insurers, however, are willing to take a view on residuals for specific types of equipment; for example, residual-backed insurance is sometimes available for printing companies, who often have little net worth but operate equipment that is more likely to attract a strong residual value.

RETURN CONDITIONS

It is not intended that the insurers should have to concern themselves with care and maintenance of a leased asset. At the time a claim is made, the asset must be of a specific, minimum standard, as defined in the insurance policy. For the purpose of assessing a claim, an independent appraiser will assume that the policy conditions with regard to maintenance standards have been met and will ignore any lower value that a lesser level of condition would attract, e.g. if engines on an aircraft have zero hours left until the next major overhaul, the appraiser would normally treat them as though they had a minimum of 'half time' remaining. The difference in such a case would otherwise amount to as much as 5–10 per cent of the aircraft value.

ASSET TYPES

RVI is suitable only for assets that are not susceptible to obsolescence. It could reasonably be argued that satellitic transponders, for example, would not be a good subject for a future asset value commitment. Assets that are subject to cyclical rises and falls in value with a tendency to a long working life are most suitable. Vehicles are not necessarily a good subject due to their rather predictable residual expectancy. Lessors often do not feel the same need for risk transfer on them as they might with aircraft or ships although they may wish to pass layers of contingent liability on to a third party balance sheet.

In general, transportation equipment has proved itself more viable than most other asset types for consideration by insurers. Some ships have proved to be worth only scrap value but RVI can provide a minimum scrap metal future value. There are, however, certain ships that could be insured at sensible levels providing an underwriter can be found who has sufficient marine financing expertise.

UNDERWRITING APPROACH

Most modern assets with a long life are, theoretically, suitable for RVI. Underwriters, however, cannot be expert in the intricacies of differing market trends of ships, containers, trucks, trailers, printing equipment, aircraft, construction equipment and cannisters. For this reason a view is sought from independent experts in each field, although appraisers are not always willing to make forecasts, and this is particularly true outside the USA. Furthermore, since appraisers cannot be found for all equipment types and the quality, background and reliability of any forecast is subject to many unpredictable influences, underwriters must nevertheless be guided by independent forecasts whenever available. They normally seek a constant currency (uninflated) probable future value, fixing a lower possible future value — which might be termed 'distress' value — to reflect a forced sale in a poor market. A distress value for an aircraft, for example, would cover an airline being forced out of business through high fixed costs and lack of passenger demand and returning, say, four 727–200s to a lessor at a time when oil prices have risen substantially.

The underwriter tends to look at the correlation between probable and distress value and decides what level of distress value to insure (see Figure 17.1). Normally the figure will fall between 70 and 110 per cent of the 'distress' figure.

The level of insurance made available or the offer of a quotation is influenced by various factors. The underwriters have to consider the spread of existing business. They need to create self-imposed limits on the number and types of asset to which they will expose their companies at any future date. The age of the asset at the termination date may affect an

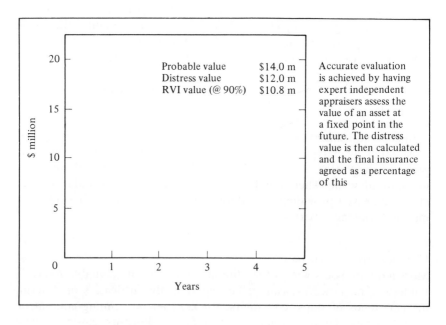

Figure 17.1 Calculating the residual value of an asset

underwriter's judgement and affect the degree of caution exercised. For example, appraisers the world over may say that a nine-year-old aircraft will be worth $15 million in constant dollars in 10 years time with a distress value of $10.5 million. The problem is that the model would be 19 years old at that time and there may be new composite materials technology that would affect the viability of the particular model. The underwriters would look at their spread of aircraft with termination dates in 10 years and their overall commitment to aircraft of that particular model and type. They would then decide whether or not they were prepared to risk residual insurance on a model approaching 20 years of age. If so, they may quote a lower percentage of distress value than if the aircraft were newer. They may even decide they have too much overall risk on the model type and refuse to tender a quotation at all.

In the case of an aircraft, the appraisers' forecasts will be affected by the type of power plant on the aircraft. If engines with a higher thrust are powering the model, this may be a positive factor. If only two airlines out of 50 ordered engines from one particular manufacturer, these aircraft may have a considerably lower market attraction than those with the other 48 airlines.

An underwriter may have personal views irrespective of the appraisers' forecasts. In the early 1980s one new technology aircraft was not attracting the orders that it subsequently achieved. Possibly it was in advance of its time. The major RVI underwriters were nevertheless taking a more optimistic stance with this model than with other new models of the period. They had apparently made up their own minds about its likely success in the future.

The most difficult aspect of an RVI underwriter's job is keeping the underwriting consistent. If an aircraft had a fair market value of $20 million five years ago, for example, and a quotation was given for $10.5 million in eight years, the underwriter will know that a quotation today for three years hence should probably be close to the $10.5 million previous figure, even if the model enjoys a vastly increased current fair market value. It goes without saying that underwriting income will, to some extent, be subject to fluctuations which closely follow cycles in aircraft values.

Cost of residual value insurance

A claim that the relative cost of RVI is too high is more often than not based on a misunderstanding of its intended purpose. The 'add-on' cost to the annual rate of interest in the leasing transaction is usually a relatively small fraction, based on an average upfront premium of between 0.5 and 2.5 per cent of the equipment cost depending on individual requirements.

Case studies

CASE STUDY 17.1

An airline wished to re-finance a seven-year-old Boeing 737–200 Advanced with JT8D–15 engines. It wanted the option to upgrade to a new-generation aircraft type when it became available in eight years, by which time the 737 would still be only 15 years old. A bid was obtained from a major Japanese trading house at the highly competitive rate of 90 basis points below LIBOR. On the basis of US$12,750,000 per aircraft, there would have been a requirement for 32 quarterly rentals of US$511,196 over the eight-year lease.

However, an alternative bidder, who included an insured residual of US$3,950,000, was able to quote a lower quarterly rental of US$449,700, which included total premium of US$217,250 financed over the 32 quarters and was still able to increase the yield by 100 basis points. This structure saved the airline US$61,496 per quarter. Significantly, the increase in the annual rate of interest resulting from the inclusion of RVI was only 41 basis points.

Although this demonstrates one use of RVI, it is somewhat simplistic in that it does not address the sharing of sales proceeds that may have been available with the first lessor. Some jurisdictions allow sharing and some do not.

CASE STUDY 17.2

A finance company wished to offer to an airline a sale and lease back arrangement on an 11-year-old wide body aircraft. The agreed purchase price was $20 million and the lessor would lease the aircraft back to the airline for eight years. Assuming the aircraft had depreciated to a book value of $1 million, and that the lease the airline has is an operating lease, the airline would show a $19 million profit on the sale.

There are three ways in which the airline could have leased back the aircraft.

1. Full payout lease:
   $20m fair market value
   Assume 8-year lease, 12 per cent annual fixed
   interest 96 monthly payments of $321,838

2. Lease with insured residual of $10.5m:
   RVI for $10.5m in eight years at cost of
   5.25 per cent
   For total premium of $551,250 loaded onto
   financed value.

Financed value	$20,551,250
Deduct PV of RVI discounted at 12 per cent	
per annum over 96 months	$4,039,591
Amount to be amortized	$16,511,659
96 monthly payments of	$265,704
Monthly cash flow benefit of	$56,134
(See Notes below)	

3. Lease with residual risk falling on the lessor:

Financed value	$20,000,000
Self-assumed residual risk	$10,500,000
96 monthly payments of	$256,834
Difference per month between example 2 and 3	$8,870
(See Notes below)	

Notes: In example 2 and 3 above, the lessee would have an operating lease and therefore off-balance sheet finance.

In example 2, the RVI element changes the lessor's accounting to that of a finance lease.

In example 3, the lessor will have a $10.5 million residual exposure in respect of what will be an operating lease.

Accounting for leases with RVI (see Chapter 16)

Paragraph 9 of SSAP 21 reads:

> Sometimes, the lessor may receive part of his return in the form of a guarantee from an independent third party, in which case the lease may be a finance lease as far as the lessor is concerned, but not from the lessee's point of view.

The effect of the application of SSAP 21 where there is an independent third party involvement, e.g. in the form of a residual value insurer, can be to alter the lessor's accounting to that of a finance lease and for the lessee to have an operating lease that is therefore off-balance sheet.

An example of this is as follows:

Purchase price	$1,000,000	Interest rate implicit	
Term	5 years	in the lease	15%
Residual value insurance of 15%	$150,000	Residual value	30%
(5% premium: $7,500)			
Annual rental with RVI	$220,713		

PV of rentals at 15%	$850,846 ⎫ $1,000,000
PV of residual at 15%	149,154 ⎭

LESSOR:	PV of rentals	$850,846	
	PV of residual	74,577	
	(Gross 150,000)	925,423	= 92.5% of fair value (finance lease)
LESSEE:	PV of rentals	$850,846	= 85.1% of fair value (operating lease)

The future for RVI

From the early to mid-1980s, changes in tax legislation, notably in the USA, the UK and Australia, removed many of the substantial tax benefits previously enjoyed by airlines and other equipment users and investors. This removal of cross-border and domestic tax subsidies coupled with new, restrictive lease accounting standards in some countries led to the increased use of operating leasing where the full value of the asset is not recoverable during the term of the lease. This encouraged many cautious bankers, the Japanese in particular, to seek a third party asset value guarantor or insurer to cover the outstanding balance, even though at the time aircraft were steadily rising in value and residuals were rising to an all-time peak.

Many conservative funders and lessors knew that, whatever the fluctuations in values, their prime business would always be credit lending and that uncertain residuals should be a contingency of concern only to third parties. Some less cautious bankers chose to 'insure' their own and others' future asset values, sometimes at over-optimistic levels, despite warning signs of excessive equipment supply, strong competition from their rivals in the market and the likelihood of extreme volatility in oil prices which would affect the viability of certain aircraft types.

In a less dramatic entry into the area of residual risk with a view to a longer term bond between insurance and banking, there was a joining together of a new breed of specialist broker expert with experienced and responsible financial institutions prepared to act as underwriters. It is this element of the residual value insurance market that is likely to continue to develop the product with a carefully calculated balance between risk and reward.

The future will bring about opportunities for new kinds of investors wishing to participate in new types of leasing instruments. On the one hand, there will be those institutions and private investors looking for high returns from participation in companies who speculatively purchase equipment for short-term operating leases to others. On the other hand, the more cautious investors will seek means by which to participate in lease transactions where downside risk on asset value will be insured but excess residual profit will remain intact.

Aircraft leases are most likely to continue to take the form of operating leases where speculation in the future value of equipment is an inherent ingredient. Banks and other lessors may well lose their appetite for 24-year leases with small residuals, particularly where the residual is the difference between profit and loss. Those responsible for arranging such leases in the past will have retired long before their lease-funding structures are called into question and it is pure speculation at this time as to whether their residual value judgements will be correct.

Banks and lessors who used residual value insurance, however, will find themselves in the happy position of having limited their liability. There are two major areas of concern which lessors must address before embarking on residual value insurance.

Apart from the usual due diligence required towards the complex wording of insurance policies, the lessor should look carefully at the strength and credit standing of the insurer. As with financial institutions, there are differences and care must be exercised to ensure the most appropriate arrangements.

The second need for caution, particularly in the UK market, is the eligibility of the insurance premiums for tax relief. The question arises as to what is being insured, a potential loss or the repayment of capital. The Inland Revenue in the UK have some reservations as to whether it is the latter.

The concept of spreading risk through the insurance market will, nevertheless, prevail. It is increasingly likely that, when a lessor accepts a residual, all or a part of that liability will be passed on to third parties. The leasing market in the United States already sees a great deal of this secondary market activity.

18. *Capital grants*

Grants for capital expenditure by government and other sources can have a bearing on the decision to lease. In practice, however, grants have been less critical than taxation factors in shaping the use of leasing in the UK.

Where assets are financed by leasing, grant aid may in some cases be payable to lessors, and in others to lessees. All grants schemes can be classified for these purposes into the following categories:

1. Under the legal ownership principle, some types of grant are payable to the lessor and not the lessee.
2. Other types of grant, on the user basis, may be payable to the lessee rather than the lessor.
3. A third category, where the grant administration system cannot readily cope with the leasing finance option, may be unavailable where leasing is used.

In recent years the UK authorities have generally been aware of the role of equipment leasing in structuring the administration of grant schemes. Examples of the third category above, where the grant system itself discriminates against the leasing option, are therefore few. One such — of relatively little importance because of the small amount of funding involved in the scheme — is the Agriculture and Horticulture Development Scheme funded by the European Community.

The principal grant scheme of relevance to leasing in the UK is the regional enterprise grant (REG) system which in April 1988 replaced the former regional developments grants (RDG) scheme. Both these schemes have been restricted to 'development areas' — i.e. designated regions of the UK, with relatively high unemployment.

When 100 per cent first-year allowances on plant and machinery were introduced into the tax system in 1971 (see Chapter 5), they replaced a more widespread scheme of investment grants that had been introduced in 1966, whereby expenditure on industrial buildings and plant had attracted grant aid across the UK. The emphasis of official policy at the time was very much on stimulating capital investment in manufacturing industry, and more generally throughout industry and commerce. When FYAs were substituted for investment grants in 1971, the intention was to restrict Exchequer support to more profitable types of investment. The incentive element in the advantageous tax allowances depended on the recipient being in a taxpaying position, so that government support might depend on capital projects being profitable, or at any rate being undertaken by a profitable enterprise. In effect, however, the use of tax-based leasing by tax-exhausted lessees during the 1970s served to negate this element of the rationale for the tax allowances alternative to grants.

The grant principle reappeared in a more limited form very soon after the ending of investment grants. RDGs were introduced in 1972, with the emphasis still on capital expenditure but with only certain regions of the UK benefiting from the scheme.

By the 1980s the stance of government industrial policy had become less 'interventionist' in general. While government was still concerned to underpin the level of employment in the disadvantaged regions, there was a clear move away from the incentives targeted at capital expenditure. The ending of FYAs in the tax system in 1984–86 was presented by the authorities as a move to eliminate an artificial stimulus for capital projects that might be of relatively low quality in terms of adding to productive capacity. The RDG scheme was itself restricted in scope by various moves in the early 1980s. In 1985 'grant per job' limits were introduced, which tied the grant aid to the creation of new employment opportunities in the assisted projects. Finally, in 1988 the RDG scheme was replaced by REGs, which were no longer specifically capital-related, though they could still be paid in support of certain capital expenditure projects.

Payments of RDG were to lessors rather than to lessees. The authorities often prefer the 'legal ownership' approach since leasing companies, many of which are in the banking sector, are seen as more credit-worthy than lessees in many cases, and might more easily be pursued for refunds of grant where conditions of grant aid have not been complied with. The leasing companies, of course, had to take account of the value of grants in their leasing evaluations, and in the terms offered to lessees, to ensure that leasing would be competitive with alternative financing options where the potential lessee would claim the grant as owner. A particular complication was that RDGs were free of tax in the hands of the recipient, whether the latter were the equipment user or the lessor; while other elements in a lease evaluation would relate to taxable income streams or tax-allowable outgoings.

The benefit of RDG was passed on by lessors to lessees in one of two ways. Either the lessor estimated the time at which the grant would be received, included the payment as part of his or her cash flow, and reduced all the rentals payable by the lessee by an appropriate amount; alternatively, the lessor would wait until the grant was received, and pay a 'grossed up' amount to the lessee at this stage. The latter method could sometimes lead to complications. Because of the nature of the leasing contract, the refund to the lessee had to be classed as a refund of rentals paid. If insufficient rentals had been paid, the full refund could not be made as lessors were advised that the concept of negative rentals might strike at the root of the transaction. Some leases were, therefore, structured so that large amounts of rental were payable at the time, or just before, the refund was made. These arrangements were commonly known as 'grant swap' structures.

When 'grant per job' limits were introduced into RDGs in 1985, the complications were exacerbated because the grant conditions were such that lessors could not take responsibility for compliance. As a result, many leasing companies withdrew from the market in relation to projects eligible for RDG support, and the whole scheme threatened to become discriminatory against the use of the leasing option.

When REGs were introduced in 1988, the Department of Trade and Industry reached agreement with the Equipment Leasing Association for grant payments to be made directly to lessees. This brought them into line with other DTI industrial support schemes, such as regional selective assistance under the Industry Act 1972, where payments had always been made direct to lessees.

Wherever lessees are entitled to claim grant aid direct, their percentage grants are payable not on their lease rental payments but on the cost of the asset as if the lessee were buying outright. This greatly simplifies the grant administration where the leasing option is used. The business asset user can assess the cost of leasing against other options in the knowledge that the choice of financing method will not affect an entitlement to grant aid. With REGs, as with other user-based grant schemes, full payment of grant can be withheld by the authorities until the lessee has paid lease rentals up to the amount of the grant itself.

A further limitation with REGs is that payments to lessees are restricted to the case of finance leases; assets financed by operating leases are not eligible for grant aid, even where they meet all other criteria for support. This restriction is of relatively little significance, however, given that the operating lease structure lends itself most readily to vehicles and other movable plant, which might not be eligible for grant aid in any event.

Increasingly, schemes of grant aid to industry and commerce are coming within the ambit of European Community policies and programmes. The community has in recent years adopted a number of decisions to restrict the scope of national government schemes like REGs and RDGs on competition grounds. At the same time the EC is developing programmes of its own for grant-aiding certain projects on a basis that effectively favours disadvantaged regions but is applied in all EC member states. Some such schemes, as in the agricultural sector, are operated by national government agencies but funded and effectively controlled by EC institutions through the Community Budget. Other grant schemes are directly administered by EC agencies, such as the European Regional Development Fund and the European Social Fund.

Since the beginning of 1990, the Financial Control Directorate of the European Commission has been formulating proposals for the application of EC grant aid schemes to projects financed by leasing. Though some details are still to be finalized, the Commission's proposals at present appear very helpful to leasing. They envisage that grants may be claimed alternatively by lessors or lessees; and that pro-rata grants on a proportion of the cost of an asset might be paid in the case of operating leases. If these proposals are eventually adopted, UK lessors will prefer to encourage direct grant applications by lessees, in order to avoid the complications of bringing the grant factor into lease terms and evaluations.

19. *The leasing contract*

Leasing covers a wide range of financial services, the scope of which is continually growing. Examples include: finance leasing of plant; operating leases with dealer tie-ups, residual value insurance or short-term hire; finance or operating leases of property, ships, and aircraft. These give but a partial picture of the scope covered by leasing or hiring agreements. First-year allowances having largely disappeared since 31 March 1986, a discussion of leasing may again include lease purchase, or hire purchase as it is more accurately described, as in most legal and commercial contexts such an agreement is simply a hiring coupled with an option to purchase.

Agreements drawn to reflect these various commercial arrangements are very different from one another, seeking as they do to achieve totally contrasting commercial purposes. The people who draft charterparties, small unit leases for television rentals, and property financing leases must address widely differing legal, commercial and theoretical considerations. The Equipment Leasing Association has for this very reason resisted the publication of a standard leasing agreement.

It may be surprising, therefore, to discover that the basic core of the terms of all hiring agreements are similar. All leases reflect the need to govern the relationship between the lessor and the lessee: the agreement to hire; payment; who does what; and how the arrangement may be terminated. All the other terms are embellishments of this central core. Additional contractual arrangements may include third party buy-back contracts and maintenance provisions, or terms for funding the lease, say by way of drop-lock option. Additionally, the lease may contain detailed money cost and taxation assumptions. All this is additional to the obvious need for the agreement to reflect the transaction in hand — a charterparty needs to reflect marine matters and an aircraft lease must reflect aviation matters.

While this chapter is primarily concerned with the expressed terms of the lease, the common law and specific statutes imply extensive terms into leasing agreements covering not only the condition and merchantability of leased assets but also the responsibility of the lessor in respect of defective premises and the right of the lessee to quiet possession. These implied terms are concerned with the protection of the lessee whereas the terms expressed in the leasing agreement, being generally drafted by the lessor, are intended to govern the relationship between lessor and lessee in such a way as to protect the lessor's right of ownership of the leased assets and to ensure that the lessor receives the rentals and is protected should the lessee default in carrying out the obligations under the leasing agreement.

In a finance lease, generally nothing further is required of the lessor following the delivery of the leased assets to the lessee save for dealing with possible variations in the rentals. It is almost wholly up to the lessee to carry out the expressed terms. However, this is not the case in other types of lease. In short-term car hiring it is the lessor who is responsible for taxing and maintaining the car; in the hire of a chauffeur-driven car, the lessor provides the driver and, in the time charter of a ship, provides the crew. What terms then, are common to all leases? Many provisions may be included in leasing agreements to reflect the particular transaction contemplated, but the most commonly used contractual obligations are detailed below.

The lessor's agreement to hire

This generally comprises a statement that the lessor agrees to hire the leased assets to the lessee for a particular period or periods of time upon the terms and conditions of the leasing agreement. Finance leases of plant and machinery do not generally deal with delivery of the leased asset to the lessee at the commencement of the hiring but provide that the hiring commences on delivery, leaving the arrangements for delivery to be settled between the lessee and the supplier. In contrast, where the lessor funds the construction of the leased asset the lease contains detailed provisions relating to the period up to and including delivery. During the construction period the lessee is either the bailee of a partially completed leased asset, e.g. a ship, or has with the lessor an enforceable agreement to lease once the leased asset is complete. These agreements also contain terms under which construction, delivery and acceptance are supervised by the lessee; the insolvency of the constructor or lessee and the destruction of the leased asset during construction is also considered.

In law, delivery need not be the physical delivery of the goods. It can be effected by making available a token of possession such as a key to a motor vehicle, or if the leased assets are in possession of a third person by the acknowledgement by that person that the leased assets are held on the hirer's behalf. If, as is common with finance leases, the hirer is already in physical possession of the leased assets when the lease is signed — because, for example, they required construction and/or installation, or the transaction is a sale and leaseback — 'delivery' is completed when the lease is entered into. It is normal in such circumstances for the lessee to sign a delivery note acknowledging that the leased assets are accepted and are in good condition.

Finance lease agreements generally provide that the leased assets are hired to one lessee for an agreed fixed or primary period of hire during which time the lessee will, by payment of the rentals agreed during this period, pay the cost of the leased asset to the lessor together with the profit the lessor expects to make from the transaction. Thereafter it is common for the hiring to continue for a secondary period of hire for the full useful life of the leased assets at a nominal rental. Operating leases may also have a fixed period of hire but there may not be scope for an extension of hire because, for example, a manufacturer's buy-back may have been negotiated. For some types of hire, a fixed term may not be appropriate, for example, in the case of short-term hire of cars or construction equipment.

The lessee's covenants

(a) *To pay rentals*. In a simple finance lease the covenant is a statement of the amount of each of the rentals payable during the primary and secondary periods of hire and whether value added tax is to be added. More sophisticated leases may include provisions for: rental-free periods at the beginning of the primary period when the leased asset may not yet have realized its earnings potential in full; balloon rentals at the end of the primary period intended to be paid out of the sales proceeds of the leased assets; rental variation provisions dealing with the lessor's funding of the lease; money cost variations and variation terms for capital allowances and corporation tax rate changes. Sometimes these variations appear in separate appendices to the leasing agreement.

It is in evaluating the rentals and constructing the rental payment provisions where the commercial inventiveness of the leasing executive comes to the fore and where the skills of maximizing the benefits of cash flow are expressed. This is the area of the leasing agreement that most reflects the creative financing techniques that have led to the growth of leasing.

(b) *To maintain and repair the leased assets*. These are two separate obligations. Sometimes leases will place the obligation to repair the leased asset not with the lessee's covenants but in the insurance clause, thereby reflecting the requirement for the lessee to insure the leased assets, the proceeds of insurance being applied directly to their repair.

It is more common, certainly in finance house leasing agreements, for the repairing covenant to be joined with that obliging the lessee to maintain the leased assets. In certain operating leases, e.g. short-term car rental, television rental and certain computer leases, the lessee will not be obliged to maintain and service the leased assets as this will be the responsibility of the lessor. In some of these cases, e.g. short-term car rental, the responsibility for the condition of the leased asset will remain that of the lessor. However, even if this is the case the lessee will be ultimately responsible for the condition of the leased assets on re-delivery at the end of the hiring by virtue of the lessee's indemnity against the lessor's loss (see (g) below).

The standard of maintenance (and repair) is generally that necessary to ensure that the leased assets may be lawfully, safely and efficiently used during the period of hire and that at the end of the lease they are re-delivered to the lessor in the same condition as at the beginning of the hiring. Some agreements require that on re-delivery the leased assets may be in a condition that is subject to fair wear and tear.

This is intended not only to reflect the wear and tear that must have taken place over the period of hire, but also to ensure that the lessor bears the burden of wear and tear for capital allowance purposes. However, in some cases, such as leases of aircraft, such a provision would be wholly inappropriate, because in order to be lawfully operated the aircraft must be free from time-expired components and not subject to wear and tear.

(c) *To bear the cost of all taxes, expenses and outgoings relating to the leased assets, their operational use and their acquisition whether attributable to the lessor or to the lessee.* This reflects the fact that such expenses would accrue to the lessee if the assets had been bought instead of leased. It is important that the clause should cover all costs, expenses, taxes, customs, duties, stamp duties and rates and that these should be payable in relation to the purchase, construction, use, operation, leasing and dismantling and disposal of the leased assets. In other words, in relation to all aspects of the transaction from inception to disposal.

The covenant should cover not only those taxes with which the lessee would normally be charged as operator of the leased assets, e.g. rates or road fund licences, but also those charged to the lessor as owner, e.g. stamp duty on the acquisition of the leased assets or value added tax on the rentals. Such a covenant is, of course, not intended to, nor does it, cover corporation tax on the profits accruing to the lessor in consequence of the leasing.

(d) *To use the leased assets lawfully, with care and by properly trained and qualified personnel.* This clause is intended to ensure that the leased assets are operated safely by the lessee and that the lessee is made responsible for so doing. While there are circumstances in which the lessor as owner may incur civil and possibly criminal liability for the unlawful or negligent use of the leased assets (e.g. if unexcised fuel is used in leased commercial vehicles), it is primarily the lessee's responsibility to operate the leased assets lawfully and in accordance

253

with the manufacturer's instructions and safely in accordance with the Health and Safety at Work Act 1974.

The requirement for properly trained and qualified personnel is a requirement not only of the Health and Safety at Work Act but is also a separate statutory requirement when, for instance, operating aircraft or ships.

(e) *To insure the leased assets against material damage and for third party risks.* These are separate obligations, though the distinction between the two insurances is often blurred if contained in one clause. It is important that these two obligations are made clear.

In finance leases the lessee insures the leased assets against material damage. The covenant to insure against third party is quite different. If the leased asset should injure a third party then the lessor as owner, as well as the lessee, may be tortiously liable to the third party. The level of third party insurance required by the lease may be of an unlimited amount for, say, motor vehicles or may be fixed by agreement between the lessor and the lessee in other cases.

The provision of insurance is dealt with more fully in Chapter 20. It is, however, important to note that in the case of a mere notification of the lessor's interest on the policy of insurance, such provisions are often unenforceable against the insurers even if acknowledged because there is often no consideration for the variation of an existing insurance contract in this way. The only way the lessor can be certain of obtaining the protection required is to become a joint assured or by a loss payee arrangement direct with the insurer who enters a contract with the lessor. Otherwise the arrangements are not legally binding. The disadvantage of being a joint assured is that the lessor's cover may be affected by the acts and omissions of the lessee (though this may be altered by negotiation with the insurer) and the lessor will be liable for premiums.

(f) *To apply the insurance proceeds to the repair of the leased assets or in reduction of future rentals.* This is the corollary to the obligation to repair the leased assets, if they are capable of repair. If it is not possible to repair them, they are then likely to be regarded by the insurers as a total loss in which case the hiring would come to an end and any shortfall after the insurance proceeds have been applied to the reduction of the future rentals would, under this clause, be required to be made up to the lessor by the lessee. Alternatively, it may be that a total loss does not occur and the leased assets, the subject of the occurrence, are capable of being repaired but not to their former condition and capability, e.g. after repair the machine tool produces less per hour than formerly or the ship cannot sail as quickly as previously. In such circumstances the lessor's assets have been reduced in value and it is necessary to reduce the financial liability of the lessee in respect of those assets. Accordingly, the lease may provide that the leased assets should be repaired from the lessee's own resources, the insurance proceeds being paid to the lessor in reduction of future rentals.

(g) *To indemnify the lessor against any loss incurred as a result of the acquisition, hire and disposal of the leased assets at the end of the lease.* In the case of finance leases of assets costing relatively large amounts this would extend to include an indemnity against loss through a change in the capital allowance system or in the rate of corporation tax.

Finance leasing is intended to be a method of finance whereby the responsibility for the leased assets is placed, as far as possible, upon the lessee. The amount of the rentals is reflective of this. Such leases are not point of sale transactions but concern leased assets specifically selected and purchased by the lessor at the request of the lessee. The indemnity is intended to reflect this and to ensure as far as possible that any liability or loss affecting the lessor as the result of the transaction and any of its constituent parts is passed on to and indemnified by the lessee. An application of this principle is the taxation indemnity clause, which is the means by which the lessor's rate of return is maintained despite variations in corporation tax rates or capital allowances from those assumed. Such provisions are often included separately either in the rentals payment clause or, in multi-million pound leases, in a separate appendix. The lessor's net rate of return is maintained by adjusting the rentals as the hiring continues or by payment of an additional rental or a rebate of rental if the hiring has terminated.

(h) *To keep possession of the leased assets and not to underlet or mortgage them or create any lien over them.* This provision also prohibits assignment and any other form of alienation and is concerned with ensuring that the lessee does not encumber the leased assets so as to create rights over them in favour of a third party to the detriment of the lessor's interest. The lessor wishes to hire to the lessee and not to an unknown third party; nor does the lessor wish third parties to acquire rights over the leased assets or the leasing agreement.

It should be noted that a prohibition against the creation of liens does not conflict with the requirement that the leased assets should be passed to a third party for repair. Delivery to a repairer does not pass legal possession of the leased assets and a repairer's lien will only arise if the repair charge is not met when the bill is tendered.

255

In contrast, the lessor may intend to discount all agreements to a third party, e.g. in television rental agreements. Occasionally, in large-scale finance leases, the lessor may also be obliged to agree to restrict his or her right to alienate any interest in the reversion of the leased assets at the end of the lease because the lessee would not wish to lease from an unknown lessor.

Some finance leases allow the leased assets to be sublet. This is generally the case if, for credit reasons, the leased assets are hired to a holding company rather than to the individual operating company who will actually use the leased assets. The fact is generally recorded in a licence to under-let to which the under-lessee is often a party.

(i) *To ensure that the lessor's rights in the leased assets are not prejudiced by their becoming a fixture.* It is important for the lessor to be satisfied that the leased assets, if plant and machinery, remain in his or her ownership. If they become a fixture then title will automatically pass to the freeholder. As a result, the lessor's rights under the leasing agreement to recover rentals may be affected and the taxation effect of the transaction may also change with the result that the lessor may not be entitled to capital allowances in relation to the leased assets. The provisions of Schedule 17 to the Finance Act 1985 need to be strictly adhered to if the lessor's right to capital allowances is to be preserved (see Chapter 21).

If the leased assets are of a nature that they are likely to become a fixture, then the lessor's ownership of those assets can be protected by means of a landlord's waiver and/or a debenture holder's waiver. These will prevent the relevant third party from assuming rights over the leased assets.

The question of waivers will not, of course, apply if the leased assets are land or buildings.

(j) *To redeliver the leased assets to the lessor at the expiration of the hiring.* All forms of hire agreement, except hire purchase, contain a provision for re-delivery. Large-scale finance leases usually contain detailed provisions relating to the leased assets being kept or stored at the lessee's premises until arrangements have been made for their disposal, whereupon re-delivery will take place at the lessee's premises. In, for example, car leasing, where the lessor is more likely to control the disposal, it is more usual for the lessee to be obliged to re-deliver the leased assets to the lessor's premises.

The lessee's right to terminate the hiring

Leasing agreements sometimes give the lessee the right to terminate the hiring of the leased assets before the end of the primary period of hiring.

This is often subject to the payment by the lessee of the balance of the lessor's financial interest in the leased assets. Such a right to terminate is most common in operating leases, e.g. car leases and television rental agreements, but less so as the size and scale of transactions increase.

The lessor's right to terminate the hiring

All leases contain a termination clause enabling the lessor, in the event of a default in payment or breach of the terms of the lease or insolvency of the lessee, to terminate the hiring and/or repossess the leased assets and/or recover damages for breach. The complexity of such a clause generally increases with the size of the transaction. Operating leases, e.g. of cars, are mainly concerned with the lessor recovering possession of the leased assets and arrears of rentals. Finance leases, which involve the leasing of equipment for which there is no ready second-hand value, often provide stipulated loss values to apply at specified periods during the hiring, e.g. quarterly. These values are agreed measures of liquidated damages reflecting the amount required by the lessor to maintain a net rate of return on the transaction. Most clauses of this type seek to recompense the lessor for any loss on the transaction as a result of the default, and some clauses attempt to follow the judicial guidelines set down in the case of Robophone Facilities Ltd v Blank ((1966) 3 A11 ER 128) where an operating lease provided that upon default the lessee should pay liquidated damages calculated by discounting the rentals (other than arrears) remaining unpaid at the date of termination to reflect their present value.

In contrast, other clauses — even in finance leases of leased assets costing quite substantial sums — are simple and provide primarily for the payment of arrears. These rely upon damages being awarded to the lessor by the courts under the common law should the leasing agreement be repudiated by the lessee failing to make payment under it.

Exclusion clause

A clause excluding the lessor's liability for defects in the leased assets or for their operation is usually included. This will not, of course, cover responsibilities specifically assumed by the lessor, e.g. maintenance, insurance, etc., under some operating leases. A considerable amount of legislation has restricted the ability of a lessor to exclude terms that would otherwise be implied in the agreement. In particular, the Supply of Goods (Implied Terms) Act 1973 (Section 12) and the Supply of Goods and Services Act 1982 (Section 11) provide for the exclusion of implied terms, but these rights are restricted by the Unfair Contract Terms Act 1977 as follows:

257

(a) the exclusion of the implied terms as to title, quiet possession and freedom from encumbrances is void as against a party to a contract who 'deals as consumer' (Unfair Contract Terms Act 1977, Section 12) and is valid only against others if the exclusion satisfies the requirement of reasonableness;

(b) against parties who 'deal as consumer' a term purporting to exclude any of the implied terms as to description of the leased assets, merchantable quality and fitness for purpose is void. Where the lessee does not deal as consumer, these implied terms may be validly excluded only if the exempting term satisfies the test of reasonableness, although liability for death and personal injury may in no circumstance be excluded (Unfair Contract Terms Act, Section 2(1)).

Such exclusions may be reasonable where the lessee selects the leased assets and relies on his own skill and judgement, but where the lease deprives the lessee of his or her rights in respect of the leased assets the court may not consider it reasonable. Schedule 2 of the Unfair Contract Terms Act 1977 sets out guidelines as to how the lessor may show that reliance on the exclusion is reasonable in the circumstances prevailing at the date of the contract.

In an attempt to show the reasonableness of the exclusions, it has become common for the leasing agreement to provide certain benefits to the lessee such as assistance from the lessor to the lessee in prosecuting claims against suppliers.

Title

Every leasing agreement contains a provision that title will always remain with the lessor.

Re-delivery of the leased assets

A finance lease will contain provisions dealing with the disposal of leased assets at the end of the hiring. Often, these appear in a side-letter. In any case, provisions are made to appoint the lessee agent of the lessor to sell the leased assets and for most of the sale proceeds to be rebated to the lessee after the deduction of sale and repairs. Some of the sale proceeds are retained by the lessor to avoid the suggestion that the lessee has received the whole benefit of the leased assets and that the lease agreement is in fact a hire-purchase agreement. These provisions often include detailed terms as to how the lessee is to keep, store, maintain and insure the leased assets while negotiations for sale are progressed.

Other common terms

(a) Formal provisions for the variation of the rentals in accordance with fluctuations in the cost of money.
(b) A clause dealing with the treatment of government grants whether received by the lessor or the lessee.
(c) A clause prescribing the governing law of the agreement and the methods for serving notices, etc.
(d) Additional terms required for leasing agreements to which the Consumer Credit Act 1974 applies (see Chapter 22).

20. *Liberty risks under a lease*

Liability exposure

The areas of 'liability exposure' against which a lessor should obtain protection fall into four categories.

1. Contractual liabilities relating to the leasing contract
The lessor, when in breach of contract with the lessee, may be liable to pay damages or compensation to the lessee. For example, such payments can relate to compensation for loss of life, bodily injury and loss of or damage to property.

Such a situation might arise if, for example, the contract is in respect of an item of equipment of a certain type or quality but the equipment provided was of a different type or quality. The lessee may, fully believing that the equipment was of the type specified, use it for a purpose for which it was not suitable, resulting in damage to property or injury to an employee.

Situations such as this fall under that part of the Supply of Goods and Services Act 1982 which requires that the goods leased conform to description. A lessor who is in breach of contract as a result of the supply of the wrong goods may have recourse against the manufacturers or suppliers (who may have been at fault) but would, in the first instance, be required to meet all his obligations to the lessee.

The Supply of Goods and Services Act 1982 — which among other things legislates for implied terms in contracts — establishes the lessee's right to quiet possession and the fitness of leased goods for their purpose. Failure of the lessor to meet these requirements can result in liability to the lessee.

2. Liability of the lessor arising from the action of a lessee
A lessee may use leased equipment illegally or recklessly, resulting in loss of life, bodily injury and loss of or damage to property. The lessee may, for instance, disregard instructions for the proper use of the equipment. Notwithstanding the fact that the lessee may be responsible for the injury caused, the lessor as owner of the equipment may be required to pay compensation to the extent that the lessee was uninsured, inadequately insured and unable to pay from his or her own resources.

260

Where the lessee's action results in a claim, the claimant, influenced by the 'deep pocket' philosophy, may demand compensation directly from the lessor. Should this action succeed the lessor may subsequently be able to obtain compensation from the lessee or the lessee's insurers, but in any case may incur legal costs that will not all be recoverable.

3. Contractual liability arising after the termination of the leasing contract

At the expiry of the leasing contract it is common practice for the goods to be sold — often with the lessee acting as an agent of the lessor for this purpose.

The lessor will therefore be subject to the obligations arising from the contract of sale and the Sale of Goods Act 1979.

The fact that the lessee has sold the goods on behalf of the lessor does not afford the lessor a defence. The lessor will be held liable as the principal and as a party to the contract entered into by the lessee acting as agent for and on behalf of the lessor.

Suppose, for example, that a vehicle was sold by the lessee (as agent for the lessor) at the termination of the lease and the vehicle was not in road-worthy condition. If, say, the brakes failed, resulting in the death of a pedestrian, then the lessor as vendor could be held liable.

4. Liability to third parties

Claims may be made by third parties under statute or common law and in circumstances different from those already described. Equipment such as lifts, electrical apparatus and machinery used by the general public may give rise to a third party claim if injury results from its failure in normal use.

There are many other categories of claim that may arise from the use of the leased equipment. For example, ships may cause pollution which may lead to substantial claims. Ship operators are normally shielded by Mutual Insurance Associations (P&I Clubs) against these and other liability risks, and some oil pollution risks are covered under various international arrangements. However, the lessor as the shipowner could be potentially exposed.

LEGAL COSTS

Defending the lessor's position against a claim, however weak the claim may in fact be, can give rise to legal costs and these can be considerable. The lessor's insurance cover should therefore include the costs and expenses incurred in defending or settling a claim.

261

Other risks of the lessor

In addition to liabilities there are other risks to be considered, the most common of which are as follows:

- *Theft* Goods may be stolen prior to delivery to the lessee, or while in the lessee's possession or after the lease has been terminated. Despite any contractual obligation of the lessee to insure the goods against theft, contingent cover must be considered by the lessor to allow for:

  (a) failure of the lessee to insure; or
  (b) failure of the lessee's insurance; and
  (c) inability of the lessee to compensate the lessor for the loss from the lessee's own resources.

  In an actual case the leased goods disappeared and were believed to have been stolen at the same time as the lessee became bankrupt and also disappeared. The lessor was not insured and suffered the loss of property without compensation.
- *Special perils* for example, malicious damage, burst pipes, sprinkler leakage or malfunction and storm.
- *Fire*
- *Accidental damage* Most of the same considerations apply in this last category of risk as in the first. Insurance cover should take account of when the incident may occur as well as the possible failure or inability of the lessee to meet obligations.

The lessee's liabilities

Many of the lessee's liabilities match those of the lessor. The lessee will have contractual obligations to the lessor and normally the contract will stipulate the insurance that the lessee must arrange. The liabilities that the lessee must consider in addition to contractual obligations to the lessor are:

- Liabilities to subcontractors and their employees.
- Liabilities to customers.
- Liabilities to authorities; for example, in the case of companies operating ships and aircraft, liabilities can arise in respect of such problems as abandoned cargo, wreck removal and pollution.
- Liabilities to other third parties.

Product liability

The gradual move in EC countries towards adoption of the 'strict liability' doctrine imposes greater burdens on lessors as well as on manufacturers. It is no longer a defence to a claim resulting from the failure of a product to show that there was not negligence contributing to the loss. In addition, the lessor can be placed 'in the shoes' of the manufacturer of a faulty product and suffer the consequences. The following example is an imaginary scenario illustrating the position.

Example 20.1
ABC Leasing Ltd purchase a light aircraft made by Highflight Ltd. The aircraft is leased to Smith's Airtaxis Ltd. The aircraft crashes during its first commercial flight killing the four passengers, the pilot and five people standing in a bus queue. The impact also results in a fire which destroys an office block and two expensive cars parked outside. Investigations showed that the accident was caused by a fundamental fault in the construction of the aircraft that would not have been revealed by normal inspection and testing — all of which had been carried out in accordance with the regulations.

Highflight Ltd has, in the meantime, gone into liquidation and their product liability insurance has lapsed prior to the accident due to non-payment of premiums. Lawyers for the victims of the accident decide to sue ABC Leasing on the grounds that the product was unsound and that the lessor stands in the shoes of the manufacturer.

All lessors are, to a greater or lesser degree, exposed to a product liability claim — more especially if the goods originate from a manufacturer in a country where it would be difficult to obtain compensation. Notwithstanding the fact that the manufacturer may have adequate product liability cover, lessors should consider the need for contingent cover for defective design, faulty workmanship or faulty materials.

The risk is clearly greater in some areas than others, and will be determined by:

- the nature of the goods
- the use to which the goods are put
- the standing of the manufacturers.

Lessors should err on the side of caution, bearing in mind that even the most prestigious manufacturers can make a serious mistake and/or can go out of business. The lessor could then be held responsible whether or not he or she was in any way to blame.

Insurance

There are several types of risk arising from the ownership or use of equipment, and insurance is available in the market to cover most risks of

263

loss or damage and against claims by third parties. The separation of use and ownership makes no significant difference to the overall degree of risk, but it is necessary to ensure that the interests of both lessees and lessors are protected by the insurances effected. One of the common features of a leasing contract is that the lessee is required to bear the financial consequences of any physical loss or damage to the leased equipment and of any third party claims arising out of its use, to the extent that these are not covered by insurance.

The insurable interest of a lessee in equipment that is the subject of a leasing contract is similar to that of a purchaser in equipment that is purchased, and the lessee will wish to arrange insurance on the same basis. The lessor will, nevertheless, be concerned to obtain the collateral security afforded by the insurances arranged by the lessee. Insurance provides lessors with both direct protection against any claims made by third parties and an assurance that, in the event of a loss, there will be sufficient funds to pay the current value of rentals in respect of the unexpired portion of the primary lease period and any other liabilities.

Normally, the lessee is responsible for arranging suitable insurance. Often, the leased asset will be one of a group for similar items used by the lessee for which it is appropriate to have a blanket policy in order to qualify for the lower premium arising from the spread of risk. Under some leasing arrangements, the lessor is prepared to allow the lessee to self-insure, should the lessee wish to do so.

Neither a lessor nor a lessee is under any statutory obligation specifically to insure leased equipment. However, in the case of motor vehicles, it is unlawful for a person to use, or permit any other person to use, a motor vehicle on a road unless the use of the vehicle is insured against liability in respect of death of or personal injury to third parties. The effect of this is to make a lessor criminally liable if the vehicles are permitted to be used without such insurance and, possibly, also liable for damages awarded against the uninsured lessee of the vehicle to the extent that the lessee is unable to satisfy any claim. A lessor may be able to avoid this liability by inserting a provision in the leasing agreement prohibiting the lessee from using the vehicle without third party cover which complies with the statutory requirements. If the lessee then uses the vehicles without the requisite insurance cover, it is being done without the permission of the lessor.

POLICY CONDITIONS

Leasing agreements generally contain detailed provisions concerning the insurances which lessees are required to effect at the start of the lease and to maintain throughout the lease period. The conditions imposed vary between leasing companies and may also depend on the type of equipment being leased. There are special requirements and arrangements in the case of mobile assets such as ships and aircraft. For example, it is usual to cover liabilities to third parties arising out of the ownership or use of a ship by entering the vessel with a Protection and Indemnity Association.

Insurance covering equipment against loss or damage is normally arranged on an agreed-value basis for the greater of the market value of the equipment and the amount stipulated in the lease to enable the lessor to recover the unamortized cost at the date of the loss of the equipment. The stipulated amount is most commonly determined by discounting future rentals at a specified rate; alternatively, a schedule of amounts or percentages of total cost applying at each stage of the primary lease period is appended to the lease. (The methods of calculating these and other types of terminal payments have been considered in Chapter 9.)

The amount of insurance cover to be provided for liability policies may also be stipulated by the lessor or, in the absence of any figure being specified, will be for whatever amount the lessee regards as prudent in the circumstances.

Certain risks are normally excluded from insurance policies, although cover can sometimes be arranged by endorsement or by the issue of a separate policy, such as one of the war risk policies for ships and aircraft which cover damage arising from war or war-like actions, either world wide or, for a lower premium, in the particular geographical areas in which it is proposed to operate the ship or aircraft. The lessee may be required to obtain the lessor's approval to any particular exclusions that are normally insurable. Some types of risk are completely uninsurable, such as nuclear detonations, criminal liabilities, and the insolvency of an insurer.

Most policies also incorporate exclusions regarding the uses of equipment and who may operate the equipment. The use of leased equipment for an illegal purpose or its operation by an unqualified machinist may, for example, invalidate a policy. The lessor is protected in these circumstances if the policy covers his or her interest and contains, for the lessor's benefit, a 'breach of warranty' clause stating that the insurance provided under the policy for the lessor is not invalidated by any act or omission on the part of the lessee or servants or agents of the lessee.

Some or all of the following general requirements may also be included in the insurance clause of a leasing agreement:

1. The policy either will be effected in the joint names of the lessor and the lessee or will note the interest of the lessor. Additionally, for large-valued items such as aircraft or ships, the lessor may require the lessee to assign all rights and interest in the insurances and to warrant that he or she will not assign, charge, or pledge the policies to any other person.

2. The policy will provide that any payment made pursuant to a claim is to be made direct to the lessor or, in the case of liability policies, will be applied directly in or towards satisfaction of the relevant claim.
3. The policy, and the receipts or other evidence of payment of premiums, will be produced to the lessor on request.
4. The policy will be in a form approved by the lessor.
5. The policy will be with such insurers as the lessor may approve.
6. The policy will provide that it may not be cancelled or materially modified until a specified time after prior written notice of intended cancellation or modification has been given to the lessor.
7. No other insurance will be effected by the lessee if a claim under such insurance could result in the operation of any average clause in the policy taken out by the lessee in accordance with the provisions of the leasing agreement.

TREATMENT OF PROCEEDS

Under a financial lease, the lessee is liable for any loss or damage to the leased equipment during the lease period. In the event of there being any repairable damage to the equipment, the lessor has a responsibility (subject to any contractual right permitting any sums that may be due from the lessee to be set against insurance proceeds) to apply any insurance moneys received towards the lessee's expenditure in making good the damage.

In the event of a total loss of leased equipment, the lease terminates and the lessee is required to make a lump sum terminal payment to the lessor. Normally, a lessee is discharged from this obligation by the lessor receiving the proceeds of the insurance policy covering the equipment against physical loss or damage. However, in the absence of sufficient insurance proceeds, all or part of the terminal payment has to be found by the lessee.

The amount for which the equipment is insured may exceed the amount of the stipulated terminal payment, for example, because the insurance additionally covers consequential losses of the lessee or the market value of the equipment is greater than the lessor's unamortized capital cost. The lessor is accountable to the lessee for any excess proceeds received by the lessor relating to consequential losses of the lessee. In the case of excess proceeds relating to the value of the equipment, the lessor normally accounts to the lessee either for the whole of the excess or, more logically, for the same proportion as is set out in the leasing agreement for sharing sales proceeds.

LESSOR POLICIES

Leasing companies undertaking financial leasing business are acting as financial institutions and, as such, normally accept the credit risks involved. Credit insurance of rental payments is not generally sought, though it is available.

21. *The treatment of fixtures*

The question of the annexation of equipment to real property and the consequences form a complex legal subject. Broadly, any item of equipment, if it is affixed to land or buildings, becomes part of the freehold property and a fixture in such circumstances ceases to be a personal chattel in law. Whether or not this occurs in any particular case is often determined partly (but not exclusively) by the intention of the person who does the affixing, but once affixed a chattel may be claimed as a part of the real estate by a third party such as landlord or mortgagee of the property. In the past this has led to considerable confusion in the leasing of fixtures but the current tax position is now set out reasonably comprehensively in the Finance Act 1985.

In any study of the legal treatment of fixtures an outline of the history of the subject is helpful in understanding the current situation. Prior to the Finance Act 1985 the argument used in considering questions of title was that, as the prerequisite to claiming capital allowances, the lessor was not looking solely at the requirement in Section 41 of the Finance Act 1971 that the asset should 'belong' to the leasing company. There was and still is a much wider requirement that in order to lease an asset (be it unaffixed plant or fixtures), including land, the leasing company must have an interest in the asset. The asset need not 'belong' to the leasing company for this 'interest' test to be met but the leasing company must have something it can lease.

Thus, turning to the question of passing title it was considered that if the plant was, or was to become, a fixture and the lessor was not the freeholder the following would hold:

(a) If the plant was to be supplied by an independent manufacturer or supplier the leasing company could purchase it direct. This would be an ordinary contract for the sale of goods and title could be made to pass to the leasing company either on delivery or at such other time as the contract provides. Normally a sale agreement will provide for title to pass ex-works and subsequently the plant could then be installed and affixed by the lessee or a third party, but provided that there was a reasonable period of time between title passing to the leasing company and installation there would be some reality in saying that plant belonged to the leasing company. (The leasing company could, for the purpose of the purchase, act through the lessee as agent without jeopardizing this claim.) Thus the leasing company would own the equipment and the lease would start on delivery ex-works. When the plant was installed it would become a fixture and therefore, from a legal standpoint, the very subject matter of the lease would cease to exist but it was agreed that, subject to the individual circumstances, the obligation to the lessee under the equipment lease should as a matter of contract law stand and remain valid. (However, here the leasing company would no longer have any security and perhaps would not have the ability to sell if the lease were terminated.)

(b) The premise in paragraph (a) applied to identifiable pieces of plant, but in the more usual situation the plant (fixture) would be supplied as part of a building contract and the value of such a contract would be represented by the provision of services in assembling and installing a variety of individual pieces of equipment. The legal title to the material supplied under the building contract would initially be with the contractor, and once affixed the legal title is probably lost in favour of the landowner. In such a situation, a leasing company with no interest in the underlying land, even if it became a party to the building contract, would never own the fixtures and therefore would have nothing to lease. The special problem with many types of fixtures is that they become so bound up with the fabric of the building it is difficult to see how they could be dealt with separately.

In response to this problem and where it was not practical for the lessor to take the freehold or even the long leasehold interest in the land to which the chattel was to become affixed, the contrary intention or waiver route evolved. This involved the person to whose land the plant was affixed, waiving any right to it or saying that, notwithstanding the general law, it was the intention of the parties that the title to the plant should not pass to the landowner. This premise was backed up with a right for the leasing company to enter and remove the plant. The fundamental deficiency with this route was that although it probably worked as between the parties as a matter of contract law there was no guarantee that it would work against a liquidator or mortgagee and, more importantly, the interest of the leasing company as a matter of land law was so remote that it would be difficult to see how the plant could be said to belong to the lessor or for an appropriate interest to be available to anyone but the landowner.

This unsatisfactory and confused situation was made considerably worse by the decision in 'Stokes v Costain', where in the course of a long and complex judgment, it was ruled that in most cases the contrary intention route was ineffectual and allowances essentially fell to the freeholder.

This decision in 'Stokes v Costain' clearly caused major problems for various types of bona fide property-leasing arrangements and in some circumstances could have prevented lessees claiming allowances on equipment provided by them that became attached to buildings, even though the equipment was provided for their own use and exclusively for their trade. Section 59, and paragraph 17, in the Finance Act 1985 were an attempt by the Inland Revenue to correct this wholly unsatisfactory state of affairs. The relevant section of Schedule 17 concerning lessors is paragraph 3, the relevant provisions of which are set out in paragraph 3.1 as follows:

In any case where:
(a) a person ('the equipment lessor') incurs capital expenditure on the provision of machinery or plant for leasing; and
(b) an agreement is entered into for the lease, directly or indirectly from the equipment lessor, of the machinery or plant (otherwise than as part of the relevant land) to another person (. . . 'the equipment lessee') for the purposes of the trade carried on by the equipment lessee or for leasing otherwise than in the course of a trade; and
(c) the machinery or plant becomes a fixture; and
(d) if the expenditure referred to in paragraph (a) above had been incurred by the equipment lessee, the fixture would, by virtue of paragraph 2 above (expenditure incurred by holder of interest in land), have been treated for material purposes as belonging to him in consequence of his incurring the expenditure; and
(e) equipment lessor and the equipment lessee elect that this paragraph should apply;

then . . . on and after the time at which the expenditure is incurred the fixture should be treated for material purposes as belonging to the equipment lessor in consequence of his incurring the expenditure.

Here the legislation can be seen to have regularized the contrary intention or waiver route, and at paragraph 4 the schedule does the same thing for equipment already affixed and acquired as part of a land interest. However, unfortunately there are still problems, particularly the general nature of the drafting which may capture items whose status is on the borderline of the classification, where subleasing is involved, and from the nature of the wording it appears that the provisions will not be applicable where an existing fixture is purchased by an equipment lessor for leasing.

The law covering fixtures continues to evolve and doubtless these problems will be solved in time. For the present, the procedure would appear to be to enter an appropriate election in the case of a lease of any equipment that might, in some circumstances, be deemed a fixture and rely on the general intention of the Inland Revenue to treat it as such.

22. *Consumer Credit Act*

It may be thought surprising to find a chapter on the Consumer Credit Act 1974 in a book devoted to leasing, particularly as the government have announced the intention to exclude hire for business purposes from the scope of the Act. However, a study of the Consumer Credit Act (CCA) will show that it is restricted neither to a consumer in the usual sense of the word nor to credit. The extension of the legislation to consumer hire, in the non-business sense, is eminently logical. Prior to the Act protection was only afforded to certain types of instalment credit transactions, so that if a consumer wished to rent a television rather than to acquire it on hire purchase or conditional sale, he or she obtained no specific protection. The form of the transaction governed the applicable law. This seemed illogical to the Crowther Committee, upon whose report the CCA was based. However, the legislation adopted the definition of a consumer found in earlier hire-purchase legislation, which was, in effect, anyone who was not a body corporate. While such a definition is free from ambiguity, it does mean that hire or leasing agreements with sole traders and partnerships, including professional partnerships, such as solicitors and accountants, are regulated by the Act — assuming they fall below the relevant monetary limit, which is currently £15,000.

The Equipment Leasing Association, together with the Finance Houses Association, the British Vehicle Rental and Leasing Association and the Consumer Credit Trade Association, have argued strongly that business transactions should be outside the scope of the Act. These representations have been accepted and it was announced in November 1987 that the government

> have therefore decided that the Act should be amended to exclude all credit and hire for business purposes and we will make this change to the Act, together with other changes to simplify and clarify the Act's provisions, as soon as there is a suitable opportunity.

As the proposed changes can only be made by way of primary legislation, business hire or leasing will not be excluded from the scope of the Act until such time as Parliamentary time is available. How the government intend to exclude business transactions remains to be seen. It may well be that they will amend the definition of 'individual' to be found in Section 189 of the Act which, at present, is stated as including 'a partnership or other unincorporated body of persons not consisting entirely of bodies corporate'. It is this definition that has brought in business transactions as 'an individual' can include a sole trader or partnership and the purpose of the leasing is ignored. It is possible that a definition of 'individual' could follow that set out in the EC Council Directive of 22 December 1986 for the approximation of the laws, regulations and administrative provisions of the Member States concerning consumer credit. That directive does not apply to hiring, but it restricts its application to credit agreements for non-business purpose. It achieves this by defining 'consumer' as 'a natural person who, in transactions covered by this Directive, is acting for purposes which can be regarded as outside his trade or profession'. If such a definition was applied to an individual then the vast majority of business transactions would be clearly outside the scope of the Act. There would, of course, remain some grey areas where a customer was leasing, say, an estate car partly for business use and partly for domestic purposes. However, similar problems arose some years ago in relation to the interpretation of the terms controls which regulated deposits and periods of leases for non-business purposes, so it is hoped that the grey areas will be few and easily resolved.

The following presents an outline of the requirements of the Consumer Credit Act and the regulations made under it. It is intended that this outline will act as a guide, or pointer, to those areas that need further consideration by a lessor. If a leasing company therefore identifies that it enters into transactions that are regulated by the Act, then further detailed reference should be made to the Act itself and the regulations made thereunder.

Neither the Act nor the regulations refer to leasing as such. The Act adopts the more usual domestic terminology of hire and refers to the bailment or hiring agreement which falls within the scope of the Act as a consumer hire agreement. The lessor is referred to as the owner and the lessee is referred to as the hirer. However, for the sake of consistency, in this chapter the more usual terms of *lease*, *lessor* and *lessee* will be used.

Leasing

A lease will be regulated by the Act if it is made with a non-corporate body for the leasing of goods, is not a hire-purchase agreement, is capable of subsisting for more than three months and does not require the lessee to make VAT inclusive rental payments totalling more than £15,000.

In determining whether a lease falls within the financial parameters of the Act the value of the rentals at the date the lease is made is the all-important factor. Thus, if a lease permits the lessor to vary rentals consequent upon a change in corporation tax or money costs then any subsequent variation can be ignored when calculating the value of the rentals. However, care has to be taken in relation to an agreement that confers an option to terminate on the lessee, say, at the expiration of one year, as the lessee is only required to make the payments for that period and therefore only the first year's rentals will have to be taken into account when calculating if the agreement falls within the scope of the Act. Any balloon payment payable on early termination is excluded from the calculation.

LICENSING

If it is identified that the lessor, in the course of business, wishes to lease goods by way of regulated leases (consumer hire agreements) then the lessor must obtain a licence to do so before commencing business. A licence will be needed whether or not the consumer hire business is the totality of the lessor's business or just forms part of it. However, a person is not to be treated as carrying on a leasing business for the purposes of the Act merely because transactions of that type are entered into occasionally.

Licences are of two types: a standard licence and a group licence. A standard licence is issued to a named person, authorizing that person to carry on business under the name or names specified in the licence, but not under any other name, whereas a group licence is intended not for a group of companies but merely to identify a group of like persons or bodies, such as the Law Society and the Citizens' Advice Bureaux, and is therefore of no import for lessors.

There are six categories of licensable activity and the lessor will require to obtain from the Director-General of Fair Trading a licence in category B which would enable the lessor to carry on 'a consumer hire business', together with the right to canvass regulated consumer hire agreements off trade premises. The right to canvass will be required if the lessor's staff wish to visit the premises of customers in order to seek business. Canvassing means any 'oral communication' inviting a prospective lessee to enter into an agreement where the communications are made other than at the trade premises of the lessor, the supplier of the goods, the canvasser or the canvasser's agent or the business premises of the consumer. The only exemption is if the call is made 'in response' to a request made on a previous occasion by the prospective lessee.

Seeking business

The Act is structured so that the major part of it follows, in chronological order, the steps taken in relation to a usual business transaction. The Act therefore, in effect, starts with the seeking of business and then goes on to deal with the entry into the leasing agreement, followed by matters that can arise during the currency of the agreement, and then default and termination.

Control by the Act in relation to the seeking of business is directed at two areas: advertising and quotations. The advertising is governed partly by the Act and partly by the regulations. However, advertising is one of the few areas of the legislation where business transactions have already been exempted. By Section 43(4) an advertisement which indicates that the advertiser is not willing to enter into consumer hire agreements is outside the scope of the Act. However, this would mean that the advertiser only intended to enter into leasing transactions with corporate bodies or transactions above the financial limit of the Act. As a result the Consumer Credit (Advertisements) Regulations 1989, in effect, extend the exemption to all business advertising whether in relation to a regulated leasing agreement or not in that the regulations do not apply to leasing adverts where the advertisement expressly or by implication indicates clearly that the advertiser is willing to enter into leasing agreements for a purpose of a person's business and does not indicate either expressly or by implication a willingness to provide such a facility for non-business transactions even if the lessor is willing to do so. In short, therefore, provided that the advert makes it clear either expressly or by implication that it relates to a business facility only then can the lessor ignore the advertising regulations. If the lessor does not fall into that category then he or she must comply with the regulations as to form and content.

Even if the advertisement is exempt from the Advertising Regulations it is not totally exempt from the Act. Section 46 of the Act will apply, so that if the advertisement conveys information that, in a material respect, is false or misleading the advertiser commits an offence.

Although a lessor's affairs can be so ordered as to avoid the detailed requirements of the advertisement regulations in relation to business transactions, there is no similar line of escape in relation to the obligation to give quotations. It follows, therefore, that the lessor, or the lessor's credit broker (i.e. the person introducing the regulated business to the lessor), must be in a position to give a prospective customer a written quotation in the prescribed form upon request. Reference should be made to the Consumer Credit (Quotations) Regulations 1989 for the detail as to the prescribed form and content of a quotation and whether or not there is a statutory obligation to supply one.

The form and content of a regulated leasing agreement

The Act superimposes upon the common law relating to leasing agreements generally certain requirements as to form and content. These apply, unlike in relation to the advertising regulations, irrespective of whether the lease is for business or domestic purposes.

The provisions governing the form and content of regulated leasing agreements are contained in Sections 60–64 of the 1974 Act and also the Consumer Credit (Agreements) Regulations 1983 (the Agreement Regulations) and the Consumer Credit (Cancellation Notices and Copies of Documents) Regulations 1983 (the Copy Document Regulations). If the Act or the regulations are not complied with then the agreement can only be enforced (provided that certain basic provisions called 'prescribed terms' are included) on an order of the court.

The requirements imposed by the Act and the regulations major on the information that must be given to the lessee. There are two ways in which this is done: first, there is the information that must be contained in the agreement itself; secondly, there is the necessity to supply copies of the agreement so that the lessee will, in theory, have the information of the essential terms of the lease readily to hand.

The information that must be contained in the lease is little more than the details that are normally found in the well-drawn non-regulated document and must contain the following principal groups of information:

1. The statutory heading 'Hire Agreement regulated by the Consumer Credit Act 1974', must be shown prominently on the first page of the document. Only these words can be used, so the term 'lease' or 'leasing' cannot be used.

2. What are called in the regulations, 'Financial and related particulars', must be shown 'together as a whole and not interspersed with other information apart from sub-totals and cross references'.

   The information must be precise, except that when exact information is not available estimated information can be included in respect of the rentals, but if that is done then an indication of the assumptions on which the estimation is made must also be included.

   Briefly, the information that must be included as 'financial and related particulars' and shown 'together as a whole' is a description of the goods, details of any advance payment and, where the agreement is cancellable, the nature of such payments, the amount of each hire payment other than the advance payment and the timing of such payments. There is considerable flexibility in relation to the expression of such sums allowed by the regulations. There must also be information as to certain other types of payments that are to be made under the agreement. The types of payments caught by this requirement are those relating to a payment to the lessor under any arrangements for the installation, care, maintenance or protection of the goods, any premium under a contract of insurance or any payment payable on termination of the agreement other than a default charge. The timing of these payments must also be shown. If any of the rentals or other payments are variable and the amount of the varied payment cannot be ascertained at the time of the making of the agreement, then the agreement must contain a statement indicating the circumstances in which any rental or payment may be varied and, if known, the time in which any such variation may occur. Finally, and not unnaturally, the agreement must state whether the goods are to be leased for a fixed period or a minimum period, and the duration of that period.

3. Information must be given as to whether any security is to be provided by the lessee or additional charges payable on default; for example, interest on overdue rentals.

4. The appropriate statutory form of statement of protection and remedies available to the lessee under the Act must also be set out. In addition to the information that is to be given to the lessee, it is necessary for both parties to the agreement to sign it, the lessee will sign it in a statutory form of signature box and the lessor will sign it outside the box. If the agreement is cancellable then the date of signature by the lessee must be shown within the signature box and the lessor outside the box, but in the case of non-cancellable agreements only one date is necessary, to be shown outside the box, and that is the date on which the agreement becomes an executed agreement.

Administrative problems

The Act creates new areas of administrative problems for the lessor that do not exist in relation to non-Act transactions. In common law, it is open to a lessee to withdraw from an agreement before the agreement is made, which is usually when the lessor signs the agreement. However, the CCA converts this common law right into a statutory right. In the case of a prospective regulated lease, therefore, the lessee can withdraw from the agreement by a written or oral notice indicating the intention to withdraw. Like the common law withdrawal, but unlike the provisions relating to cancellation, notice of withdrawal must be received by the lessor or a statutory agent. While it would be expected that the credit broker or supplier who is the negotiator in antecedent negotiations (a technical term defined by Section 56) relating to the leasing agreement, would be the agent of the lessor for this purpose, the Act rather surprisingly extends the statutory agency to any person who, in the course of a business carried on by the lessee, acts on behalf of the lessee in any negotiations for the agreement. Thus, not only would the dealer concerned in relation to, say, the hire of a car, be the agent of the lessor but also the lessee's own solicitors if they were engaged in the negotiations on the lessee's behalf.

If an effective notice of withdrawal is given by the lessee, then the lessee is in the same position as if the agreement had been made and then cancelled under Section 69. The effect of this rather odd provision is that any transaction that is intended to be linked to the leasing by reason of Section 19, e.g. a maintenance agreement, is also cancelled. There are exceptions to this relating to contracts of insurance, guarantees of goods and transactions under agreements for the operation of a deposit or a current account.

While lessors have always been vulnerable to a prospective lessee withdrawing from a transaction, the CCA imposes a new concept in relation to leasing transactions, namely that of cancellability. This concept had existed since 1965 in relation to certain instalment credit transactions and since July 1988 in relation to certain cash transactions.

The concept of cancellability of a lease presents problems for the lessor. The circumstances in which a regulated lease may be cancelled by the lessee are as follows:

- if the antecedent negotiations included oral representations made in the presence of the lessee by an individual acting as, or on behalf of, the lessor

- if the agreement is not within a category excluded by Section 67 of the Act from the cancellation provisions

The main exclusions from the right to cancel are, in relation to leasing agreements, agreements secured on land or agreements signed at the business premises of the lessor or any party to a linked transaction. However, if a lease is signed on the business premises of the lessee and the other requirements are met, then the agreement will be cancellable.

- if the time for cancellation has not expired

In the normal situation where the agreement is made on the signature of the lessor, the lessee has until the end of the fifth day following the date of receipt of the second copy agreement within which to serve the notice of cancellation. If it is one of those unusual types of agreement where it is concluded by the signature of the lessee then, instead of getting a second copy of the agreement a separate notice advising the lessee of his or her cancellation rights has to be sent by post. The lessee then has until the end of the fifth day following the date of receipt of the notice within which to serve a notice of cancellation. Unlike the notice of withdrawal, the notice of cancellation is served as soon as it is posted and is effective even if not received by the lessor.

If a lessor identifies that it is likely to carry on business transactions that are cancellable then this has a direct impact upon its documentation. Not only will it have to prepare documentation for use in non-cancellable situations, but it will also require documentation for use in cancellable circumstances. The Act and regulations require certain additional information to be given in cancellable agreements setting out in simple terms the right of the lessee to cancel and the consequences of taking that action. In addition to the statutory notices, which differ for the original agreement and the two copies, the second statutory copy of a cancellable agreement must also be accompanied by a cancellation form. The contents of the statutory notices and the cancellation forms are set down in regulations.

However, the lessee is not obliged to use the statutory cancellation form and can express the intention to withdraw from an agreement in any form of notice given either to the person specified by the lessor in the statutory notice or to any person acting as the lessor's agent. One practical problem that can arise is that the lessee may not wait until the second copy of the agreement is received and that an informal notice may be received by the lessor or lessor's agent before the transaction has been processed. A system is necessary, therefore, for identifying such transactions, particularly if they are likely to be dealt with within a branch network.

If a lessee legitimately cancels an agreement, then the notice operates to cancel the leasing agreement and any existing linked transaction other than those already referred to above in relation to withdrawal. It is important to remember that the cancellation of the leasing agreement does not operate to cancel the sale agreement between the dealer and the lessor as such an agreement is not a linked transaction within the meaning of Section 19. A lessor must, therefore, consider how to deal with the possibility of being left with goods, albeit virtually new goods. The most common form of avoidance that has been adopted by the industry is to arrange with the dealer to postpone delivery of the goods until the possibility of cancellation has passed, so that the lessor's obligation to pay will not arise until the goods have been delivered. Alternatively, the lessor may enter into a master agreement with the supplier of the goods whereby if a sale to a lessor results in a cancellable transaction, which in the event is cancelled, then the dealer will buy the goods back at the original cash price.

Upon cancellation of the agreement and any linked transaction, the lessee is entitled to repayment of any sums that have been paid in contemplation of the agreement or any linked transaction and to recover any goods tendered in part-exchange or their part-exchange allowance. If the goods are not restored within ten days in substantially the same condition, then the lessee has a lien on any goods that have been delivered under the leasing agreement for repayment of the moneys that have fallen due to him or her as a result of the cancellation. Naturally, the lessee is also discharged from any liability for payment under the agreement or any linked transaction.

Any security that has been given in relation to the cancelled agreement is treated as never having taken effect and any property that has been lodged with the lessor to give effect to the security has, therefore, to be returned. Until the lessor has complied with these provisions the lessee cannot be obliged to surrender the goods under the cancelled agreement.

Finally, the lessee is under a duty pending the surrender of the goods to retain possession of them and to take reasonable care of them, but need only deliver them up at the lessee's own premises and then only in pursuance of a lessor's written request served on the lessee before it is time for the lessor's collection of the goods; alternatively, the lessee may deliver or send the goods to the lessor's nominee for receiving notice of cancellation.

Lessee's right to terminate

The Hire Purchase Acts have always included the right of a debtor under a hire-purchase agreement, or latterly under a conditional sale agreement, to terminate the agreement and return the goods before the end of the agreement. This concept has now been imported into leasing agreements by Section 101 of the CCA. However, the section does endeavour to exclude from the operation of right of termination, with one important exception, the traditional form of business lease. The lessee, therefore, has no right to terminate the lease under the statutory powers if the lease falls into one of the following categories:

1. The lease obliges the lessee to make payment which, in total (and without breach of the agreement), exceeds £900 in any year.
2. Any lease under which the goods are leased for the purposes of a business carried on by the lessee or where the lessee requires them for business purposes and the goods are selected by the lessee and acquired by the lessor at the lessee's request from a supplier who is not an associate of the lessor. The expression 'associate' is very widely defined by Section 184 and would include, for example, a member of the same group of companies. It follows, therefore, that a manufacturer who intends to lease directly to its own customers or lease through a subsidiary or even perhaps a joint venture company will not be able to take advantage of this exception to business use. Such a manufacturer or supplier must of necessity, if it wishes to avoid the provisions of Section 101, arrange its leasing facilities through an independent lessor.
3. Any lease where the lessee requires, or holds itself out as requiring, the goods for the business purposes of sub-letting. In this instance,

however, it does not matter whether the supplier is an associate of the lessor or not.

4. A lease in respect of which the Director-General of Fair Trading has made a direction following the lessor's application that it would be in the interests of lessees for Section 101 not to apply to the lessor's agreements (Section 101(8)). It should be noted that the direction will only be made when it is in the interest of lessees to do so, so that mere inconvenience to the lessor in complying with the Act and the regulations is not sufficient grounds for the Director-General to make an order. If the Director does make an order, it can be made subject to conditions.

If a lessor's agreements do not fall under any one of the four categories listed above then the lessee will have the right, upon giving written notice to the lessor, to terminate the agreement but not within the first 18 months after it was made. The period of notice, if the rentals are paid at equal intervals, will be the length of one interval or three months, whichever is less, or if the rentals are payable at differing intervals then the period of notice will be the length of the shortest interval or three months, whichever is less. In any other case, the minimum period of notice is three months. Finally, it should be noted that this statutory right of termination cannot be taken from the lessee by any term in the contract, nor can any liability be imposed on the lessee in respect of rentals that fall due after the lessee's statutory right has been exercised (Section 173).

Varying the agreement

There are many occasions that can arise during the currency of a lease where the lessor may wish to vary the terms of the agreement; for example, upon change in fiscal legislation relating to corporation tax or capital allowances, or at the request of the lessee where, for example, a sole trader wishes to transfer his or her business to a corporate body. In the case of a lease that falls outside the scope of the CCA, such variations are often dealt with quite informally by way of a simple memorandum or even exchange of letters. The CCA, while recognizing the necessity for allowing variation of the lease during its currency, to a large extent formalizes the various methods of variation. The formalities arise out of one of the key objectives of the Act, namely, that the lessee must know at least the basic details of the transaction as varied, particularly at the time of the variation, and receive written information as to the revised terms of the lease.

The Act lays down several ways in which a lease can be varied. It recognizes that provision is often made in leases whereby a variation of its terms can be triggered by an external event, e.g. change in the rate of corporation tax or money costs to the lessor. The Act and the regulations do not impinge on such a clause provided that the triggering event is outside the control of the lessor or any associate of the lessor. The essential ingredient of this type of variation is therefore its automatic nature. If, however, the lessor has merely reserved a right in the agreement to vary certain terms, which may be in relation to fiscal matters or money costs, then it is permissible to have such a clause in the agreement, but any variation cannot take effect before at least seven days' written notice is given to the lessee. The one relaxation in this respect relates to VAT where a VAT rate change is passed on to the lessee. Any power reserved by the lessor to vary payments is a prescribed term of the agreement and, as such, must be set out in the agreement itself. If it relates to any payments it will, of course, form part of the financial and related particulars.

There are, however, many occasions on which it is not possible to cater for a variation or modification of an agreement whether by automatic provision or upon notice. The lessee, as already suggested, may wish to transfer his or her business to a limited company, or may wish to update equipment by the addition of further goods, in which case there are only two options open to the lessor. The lessor — depending on the circumstances surrounding the transaction, particularly in relation to tax — may be able to terminate the original agreement and enter into a completely new agreement with the lessee, or a new agreement simply for the additional goods if that is the case. If this alternative is not available to a lessor and the variation varies or supplements the earlier agreement, the lessor will have to enter into what the Act refers to as a 'modifying agreement' (Section 82(2)). The modifying agreement is treated by the Act as revoking the earlier agreement and reproducing the combined effect of both the earlier agreement and the new agreement in one document, with the result that outstanding obligations under the earlier agreement are carried forward into the modifying agreement.

When considering the question of the variation of an agreement the lessor must always bear in mind that, notwithstanding the fact that the rentals payable under the modifying agreement may exceed £15,000 or the agreement is to be with a limited company after the transfer from an individual, the modifying agreement will remain a regulated agreement. Computer systems must be geared to the identification of regulated agreements to take this factor into account. If they do not then the lessor may fail to identify the agreement as regulated, with the result that they may fail to comply with the Act in some material respect, for example, in relation to the service of a default notice.

If a lessor decides to enter into a modifying agreement rather than a replacement or an additional agreement, then the lessor must appreciate that all the formalities of the Act must be complied with both as to the form and content of the agreement and as to the provision of copies.

It will be seen, therefore, that there is little advantage, other than perhaps for tax reasons, in following the modifying agreement route if it is possible to have an additional or replacement agreement. The avoidance of modifying agreements merely means that additional documents become unnecessary.

ABILITY TO SUPPLY INFORMATION

Having ensured that the lessee will be fully aware of any rights and obligations at the time of entering into the agreement or upon any variation of the agreement, the Act goes on to require the lessor to provide the lessee with information during the currency of the agreement. Not only must the lessor be aware of the ongoing problems of variation of agreements and provide for the variation in its systems, but it must also cater for the provision of information and copy documents to the lessee. The Act's requirements are not over-stringent in that a lessor will have 12 working days after the receipt of a written request, together with the payment or tender of a fee of 50p, in which to supply a copy of the executed agreement and of any other document referred to in it, together with a statement that has to be signed by the lessor. The statement must show, according to the information to which it is practicable for the lessor to refer, the total sum that has become payable under the agreement by the lessee but remains unpaid, usually the arrears, and the various amounts comprised in that total sum with the date when each became due. The statement should be accurate as it is binding on the lessor. If the request is not complied with within the time limit and the agreement is in default, it is unenforceable by the lessor, and if the lessor fails for one month to supply the statement then the lessor commits an offence and is liable upon summary conviction to a fine not exceeding £1,000.

There is also a duty on the lessee to disclose the whereabouts of the goods, which are the subject matter of the lease, within seven working days after the lessee has received a request in writing to that effect, provided that it is a term of the lease that the goods must be kept in the lessee's control or possession. Again, failure to comply with that notice for a period of days will result in the lessee committing an offence.

Default and termination

The well-drawn lease will provide for the remedies available to a lessor upon default being made by the lessee. The traditional remedies include the power to terminate the agreement or the hiring, to repossess the goods and in many instances to recover compensation for loss of profit by way of a precalculated liquidated sum. Subject to the common law as to penalties, the rights of the lessor are usually unfettered. In order to redress what has been felt to be an imbalance in favour of the lessor, the Consumer Credit Act imposes constraints upon the exercise of the traditional remedies under a regulated lease.

The Act sets out procedures whereby the lessor is precluded from taking action in most of the traditional default events until a statutory notice has been served upon the lessee in the prescribed form (see Consumer Credit (Enforcement, Default and Termination) Regulations 1983).

The Act divides up default events into those that arise by reason of a breach by the lessee of the terms of the agreement and those that do not. Where it is necessary to exercise a remedy for a breach, Section 87 relating to default notices applies, but in other cases Section 76 is applicable, e.g. the lessee becomes bankrupt or an execution is levied against the lessee's assets.

In the case of a non-breach default event, the lessor is not entitled to enforce a term of a regulated lease by demanding earlier payment of any sum or recovering possession of any goods or land or treating any right conferred on the lessee by the agreement as terminated, restricted or deferred except by or after giving the lessee not less than seven days' notice of the intention to do so. An enforcement notice under Section 76 is not required where a period for the duration of the agreement is not specified in the agreement. It should also be noted that if the agreement itself is to be terminated and the goods repossessed, then a seven days' notice of termination has to be given under Section 98(1) and at least seven days' notice of the intention to repossess under Section 76(1b), although the two notices may be combined in one document and the seven-day periods may run concurrently. The form and contents of the Section 76 notice are set out in the Enforcement Default and Termination Notices Regulations which must be complied with.

If the default event is a breach of the agreement then service of a default notice is necessary. By Section 87(1) the lessor must serve a default notice before it can become entitled by reason of a breach by the lessee, to terminate the agreement, demand earlier payment of any sum, recover possession of any goods or land, treat any right conferred on the lessee by the agreement as terminated, restricted or deferred, or enforce any security. It should be noted that Section 87 is considerably wider than Section 76. No notice is necessary, however, if the lessor merely wishes to recover accrued arrears or damages, unless it also intends to proceed against a surety, in which case it must serve a default notice on the lessee and a copy on the surety. Again the default notice must be in the prescribed form and comply with the appropriate regulations.

In the usual case, therefore, when the lessor wishes to terminate the agreement and repossess the goods by reason of default, a default notice must be served and must expire. The lessor may either state in the default notice that the agreement will come to an end automatically if the notice is not complied with, or give a separate notice of termination after expiry of the default notice. Once the right to repossess has arisen, the lessor can then repossess the goods but cannot enter any premises to do so without the consent of the lessee or a Court Order. If the goods are repossessed, or are ordered to be returned by the court, the court is given the power by Section 132 to release the lessee from the whole or a part of the outstanding liability and to order the return of all or any part of the rental payments.

Judicial control

All actions by the lessor to enforce a regulated agreement, any security relating to a regulated agreement or any linked transaction against the lessee must be brought in the applicable County Court if the action arises in England or Wales. In Scotland the applicable Court is the Sheriff Court and in Northern Ireland it can be either the High Court or the County Court.

The Act does not only restrict the right of action to the applicable court, but creates several new forms of action, which are summarized below.

1. AN ENFORCEMENT ORDER

Such an order is necessary before a lessor can enforce, for example, an improperly executed agreement or security instrument or after failing to serve a copy of a default notice on a surety.

If a lessor applies to the court for an enforcement order because the regulated lease has not been properly executed because of non-compliance with Section 61(1a), the court is precluded from making such an order unless a document (whether or not in the prescribed form and complying with the Agreement Regulations) itself containing all the prescribed terms of the agreement was signed by the lessee (whether or not in the prescribed manner). Thus, if a prescribed term or the lessee's signature are omitted from the document, it can never be enforced.

The court is also precluded from making an enforcement order in the case of a cancellable agreement if the provisions of the Act relating to the supply of copies have not been complied with, unless the failure has been rectified by giving a copy of the executed agreement to the lessee before the commencement of the proceedings in which the order is sought. This is double-edged in that if such a copy is given the lessee will then have the right to cancel the agreement.

Subject to the three exceptions mentioned above, the court on hearing an application for which an order is required is to dismiss the application if, but only if, it considers it just to do so having regard to, first, the prejudice caused to any person by the contravention in question and the degree of culpability for it and, secondly, the powers conferred on the court by Sections 127(2), 135 and 136.

2. TIME ORDERS

A court is empowered to make what is called a 'time order' if it considers it just to do so, first on the application for an enforcement order by a lessor or on the application made by a lessee after being served with a default notice or a notice under Section 76(1) or 98(1) or, thirdly, in an action brought by a lessor to enforce a regulated agreement or any security or to recover possession of any goods or land to which a regulated agreement relates.

A time order must provide for one or both of the following as the court considers just:

(a) payment by the lessee or any surety of any sum owed under a regulated agreement or a security by such instalments, at such times, as the court having regard to the means of the lessee and any surety, considers reasonable;

(b) the remedy by the lessee of any breach of the regulated agreement (other than non-payment of money) within such period as the court may specify.

If an offer to pay by instalments is made by the lessee and accepted by the lessor, the court may make a time order giving effect to the offer without hearing evidence of means and the making of an application for a time order will enable the court to make an order for delivery of goods the subject matter of the agreement under the Torts (Interference with Goods) Act 1977 which can be suspended upon the operation of that order.

If, when the time order is made, the lessee is still in possession of the goods, then the lessee is treated as a bailee under the terms of the agreement notwithstanding that the agreement has been terminated. The time order can only deal with arrears of rentals, but presumably the contractual rentals will continue under the statutory bailment as do the other obligations, e.g. maintenance or insurance.

If the breach of the agreement has been non-monetary and the agreement is still in force when the time order is made, i.e. it has not been terminated, then the lessor's remedies are frozen for the period specified in the time order, e.g. the lessor is unable to terminate the agreement or serve a default notice.

If the agreement has been terminated, however, prior to the making of the time order and the lessor has exercised other remedies under the contractual terms of the agreement, e.g. repossessed the goods, the position is extremely complex and the Act should be studied carefully.

3. PROTECTION ORDERS

A court on the application of the lessor in relation to a regulated agreement may make such orders as it thinks just for protecting any property of the lessor, or any property subject to any security, from damage or depreciation pending the determination of any proceedings under the Act, including orders restricting or prohibiting use of the property or giving directions as to its custody. The court, however, cannot make an order for the sale of the goods.

4. REPAYMENT TO LESSEE

Section 132 empowers the court, on an application by a lessee in relation to a regulated agreement, to grant financial relief if the lessor has recovered possession of the goods otherwise than by court action. The application can be, not only for relief from payments of sums owed by the lessee in respect of the goods, but also for repayment of the whole or part of the rentals (or other sums) already paid, e.g. a substantial deposit. The court may make the order applied for if it considers it just to do so 'having regard to the extent of the enjoyment of the goods' by the lessee.

If the lessee brings proceedings for wrongful interference and the court makes an order for delivery of goods to the lessor (Section 3 of the Torts (Interference with Goods) Act 1977) the court can include in that order a provision of the kind referred to above.

23. *Banking supervision*

There are no prima facie reasons why a leasing company simply as a provider of finance should need to be directly subject to regulation or supervision, although under the provisions of the Consumer Credit Act 1974 any company wishing to provide finance, whether by way of loans, leases or hire-purchase facilities, with transactions of an individual value of up to the amount specified, must obtain a licence for consumer credit activities from the Office of Fair Trading (see Chapter 22).

However, a large number of leasing companies in the United Kingdom and elsewhere are subsidiaries of banks or other deposit-taking institutions, and in some instances are deposit-taking institutions themselves. Such leasing companies are, therefore, directly affected by the supervision imposed by national and supranational bodies on banks. Furthermore, as major users of credit provided by the banking sector, even those leasing companies not directly subject to banking regulations or supervision will nevertheless be affected by such supervision in respect of the availability of credit facilities, and the terms thereof, from banks or other financial institutions.

The supervision of banks and other deposit-taking institutions has a number of different objectives; the primary ones are the protection of depositors and the protection of the banking and financial systems, both national and international. Banks are also often used by governments as a medium for implementing certain fiscal and monetary policies, including exchange and credit controls, although these two particular governmental policies have not been applied in the United Kingdom since the 1970s. Supervision of banks, and other financial institutions, is carried out on a national basis. Although the method of exercising supervision will vary from one authority to another, it will normally encompass the authority, first, establishing certain criteria for initial authorization; secondly, ensuring the maintenance by each institution of such criteria; and, thirdly, monitoring that each institution conducts its business in a prudent manner, and maintains sufficient capital and liquidity, having regard to the nature of its assets and liabilities, and adequate accounting and other records and systems of internal control. The single most important aspect of an institution for supervisory authorities is probably the competence and probity of its management.

During the 1980s the nature and depth of supervision applied to banks in the United Kingdom has increased considerably, both by direct legislation (Banking Acts 1979 and 1987) and by notices issued by the Bank of England under powers granted to it under the Banking Acts. However, much of the momentum for such supervision has come from two international bodies, the European Commission and the Committee on Banking Regulations and Supervisory Practices (the Basle Committee, which meets at the Bank for International Settlements in Basle, Switzerland). The principal aspects relating to banking supervision which are now covered or planned to be covered by these two bodies, is increasing all the time, the principal issues at the time of writing being:

- Consolidated supervision
- Minimum level of capital
- Capital adequacy, involving the calculation of own funds, the application of risk weighting and credit conversion factors, in order to establish solvency ratios
- Large exposures
- Liquidity and reserve assets
- Sovereign debt provisioning
- Deposit guarantee schemes
- Authorization, harmonization and mutual recognition
- Annual accounts of banks
- Branch accounts of institutions having head offices overseas
- Composition of board of directors and management
- Controlling shareholders
- Reorganization and winding-up of credit institutions

The majority of these issues have been covered in the United Kingdom by legislation or notices issued by the Bank of England.

The role of the Bank of England

The Bank of England (the Bank) has acted as the supervisory authority for the UK banking system for many years, but it was not until the enactment of the Banking Act 1979 that the Bank had statutory powers in discharging its supervisory role, such powers being deemed to be necessary in response to the secondary banking crisis of 1973/74 and the harmonization requirements of banking directives issued by the European Commission. Following the problems experienced by Johnson Matthey Bankers in 1984 and other developments and events, the Bank's supervisory activities and its approach to banking supervision were reappraised, resulting in stronger and wider powers being given to the Bank by the Banking Act 1987.

One of the changes made in the 1987 Act was to end the distinction between the banks and licensed deposit-takers, replacing them with a single category of 'authorized institutions'. However, the Act includes a wide prohibition on the use of banking names, and a newly formed authorized institution incorporated in the United Kingdom may only use a banking name if it has paid-up share capital and/or undistributable reserves of at least £5 million. In addition, an overseas bank may establish a representative office in the UK using the banking name under which it carries on business in its country of origin, on giving two months' written notice to the Bank of England and providing 'such information or documents as the Bank may reasonably require'. To establish a branch or a subsidiary, it is necessary to complete a longer and more detailed authorization procedure.

Although the Bank operates under statutory powers, with a specialist Banking Supervision Division being responsible for supervision, it adopts, wherever possible, a flexible approach. Notices and consultative papers issued on various topics are designed to explain in detail the approach to specific areas and few of them prescribe specific limits or ratios.

Directives from the European Commission

The Commission's supervisory powers are largely indirect, since the method of implementing a Directive, once it has been approved, is for each member state of the European Community to pass appropriate legislation enacting the provision of the Directive into national law. The approved process for Directives is lengthy, involving first the adoption of a proposed Directive by the Commission, which submits it to the Council of Ministers. The Council will then normally agree a 'common position' on the basis of a (weighted) majority vote. The proposed Directive will then be referred by the Commission to the European Parliament and to the Economic and Social Committee, in order to achieve agreement between these three bodies. Once such agreement is achieved, the proposed Directive is re-submitted to the Parliament for a second reading, and to the Council for final approval, which can only be withheld (if both Commission and Parliament have agreed a 'common position') on a unanimous vote by the members of the Council. When this approval process has been completed, the Directive is binding on each member state of the Community, which is obliged to implement the Directive by passing national laws in accordance with its terms, which are regarded as minimum standards, within a specified time limit.

It should be appreciated that Directives from the Commission apply to what are called 'Credit Institutions', which are defined as undertakings whose business is to receive deposits or other repayable funds from the public and to grant credits for its own account. This definition obviously covers a number of different types of institutions other than banks. Certain Directives also apply to what are termed 'Financial Institutions', which are defined as undertakings, not being Credit Institutions, the principal activity of which is to grant credit facilities (including guarantees) to acquire participation or to make investments.

The principal Directives issued by the Commission to date are the Credit Institutions Directive (often referred to as the First Banking Directive) passed in 1977, the provisions of which were substantially implemented in the United Kingdom by the Banking Act 1979, the Directives on Consolidated Supervision of Credit Institutions, and on the Annual Accounts of Banks and other Financial Institutions.

The principal proposed Directives, some of which have already been adopted by the Commission and submitted to the Council of Ministers and the European Parliament, are the Directives on Own Funds, on Solvency Ratios, on Branch Accounts, and the Second Banking Directive. The Commission has also issued Recommendations on Large Exposures and on Deposit Guarantee Schemes. A Recommendation has no legal effect, but it expresses the Commission's wish that member states may decide to implement legislation reflecting the Recommendation, and is likely to be followed by a Directive at a later date.

The principal objective of the Second Banking Directive is to enable credit institutions authorized to operate in one member state of the Community to set up branches and to operate in other member states without the necessity of obtaining further authorization. The effect of this system of mutual recognition is to allow Community-based banks, including such institutions owned or controlled by a non Community-based institution, to operate in all countries in the Community under a single banking licence once authorization has been obtained from one national supervisory body. This reciprocity for a non-Community-controlled institution will not, however, apply if its home country discriminates against Community-controlled banks. It is of particular interest to leasing companies — whether based in the United Kingdom or elsewhere in the Community — that, included in those activities regarded as integral to banking and therefore within the scope of mutual recognition and automatic authorization, are financial leasing and hire-purchase and conditional or credit sale activities. Certain sections of the leasing community have protested that, as a result of this system of mutual recognition, leasing companies will be in a privileged position compared to independent lessors, by being able to set up leasing (and other) subsidiaries in other member states without obtaining local authorization. This is incorrect since the basis of mutual recognition and automatic authorization throughout the Community only applies to the establishment of branches of existing authorized institutions, who can thereby offer their services on a cross-border basis and not to the establishment of subsidiaries in another member state. The system of mutual recognition is, of course, based upon the harmonization of common standards laid down by the various Directives in relation to the authorization, supervision and capital requirements of such institutions.

The Committee on Banking Regulations and Supervisory Practices

The Basle Committee comprises representatives of the central banks and supervisory authorities of the 'Group of Ten' (G–10) countries (Belgium, Canada, France, Italy, Japan, Netherlands, Sweden, Switzerland, UK, USA, Germany and Luxembourg). Its supervisory powers (like those of the Commission) are indirect, although since the supervisory authorities themselves are represented on the Committee its proposals and recommendations are likely to be acceptable, in principle, to those countries involved.

Although the Basle Committee has issued reports on different issues over a number of years, the Committee's most important (and its most recent) paper is its Report entitled *International Convergence of Capital Measurement and Capital Standards*, issued in July 1988 following a consultative process involving the G–10 countries; the contents of the final agreed paper were also endorsed by the G–10 central-bank governors. As with Directives from the Commission, national authorities were then required to prepare papers setting out the timetable and the manner for implementing the recommendations of the Report in their respective countries. The Report was also circulated to banking supervisory authorities world wide to encourage its adoption in other countries in respect of those banks conducting substantial international business.

The Report sets out the details of the agreed framework for measuring capital adequacy and the minimum standard to be achieved. The two fundamental objectives of the Report were 'to strengthen the soundness and stability of the international banking system',[1] and to establish a framework that is 'fair and has a high degree of consistency in its application to banks in different countries with a view to diminishing an existing source of competitive inequality among international banks',[2] the concept of convergence (or the level playing field).The framework laid down by the Report does, however, allow a degree of discretion in certain very limited respects in the way in which it is applied by each national supervisory authority. The Committee also maintained close contact with the authorities of the European Community in Brussels with the aim of ensuring 'the maximum degree of consistency between the framework agreed in Basle and the framework to be applied in the Community'[3] under the Commission's proposed Directives on Own Funds and on Solvency Ratios. It should be noted that, while these Directives will apply to all credit institutions in the European Community, the Basle Committee's framework for capital adequacy was directed more specifically with banks undertaking international business in mind.

Principal aspects of banking supervision

As a result of the diversified framework under which banking supervision is implemented, and the different approaches and policies adopted by the various bodies involved in banking supervision, it is difficult to provide comprehensive summaries of all the various topics and issues dealt with by supervisory authorities. Set out below are summaries of the principal aspects of banking supervision, with particular regard to the policies adopted by the Bank of England.

CONSOLIDATED SUPERVISION

The purpose of applying consolidated supervision is to ensure that the business undertaken by a bank and other credit/authorized institutions controlled by it are managed in accordance with, in particular, two of the other major tenets of supervision, capital adequacy and large exposures. However, the Bank of England also supervises authorized institutions on an individual basis (solo supervision), in order to ensure that each individual institution meets the Bank's minimum requirements regarding matters such as capital, liquidity and large exposures.

Many banking groups in the United Kingdom have a number of different authorized institutions within the group, with the result that each authorized institution (including most finance houses) are subject to regulation on both an individual basis under solo supervision and on a consolidated basis with their parent banks. However, very closely related subsidiaries who have no creditors other than the parent bank itself may, with the agreement of the Bank of England, be regarded as part of the parent bank itself for the purpose of solo supervision.

CAPITAL ADEQUACY

This is perhaps the most important single aspect of banking supervision, since the financial strength of a bank is fundamental to its ability to fulfil its important position in the financial system of a country and to be regarded as an acceptable receiver of deposits from the general public. The method by which the capital adequacy of authorized institutions is monitored is to test the adequacy of a bank's capital in relation to the risk of losses that may arise by measuring the ratio between (1) the capital (or own funds) held by an institution to support the business and (2) the assets of the institution. Both the Basle Report and the Commission's proposed Directives on Own Funds and on Solvency Ratios developed a framework for establishing the constituents of capital and, since a simple calculation of capital to total assets would be rather meaningless as it would ignore the nature and quality of the risk inherent in specific assets, also a system of weighting such assets.

In accordance with the stated intention that national authorities would prepare papers setting out, *inter alia*, the manner in which the Basle Report would be implemented in their respective countries, and bearing in mind that the agreed framework set out in the Report was designed to establish minimum levels of capital and that a degree of national discretion was allowed in a number of (limited) respects, the Bank of England issued in October 1988 a Notice to institutions authorized under the Banking Act 1987 entitled *Implementation of the Basle Convergence Agreement in the United Kingdom*, the contents of which will replace the Bank's previous arrangements for supervising capital adequacy. In addition to reflecting the basis on which the Bank intends to implement the Basle Report, the Notice also recognizes the need to meet the requirements of the Directives from the European Community. In this Notice (Ref.: BBSD/1988/3) the Bank indicated that it intended to apply the agreed framework to all UK institutions authorized under the Banking Act, and not just to banks with an international range of operations, and in accordance with its policy of both consolidation and solo supervision, while the proposals were to be applied on a consolidated basis, that the Bank would continue to assess capital adequacy on an unconsolidated basis to ensure that there was a reasonable distribution of capital within a group. As stated above, since the finance house subsidiaries (*inter alia*) of a number of UK banks are themselves authorized institutions, they will be subject to assessment of their capital adequacy on both an individual basis under 'solo' supervision and on a consolidated basis. However, certain authorized institutions which are regarded as specialist, such as discount houses and money funds, are exempt from the provisions of the Notice, and therefore presumably leasing (and other) subsidiaries of such institutions will only fall under these particular capital adequacy regulations if they themselves are authorized institutions.

As in the Basle Report, the Bank's Notice addressed the principal aspects of capital adequacy regulation, which are:

1. definition of capital;
2. risk-adjusted weights to be applied to assets (both on and off-balance sheet); and
3. minimum risk-adjusted capital ratio.

Full details of the different categories for 1. and 2. above are set out in Annex I of the Bank's Notice.

1. Definition of capital

This has become substantially more complex and less flexible than under the Bank's previous arrangements, the most important aspect being the division of capital into two tiers, with a strong emphasis on equity capital and reserves. Tier 1 (referred to as Core Capital) comprises fully paid share capital and preferred stock, which must be perpetual, non-cumulative and irredeemable or convertible at the issuer's option into common shares with the prior consent of the Bank, together with disclosed general reserves, which include retained earnings (including those having arisen during the current year if published by way of an interim statement), share premiums and capital reserves. From these must be deducted goodwill (and other intangible assets) and current year's losses. Retained earnings will, of course, be calculated after taxation, including provisions for deferred tax, and the Bank will no doubt ensure that authorized institutions make full provision for deferred taxation liabilities, including those arising from leasing activities. Tier 2, called Supplementary Capital, may not exceed Core Capital, and consists of undisclosed reserves (including unpublished current year's retained profits), fixed asset revaluation reserves, general provisions, hybrid capital (e.g. perpetual cumulative preferred shares, and convertible or perpetual subordinated debt), and subordinated term debt, subject to straight-line amortization over the five years preceding maturity. In addition to the overall limitations that Tier 2 capital may not exceed the total of Tier 1, subordinated term debt should not exceed 50 per cent of Tier 1 and general (bad debt) provisions should not exceed 1.5 per cent of weighted risk asset (1.25 per cent from 1 January 1993).

The comparative importance placed upon Tier 1 capital has resulted in many banks making strenuous efforts to increase this category of capital, for instance by the capitalizing (by way of a rights issue) of reserves otherwise categorized as Tier 2 capital or by structuring new capital issues to ensure that they are characterized as Tier 1 capital. Actions such as these will probably be of particular importance to banks in a number of OECD (and even G–10) countries who do not enjoy the access to new equity that is available in the United Kingdom and, for example, Japan, the United States of America and Germany.

Minority interests arising on consolidation from interests in shareholders' equity or in Tier 2 preference shares are eligible for inclusion in the appropriate tier, but investments in unconsolidated subsidiaries and associates, connected lending of a capital nature, and (most importantly, particularly since this was subject to the Bank's discretion) all holdings of other banks' and building societies' capital instruments, including perpetual floating rate notes (except those held by a bank acting as a market maker) are to be deducted from the total of Tier 1 and Tier 2. Another element of discretion where the Bank has taken the most conservative approach relates to the exclusion by the Bank from Tier 2 capital of 'latent' revaluation reserves (after applying a 55 per cent discount factor) arising from long-term holdings of equities.

2. Risk-adjusted weights to be applied to assets

When calculating a bank's weighted risk assets, both assets and off-balance sheet exposure are to be included and weighted according to broad categories of relative riskiness. In the Basle Report, the benchmark of weights to be applied, was kept as simple as possible, with five different weights being used, viz: 0, 10, 20, 50 and 100 per cent. The framework adopted by the Basle Committee focused on two principal different kinds of risk — credit risk and country (transfer) risk — while also taking account of other risks such as investment risk and interest and exchange rate risks. These broad categories of credit (or counterparty) risk were established to which different percentage weightings were given for calculating a bank's weighted risk assets as follows:

- Claims on domestic governments — nil weight
- Short-term claims on banks — 20 per cent weight
- Claims on the private sector — 100 per cent weight

On this basis was built a more complex structure, including the introduction of a 50 per cent weight for loans secured on residential first mortgages. Also, because the other risks referred to above needed to be reflected, proxy weights can be given for assets that would otherwise attract no capital requirement, e.g. fixed rate government securities. For example, the Bank of England has applied a 10 per cent weighting to fixed interest government securities with a remaining term to maturity of under one year and floating rate paper of any maturity, and 20 per cent for similar fixed interest paper with a remaining term to maturity of one year and over.

With regard to country transfer risk, the Basle Report concluded that those countries that are either full members of the Organization for Economic Co-operation and Development (see Table 23.1) or have concluded special banking arrangements with the International Monetary Fund (the IMF) associated with the IMF's General Arrangements to Borrow (which currently only applies to Saudi Arabia) (together referred to as the OECD) should be adopted as a basis for applying differential weighting coefficients for a number of aspects in calculating weighted risk assets. As a result, preferential weighting applies to risks (or claims) on three specific categories of OECD-based parties, being central governments, non-central government public-sector entities and banks. Claims on central governments within the OECD are to attract a zero weight, while claims on OECD non-central government public-sector entities (such as

Table 23.1 Members of the Organization for Economic Co-operation and Development (the OECD)

Australia	Greece	Norway
Austria	Iceland	Portugal
Belgium	Ireland	Spain
Canada	Italy	Sweden
Denmark	Japan	Switzerland
Finland	Luxembourg	Turkey
France	Netherlands	United Kingdom
Germany	New Zealand	United States

local authorities and development agencies) attract a low weight, recommended to be 20 per cent but permitted at between 0 and 50 per cent. Commercial companies owned by the public sector attract a uniform weight of 100 per cent, in order *inter alia* to avoid competitive inequality *vis-à-vis* similar private-sector commercial enterprises, unless of course guaranteed by the central government or other low-weighted party. To reflect the absence of risk relating to the availability and transfer of foreign exchange, claims on central governments and central banks outside the OECD will also attract a zero weight provided that such claims are denominated in the national currency and funded by liabilities in the same currency.

As regards the treatment of claims on other banks (in which category the Bank of England has effectively included UK building societies), as stated above, a 20 per cent weight will be applied to claims on all banks, wherever incorporated, with a residual maturity of up to and including one year, while longer term claims on OECD incorporated banks will also be weighted at 20 per cent, but on banks incorporated outside the OECD at 100 per cent. These weightings apply regardless of where the parent or controlling company of the bank is incorporated. Thus a claim against the UK-incorporated subsidiary of a non-OECD bank will attract a 20 per cent weighting for a transaction of greater than 12 months, while such a claim against the non-OECD parent bank itself or a subsidiary of an OECD bank incorporated in a non-OECD country would attract a 100 per cent weighting.

The inclusion of off-balance sheet transactions, including both contingent liabilities and commitments to reflect a bank's underlying exposure, is particularly important. This is effected through the application of a credit conversion factor, which may reduce the notional value of the exposure before the normal counterparty risk weight is applied.

The following is a summary of the principal risk weight categories for on-balance sheet assets set out in the Bank's Notice:

0%
- Cash, gold and other bullion held in vaults.
- Loans to OECD central governments and central banks.
- Loans to non-OECD central governments and central banks denominated and funded in local currency.

10%
- Loans to discount houses, gilt-edged market makers, etc., secured on gilts, UK Treasury bills, eligible local authority or bank bills, or London CDs.
- Holdings of OECD central government fixed interest rate securities with a residual maturity of up to one year, and floating rate securities of any maturity, and of non-OECD central government securities with a residual maturity of up to one year denominated and funded in local currency.

20%
- Holdings of OECD central government fixed interest rate securities with a residual maturity of one year and over, and of non-OECD central government securities of a maturity of one year and over denominated and funded in local currency.
- Claims on multilateral development banks (IBRD, IFC, IADB, AsDB, AfDB, EIB and CDB), on OECD incorporated banks (including UK building societies and discount houses), and non-OECD incorporated banks, with a residual maturity of up to one year.
- Claims on OECD public-sector entities (PSEs). In the UK, PSEs are local authorities and other non-commercial public corporations. At Table 23.2 are listed PSEs in the UK, as set out in Annex III to the Bank's Notice.

50%
- Loans and securities fully secured by a first equitable or legal charge over occupied residential property.

100%
- All other loans, claims and assets, including:
  – Claims on non-OECD incorporated banks with a residual maturity of one year and over.
  – Claims on non-OECD central governments or central banks not denominated and funded in local currency, and on non-OECD PSEs.
  – Claims on commercial companies owned by public sector (see Table 23.3 for UK companies, as set out in Annex III to the Bank's Notice).
  – Premises, plant, equipment, real estate, trade investments and fixed assets.

Note: 'Claims' include net amounts receivable under leases.

Table 23.2 UK public bodies classified as public-sector entities

Local authorities
London borough councils, county and district councils in England, Northern Ireland and Wales, and district and regional councils in Scotland, together with their departments (e.g. gas departments and water service departments but not transport departments); those bodies formed on 1 April 1986 to take over the assets and functions of the former metropolitan councils and the GLC; the state governments in the Channel Islands, the Isle of Man Government; and the following local bodies:

Central Scotland Water Development
  Board
Fire services
Fire services colleges
Forth Road Bridge Joint Board
Humber Bridge Board
Magistrates' Courts
Markets (municipally owned)

Police Colleges
Police Forces (including Metropolitan
  Police)
Polytechnics
Probation Service in England and
  Wales
Quarries (municipally owned)
Scottish River Purification Boards
Teacher-training colleges

Non-commercial public corporations
The Audit Commission
Cable Authority
Covent Garden Market Authority
Development Board for Rural Wales
English Industrial Estates Corporation
General Practice Finance Corporation
Her Majesty's Stationery Office
Highlands and Islands Development
  Board
Housing Action Trusts
Independent Broadcasting Authority
Letchworth Garden City
National Dock Labour Board

New Town Development Corporations
  and Commission for the New Towns
Northern Ireland Housing Executive
Oil and Pipeline Agency
The Pilotage Commission
Royal Mint
Scottish Development Agency
Scottish Housing Association
UK Atomic Energy Authority
Urban Development Corporation
Welsh Development Agency
The Welsh Fourth Channel Authority

It should also be noted that claims and loans guaranteed or collateralized by any of the above will attract the lower risk-weighting applicable in respect of the primary obligor and the guarantor and the collateral, i.e. ECGD and SMFC loans guaranteed by the UK Government will attract a 0 per cent weighting. However, any exposure to the private sector (unless guaranteed by a lower risk-weighted counterparty) is weighted at 100 per cent resulting in a loan or lease to (for example) British Petroleum or a petrol-filling station attracting the same risk-weighting.

In the case of the leasing and finance market, it should be noted that plant and equipment, which were previously deducted in calculating the net capital available for a bank, are now treated as ordinary assets as are all

Table 23.3 UK public bodies not eligible for classification as public-sector entities

Nationalized industries

British Coal Corporation	London Regional Transport
British Railways Board	National Bus Company
British Shipbuilders	North of Scotland Hydro-Electric
British Steel Corporation	Board
British Waterways Board	Post Office
Civil Aviation Authority	Scottish Transport Group
Electricity England and Wales —	South of Scotland Electricity Board
including Central Electricity	Water England and Wales — including
Generating Board and Area Boards	Regional Water Authorities

Other public corporations

British Technology Group (including	Crown suppliers
NEB and NRDC and their	Northern Ireland Electricity Service
subsidiaries)	Northern Ireland Transport Holding
The British Broadcasting Corporation	Company
The Crown Agents	Passenger Transport Executives
The Crown Agents Holding and	
Realization Board	

Other local authority bodies

Airports (municipally owned)	Kingston-upon-Hull Telephone System
Airport companies	Local authority passenger transport
Ferries (municipally owned)	departments
	Ports and harbours (municipally owned)

The following bodies are not in the public sector and should be classified as non-bank private sector:

Air Travel Trust	Council of Industrial board
British Agricultural Export Council	Marketing boards
British Institute of Management	National Building Agency
British Standards Institute	Western Hemisphere Export Council

Note: Since the issue of Annex III to the Bank of England Notice of October 1988, there have been a number of changes to the names and the structure of bodies listed.

real estate holdings, which had previously been weighted 200 per cent. Such assets include (for UK institutions) assets leased by the institution on a finance lease basis, but not those leased under an operating lease. This may therefore increase the attraction to such institutions of leasing assets on an operating lease basis, rather than under a finance lease, or of purchasing them outright.

It is perhaps of greater importance, however, to note that no differential weighting is applied to transactions involving asset risk, such as operating leasing and asset underwriting facilities, where there is no recourse to a third party for recovery of the lessor's (or bank's) investment. As a result, there is no specific discouragement by either the Basle Report or the Bank of England of operating leasing by lessors that are members of an authorized institution's group. This is in contrast to regulations issued in the United States by the Federal Reserve Board and the Comptroller of the Currency, which limit the levels of residual values that may be assumed by banks (or bank-holding companies) and their subsidiaries regulated by these bodies to 20 and 25 per cent respectively of the price paid by such an institution for an asset.

The importance accorded to the OECD group of countries, in respect of claims against both the central government and central banks, and commercial banks incorporated therein, also deserve careful attention. While the member countries of the OECD certainly include the strongest economies in the world, there are a number of OECD countries that are rated below certain non-OECD countries, in particular countries in South-East Asia. Taiwan, South Korea and Singapore were all rated in the top 20 countries and a number of Comecon countries were in the top 30, while Greece and Turkey were rated 33rd and 47th respectively (Euromoney in its table published in September 1988).

With regard to off-balance sheet items, the Credit Conversion Factors by which the face value of each item is multiplied, before applying the normal counterparty risk weights, are as follows:

100%
- Direct credit substitutes, e.g. guarantees, standby letters of credit serving as financial guarantees, and acceptances.
- Sale and repurchase agreements, and asset sales with recourse.
- Forward asset purchases, forward deposits and the unpaid part of partly paid shares and securities.

50%
- Performance and bid bonds, warranties and standby letters of credit for similar purposes.
- Note issuance facilities (NIFs) and revolving underwriting facilities (RUFs).
- Other commitments (e.g. formal standby facilities and credit lines) with a residual maturity of one year and over.

20%
- Short-term self-liquidating trade-related contingencies (e.g. documentary credits collateralized by underlying shipments).

0%
- Standby facilities and credit lines with a maturity of up to one year, or which can be cancelled at any time (except on a *force majeure* basis only).

The third category of claims or exposures for which a bank must calculate its risk-weighted assets relates to interest and foreign exchange rate related instruments, including swaps, currency and interest rate futures and options and forward rate agreements. Higher conversion factors apply to those contracts based on exchange risk to reflect the greater volatility of exchange rates. The Bank accepted the position agreed by the Basle Committee that, since most counterparties in these markets, particularly for long-term contracts, tend to be first-class names, a 50 per cent weight would be applied in respect of counterparties that would otherwise attract a 100 per cent weight.

In order to calculate the credit equivalent amount of these instruments, a bank should add together (i) the total replacement cost (obtained by 'marking to market') of all of its contracts with a positive value, and (ii) an amount for potential future credit exposure which reflects the residual maturity of the contract, calculated as a percentage of the notional principal amount according to the following matrix:

	Interest rate contracts	Exchange rate contracts
Less than one year	Nil	1.0% (greater than 14 days)
One year and over	0.5%	5.0%

This method of calculating credit risk equivalents was preferred by the Bank to the alternative method permitted under the Basle Report called the 'original exposure method', under which no 'revaluation' of the contract is made but an annual conversion factor is applied.

3. Minimum risk-adjusted capital ratio

The Notice states that the Bank's capital requirements will continue to be specified as trigger and target ratios. The 8 per cent minimum standard (as laid down by the Basle Report, although to be achieved over a transitional period by end–1992, with an interim ratio of 7.25 per cent to be achieved by end–1990) will become the base line for the Bank's discretion in setting the requirements of both consolidated and individual authorized bank levels. It is not intended to alter the levels of trigger and target ratios agreed with each bank (determined by the Bank with regard to the size of a bank, the mix of its business, the experience of its management, etc.), and these ratios will continue to reflect each bank's particular cicumstances. In most cases these will be considerably higher than the 8 per cent minimum; figures published by the Bank showed that the aggregate capital ratio of the eight largest British banks in 1987 was 9.8 per cent. Any change in a bank's actual ratio arising from switching from the old to the new framework will not be regarded in itself as justification for revising a bank's trigger or target ratio (either downwards or upwards).

With regard to the timing of the implementation of the provisions of the Bank's Notice, the Bank indicated that it wants banks to report on the new basis as quickly as possible, and that it was aiming for first reports to be

301

made as at 30 June 1989, with all reporting by all authorized institutions to have been changed from the framework based on the Bank's 'The Measurement of Liquidity' paper by no later than the end of 1989. In December 1990, the Bank issued two further notices (BSD/1990/2 and 3) to formally implement in the United Kingdom the EC Directives on Own Funds and on Solvency Ratios, both of which required implementation in each member state by no later than 1 January 1993. However, the content of the Directives differed little from the Basle Convergence Agreement, and implementation implied minimal change to the existing capital adequacy regulations in the United Kingdom, and none to the Bank's overall policy for this area.

Under 'The Measurement of Liquidity' referred to above, the Bank considered, in addition to a 'risk asset ratio', the gearing ratio of each bank defined as the ratio of deposits and other non-capital liabilities (excluding liabilities on acceptances and contingent liabilities) to the bank's 'adjusted capital base'. Since no mention of this ratio is made in the Bank's Notice, it is assumed that the Bank will not continue to apply this ratio, which was designed primarily to ensure that the capital position of an institution was regarded as acceptable by its depositors (and other creditors).

LARGE EXPOSURES

As well as assessing the capital adequacy of banking institutions generally, under powers granted to it under the Banking Act 1987 the Bank has developed policies regarding large exposures to try to ensure that no one problem can result in the failure of a bank. These policies are detailed in a notice issued by the Bank in September 1987 (and by subsequent amendments) entitled 'Large exposures undertaken by institutions authorized under the Banking Act 1987' (BSD/1987/1), and were introduced in particular as a result of the near failure of Johnson Matthey Bankers, many of whose problems stemmed from large exposures to connected borrowers. The Banking Act 1987 requires authorized institutions to inform the Bank after the event on each reporting date of any exposure to an individual non-bank customer, or group of closely-related customers, in excess of 10 per cent of a bank's capital base (after adding back holdings of other banks' capital) and to report in advance any exposure in excess of 25 per cent of capital. In practice, the Bank also limits the number of exposures in excess of 25 per cent except in the most exceptional circumstances. Futhermore,unlike its application of the regulations relating to capital adequacy, the Bank takes the most pessimistic view of any exposure and does not accept that security serves to reduce any exposure since it is concerned that there exists a risk in respect of the lender's arrangements for controlling security in such circumstances. In its September 1987 Notice, the Bank stated that 'it is difficult to determine with certainty what constitutes a well secured exposure. The worth of security can never be fully tested until it is realised'. While the Bank accepts that security can mitigate large exposures, it is unlikely that, in particular, security would be taken into account with regard to exposures over 25 per cent. Where ownership of an asset is held (rather than a charge over an asset as security), the Bank has not indicated whether it regards such ownership, as would be held by a lessor, as being more satisfactory than a mortgage or other charge being taken over the same asset as security.

Excluded from exposures of greater than 25 per cent of a bank's capital base requiring pre-notification are inter-bank loans of up to one year, and exposures to overseas central governments, provided lending limits for these have been pre-notified to, and accepted by, the Bank. Similarly, exposures to local authorities, nationalized industries, and other PSEs are excluded if all such an entity's liabilities are guaranteed by the central government.

Exposures include not only loans, overdrafts, leases and other on-balance sheet items but also guarantees on behalf of a customer, undrawn commitments and other contingent liabilities. As well as monitoring exposures to connected parties, banks are also expected to set limits for both individual country exposures and different economic and industrial sectors. Special arrangements apply to large exposures, whether in respect of equity or debt securities, arising from securities' underwriting or market-making.

It is possible that this policy relating to large exposures could cause some problems to smaller institutions in the leasing market. While most banking transactions can be sub-participated or funded without recourse, and consequently can escape the large exposure rules, in a lease in order to continue to be entitled to claim capital allowances a lessor must retain beneficial ownership of an asset. The only way for the risk in such a transaction to be shared is for another party (or parties) to provide a guarantee of the obligations of the lessee, but under the large exposure rules the guarantee would only be regarded by the Bank as some mitigation of the exposure, which could not in practice exceed 25 per cent of the lessor group's total capital. This could limit the size of any one transaction which, in particular, a small or medium-sized institution might wish to write, even if the credit risk has in practice been removed. The Bank's Notice recognizes that certain types of security should be considered as sufficient justification for an exposure to exceed 25 per cent of the bank's capital base. It notes three acceptable categories (subject to certain conditions and provisos), namely British Government Stock (amended under Notice BSD/1992/2 issued in February 1992 to OECD central government securities), cash deposits held with the lender, or an ECGD bank guarantee.

Not surprisingly, the European Commission has also developed a policy in respect of large exposures, at this time only in the form of a Recommendation. The provisions of this Recommendation are, however, almost entirely less restrictive than those of the 1987 Banking Act and the Bank's Notice.

LIQUIDITY

The Bank's paper ' The Measurement of Liquidity' was published in July 1982, and in March 1988 a new consultative paper on liquidity was issued. While of little direct concern to many leasing companies, the terms of these papers naturally need to be followed by those leasing companies that are authorized institutions and/or by their parent or lending banks. The Bank requires that such an institution has sufficient immediately available cash or liquid assets, an appropriate matching future profile of cash flows from maturing assets and liabilities, and a well-diversified deposit base in terms of both maturities and range of depositors. Although this policy is adopted on a consolidated basis of all currencies, the Bank expects an institution with substantial foreign currency loans and deposits to monitor different currencies individually.

RESERVE ASSETS

Although not strictly an aspect of supervision, since the administration is carried out by the Bank's Money Market Operations Division, the requirement of the Bank for each authorized institution that has eligible liabilities of £10 million or more, to hold non-operational, non-interest-bearing deposits with the Bank, is of greater importance to lessors, whether authorized institutions themselves or not. These deposits provide resources (and income) for the Bank to enable it to participate directly in the sterling money-market. The level of such deposits to be maintained is set at 0.45 per cent of an institution's average eligible liabilities (established every six months), eligible liabilities being broadly sterling deposit liabilities other than those with an original maturity of two years or more, less funds lent by an institution to another in the monetary sector and money at call placed with money brokers or gilt-edged jobbers and secured by gilt-edged stocks, Treasury bills or local authority and bank bills. Futhermore, the Bank can call for further special deposits, although these bear interest at the Treasury bills' rate.

The impact of this requirement to hold 'reserve assets' at the Bank is well known, in both the banking sector in general and the leasing market. 'Big ticket' leases in particular often include a provision to compensate a lessor for either the cost thereof or for any increased costs resulting from changes in the regulations or effect thereof upon the lessor.

304

SOVEREIGN DEBT PROVISIONING

As leasing becomes a more and more popular method of providing finance internationally, and with its being of particular interest to institutions providing finance for developing countries, some lessors will need to assess the possible impact of the Bank's paper on debt provisioning issued in August 1987. This paper sets out a matrix framework of 15 different factors (economic, monetary, regulatory, etc.) intended to indicate the likelihood and ability of a particular country to service its debts or to permit borrowers resident in the country to repay borrowings. The most important factor is whether debt repayments from that country are (or have been) subject to rescheduling or a moratorium. On the basis of the total number of points allocated, the Bank recommends the appropriate range of levels at which provisions should be made. This system applies to both existing and new loans to the countries concerned, and can therefore now result in an authorized institution being recommended by the Bank to make provisions on such a loan as soon as it is made.

ADVERTISING FOR AND PROTECTION OF DEPOSITS

One of the most important provisions of the Banking Acts relates to the Deposit Protection Scheme. Much of the purpose of banking supervision is, of course, directed towards the safeguarding of an authorized institution's depositors, and in addition the Treasury, in consultation with the Bank and the Building Societies Commission, can issue regulations covering the content and form of advertising for deposits.

All authorized institutions are required, whether or not they accept sterling deposits, to contribute to the Deposit Protection Fund, subject to certain minimum and maximum levels. If an authorized institution becomes insolvent, a depositor, other than another authorized institution and certain connected parties, will be paid out of the fund 75 per cent of protected deposits up to £20,000, i.e. a maximum receipt of £15,000 by each depositor. Secured deposits, deposits with an original term of more than five years and certificates of deposit are excluded from this protection.

AUTHORIZATION OF INSTITUTIONS

The Banking Act 1987 provides for the prior authorization and continuing supervision of institutions which wish to carry out a deposit-taking activity. The initial authorization is carried out on the basis of an application to the Bank, which needs to be satisfied that the specific requirements set out in Schedule 3 to the Act, covering six principal areas, are met:

- Competence, experience, judgement and (perhaps most important) probity of directors, controllers and managers ('fit and proper person to hold the particular position which he holds or is to hold').

- Business to be directed by at least two individuals.
- Composition of the board of directors, including such number (if any) of non-executive directors considered appropriate by the Bank having regard to the circumstances of the institution, and the scale and nature of its operations.
- Business to be conducted in a prudent manner, such as maintaining net assets, other financial resources, liquidity, adequate provisions, and adequate accounting and other records and systems of control.
- Business to be carried on with integrity and appropriate professional skills.
- Minimum net assets (paid up capital and reserves) not less than £1 million (£5 million if a banking name is to be used).

In addition, the Bank operates a system of pre-authorization of 'shareholder controllers' (defined as a person or corporation, acting either alone or with associates, who can control 15 per cent or more of the voting power of an institution). Significant shareholders, being those who control between 5 and 15 per cent, are required to advise the Bank in writing within seven days of taking such an interest. Authorized institutions themselves have the obligation to notify the Bank of any changes in control.

ACCOUNTING RECORDS, REPORTS, RETURNS AND INTERNAL CONTROL
In addition to their obligations to maintain and prepare accounts under the Companies Acts, and in accordance with Statements of Standard Accounting Practice, and to provide information and returns to the Inland Revenue and HM Customs and Excise, authorized institutions have a number of further obligations under the Banking Acts, under papers issued by the Bank, and under the Commission's Directive on the Annual Accounts of Banks and other Financial Institutions. This Directive was approved by the Council of Ministers in 1986, and member states are required to bring the Directive into national law by 31 December 1990, with implementation for accounts for financial years beginning on or after 1 January 1993. While the overriding requirement of the Directive is that the accounts show a true and fair view, there are a number of requirements for disclosure greater than that currently required under UK legislation and different rules regarding the valuation of certain classes of assets and foreign currency assets and liabilities. Futhermore, the Directive (with certain minor exceptions) forbids the creation or use of hidden reserves.

All authorized institutions are required to submit regular returns for prudential purposes ('prudential returns') based around a detailed monthly balance sheet. The information provided permits the Bank to assess the nature and spread of the institution's business, ratios of capital adequacy, liquidity and the maturity profiles of assets and liabilities. The Bank also holds regular meetings with the senior management of each institution and makes visits to the institution to assist the Bank's understanding of the institution's operations, controls and policies, and most importantly of the competence and quality of management.

In addition, the Bank requires independent reporting accountants (who will probably be the institution's auditors), to carry out independent reviews of accounting and other records, of internal control systems and of the prudential returns themselves, with regular trilateral meetings being held between the Bank, the institution and the accountants. The reporting accountants may also report direct to the Bank without first referring to the client in certain circumstances where, in particular, the accountants believe that depositors may be at risk. The Bank has also laid down a number of general principles in relation to an institution's internal controls and systems, one of the principal purposes of which is to ensure that the Bank's supervision is carried out on a prudent basis through its ability to monitor and control the quality of the institution's assets and its risk exposures. The internal control systems should be aided wherever possible by an internal audit function. Finally, in a consultative paper issued in January 1987, the Bank has indicated that it wishes to see audit committees, or for smaller banks committees comprising non-executive directors, established to review *inter alia* the institution's risk profile, its management procedures and its compliance with the various regulatory and financial reporting requirements.

Conclusion

What are the consequences of this comprehensive framework of supervision on the leasing activities of, in particular, authorized institutions? Supervision is intended to ensure that authorized institutions conduct their business prudently in order, above all, to protect depositors. The single most important aspect is probably capital adequacy, where the full impact of the new regulations being applied, both in the UK and world wide, will not be known for many years. It can, however, be said that major steps have been made to achieve the stated aim of 'convergence', or the level playing field, for banks and other financial institutions operating internationally, although there remains a number of areas where national supervisory authorities can exercise fairly wide discretion. Although it might be said that non-bank leasing companies will enjoy an advantage from not having to comply with these banking regulations, such lessors will of course need to raise finance from banks and other financial institutions, particularly since they are by definition unable to raise funds by way of deposits from the public. Such commercial providers of finance will doubtless be unwilling to provide funds above prudent commercial levels to such lessors, especially if any excessive growth of an independent leasing company were to be at the expense of their own group leasing companies.

One particular impact upon the leasing industry of the new capital adequacy regulations may be that, as a result of the inclusion of 'off-balance sheet' exposures in calculating a bank's weighted risk assets, pressure will increase not only for all countries to require lessees to capitalize finance leases, but also for lessees to capitalize (in line with the philosophy of ED 49) their minimum lease obligations under operating leases. Whatever the impact, lessors will need to place a greater emphasis on playing to their strengths in attracting business, on the structuring of transactions and on the raising of funds at the lowest rate possible in order to generate the premium returns traditionally generated by lessors.

NOTES

1. *International Convergence of Capital Measurement and Capital Standards*, Committee on Banking Regulations and Supervisory Practices (the Basle Committee), July 1988, paragraph 3.
2. Ibid.
3. Ibid., paragraph 4.

24. *Main markets*

Computer leasing

Operating leasing has in the past tended to be a minority sector in equipment leasing, primarily because most providers of equipment finance have not been prepared to take risks on the ultimate value of equipment. Within the operating-leasing category, computer leasing, and almost specifically the leasing of IBM computers, has become the most developed and mature. By the late 1980s, it was estimated that the leasing of IBM computers world wide had a value probably well in excess of US$10 billion per annum, and it is a market that is continuing to grow.

The leasing of IBM computers started in the early 1960s and its growth was the result of a combination of factors that made this business very attractive. In 1964 IBM announced its 360 series, and for the first time decided that they were standardizing the internal architecture of their computers so that all future large IBM mainframes would be compatible with the original 360 system. Users therefore were secure in the knowledge that software written would be transferable to any future series and, from the point of view of the investor in this equipment, it meant that a ready market for the second-hand product would be available.

Eight years previous to the announcement of the 360 series, IBM had made a settlement with the US Department of Justice, which was prosecuting the company for alleged breaches of the Anti-Trust legislation. IBM reached a Consent Decree with the Department of Justice under which they agreed henceforth to abide by certain principles of business. In particular, they agreed to offer their equipment for sale as well as for rent. Prior to that time IBM would only offer their machinery on a rental basis. It was stipulated that the sale price had to bear an economic relationship to the monthly rental charge. Other provisions under the Consent Decree were that IBM were not allowed to discriminate between new and second user equipment, in that they were obliged to provide identical levels of maintenance and software support.

The result of this combination of events was that potential investors were able to quantify the value of equipment at a future date, with the certainty that IBM would continue to support that equipment, even if they had superseded these machines with more advanced computers.

In the 1960s, in the United States in particular, the computer-leasing business grew at a rapid rate and was pioneered by entrepreneurial companies such as Leasco, Greyhound Computer, DPF&G, and Boothe Computer. All of these operations achieved great prominence during the late 1960s, becoming public companies in their own right based on their very rapid growth.

In 1970 IBM announced their 370 series of computers which effectively replaced the 360. For those computer-leasing companies that had been assuming unrealistic periods of depreciation, the introduction of the 370 was catastrophic. Massive write-downs in the value of equipment were made and the computer-leasing industry suffered its first public loss of confidence. Nevertheless, during the 1970s, many large and traditional financial institutions became aware that computer-leasing offered a vast and effective method of deploying funds and they entered the business. Examples were Citibank, Bank of America, Chemical Bank, and Standard Chartered Bank. Not only were computer-leasing companies able to deploy funds quickly, but because the products being leased were very large computer systems, their customers were almost exclusively blue chip operators. It was a source of pride to the computer-leasing industry that bad debts were negligible and in some cases even nil, and for many financial institutions computer-leasing offered the opportunity to gain access to corporate clients that had previously not been available.

The rate of growth of computer-leasing by the mid-1970s was so rapid there were fears that the risks involved in assuming over-optimistic residual values for the equipment were rapidly leading to a major crisis. An alternative source of risk coverage was, therefore, sought.

American banks in particular were prohibited by 'Regulation Y' issued by the Federal Reserve Bank, which precluded them from taking substantial risks in capital equipment. To fulfil this need for risk coverage, underwriters at Lloyds of London offered residual value insurance on IBM equipment using the 'J' policy.

The availability of this cover was misunderstood by several computer-leasing companies who saw the policy as quasi-equity and not, as was the case, insurance for residual risk. Business was written that was highly imprudent and by the end of the 1970s it was becoming evident that a major crisis was in the offing. In 1979 IBM announced their 434X series of computers which very rapidly made obsolete the middle range of computers that IBM had introduced as part of their 370 series and, in consequence, massive claims were made under the Lloyds 'J' policy. It is estimated that underwriters suffered losses in the region of US$500 million, making it the largest loss that Lloyds had suffered at that time. It also led to the demise of the international leading computer-leasing company, the Itel Corporation.

In the 1980s computer leasing grew rapidly again and, in Britain in particular, computer-leasing companies looked towards publicly supplied funds to meet their equity requirements. United Leasing was the first computer-leasing company to obtain a full quote on the London Stock

310

Exchange, followed rapidly by Atlantic Computers, IBL, Dataserv, Computer Capital and CPS. From the beginning the City had difficulty in understanding the concept of residual value accounting which was interpreted, in principle, as the taking of profits before they were realized. It was a problem that continued to affect all the computer-leasing companies.

In the 1985–86 period, there was some public controversy concerning the residual value accounting policies of a number of then independent specialized computer lessors in the UK, which were publicly quoted companies and whose stock market valuations were felt in some cases to be influenced by optimistic residual value accounting. The problem tended to recede in the following years, as some of these computer lessors appeared to move towards more conservative accounting policies and most of them were merged into larger international companies, within which the computer residuals formed a relatively small part of total group assets.

By 1988 only Atlantic Computers, of the original six publicly quoted computer-leasing companies, existed in its own right. United, IBL and CPS had each in turn been acquired by the Inspectorate Group, based in Switzerland; Dataserv had been acquired by Bellsouth based in Atlanta; and Computer Capital was in turn acquired by Atlantic. The rationalization had occurred because computer-leasing had grown so fast, and the funding requirements were so great, that requirements were vast and only large corporate funding could provide the secure equity base necessary to develop the business. In the United States, Comdisco continued to be the market leader.

UK computer-leasing companies had developed complicated structures to finance their business. In general the computer-leasing companies would enter into a lease with their customers and would then either assign that lease to a traditional equipment-leasing company, or enter into a head lease/sublease arrangement, again with a traditional equipment-leasing company. Unlike most traditional lessors, computer-leasing companies were not in business to maximize their margins, but to realize their profits from residual values. Therefore it made sense for the computer-leasing companies to lay off the secure part of their lease with a general equipment-leasing company that was able to provide tax-based funding at the most advantageous rates.

The problem of residual value accounting resurfaced in a much more dramatic form in April 1990 with the failure of Atlantic Computers. Atlantic had specialized in writing particular types of upgrade and termination options for computer users, which allowed the latter to classify leases as operating leases and thus keep them off-balance sheet. Typically, a full payout finance lease would be written on new IBM or DEC mainframes, covering a period of seven years, but with break points at the lessee's discretion in the form of:

(a) a 'flex' option to upgrade the user's equipment after three years, usually through dispensing with the originally leased equipment and replacing this with a more up-to-date mainframe on a new lease;

(b) a 'walk' option, available after five years from the date of the original lease agreement, to terminate the lease and dispense with the equipment with no commitment to take a new lease from Atlantic.

Under both these options, Atlantic would regain possession of the originally leased asset where the lessee exercised the option, financing a full termination payment on the original finance lease from the value of the residual, which Atlantic then had to realize by a sale or lease of the second-hand equipment. The parties involved in such a lease varied in different cases. In most of these deals, which were known as an 'arranged lease', Atlantic was not acting as a lessor, but simply as a broker and as a dealer assuming residual value risk. A financial sector lessor introduced to the customer by Atlantic would write the original seven-year lease with the usual provisions for substantial amounts to be payable by the lessee on early termination. The 'flex/walk' options would be offered through a separate contract between Atlantic and the lessee, of which the financial lessor might have no knowledge. In some other cases, Atlantic itself took a head lease from a financial lessor and wrote the lease to the customer on a back-to-back basis; or took hire-purchase finance from the financier and wrote a 'tax-based' lease to the lessee; and in a few cases Atlantic wrote 'own book' leases from its own funds, with no asset-based finance from a third party. A consistent feature of all such deals, however, was the 'flex/walk' option structure, which allowed the lessee to treat the commitment as an operating lease.

The problem was that Atlantic had factored into these arrangements over-optimistic residual values. The customer would have expected to exercise one or other of the break options in virtually all cases, so that the final years' rentals would never be paid, and termination payments to clear these obligations were to be funded from the residual values. Atlantic was able to continue trading on these terms for a number of years, as long as most customers exercised the 'flex' (i.e. upgrade) option rather than the 'walk' option for a termination with no new Atlantic agreement. In the former case, unrealistic residuals could again be factored into a new lease written at the 'flex' point.

The structure finally collapsed with the exercise of 'walk' options by a number of customers, when it became apparent to Atlantic's auditors that the true residual values were insufficient to match the lease termination payments to which Atlantic was committed.

In 1987, while still trading apparently profitably, the holding company Atlantic Computers plc had been sold for more than £400 million by its directors, who had held most of the equity, to British and Commonwealth Holdings plc, a major 'conglomerate' group with a number of activities mainly in the financial sector, including a merchant bank and other companies active in the trading of financial securities and commodities. British and Commonwealth was in fact the largest non-bank financial company in the UK. This parent company responded to the emerging problems at Atlantic in April 1990 by placing Atlantic Computers plc and the latter's subsidiaries into administrative receivership under the Companies Act 1989. It very soon became apparent to the administrators that, though some overseas subsidiaries of Atlantic could be sold as going concerns, the core UK computer-leasing business vested in Atlantic Computers Systems plc was hopelessly insolvent. Returns to unsecured creditors in Atlantic would obviously be extremely small, and its equity had no value. For British and Commonwealth itself, the loss of its assets in Atlantic, in spite of the attempt to 'ring fence' these through the administration order, was so serious that its own credit lines soon began to collapse and the company was placed in administrative receivership in June 1990.

The failure of Atlantic as a computer lessor left a number of other parties seriously exposed to risk. The funding lessors on the 'arranged leases' — some of whom were long-established UK leasing companies, while others were international banks with only a limited involvement in the UK leasing market — were contractually protected in that the lessees were bound under the terms of the lease agreement to make rental payments for the full period of the finance lease. By the same token, however, the lessees (most of whom were substantial 'blue chip' industrial or commercial companies) were exposed to payments on later years' rentals, or termination payments, that they had never expected to incur because of the 'flex' or 'walk' options, having had no intention of retaining equipment in use for the full seven years of a finance lease; and were required to bring on to their balance sheets, as finance leases, commitments that had previously been off-balance sheet as operating leases. This problem for the lessees gave rise to potentially serious credit risks for the lessors, in the event that some lessees might default on the finance leases.

Most of the Atlantic lessees have made arrangements to replace their collapsed Atlantic options with alternative upgrade or termination facilities negotiated with other parties — in most cases with IBM and other manufacturers — which, while inevitably on less attractive terms than the original 'flexes' and 'walks', will nevertheless offer viable solutions to their equipment problems.

The practices used in the Atlantic group, whereby substantial annual profits could be reported over a long period on what was essentially unprofitable business, involved a combination of assuming unrealistic figures for residual values, and of unduly 'front-loading' these residuals by

313

taking a large proportion of them into the profit and loss account from the first year of the original lease period. The scope for such practices is by no means confined to computer-leasing, though the rapidly expanding nature of the computer market does give rise to particular uncertainties on second-hand values in this sector. There have been parallels in other sectors. A company that was in many ways similar to the Atlantic Group, though operating on a smaller scale — Blackspur Leasing Ltd, which had assumed residual value risk through 'flex' and 'walk' options on leased printing machinery — went into receivership in June 1990, for much the same reasons as Atlantic.

It seems clear that the principal deficiency that permitted the Atlantic type of abuse to be practised, lay in the accounting policies adopted for residual values, whichever party in a lease or associated arrangements is assuming such risks. In 1986, in response to earlier concerns surrounding computer lessors, the ELA established a joint working party with the Institute of Chartered Accountants in England and Wales (ICAEW) to examine the issues involved in residual value accounting on operating leases. This review undertook some analytical work on the accounting practices in use at the time on computer-leasing but was terminated at the instance of the ICAEW in the hope that the Accounting Standards Committee (ASC), representing all the professional accountancy bodies — which then held the responsibility for developing binding accounting standards — would itself take up the matter. No such action was taken by the ASC, and its former role in the formation of accounting standards has been taken over since 1 July 1990 by the statutory Accounting Standards Board (ASB). In response to a new approach from the ELA at the beginning of 1990, before the problems at Atlantic came to light, the ICAEW acted to commission a research study from a team of academic accountants at the University of Lancaster, on all the issues involved in residual value accounting. At the time of writing, the Lancaster study has not reached any conclusion, and the Finance and Leasing Association is proposing to formulate some substantive recommendations on residual value accounting for possible adoption by the ASB later.

Apart from residual value accounting policies, a characteristic of computer-leasing companies has been their deep involvement with the equipment itself. Profits were derived often not from the original lease but from the ability of the computer-leasing company to offer its customers facilities to terminate early. Such customers could replace their equipment with new equipment from IBM, or with second-hand equipment, or even with new equipment which the leasing companies had obtained from IBM in other countries (cross-border shopping) where perhaps a temporary exchange rates movement had given a pricing advantage that was eagerly taken up.

Most computer-leasing companies have departments involved in installation planning, maintenance, equipment, advice, and software servicing. They could differentiate their product from that offered by a general equipment-leasing company because they were totally conversant with IBM computers and could help the data-processing manager solve the inevitable problems associated with a growing department and equipment that was rapidly becoming obsolete.

By the end of the 1980s, many computer-leasing companies had come to realize that their customer base provided them with the opportunity to supply a greater breadth of service than just the leasing of IBM computers. The provision of software, other equipment apart from IBM (such as DEC), full maintenance services and communications facilities, have all been pursued by the computer-leasing companies with a degree of success.

The aviation lease market

Air transport represents one of the few industries with a record of continuing growth over the last two to three decades and the international banking community finds aviation to be an attractive area for investment, within which leasing plays a significant role. Expressed in terms of tonne kilometres, over the last ten years, the compounded annual increase in air traffic has been over 6 per cent and projections indicate similar figures for some time to come. There have, of course, been mild recessions and smaller increases in some areas of the world in some years, but the underlying trend is upwards.

The lease principle can be split into three broad classifications. Firstly, there is the 'wet' lease which literally requires the lessor to supply a completely operational aircraft and all the lessee has to do is to embark and disembark the passengers or freight for each flight. On the whole, this tends to be a short-term arrangement as the only assets the lessee possesses are the traffic rights. A number of carriers started this way, Caribbean Airways in Barbados for example, using the former Laker Airways' Boeing 707 aircraft. The intermediate stage is the 'damp' lease, for want of a better description, whereby the lessee may provide only some of the additional services such as the flight deck crew or carry out some of the maintenance checks. Finally, there is the dry lease which follows the basic lease principle: the lessor has title while the lessee has possession. It is this lattermost type of transaction which principally concerns the lessor community, many of whom are also willing to write operating lease transactions where they take substantial residual value positions at future dates.

In simple terms, the difference between the buying of an aircraft using equity and loan capital as compared with leasing over an equivalent term is the incidence of taxation both for the lessor and the lessee and the extent to

315

which leasing may reduce the effective cost to the airline while possibly improving the return to the financial institution. Any aircraft operator able to utilize whatever taxation incentives exist would normally expect to purchase the equipment and benefit thereby. In general, financial institutions are labour intensive and not capital intensive, whereas airlines are the reverse. By marrying the two, the financial investor is able to absorb the taxation incentives and pass at least part of the cost benefit to the airline, which can then charge all or at least a substantial portion of the rental against corporate taxation.

Since nearly half the world's airline traffic originates in the US, it is not surprising to find that the first major tax-based leases were negotiated in the 1960s, when the then investment tax credit structure made it attractive for Pan American, Eastern, and Trans World, among many others, to lease up to 25 per cent of their fleets over terms of 15 years and longer, a practice that has continued with their latest acquisitions, although investment tax credits have now been phased out by the US tax authorities. The pattern was soon followed in western Europe with major carriers utilizing benefits from both the US and their own taxation regimes. Today, very few airlines own all their fleet as it would not be tax-efficient to do so. KLM, for example, leases some 50 per cent of its fleet of some 60 aircraft, British Airways and Britannia all have major lease commitments. Similarly, Varig, the major Brazilian carrier, and Qantas in Australia. So the practice is well established world wide, following the international pattern of airline investment.

In recent years, due to the increasing importance of aviation in the world's economic growth, financial institutions have taken a more mature view of investment in the industry and more account is taken of the value of the asset — the aircraft and ancillary equipment. From the leasing aspect, this has resulted in increased financing of time charters or operational leases which, in effect, amortize the cost of the aircraft down to a residual value rather than to a full write-down. Furthermore, under most existing accounting standards, this shorter term finance does not require full disclosure in the accounts but can be dealt with in the notes to the accounts.

The whole question of whether to buy or lease will continue to be decided by detailed evaluation techniques which compare each financial alternative by either a present value or internal rate of return measurement including termination arrangements. While the tendency of governments is to remove some of the subsidized incentives for investment thus reducing the difference between purchasing and leasing, there is little doubt that lease finance will continue be a major source of funding for aviation investment.

Ships and oil rigs

Many types of ship, from the smallest coaster to the largest product carrier, and not least the cross-Channel ferry vessel, have featured in leasing transactions over the last 20 years. In the gathering of the fleet for the South Atlantic war more than one UK leasing company found that it was represented. Although the special features of ship leasing, mainly deriving from maritime law, are outside the scope of this book, the financial provisions of demise as opposed to time charters correspond closely with those applicable to equipment leases, although the terminology differs; a lease becomes a charter, a leasing agreement a charterparty, rentals become charterhire, and so on.

Ships have traditionally been favoured assets for leasing. In an inflationary era many shipping companies found it difficult to maximize available tax allowances, despite the special rules that allowed them to elect to postpone the whole or part of the 100 per cent allowances on expenditure on the acquisition of a new ship and claim the amount postponed at such future period or periods as they wished (see Chapter 13). Shipping companies were better served by having the benefits passed on to them through a leasing company.

While the ships in the UK leasing environment may have been built in every corner of the world, they will all have had a UK operator, which is one of the key requirements for the granting of allowances. As the years have progressed, not necessarily all have been registered under the UK flag. The Finance Act 1982 introduced controls to put an end to the practice, which the Inland Revenue thought had become prevalent, of UK financial lessors arranging charters of ships to non-resident shipping lines through a UK company specially set up for the purpose of complying with the requirement of Section 64(5) of the Finance Act 1980.

To the lessor, ships provide a readily identifiable, long-life, realizable asset, although in the lattermost context economic and political circumstances have caused wild fluctuations in values. This effect has been well demonstrated in recent years by the depressed world economy, war zones, and ship capacity ranging from extreme shortage to extreme surplus.

The ready identification of the asset does, however, allow lessors to spread the basic credit risk by means of guarantees, and during the 1970s and 1980s this was particularly prevalent with non-financial institutions who undertook leasing of ships on this basis.

Subsidized finance, available from many countries to purchasers of new ships, provides a further attraction to the lessor in designing a leasing package.

Early large shipping charters were inclined to be syndicated, the Airlease partnership exemplifying this, and even in 1977, when it was announced that two LPGs were to be built at the Harland and Wolff shipyard in Belfast at a cost of £70m, this was coupled with the announcement of a new leasing consortium of four UK clearing banks to undertake the financing.

The advantages of leasing have not been lost on shipbuilders who, when quoting for new business, regularly include in their submissions a leasing offer (in conjunction with their financial advisers).

While oil rigs tend to have similar attractions as ships, by their nature there are fewer of them and the number of major transactions has been smaller; despite the greater risks attached, these appear to have been dealt with mainly by single-leasing companies rather than on a syndication basis.

In 1976, in one of the largest transactions undertaken by a single-leasing company at that time, Lloyds Leasing provided £20 million for a semi-submersible oil-drilling unit, Sedco 707, which was then leased to a major oil company. As a measure of the growth of this market, coupled with the willingness of lessors to accept increased exposure, the same leasing company in 1982 announced the facility of £80 million for an advanced semi-submersible drilling rig for oil exploration for the British National Oil Corporation. In the meantime a number of similar transactions had been undertaken by other major leasing companies.

Where rigs have been commissioned for special purposes the covenants of the user and not necessarily the lessee have been available to enable a satisfactory package to be effected.

The long life and/or high cost of these assets means that even with 25 per cent writing-down allowances, attractive long lease finance packages can be structured. In undertaking these transactions a lessor has to assess the substantial third party liabilities that can arise from ownership and operation of the assets. In a world ever-increasingly aware of the effects of pollution upon the environment, the need to have operators of a high technical skill is as important as the need for a very strong financial structure. Major accidents, though fortunately few, can be expensive.

In acquiring ships and oil rigs the leasing companies have had to acknowledge that they are bound by maritime laws and that the exposure of their assets will not be restricted to UK regulations. This can add an administrative burden both during the period of the lease and in the event of termination under a default, particularly if the default happens when the ship or rig is out of UK jurisdiction. The future of UK tax leasing in the shipping industry is difficult to assess but it will no doubt continue to play an active part in an industry that has seen a substantial decline in recent years.

Car leasing

The leasing of fleets and cars has enjoyed significant growth, in line with the rapid development of the company car market. It is estimated that at least 60 per cent of all new cars are registered in the name of companies. Probably 40 per cent of new cars acquired are financed by way of leasing or contract hire facilities.

For cars, operating leasing is as widely used as finance leasing and the operating leasing of cars (frequently called contract hire) has achieved wide popularity because it enables the fleet user to shed the administrative burden and to avoid the maintenance costs and residual value risk. Contract hire received an added boost as a result of accounting standard SSAP 21, under which operating leases do not have to be capitalized by the lessee, and therefore remain an off-balance sheet item.

Many lessors are willing to provide the various features contained in contract hire in an 'unbundled' form. For example, transactions are being written where the balance sheet consequences of a contract hire arrangement are achieved without the contract containing such items as maintenance, road fund tax, replacement tyres, etc. Lessors frequently provide a 'shopping list' so that lessees can choose the various features to make up the extent of services required.

Off-balance sheet treatment can also be achieved for transactions which contain pure financial terms and have no element of any of the available contract hire services. An increasing number of lessors are willing to take substantial residual value risk in respect of the sale proceeds of the motor cars at the end of the lease period. This is primarily because of the substantial quantity of information that is available from the motor trade regarding second-hand car prices. *Glasses Guide* and a similar informative booklet produced by British Car Auctions are published monthly and give actual market prices for all makes and models of cars.

Finance leasing is also widely used for car fleets, and although this form of lease must be capitalized in the lessee's balance sheet it is nevertheless popular for reasons of cost and cash flow.

Most finance leases for cars are 'balloon rental' leases. Reduced rentals are paid during the primary period, followed at the end of that period by a final rental equivalent to the anticipated disposal proceeds of the car. Expressed as a percentage of the original cost of the car, a typical residual value would be 40 per cent after two years or 30 per cent after three years, depending on the make and model concerned. The size of the residual value anticipated by the contract will have a cash flow effect as well as having a significant effect on the pricing of the lease.

The finance leasing of a car leaves the user with the fleet management responsibilities. The lessee must therefore locate the cars and negotiate discounts. The lessee arranges and pays for insurance, road fund licence, maintenance, repairs and other running costs. At the end of the lease, the lessee normally acts as the agent of the lessor for the purpose of selling the car at the best price available. The lessee retains a substantial percentage of the sale proceeds as a rebate of rental. It follows that if the sale proceeds fall short of the balloon rental, the lessee must make up the difference.

Finance leases for cars often permit the lessee to extend the lease and to continue paying the same primary rental (or a reduced rental) beyond the end of the lease period in lieu of paying the final balloon rental. This is usually termed an open-ended lease and is designed to give the lessee maximum flexibility in choosing the optimum time to dispose of the cars.

Where a fleet user wishes to avoid the administrative burden and risk associated with the use of the cars, the user may choose the services of a fleet management company rather than move to a full contract hire arrangement. This will enable the user to separate the funding source from the service contract, an arrangement frequently chosen by those fleet users who have substantial borrowing powers and can lease or borrow at better rates than the contract hire company.

Fleet management companies are in business to perform all the duties associated with the running of a fleet for a fee. Their services will normally include the following:

- Locating and buying a car of the hirer's choice.
- Control of maintenance and repair costs, including tyres and batteries.
- Vehicle licensing.
- Providing a replacement car when the hired vehicle is off the road for major repairs.
- Roadside assistance and recovery services.
- Disposal of the car at the end of the hire period.

Some fleet management and contract hire companies also include insurance and the provision of fuel in the services provided, although these are always on an actual cost basis.

The vehicle user will specify the anticipated annual mileage and hire period and pay a fixed monthly all-inclusive rental. This rental may only be increased as a result of cost increases outside the management company's control, such as increases in vehicle licence, insurance premium and fuel. Frequently the risks and rewards that result, in the event that the anticipated maintenance and the residual values turn out to be inaccurate, fall upon the fleet management or contract hire company.

Both fleet management and contract hire have the perceived advantage that the cost of running each car can be accurately budgeted in advance. In return for the monthly rental, which may be to a combination of lessor and fleet manager or contract hire company, the vehicle itself is provided. In addition, when it needs to be maintained or repaired it is taken to a garage, usually nominated by the user, where a replacement car can be made available if required. Fuel can be obtained at a network of outlets around the country and licensing and insurance of the vehicle is dealt with centrally. At the end of the contract hire period, the car is returned with no further obligation other than to pay a predetermined excess mileage charge and to make good the cost of any abnormal wear and tear or damage.

A more recent concept has been introduced into the market whereunder the lessor discloses the method in which the rental for the car has been calculated and at the end of the hire period shares with the lessee any excess profits that may have arisen on the operation of the vehicles or their sale.

Many major leasing companies have close relationships in the form of joint companies or trading arrangements with vehicle suppliers. Most motor manufacturers and importers also have fleet leasing operations, while many motor dealers either own leasing or contract hire subsidiaries.

COMMERCIAL VEHICLES

As in the case of fleets of cars, finance lease and operating lease facilities are both widely available in respect of commercial vehicles.

Light vans are often treated as if they were cars for finance lease or contract hire purposes. The maximum period is usually three to four years and, as for cars, the rental will reflect the assumed residual value of the vehicle.

Heavier commercial vehicles are commonly leased for longer primary periods of up to seven years, usually on a full payout basis. A finance lease for a heavy truck is therefore no different from the lease of any other item of plant and machinery.

The contract hire of heavy commercials is, however, quite distinctive. The contract hire company not only supplies the vehicles but also takes full responsibility for maintenance and repairs, heavy goods vehicle (HGV) licensing, the provision of a replacement vehicle in the event of breakdown or accident, and possibly insurance, fuel and the supply of drivers. Some contracts even embrace the provision of distribution premises and staff.

Fleet management advice is often part of the package. The selection of the most appropriate commercial vehicle for the job for which it is required is usually of far greater importance than the selection of makes and models of cars. The costs of running commercial vehicles are also substantially higher than those of running a car fleet, so that the application of fleet management expertise can produce significant savings.

321

Contract hire companies can purchase commercial vehicles at preferential prices and can identify the disposal method which, at the end of the hire period, will produce the highest resale price. Servicing and repairs can often be carried out in the contract hire company's own workshops and replacement vehicles can be provided from its own short-term rental fleet.

Sale and leaseback transactions are a means whereby a vehicle fleet user can realize the capital locked up in its vehicles and also implement a change of financing policy on the total fleet when the decision is made. The leasing or contract hire company purchases the entire fleet, often at the user's net book value, providing a normal depreciation policy has been followed, and then leases or hires the vehicles back to the user over periods equivalent to the remaining useful lives of the vehicles.

Small-ticket leasing

The corporate tax changes contained in the Finance Act 1984 have considerably heightened lessors' interest in small-ticket leasing, which is not basically a tax-sensitive sector of the leasing market. This interest has been highlighted by the formation within the Equipment Leasing Association of a Small Ticket Sub-Committee and externally by the formation and acquisition of a number of small-ticket leasing companies by many of the well-known merchant banks, foreign banks and others who previously showed little or no interest in this sector of the industry. Further, the major finance houses have reorganized part of their operations, forming specialist teams to concentrate in this sector.

Small-ticket leasing has never previously been formally defined and in 1985 the newly formed Small Ticket Sub-Committee of the ELA, after some debate, arrived at a definition of small-ticket leasing, which is as follows: 'leases below £50,000 in value, written by a lessor predominantly writing leases below that level.' Armed with this definition, the ELA tried to estimate the size of the small-ticket market and reached the conclusion that during 1984 the total of such business written by members was approximately £580 million, compared to a total leasing volume for members that year of £4,012 million. The figure was almost certainly higher than that, with a number of companies who would have written some small-ticket business, being non-members. This is the sector of the business that many foreign-owned lessors first enter as it most closely resembles their home-based business, which is true of most European lessors.

It should be noted that a large proportion of small-ticket leasing is carried on via sales-aid-leasing schemes, which are leasing plans designed to help manufacturers or vendors sell their equipment to customers and are referred to in more detail later.

The small-ticket sector places a strong emphasis on marketing and operates on a money-on-money basis. Margins have to be adequate enough to cover substantial overheads incurred in securing and administering the business and it must be written in a manner that ensures that future collection costs are minimized.

Specialist computer and communications systems have been developed to cope with the high volume of business that will be written by a successful lessor, who is virtually running the business on a production line basis. The administration systems must be flexible enough to deal with such diverse matters as Regional Development Grants (see Chapter 18) and the requests for information that may arise as a result of the Data Protection Act.

Documentation tends to be based on a standard format and is not subject to negotiation between lessor and lessee. Recently a number of lessors have introduced a tax variation clause into the lease document, which allows an upward variation in rental payments in the event of a future rise in the corporate tax rates. This in no way rescinds the earlier statement that the sector is not tax sensitive but purely reflects a view that a return to tax rates of, say, 50 per cent would render many existing contracts unprofitable.

Small-ticket leases are, as might be expected, written at much higher interest rates than the larger ticket transactions, for several reasons:

1. The lessor needs to ensure that the rate charged covers all overheads, including the costs of: money; new business acquisition; administration and collections; bad debts; and, of course, an element of profit.
2. Lessors are not writing the business to obtain the tax allowances, but to achieve a money-on-money profit.
3. Lessees often enter into small-ticket leases simply because they provide a simple and efficient alternative to paying cash: i.e. the documentation is fairly standard and therefore easy to agree, it is relatively straightforward to obtain credit clearance for these small transactions; and, in theory, this does not affect a lessee's existing credit facilities. Cash flow benefit is mentioned by many lessees as their main attraction to leasing.

Under the old tax regime, some small-ticket leasing companies were perhaps more interested in the tax benefits rather than making a straightforward money-on-money profit. Consequently, opportunities for making profit in such areas as renewal rentals or terminations were either ignored or all the potential profit was passed to the lessee. Now that the tax system has changed and margins have been reduced, these areas of profit opportunity are being more fully exploited.

TYPES OF EQUIPMENT AND LESSEES

The types of equipment that are leased at the small-ticket end of the leasing market are very varied. As long as the covenant is acceptable, many small-ticket lessors will be happy to lease almost anything. The equipment can vary from plant and machinery to computers, office equipment, cars and commercial vehicles. Office equipment and furniture tend to be financed mainly on sales aid schemes.

The main types of assets leased fall under the following headings:

1. Computers and office equipment: for example, this category will include micro and mini computer systems with an element of software, office furniture, photocopiers, facsimile machines and communications equipment.
2. Commercial vehicles: trucks, trailers and vans.
3. Plant and machinery: printing equipment, excavators and agricultural equipment — tractors, combine harvesters.
4. Cars.

The type of equipment being financed may affect the lessor's underwriting decision and the following two important considerations will be borne in mind:

1. The expected life of the equipment: it would not make sense for the primary period of the lease to exceed the expected useful life of the equipment.
2. The ability of the lessor to remarket any piece of equipment should that need arise, i.e. is there an established second-hand market for the goods?

The types of lessee involved in this sector of the market are very varied in their nature. Almost all businesses will fall into the following categories:
- Sole traders, e.g. farmers, painters and decorators, etc.
- Partnerships, e.g. accountants, solicitors, surveyors, etc.
- Limited companies, both private and public
- Trading arms of overseas companies
- Local authorities.

All these different types of lessee form the market for small-ticket leases, usually because it is an easier and quicker way of obtaining the equipment than paying cash, particularly where an individual manager requiring the equipment may be able to authorize revenue expenditure but not capital expenditure.

There are, however, a number of difficulties when leasing to individuals such as in a partnership, rather than to a limited company, as these transactions will fall under the Consumer Credit Act (see Chapter 22).

Lease brokers are playing an increasingly important role in the small-ticket sector for the following reasons:

1. The use of brokers helps to keep costs under control, because it reduces the need to have a branch network with a direct salesforce. Most brokers work on a commission basis and if they do not produce the business, they do not earn the commission.
2. The brokers are usually locally based with their own client and supplier contacts.
3. The number of brokers in the marketplace has been increasing because many of the major finance companies have reduced the size of their branch networks and some of the affected staff have decided to establish themselves as independent brokers. They frequently work with a client and supplier base that they have built up over a number of years.

Sales-aid leasing

Sales-aid leasing, sometimes referred to as vendor leasing, is essentially a series of leasing schemes designed to help manufacturers or suppliers to sell their equipment to customers who prefer to pay for it over a period of time. In other words, it provides the vendors' salespeople with an alternative 'close' to the sale, particularly where the customer would otherwise defer the completion on the basis of a price objection.

If a sales-aid-leasing plan is set up properly, not only does it help a vendor to sell the products, it also enables the lessor to market its facilities and services in an economic manner, using the vendor's salespeople for this purpose. It thereby increases the size of its customer base. In order to derive the maximum benefit from any sales-aid-leasing scheme, however, both parties need to be fully committed to it and play an active role in its construction.

The main development of sales-aid leasing has taken place in the small-ticket sector of the leasing market; however, there are some well-known schemes for equipment, particularly computers, that are at the medium- to large-ticket end of the spectrum.

The type of supplier or manufacturer who makes use of sales-aid-leasing schemes can be selling anything from computers and office equipment through to plant and machinery such as agricultural or printing equipment. Lessors are particularly attracted to sales-aid schemes for equipment which retains its value and where there is an established second-hand market, as this represents much of the lessors' collateral. Suppliers who make the most use of sales-aid-leasing plans are in the business of selling computers and office equipment. This latter category will include photocopiers, facsimile machines, typewriters, word processors, furniture and partitioning, telephone systems and communication equipment. For example, both Canon and Rank Xerox, who supply many different office products, use leasing as a selling tool, as do British Telecom and many others.

Benefits to the supplier

There are a number of benefits that will accrue to a supplier or manufacturer from a properly structured sales-aid scheme:

- a shortening of the sales process
- an alternative method of closing the sale
- the overcoming of objection to the cost of equipment
- the lowering of the buyer decision threshold
- credit decisions are undertaken by the lessor who is equipped to make them
- prompt settlement of the sales invoice leading to an improved cash flow
- repeat sales, on the expiration of the primary period of the lease.

Drawbacks for the supplier

The main drawback for the supplier is that a proposed customer may be declined by the lessor — this leaves the supplier with several options:

- try another leasing company — some suppliers will use several leasing companies and not get tied in with any particular one
- try to persuade the customers to pay cash or to make use of their own finance facilities
- offer to buy-back or to remarket the equipment on behalf of the lessor should the customer default
- move on to the next customer.

Lessor requirements

Any lessor providing sales-aid plans would usually be expected to have the necessary technical back-up to provide the following:

- fast credit underwriting of lease applications — suppliers want a quick response even if it is a decline
- straightforward and easy to understand lease documentation — which may be personalized and should be easy to complete
- easy to use rate or rental charts — some lessors now provide pre-programmable calculators to supplier salesforces which can be used for set rental periods on a predetermined basis

- classroom and field training — so that the vendor's salesforce is equipped to maximize the benefit of the leasing facilities
- a nationwide service to meet the requirements of a national salesforce
- efficient administrative back up — to assist the vendor by providing prompt settlement of the supplier's invoice upon delivery of the equipment and to ensure receipt of properly completed lease documentation
- technical sales support — continuing liaison to improve the scheme and overcome any initial problems quickly as they arise.

In addition to the above criteria, the lessor should have the necessary administrative back up in the areas of accounts and collections as both the lessor and the vendor will require prompt statistical information to enable them to control the business relationship.

ADDITIONAL CONSIDERATIONS

There are a number of other factors that need to be taken into account when establishing a sales-aid scheme.

1. The vendor and the lessor may enter into a remarketing agreement or a buy-back agreement that is designed to cover the situation where a lessee defaults. This will provide the lessor with extra comfort when it is considering marginal credit applications and it may also give the supplier some extra control over the second-hand market.
2. There are certain attractions to a lessor if, at the end of a lease term, the original equipment supplier repurchases the goods. This may appear doubly attractive in the light of the de-pooling concessions introduced in the Finance Act 1985, as it is an ideal way to clear the asset from the lessor's books and simultaneously crystallize the flow of capital allowances. It will be appreciated by most suppliers that the main benefit they obtain from a buy-back arrangement is that of protecting their second-hand market by preventing their used equipment falling into the hands of competitors.

ABUSES OF SALES-AID LEASING

The majority of sales-aid schemes are quite straightforward and achieve the aims of both lessor and supplier, which is to increase both volume and profits. Unfortunately over the last decade certain sales-aid schemes have developed in such a way that they may detract from the future sales performance of the supplier. There are two main abuses that bring the good reputation of leasing into doubt.

Inflated pricing

A system of upgrading has developed, whereby the settlement figure of an old lease from one lessor is rolled up into the cost of the new equipment to be leased by another lessor. The effect of this is that the new lease is therefore funding an inflated price for the goods and the lessor is entering into the business of unsecured lending. Some leases have been upgraded a number of times over a fairly short period, creating the situation where the upgrade is several times higher than the cost of the new equipment.

As an example of this practice, photocopiers which probably have a real life of 30 to 36 months, are increasingly being sold on the basis of five- or six-year leases as this reduces the monthly rentals and makes them easier to sell. This is not in the interest of the user, who halfway through the lease may well require the latest model to replace an obsolete machine; nor is it in the interest of the supplier, who will then have to persuade the user to settle the old lease and enter into a new one. Any good sales-aid scheme will ensure that equipment is not leased for a period that is longer than its expected useful life.

High rentals

Another abuse that has developed in recent years is where a supplier of the equipment will write a lease agreement at a high rental and achieve a higher than normal sales price by present valuing the stream of rentals and then selling the equipment to a lessor at the inflated price.

Agricultural market

Faced with the threat of reductions in EC subsidies, as a means of cutting the European mountain of food stocks, farmers and growers are constantly seeking ways to reduce pressures on working capital. Where farm machinery is concerned, there is a fundamental requirement to maintain up-to-date equipment in order to increase productivity. With this in mind, external sources of funding are becoming more and more important.

Recent years have not been good for UK farmers. Adverse weather conditions have led to modest crop yields coupled with a fall in market prices for cereals. This has led to a substantial drop in farm incomes. Nevertheless, farmers need to keep agricultural plant and machinery up-to-date to maintain productivity.

Against this background, leasing has grown in importance as a method of finance in the agricultural machinery sector, accounting for around 55 per cent of new tractor and combine harvester sales in the UK in 1987. Used equipment and vehicles can be acquired on lease together with agricultural fixed equipment, such as milking machines and farm buildings.

However, tractors and combine harvesters attract the major proportion of leasing funds.

THE LESSORS

Leasing in the agricultural market today is very specialized and, as such, few finance companies have entered this sector of the market. Highland Leasing, a member of the Barclays Bank Group, are market leaders. Humberclyde, the subject of a recent management buyout, have the next largest market share, with the remainder taken up by Ford Motor Credit, NWS BANK (owned by the Bank of Scotland) and Farming and Agricultural Finance.

THE LESSEES

The number of farmers who use leasing has continued to grow over the last few years and leasing now penetrates the agricultural market at all levels and in all types of farming, from sheep and beef through dairies to arable farmers. Not surprisingly, it tends to be the bigger — often arable — farmers who make up the most significant proportion of all agricultural lessees, with the younger and more formally educated members of the industry being the most frequent users.

LEASE STRUCTURE

The primary period of an agriculture equipment lease will normally be based on the anticipated working life of the equipment on the farm, usually between three and five years. A nominal secondary rental comes into operation if the lessee wishes to retain the use of the machine at the end of the primary period. Otherwise, the lessee will dispose of the machine on behalf of the lessor and receive a major portion of the sale proceeds by way of a rebate of rentals.

WHY FARMERS LEASE

There are several sound economic advantages of leasing in a market where incomes are unpredictable. Accurate forward budgeting is important in today's economic climate and leasing allows the farmer to plan ahead because all rentals are usually fixed at the outset of the lease.

Specialist lessors in the agricultural market also allow rentals to be scheduled to coincide with anticipated peak cash-flow periods in the farming year. Each farm is individual in nature and a different business. Every farmer needs rental flexibility matched to the farm budget and cash flow. Most farms are faced with periods when income is low and outgoings are high — arable, dairy and mixed farms each have very different cash-flow patterns.

Therefore, many agricultural lessors have created schemes that have been specially designed to enable farmers to schedule their rentals to coincide with those times when income exceeds expenditure. In some cases, this could mean only one annual rental. Additionally, provided that the period of the lease is considered to be reasonably based on the genuine working life of the equipment, all rentals can normally be offset against taxable income as a trading expense.

Overall, leasing is growing in importance as a supplement to the farmer's traditional source of credit, the bank overdraft.

SPECIAL FEATURES OF THE AGRICULTURAL LEASING MARKET
Unlike other markets where leasing companies direct their main marketing efforts at the consumer, agricultural leasing companies must approach the market on three different levels.

The machinery manufacturer is an important partner for the agricultural leasing company with whom many joint finance schemes are operated. Machinery dealers are also crucial to lessors in the agricultural sector, as most leasing agreements are taken up at the point of sale. Farmers will be aware of leasing schemes through various direct marketing and sales promotion techniques.

Without doubt, the most important development in agricultural leasing in the last decade is the development of manufacturer-sponsored finance schemes. Today, nearly every major manufacturer offers special subsidized terms at certain times of the year. Sponsored schemes now make up a significant proportion of the agricultural machinery leasing market.

The leasing company that operates the scheme may offer to bear the cost of associated promotional material, but otherwise the cost of the subsidy lies with the manufacturer, who will include it in the annual marketing strategy and fund it from the marketing budget.

FUTURE CHANGES
The 1984 changes to the capital allowance structure still leaves the lessor the benefits of the 25 per cent annual writing-down allowances, as owners of the equipment. This is reflected in lower financing costs to the farmers. However, tax relief is not confined to the lessor. The farmer can normally off-set rentals against taxable income as a trading expense during the period of the agreement.

Today, there is an increasing tendency to take agricultural equipment on leasing contracts that include such aspects as maintenance, insurance and road tax, plus, in some cases, a replacement machine if the one on lease is out of action for more than 48 hours.

For this reason, many agricultural leasing companies are developing products to suit this change in the market. Nevertheless, farmers must continue to replace essential machinery to maintain productivity. Leasing offers forward budgeting advances and flexible payment plans, which are without doubt a viable option for most farmers and growers throughout the country.

Property market

Although the content of this book is essentially concerned with the leasing of equipment rather than property, the leasing of industrial and commercial buildings merits reference, if only because to a limited extent equipment lessors have in recent years extended their activities into this sector.

As a sector of economic activity, the leasing of property dwarfs the leasing of equipment. Probably well over half of industrial and commercial buildings in the UK are subject to some sort of a lease agreement, rather than being in the freehold ownership of the businesses that occupy them. The structure of property leasing covers a considerable range of leasing terms. At one end of the scale, there are long leases of 99 or even 999 years, where the ground rent may be of a small or nominal amount, and the ownership of the lease itself — if it still has a substantial period to run — may represent a more valuable asset, which is no less readily marketable, as compared with the gradually appreciating 'freehold reversion' held by the ground landlord. At the other end of the scale, there are monthly tenancies.

In the intermediate range, there are relatively long leases of property, possibly assigned for periods such as 10 years or 21 years, where a substantial annual or quarterly rent is payable, subject to varying conditions as to the respective responsibilities of lessor and lessee for aspects of manangement and maintenance of the buildings. In such leases, the outstanding lease may be marketable as a capital asset by a lessee who wishes to vacate the premises and assign his or her interest to a new lessee. This outstanding lease will change hands at a 'premium' value, determined by the market in the light of the current value of the location and facilities, and the amount of rent due to the lessor. Under certain conditions, a premium can be negative, so that a departing lessee has to pay a new lessee to take the lease.

On longer or intermediate property leases, the rents are usually subject to review at three- or five-yearly intervals, with a facility for a possible arbitration procedure in the light of inflation and other factors affecting the property market in the period since the last rent review. There is a limited degree of statutory regulation of non-residential property rents, under the Landlord and Tenants Acts.

In view of the range of property lease structures from long to short periods, a single property, or part thereof, may be subject to a succession of multiple property interests in the hands of different parties. A three-storey office building may, for example, be mainly occupied by one company holding a lease originally granted for 21 years by a lessor who owns a long lease originally assigned for 99 years, by a head lessor or 'superior landlord' who owns the freehold. Since the sub-lessee may not be making use of the whole of the building, that person may then assign a tenancy in respect of the first floor to another commercial tenant. The latter part of the premises would then be subject to as many as four property interests in the hands of the respective parties: the short tenancy, the sub-lease, the long lease, and the freehold reversion.

Residential property represents a separate part of the market, where leases can again range from long periods where the leasehold has a high capital value, to short weekly or monthly tenancies. The landlords of residential property include a commercial sector, as well as local authorities and voluntary housing associations. Housing rented or leased on commercial terms has been subject to a long-term decline throughout the twentieth century, under the impact of legislation that has restricted landlords' freedom to determine rents and regain vacant possession, to a point where well over half of all dwellings in the UK are now in freehold owner-occupation. Various legislation enacted since 1980 has been designed to revive the privately rented housing sector, with some limited success to date; but this sector of the property market remains distinct from others, with only a limited role for commercial leasing in any form.

Within the property market, the commercial business of holding industrial and commercial property investments for letting to business tenants or lessees is dominated by specialist property companies — who may be either 'merchant developers' (commissioning the construction or major refurbishment of property for letting on completion) or simply investors or traders who acquire property from specialist developers or casual vendors — and by the long-term investment institutions, such as pension funds and life assurance companies, who view property investments as part of an available portfolio of income-yielding assets, together with equity shareholdings and bonds and other lending instruments traded on the financial markets.

The business of property investment and property management has in general not been attractive to the type of companies who specialize in equipment leasing. Unlike plant and equipment, property is not a rapidly depreciating asset, and hence for tax purposes attracts no capital allowances or — in the case of industrial buildings — only limited annual write-offs. The banking sector cannot therefore find the tax attractions of leasing in the property market. The clearing banks play a major part in the funding of property companies, through bank advances, but have had no reason to become involved in their management.

There are nevertheless some factors that have brought certain equipment-leasing companies into the property-leasing market to a limited extent. In selected inner urban locations, where the authorities have sought to stimulate industrial and commercial employment, Ministers have enjoyed powers under the Local Government, Planning and Land Act 1980 to designate 'enterprise zones' (EZ). Within the EZ locations, a range of special incentives operates to attract private sector investment, including 100 per cent initial allowances for tax purposes on both industrial and commercial buildings, under Section 74, Finance Act 1980. A number of equipment-leasing companies have participated in the financing of major office-building projects in such areas, particularly in the Docklands EZ in East London, with a view to retaining ownership as property investors and claiming the same advantageous tax treatment that was available pre–1984 on equipment leases.

More generally, there are a number of non-tax-based property-leasing facilities with particular features which, for one reason or another, have lent themselves to the marketing skills of equipment lessors. One such structure involves a sale and leaseback transaction, where a leasing company acquires a long lease from a business which previously had unencumbered freehold ownership of its premises, and leases it back to the occupier on a shorter lease, at rents escalating at a predetermined rate, but rather lower than market rents. At some point within the leaseback, there may be a 'call option' for the occupier to repurchase the long lease, failing which the rent on the short leaseback will revert to a market level. The purpose of such a scheme is for the occupier to unlock some of the capital invested in the property, and to take the major part of the property investment off-balance sheet. The leasing company can achieve a return on its own investment through the overall terms of rents and premiums, while at the same time insuring its residual value risk with a specialist insurance company in the RVI market (see Chapter 17). In this structure, the aspect of off-balance sheet marketing, together with the use of RVI, are features which attract the equipment lessor rather than the traditional property investor.

In 1988 member companies of the ELA wrote £267 million worth of new business in the leasing of industrial and commercial buildings. This was only some $3\frac{1}{2}$ per cent of total ELA leasing business, and still less in relation to property market activity in general.

25. *International leasing*

While this work deals primarily with the UK leasing market, it is important that the latter be placed in context by comparing it with other major national markets throughout the world.

Equipment leasing can thrive in any country that combines a diverse and competitive private enterprise economic system with a framework of commercial law that can come to terms with relatively sophisticated transactions — ensuring, for example, that the lessor's ownership of fixed or movable equipment can be protected.

By no means all countries meet these conditions. Between a third and a half of the world's population could be said to be affected either by attempts at wholesale central planning of the economy, which rules out a major role for private sector companies and institutions; or by rather primitive social conditions, which do not accommodate modern financial services such as leasing. One such country in the former category — mainland China — is of such a size, accounting for nearly a quarter of the world's entire population, that even as yet very limited moves towards economic liberalization render it of some potential interest in the worldwide leasing market. Accordingly, that country is covered in the survey below of the major national markets of the Far East. Similarly, some comment is given on eastern Europe, where liberalization is at various stages but moving quite rapidly in some countries.

In other respects, it is appropriate to look mainly at those countries with a relatively advanced economic system, essentially of the western type.

General view

Among the large industrial countries, the USA and the UK stand out, with (to a lesser extent) the major economies of continental western Europe — Germany, France, Spain and Italy — as the centres where leasing has penetrated most comprehensively into the corporate financing scene. In Japan, leasing is rather less well entrenched as compared with other methods of financing. Yet the sheer scale of the Japanese economy — where a country with nearly twice the UK population now enjoys a per capita income well ahead of average European levels and where fixed investment remains exceptionally high in relation to total economic activity — means that the total volume of leasing business easily reaches second place behind the USA.

An attempt at a systematic comparison of leasing volume and 'leasing penetration' — i.e. the share of leasing in the total market for new capital equipment — is reproduced in Table 25.1, drawing on research under-taken by Dr David Porter of the UK leasing company London Financial Group Limited. Though Dr Porter's figures give by far the most compre-hensive up-to-date analysis of its kind, a word of caution should be added on the exactitude of any such comparison. Both the leasing statistics, which are derived in large part from figures compiled by the national leasing associations, and the fixed investment aggregates with which they are compared, which are from governmental sources, are subject to a degree of incompatibility from one country to another. Thus the UK figures given in the table are based on the ELA's initial calculations for 1988 of leasing by ELA members of plant and machinery (excluding buildings) as a percent-age of total UK fixed investment in the corresponding aggregate of plant and equipment. (The latest UK estimates for 1990 and earlier years (see Chapter 3) are compiled on the same basis, but incorporate a slight downward revision for the 1988 'penetration ratio', reflecting a large

Table 25.1 Leasing volume and penetration in individual countries, 1988

Ranking	Country	New leasing business (US$'000 million)	Market penetration %
1	United States	112.70	32.3
2	Japan	53.74	10.3
3	United Kingdom	16.32	20.2
4	France	15.83	16.9
5	Germany	15.65	15.2
6	Italy	9.47	12.5
7	Spain	7.90	25.8
8	Australia	7.00	33.3
9	Sweden	4.40	27.0
10	Korea	3.94	12.5
11	Canada	3.92	10.3
12	South Africa	2.65	n/a
13	Netherlands	2.32	12.0
14	Brazil	1.94	n/a
15	Hong Kong	1.55	41.3
16	Austria	1.52	12.5
17	China (People's Republic)	1.20	1.0
18	Belgium	1.15	6.8
19	Switzerland	1.15	7.4
20	Indonesia	0.89	n/a
Total of top 20 countries above		265.24	16.5
Total of top 50 countries		273.74	16.3

Source: 'LFG Global Leasing Report', London Financial Group: article by D. Porter, *World Leasing Year Book, 1990*.

upward revision by the Central Statistical Office of total UK fixed investment for that year, since its first official estimates were produced.) The USA figures include both property leasing and (for comparison) total fixed investment in non-residential construction, as well as in plant. While the UK figures exclude purchase option business, those for most other European countries include the local equivalents of both leasing and hire-purchase business; some of these countries include a certain amount of consumer hire-purchase business; while the French leasing statistics, reflecting the focus of concern of the national leasing association, only include the equivalent of UK hire purchase (i.e. 'credit bail' in France), and not the equivalent of UK leasing (i.e. 'location').

Subject to these reservations, the figures in Table 25.1 may be viewed as a very broad indication of the weight and significance of leasing business in different countries.

United States of America

Leasing in the United States has the same origins as in Britain. Its roots can be seen in the development of instalment credit and in the early methods of financing railroad equipment. Over the whole period since the mid-nineteenth century, developments in the US leasing market have closely paralleled those in the UK. However, with the American progression towards world industrial pre-eminence in the late nineteenth century, leasing and other capital financing innovations were seen to anticipate those in the UK and elsewhere, rather than following the British experience. At the time of the early development of railways, the US was still rather behind Britain. There was, however, the same initial use of leasing of railcars (in the 1860s), followed by moves in this sector away from leasing towards hire purchase and conditional sale (in the 1880s)

In the early use of leasing as a restrictive practice in the market for industrial machinery, the American experience was roughly contemporaneous with that of Britain, and was seen in many of the same sectors such as telephones and shoe manufacturing machinery. In an attempt to restrain this form of leasing through legislation, the USA was rather ahead of the parallel British experience, with the Clayton Anti-Trust Act of 1914, which had some limited success in promoting prosecutions against companies who included 'tying' clauses in leases and who made no outright sales of their machinery, such as – for example – the Xerox Corporation in the 1960s.

In the development of leasing in its present form and scale, the US was almost 20 years ahead of Britain. From the mid-1950s, American leasing was advancing very rapidly. It was used extensively as a marketing aid to increase sales of capital equipment by offering an attractive alternative to cash purchase. Taxation factors were seen as clearly helpful in this period, when the Internal Revenue Service took steps to clarify the tax status of leasing. A significant advantage for leasing appeared in the timing differences for lessees, as between attracting tax relief on rental payments and obtaining depreciation allowances where they had bought equipment.

STRUCTURE OF THE INDUSTRY

In the corporate structure of lessors, the American experience to date has remained rather different from that of the UK. In part because of the legislation restricting particular types of financial services to specified types of financial institutions, American leasing companies have tended to develop independently of the banking sector. An example is the United States Leasing Corporation (now known as United States Leasing International Inc.), which was founded by Henry Schoenfeld in 1952. It typifies the archetypal US leasing company and remains today one of the largest American leasing companies with substantial involvement in the international leasing scene.

Other major lessors are subsidiaries of industrial companies, but nevertheless function as independent leasing companies, distinct from the 'captives' which concentrate on leasing their own company's products. An outstanding example of this is General Electric Credit Corporation (GECC), which is wholly owned by General Electric Inc., one of the world's leading manufacturers of aero-engines. However, GECC obtains virtually none of its leasing business from its parent company's products and features as a general equipment lessor financing a wide range of capital assets for lessees in all industrial and commercial sectors.

These specialist lessors include a number of much smaller regionally based leasing companies as well as the major ones like US Leasing and GECC. Their funding is derived from a variety of sources, of which the commercial banks are the most significant.

However, the US financial sector, as in the UK, plays the predominant role in leasing. The companies involved can be classed in three major categories as follows:

1. The major 'money centre' commercial banks based in the largest cities, each of which operates a full range of leasing facilities across the country.
2. The smaller regional banks, which operate more selectively in terms of location.
3. The life insurance companies, which concentrate on large-ticket leasing.

Most of these financial companies operate through specialized leasing subsidiaries within their groups, though some of the banks have leasing departments within the banking company. The banks are in principle restricted by the Federal banking supervision agencies to providing full payout finance leasing, rather than operating leases with residual values. However, some are able to overcome this restriction by the use of residual value insurance arrangements, or buy-back facilities with dealers, to remove or alleviate their residual value exposures.

Among the relative newcomers to leasing in the USA, so far on a limited scale, are the 'thrift institutions' — local savings banks, and savings and loan associations which have a similar function to that of the building societies in the UK. Though the 'thrifts' are traditionally dedicated to home loans and other consumer lending, since 1981 the regulations have allowed them to deploy up to 10 per cent of their assets in corporate sector exposures; and some have now entered the leasing market.

The other substantial category of US leasing enterprises comprises the 'captive' finance companies belonging to manufacturers of capital goods, offering a choice of leasing or loan finance to customers of their parent companies. A significant feature of their capital structure is that the finance subsidiaries in the USA do not have to be consolidated with their parent companies for accounting purposes. They can thus be highly geared with external borrowings to finance their leasing and corporate lending activities, while this debt is kept off the parent companies' balance sheets.

Individual lessors, as private taxpayers taking advantage of 'tax shelters' on plant investment against their personal income — acting sometimes through limited partnerships bringing together a group of investors to acquire plant for leasing to corporate lessees — have also at times been a significant feature in US leasing. Such practices are effectively impossible in the UK, owing to the difficulty of persuading the authorities that an individual or unincorporated business can be in the 'trade of leasing' (see Chapter 1). The US Internal Revenue Service has itself been concerned at the scope for abuses in this area, and some recent tax legislation has restricted the ability of individual investors to claim the tax allowances generally available on leased assets.

THE FISCAL ENVIRONMENT

American leasing activity grew to its present scale as a result of similar tax laws in the corporate tax system to those which favoured leasing in the UK. The process started earlier in the USA but, as in the UK, the era of tax-based leasing is now giving way to a more mature phase in the leasing industry where the tax advantages are less critical.

A system of accelerated tax depreciation for plant and machinery, designed to stimulate fixed investment generally but giving particular advantages for leasing in the case of 'tax-exhausted' lessees — which, in the UK, came about in 1971 — commenced in the USA in 1954. The process was intensified in 1961 with the introduction of the investment tax credit (ITC). This was an allowance against tax paid rather than merely a tax allowance against taxable income, affecting tax payable according to the tax rate and was paid at rates of up to 10 per cent depending on plant type — in addition to depreciation on tax allowances on the same plant. The depreciation allowances were made more advantageous in 1971, and still more so in 1981 with the introduction of the accelerated cost recovery system (ACRS).

At each stage of more favourable 'tax shelter' treatment for fixed investments in plant, progressively more industrial and commercial companies became tax-exhausted, as in the UK, and turned to leasing as a means of benefiting from tax allowances and credits that could be claimed by lessors and passed on to lessees through the terms of lease rentals. The Tax Reform Act 1986 (see below) represents a major reversal of the earlier moves that created the climate for tax-based leasing, but the previous system had allowed the US leasing industry to carve out a strong established niche in asset-based financing, which is likely to be of lasting duration.

GENERAL REGULATORY FRAMEWORK

The development of leasing in the USA has been influenced by other factors in the regulatory framework for business, including accounting requirements and general principles of commercial law, apart from the tax system. On the accounting side, the key developments have paralleled those in the UK even more closely than on the tax front, though events proceeded rather earlier in the USA.

The early development of US leasing was much affected by the attraction to lessees of the off-balance sheet aspects of leasing rather than purchasing equipment. This was seen as a problem area in relation to the quality of financial information on lessee companies, for the same reasons as in the UK. From the early 1960s onwards, attempts were made to address the problem through binding accounting rules for public companies which, as in the UK, are laid down by bodies representing professional accounting practitioners.

Agreement was eventually reached by the US accountancy bodies on the terms of Statement of Financial Accounting Practice No 13: 'Accounting for Leases' (FASB 13). This standard, which came into effect in 1976, provides that leases are to be divided into 'capital' and 'operating' leases for the purpose of determining the off-balance sheet aspect for the lessee. A capital lease, which corresponds broadly with the definition of a 'finance lease' in the UK context (see Chapter 1), is defined in FASB 13.

All leases that meet none of the criteria laid down are defined as operating leases. FASB 13 requires that, in the case of the capital lease, the lessee must capitalize the future burden of lease rental payments to be reported as a balance sheet item — with much the same effect as if the assets had been purchased with borrowed funds, rather than leased, at the outset. For the operating lease, there is no such lessee capitalization requirements. FASB 13 served as the forerunner of similar accounting standards (notably SSAP 21 in the UK) in a number of other countries, which have broadly similar overall accounting practices and the same tradition of full payout finance leases as in the USA.

As with SSAP 21 in the UK, the definitions leave some scope for doubt as to the appropriate treatment of certain lease structures as capital or operating leases. There are some leasing arrangements that the lessee feels able to report as operating leases, thus allowing off-balance sheet treatment, while the lessor classifies them as capital leases, thus leaving rather more discretion on the depreciation of the leased assets in the profit and loss accounts, compared with the prescribed lessor accounting treatment for operating leases.

One important feature of large-ticket leasing in the USA, which has not so far been developed in the UK, is that of leveraged leasing. This structure, which is based on the principle of maximizing the value of tax depreciation allowances, enables the lessor to claim all the usual tax allowances on a lease in which it may have invested only 20 per cent of the capital equipment cost. This is done by bringing in a third party lender or 'debt provider' in addition to the lessor and lessee parties. This lender will usually be a bank like the lessor; but unlike the lessor, will have funds available for investment in the lease without having the 'taxable capacity' to make best use of the depreciation allowances if acting as lessor.

Under US leveraged leasing, the lessor will, in the usual way, acquire the equipment from the supplier and lease it to the lessee, but will fund the greater part of the cost with a loan from the third party debt provider, which will be on 'non-recourse' terms. Though there will be a stream of loan repayments from the lessor to the debt provider, the latter will not have recourse to the former in the sense that a commercial lender normally has recourse to the borrower, by taking a fixed or floating charge on the borrower's assets. Instead, the debt provider will have recourse to the leased assets held by the lessee, in the event of any default in payments due.

The parameters of this leasing structure are determined by the taxation and banking supervision regulations. The minimum 20 per cent of the investment in the leased asset to be financed from the lessor's own funds is laid down by the US internal revenue service as a condition of the lessor's entitlement to depreciation allowances, while the 'non-recourse' principle allows a banking sector lessor, for banking supervision purposes, to allocate the required proportion of 'free capital' against the leased asset in relation only to that part of the lease actually financed.

Leveraged leasing with non-recourse finance plays a major part in US leasing activity, whether of the 'capital' or 'operating' variety in aircraft, mainframe computers, commercial satellites and large industrial plants.

Although the taxation and accounting aspects of leasing offer very close parallels between the US and UK patterns, there are some significant differences between the two countries in terms of commercial law as applied to leasing. The US Uniform Commercial Code — a statute enacted with some variations in virtually every State of the Union — makes a distinction between 'true' and 'non-true' leases. The 'true' lease corresponds roughly with the concept of an operating lease that has now been adopted for accounting purposes — i.e. one where a significant residual value reverts to the lessor, at the conclusion of a lease agreement running for a period less than the anticipated useful life of the asset. The 'non-true', covering the case of full payout leasing and corresponding with the finance or capital lease for accounting purposes, is treated under US commercial law as a conditional sale loan financing arrangement rather than a lease in the usual sense, with the lessor retaining full rights of ownership.

As a consequence, the lessor in the case of a 'non-true' lease is required under the Code to take complex steps to perfect a security interest in the leased assets, to give a prior claim to the leased assets against creditors or trustees in bankruptcy of the lessee, or indeed a 'good faith' purchaser to whom the lessee might have purported to sell the equipment. Even if these steps are taken, the Code could override the security taken by the lessor in some eventualities in the case of the 'non-true' lease; and, because of the deemed sale principle, can make the lessor liable for performance defects in the leased assets to an extent that does not arise under the 'true' lease. Unlike the 'true' lease structure, the 'non-true' can fall foul of the usury laws which, in most States, apply an absolute maximum to the interest rate that can be charged on any loan facility. The true/non-true distinction can, in addition, affect the treatment of a lease under State sales taxes. Some States apply sales tax to the rentals under a lease, in which case all types of lease structure are treated similarly. However, others charge tax on deemed sales of equipment in the case of a 'non-true' lease only.

IMPACT OF THE 1986 TAX CHANGES

The Tax Reform Act 1986 (TRA), which for the most part became effective in 1987, contained many provisions which significantly affect the relative advantages of equipment leasing in the United States. Nevertheless, tax-oriented leasing continues to be a very attractive method for equipment financing. Briefly, the major provisions of the TRA that affect equipment leasing are as follows:

1. The corporate tax rate was reduced for a calendar year taxpayer from 46 per cent in 1986, to 40 per cent in 1987, and to 34 per cent in 1988 and subsequent years.
2. Investment tax credit (ITC) was generally repealed for equipment brought into use after 31 December 1985, subject to transitional relief or grandfathering for equipment on order at that time.
3. Deductions for depreciation (ACRS) were changed for equipment placed in service after 31 December 1986. The benefits were increased for some types of equipment and decreased for others.
4. The value of depreciation deductions was further reduced by restrictions on timing advantages where the equipment is brought into use during the fourth quarter of the taxpayer's tax year.
5. A newly enacted 20 per cent alternative minimum tax (AMT) for corporations reduced the ability of corporations to claim tax benefits from depreciation and certain other tax deductions which create a difference between taxable income and reported income for accounting purposes, on which AMT is based.

With the repeal of ITC, rates for lessees are higher under the TRA than under the old tax laws. However, pricing still continues to be attractive as compared to conventional financing for companies unable currently to claim tax depreciation benefits associated with equipment ownership. Most companies that were lessees under the old tax law are continuing to lease equipment at the present time.

AMT is in some instances resulting in new market opportunities. Capital intensive companies that are subject to AMT are finding their depreciation deductions considerably reduced. The economic cost of leasing is consequently attractive to capital intensive companies that expect to be permanently subject to AMT. Tax loss companies that expect to be taxable eventually, still face the prospect of then becoming subject to AMT, which makes them all the more inclined to lease.

The restricted tax-timing advantages, which apply to all businesses, in some cases inhibit direct purchase of equipment more than the leasing option. Another factor is that the management of foreign tax credit has become more difficult over the short term for many multinational companies as a result of the new lower federal income tax rates. Where this is a problem, leases can often be used more efficiently than borrowings to allocate financing expense to the United States.

Finally, companies concerned that corporate tax rates will rise in the future sometimes prefer to lease equipment because they believe that tax deductions for lease rentals three or four years in the future will then be more valuable than depreciation deductions.

As for lessors, the TRA has caused some reduction in numbers. Casual lessor investors found leasing attractive in the past because of the rapid recovery of their cash investment as a result of ITC. Without ITC, the time and funding exposure for a lessor to recover its investment is significantly longer. Some of these lessors are finding this exposure unacceptable and have consequently withdrawn from the market.

Some leasing companies, which are subsidiaries of large industrial companies, now find themselves subject to AMT and are no longer able to make full use of tax depreciation deductions. The depreciation rate is lower for AMT, and the difference between tax depreciation and book depreciation also affects AMT. Some companies now subject to AMT have, in the past, been leading or significant lessors and they are no longer able to price competitively. Small independent leasing companies that have had taxable income and engage in tax-oriented leasing are also finding it more difficult, or even impossible, to now offer competitively priced true leases due to AMT.

In the new environment, lessors are motivated to take larger residual risks in order to make lease pricing more attractive to lessees and in order to qualify leases as operating leases for financial accounting purposes under the FASB 13 90 per cent test for lessees.

In other cases, however, lessors are offering longer lease terms to make pricing more attractive to lessees, as an alternative to shorter term leases with larger residual assumptions.

US lessors are now under competitive pressure to grant fixed price purchase options, mid-term purchase options, and various types of renewal options, under the guise of estimating the residual value at the outset of the lease. The change in corporate tax rates has led to claims by lessors and lessees for tax rate indemnity payments under existing leases. Lump sum payments and/or rental adjustments have resulted from, sometimes, acrimonious negotiations or arbitrations. At the same time, the possibility of future upward movements of the corporate tax rate is resulting in serious disputes between lessees and lessors as to which will bear the risk. This is a relatively new phenomenon in US leases, though it is a highly developed area of negotiation in major UK leases where tax variation clauses are widely used.

Though individual lessors have largely dropped out of the market for direct leasing, managed funds engaging in non-tax-oriented equipment leasing have been formed by brokers and investment banks to satisfy the appetite of individual investors who formerly invested in tax shelters.

Lessors with the ability to shelter State income tax, in addition to Federal taxes, such as in New York and California, are able to offer more competitive rates than others under the new tax regime.

As companies drop out of the lease market or become subject to AMT, they will be inclined to sell off their leasing companies or their lease portfolios. A new market in recycling these lease portfolios seems likely to develop.

In spite of the tax changes, tax-based leasing appears set to continue as an attractive equipment-financing alternative for many companies. The after-tax cost of either leasing or purchasing equipment has increased as a result of 1986 tax changes. Where a potential lessee cannot use tax benefits currently, leasing equipment will continue to have a significant cost advantage over purchasing. Where this is not the case, the cost differential under the TRA is much smaller than previously, so that other advantages of leasing, such as off-balance sheet treatment, will have greater weight in lease or purchase decisions than in the past.

Western Europe

A review of leasing in mainland Europe has, of necessity, to adopt a broad approach as specific definitions and regulatory factors vary substantially from country to country.

Leasing has had a much slower start in western Europe than in either the United States or the United Kingdom. It is believed that this is mainly due to the fact that there have been many fewer tax advantages available to European lessors. In both the US and UK the substantial tax depreciation that is available on a group basis, has been reflected in the pricing of leases and many industrial companies, both large and small, have found that the rates being charged were substantially less than the equivalent costs of the more traditional sources of finance. As a result, many of the large investments in new plant and machinery were financed by way of leasing.

European lessors, without these advantages, have concentrated in providing leases as an alternative source of finance to the small and medium-sized companies.

The factor common to all leasing in Europe, which distinguishes it from other forms of finance, is the taxation treatment of the rental payments. These are treated as tax deductible by the lessee and as taxable income of the lessor. Lessors, in order to compensate for the taxable nature of their income, are able to take tax depreciation commensurate with the type of equipment being leased. This so-called tax depreciation figure varies from country to country — however, it is usually intended to match approximately the useful life of an asset.

Comparisons between the western European market and others are further made more difficult due to the differences in the laws relating to leasing. Codified law in such countries as France and Belgium, as opposed to that based on statute and common law such as in the UK, have led to different interpretations — thus the development of leasing has been slowed or quickened by the nature of the perceived advantages in different countries. In general, the more flexible the interpretation, the greater the development that has taken place.

Out of these different perspectives has flowed the attitudes of governments towards leasing, and in a number of countries this has resulted in particularly restrictive regulations. France and Belgium are two countries that have a large degree of governmental regulation of leasing whereas countries such as western Germany and the Netherlands have avoided substantial legislation, and thus controls, in respect of their business. It is the case, however, that the legislators are having an increasing effect and more regulations concerning leasing are being introduced than ever before.

In France the banking authorities have taken the view that leasing is tantamount to a credit transaction and thus included controls relating to 'credit-bail' in the law of 2 July 1966, which defines the principles of equipment leasing. On the other hand, they have left certain transactions — for example, those with no option to purchase the equipment at the end of the contract — outside the regulations. In essence, however, leasing companies are regulated as *sociétés financières* along with banks and other credit institutions.

In Germany, the other major market in Europe, the leasing industry has developed as a non-regulated market and the German Leasing Association are intent on ensuring that this remains the case.

All the markets in Europe have developed by directing their efforts towards the small to medium-sized companies. Concentration on the traditional advantages of leasing, rather than the price advantage produced by certain tax regimes, has produced a healthy industry in most European countries. Even with the newcomers like Portugal, the advantages such as 100 per cent financing, the flexibility of the arrangements, preservation of existing lines of credit, cash flow benefits and quick credit decisions when compared with more traditional financing sources, have assisted the growth of equipment leasing.

One major difference between the leasing industry that has developed in the UK and that in many other European countries is the area of real estate leasing. Both Germany and France, for example, have thriving real estate leasing markets whereas in the UK growth has been confined to the institutional investor whose favourable tax treatment has produced rental prices with which the traditional lessor cannot compete.

The establishment of the European Economic Community, with the signing of the Treaty of Rome on 25 March 1957, laid the foundation for the future harmonization of many of the areas of activity hitherto controlled by individual countries. Inevitably, many of the factors affecting leasing business are the subject of harmonization and it was felt important to ensure that discussions do not take place without a major contribution from the European leasing community. The concept of forming a European federation of the individual leasing associations of all European states was discussed at length in the late 1960s, and this was given effect when Leaseurope was formed in 1973 under Belgian law and confirmed by Royal decree. Although not limited exclusively to EC member states, it has set itself the target of bringing about an exchange of views and experiences among all leasing companies in western Europe.

To the present day, the topics discussed by Leaseurope address the pertinent areas common to the interest of all leasing companies who are concerned about future changes to the regulatory framework, e.g. legal issues, taxation (both corporation tax and VAT), accounting standards and the degree to which central banks may wish to supervise leasing as an activity in the future.

Eastern Europe

In eastern Europe, there are prospects for the development — quite rapidly in some places — of a western-style leasing industry, in the wake of moves towards economic liberalization following the political convulsions of the 1989–90 period.

It is likely that before many years have passed, independent privately owned financial institutions will emerge in many eastern European states, which could act as domestic lessors. In the more immediate future, it is much more likely that foreign-owned leasing companies will establish local subsidiaries in each of the more promising markets within eastern Europe, offering leasing services to the emergent independent enterprises throughout the various sectors of industry and commerce. Western German leasing companies have already made moves in this direction, and some UK leasing groups are giving active consideration to their possible participation in eastern European markets in the coming years.

The former East Germany was incorporated into the Federal Republic of Germany in 1990. The commercial laws, corporate tax system and all other economic features of the former West Germany were adopted wholesale in the east at that time. Although the fiscal and social arrangements for German unity were such as to increase unemployment and inhibit economic growth in the east in the years immediately following, the longer-term prospect is for leasing to play much the same role throughout Germany as it has to date in the west.

346

No such ready solution is available for the other eastern European countries. On the basis of economic reform programmes adopted to date, however, and the evident attitudes towards the development of a western type of economic system on the part of local governments, local public opinion, and more significantly potential entrepreneurs in both the financial and industrial sectors, it would seem that Hungary and Czechoslovakia, followed by Poland, will be among the first countries to reach the point where equipment leasing as it is known in the west becomes a significant economic factor. In the southern countries of eastern Europe — Romania, Bulgaria, the former Yugoslavia and Albania — it seems that the pace of change will proceed much more slowly, though ultimately in the same direction.

In the Commonwealth of Independent States, the former Soviet Union — theoretically the most significant potential market in eastern Europe, with a population of over 200 million — the prospects for speedy economic progress are constrained by a critical lack of awareness, among any potential local entrepreneurs, of how a market economy works after 70 years of a communist system, largely closed to information from the outside world. The emergence of modern financial services such as leasing can nevertheless be seen as a longer term possibility.

Australasia

AUSTRALIA

In Australia, leasing was pioneered in the late 1950s and early 1960s and the maturity of the industry is such that it now represents some 35 per cent of total finance company business and is believed to account for approximately a similar proportion of new private capital expenditure. The latter is high by comparison with other developed leasing markets; e.g. UK 16.5 per cent, France 8.4 per cent, Japan 7 per cent.

Since 1958 the Australian Finance Conference has served as the national association of major finance companies and has often acted on behalf of lessors. In December 1986 the Australian Equipment Lessors' Association was formed; though established by the AFC, the AELA is an independent organization with a membership that comprises lessors from all institutional groupings.

The Australian Bureau of Statistics groups lessors into the following categories: all banks; money market corporations; finance companies; and general financiers. The volume of all new lease business written in the fiscal year 1986–87 was A$5,521.4m compared to A$5,592.6m in 1985–86, the latter being some 20 per cent below the year 1984–85. The market is adjusting to reduced equipment financing demands consequent upon a lower level of economic activity, and increased volumes of capital equipment being financed from internal company sources bolstered by operating surpluses resulting from the higher economic activity of prior years.

In 1986–87 some 26 per cent of new leasing business was in new motor cars and station wagons, which is a similar percentage to the previous year, though numbers of new units leased dropped from 88,246 to 71,417. The total motor vehicle category, which includes used cars and station wagons, new and used trucks and other motor vehicles, amounted to A$2,791.2m in 1986–87 — over 50 per cent of the market. The next largest category is automatic data-processing equipment and office machines which accounted for A$766.4m, followed by shop and office furniture, fittings and equipment at A$581.1m. Both of the last named categories reflected increases of 64 and 29 per cent respectively over the previous annual period, but leasing to the construction and earth moving equipment sector was down by A$126.6m and agricultural machinery and equipment down by A$66.3m. The above figures exclude the volume of leveraged lease business, almost entirely in the transport and storage category, which amounted to A$185.6m in 1986–87 (A$280.9m 1985–86).

In the nine-month period ending 30 September 1987, total new business (excluding leveraged leasing) amounted to A$4,315.9m, of which 60 per cent was written by finance houses and 25 per cent by banks. At 31 December 1986 net finance house receivables amounted to A$8,197m out of a total of approximately A$12,000m.

Large-ticket leases apart, most leases for capital equipment items are written for periods ranging from two to five years, and rates are usually fixed for the period. Assuming the goods leased are for a qualifying commercial purpose, the lease rental is tax deductible by the lessee with the lessor able to claim depreciation and investment incentives. No option to purchase may be included in the lease contract, though the lessee can re-lease at the end of the period or make a market offer for the goods.

NEW ZEALAND

In New Zealand several finance company subsidiaries are involved in the leasing market, which, since tax changes in 1982, is principally concerned with the short-term rental and contract hire of motor vehicles. The book value of the leased assets of finance houses show how the industry is declining:

NZ$ millions					
31.12.85	31.3.86	30.6.86	30.9.86	31.12.86	31.3.87
278.5	293.7	298.0	296.4	247.4	247.7

Following a decade of high inflation and interest rates which depressed real profits, companies found themselves increasingly unable to take advantage of tax depreciation allowances on investment in plant and machinery. Finance leasing became an attractive form of financing, but the government, aware of this development and the effect it was likely to have on revenue collection, legislated to remove tax advantages on 6 August 1982. Lessors could still claim depreciation benefits on leased assets in bloodstock and livestock, but even those benefits were eliminated in the 1987 Budget.

Additionally, effective from 1 April 1986, Statements of Standard Accounting Practice issued by the New Zealand Society of Accountants followed the UK practice that a finance lease be recorded in the lessee's balance sheet both as an asset and as an obligation to pay future rentals. This has encouraged many companies to return to more traditional funding arrangements, and finance houses are offering flexible loan packages (e.g. lower interest in early years or 'even-spread' interest) as it is perceived that leasing offers no particular cash flow advantage.

In order to maintain a lease service several finance houses are now offering car maintenance and finance packages, and it is this sector that offers the best growth opportunities.

Far East

The growth of leasing in Asia has been dramatic. In the calendar year 1985 the volume of Asian leasing business amounted to US$25,855m at year-end exchange rate, for the first time exceeding the volume for Europe (US$24,705m).

Japan dominated the scene, commanding 86 per cent of the business, and continues to do so having increased its new business volume from 1985 to the fiscal year ended 31 March 1987 by 42 per cent.

The region's representative body is the Asian Leasing Association (Asialease). Membership consists of six institutional members (the leasing associations of Hong Kong, India, Indonesia, Japan, Singapore and Taiwan) and the leading lessors of Korea, Malaysia, Pakistan, Philippines, Sri Lanka and Thailand in addition to leading lessors in the countries that have institutional membership. Currently not represented is China (People's Republic) where the volume of leasing business is growing extremely rapidly.

JAPAN

In Japan the first leasing company, Japan Leasing Corporation, was established on 1 August 1963, with two other lessors being founded in the following five years. In the period 1968–74 more than 20 new lessors were established and the annual volume of new leasing contracts increased from Y bn 45 in the fiscal year 1968 to Y bn 529 in the fiscal year 1974. Lessors increased from 43 in 1975 to 155 in 1980, by which time annual volume had increased to Y bn 1,574. In the year ended 31 March 1987 the volume of leasing by Japanese Leasing Association (JLA) members had reached Y bn 4,757 (US$31.7bn) and the number of lessors had risen to 286. Computer and ancillary equipment accounted for 33.2 per cent and industrial machinery 15.7 per cent.

The above figures reflect a reduction in the rate of expansion of leasing volume. In the four years to 31 March 1985, leasing expanded at an annual rate of more than 20 per cent; the following year saw the rate drop to 17.5 per cent and in the year ended 31 March 1987 growth rate had decreased to 10.1 per cent. Many of the larger lessors no longer specialize solely in equipment financing and have expanded into general financing operations such as investment in loan issues and real estate finance. Nevertheless, the JLA forecasts demand for domestic leasing will rise to between Y bn 12,000 and Y bn 13,000 by 1995.

Most equipment leasing in Japan is financial, as operating leasing is restricted by the absence of a developed used equipment market. Competition is fierce, especially in the leasing of computers and office automation equipment, with very fine margins being enjoyed by users. Such a scenario would suggest that the number of lessors will contract, though the majority are affiliated to banks and other financial institutions. Others are subsidiaries of industrial manufacturers and trading houses and are likely to take a longer term view of prospects. Independent lessors, such as the largest (Orient Leasing) comprise the remaining group of lessors.

The top six members of the JLA in order of value of contracts in the fiscal year 1986 were:

Orient Leasing	Y bn 350 (US$2.3bn)
SB General Leasing	Y bn 210 (US$1.39bn)
Japan Leasing Corpn	Y bn 190 (US$1.2bn)
Showa Leasing	Y bn 160 (US$1.12bn)
Sumisho & Century Leasing	Y bn 160 (US$1.12bn)
Diamond Lease	Y bn 155 (US$1.02bn)

While there are no statutory regulations governing leasing contracts in Japan, and in that sense leasing companies enjoy freedom of operation, certain guidelines were issued by the Tax Administration Agency effective from 1 January 1979 to ensure fair treatment between lessees and purchasers of equipment. Generally, the lease term is related to a percentage of the legal useful life of the goods; the minimum term for the maturity of a lease contract is expressed as not less than 70 per cent of the statutory useful life of the asset. Where that is deemed to be ten years or more, the minimum lease term is 60 per cent. There is no maximum term. Purchase options afforded to the lessee would have the effect of the contract being treated as hire or instalment purchase and thus the rentals would be disallowed as an operating expense for taxation purposes.

Japanese lessors have been particularly innovative in cross-border arrangements.

CHINA (PEOPLE'S REPUBLIC)

Following a 1979 law which liberalized the environment for international joint ventures, the first leasing company, China Orient Leasing Company, was established in China in 1981. China Leasing Company Ltd has its origins in the same year and today, jointly, they command about 50 per cent of annual business volume. There are now over 30 lessors, including four banking institutions and a number of joint ventures with foreign companies.

The leasing industry has developed very quickly and in the period 1980–85 the average annual rate of increase was some 280 per cent. By the end of 1985 business volume had reached US$800m and at present is well in excess of $1bn. While a substantial proportion of the volume relates to imported equipment, the volume of leasing of Chinese manufactured equipment is increasing rapidly with the Industrial and Commercial Bank of China reckoned to have a commanding share of that sector.

Several of the leading lessors are authorized by the government to import machinery and equipment directly from abroad and users would be accustomed to approach the lessor directly, not only for the financial facility but to take advantage of the lessor's import facilities and procedures as these have come to be recognized for their speed and efficiency compared to the service provided by state-owned foreign trade corporations.

Financial leasing predominates, with lease periods ranging from one to five years. Users tend to prefer a comparatively short repayment period to minimize the interest cost, thus the average lease period is between two and three years. Quarterly, biannual and annual repayments are preferred to monthly. Upon maturity of the contract the lessee may exercise an option to purchase for a nominal sum (say $10) or re-lease for a secondary period, though the latter option is rarely taken. Contracts are frequently supported by guarantees of banks and/or the lessee's state supervisory authority.

China recognizes that much of its factory equipment is obsolete and needs to be replaced with modern plant. With bank funding being scarce and their loan procedures somewhat complicated, the prospects look assured for further substantial development of finance leasing. The state promotion of production and retooling of factories is also likely to further the development of operating leasing.

TAIWAN (REPUBLIC OF CHINA)
In Taiwan, the first equipment lessors can be traced to the late 1970s and by the end of 1978 there were three leasing companies in existence. The following two years saw the formation of a further eight companies and, by the end of 1985, 43 companies were in operation.

In 1986 the banks, finding themselves highly liquid as a result of large foreign exchange reserves, arising from a US$15.6bn trade surplus, started to offer loans aggressively to medium and small enterprises, the very group which constituted the major customer base of the leasing industry. As a consequence, 19 leasing companies ceased activities enabling the surviving 24 lessors to recover from the 55 per cent decline in business in 1985. The value of contracts in 1986 amounted to NT$8,042m, an 8 per cent growth on 1985 business of NT$7,438m.

In 1986 the value of leasing contracts was 2.9 per cent of private sector fixed capital formulation (NT$278.3bn), broadly similar to 1985 but low compared to other Asian countries. Production equipment accounted for 60 per cent of 1986 volume, followed by 28 per cent in the computer and office equipment sector. The average value of local leases was NT$4.47m, and it is interesting to note that NT$1.7bn of 1986's volume was generated by 160 off-shore leases. Of the 1,586 leases written in 1986 by members of the Taipei Leasing Association, 46 per cent were for periods under 36 months with a similar percentage recorded for the actual three-year period. Only three leases were written where the period was in excess of five years.

The future of leasing is viewed with guarded optimism. On the one hand the government has, since mid–1986, recognized the important role the industry plays in industrial and economic development and has seen fit to declare financial leasing a strategic service industry that has to be promoted; but, on the other hand, the plentiful money supply created by the excess foreign exchange reserves is not expected to recede in the near future to any appreciable extent and lessors must be concerned about the effect of continued competition from the banks.

SOUTH KOREA
In South Korea, the first leasing company, Korea Industrial Leasing Company (KILC), was established in 1973 and another two specialist leasing companies were established in 1975. By 1979, following the formation of the first domestic merchant bank in 1976, there were six

merchant banks conducting leasing and three specialist lessors. In the period 1973–79 the value of new leasing contracts doubled each year.

Subsequently, the volume of expansion of the leasing industry slackened, largely reflecting reduced industrial activity following the second oil crisis. However, in 1982 favourable legislation, which amended the Leasing Industry Promotion Act, sowed the seeds of a second phase of expansion which matched an ebullient economy, and in the following year the acquisition value of new contracts had doubled to 358,000m Won (US$460m). Since then the rate of expansion of the industry has been such that in fiscal year ended 31 March 1987 total lease contracts amounted to 1,588,695m Won (US$1.867bn) arising from 7,500 contracts; and in the same period three new specialist lessors entered the market.

With only 14 leasing companies (eight specialists and six merchant banks) South Korea has managed to become the second largest leasing market in Asia. The largest lessor appears to be Korea Development Leasing Corporation (KDLC) which increased its issued capital to 16,000m Won in May 1987. In year ended 31 March 1987 KDLC's net investment in leases had increased to 521,210m Won (US$612.6m) from 286,216m Won (US$428.4m) the previous year. KDLC reckons to have 17.7 per cent of the market in terms of contract amount and 27.9 per cent in terms of contract numbers (2,096).

There is a law that governs leasing. The main provisions cover the establishment of leasing companies; their area of operation; type of plant and equipment eligible for lease finance; repayment terms and conditions. In the case of the latter, there is a maximum rate of 5 per cent over cost of funds (LIBOR for foreign currency transactions and coupon rates on guaranteed corporate debentures for domestic local currency transactions); the lease term must be for more than 70 per cent of the legal life of the equipment where it is deemed to be five years or under, and where the legal life of equipment is deemed to be over five years the lease term must be more than 60 per cent of the life. Purchase options are not mandatory but may be permitted as a concession to the lessee.

In view of existing economic conditions and the investment climate, the leasing industry is well set to maintain growth, though price competition is expected to intensify in the future. Currently more than 50 per cent of business is derived from the manufacturing sector with the next largest sectors being transport and office equipment (mostly computers) though the market is expected to evolve towards service and high-technology areas. The government has a top priority economic objective to foster the growth of small and medium-sized enterprises (SMSE) and there is a statutory guideline to specialist lessors that 35 per cent of the value of lessors' volume should be in the SMSE category, therefore this sector is set for expansion.

OTHER COUNTRIES

There is no doubt that Japan, South Korea, China and Taiwan constitute more than 90 per cent of the total Asian leasing market. However, there are established leasing markets in a number of other countries, and brief details are given below.

Allowance should be made for the different market sectors in which countries classify equipment leases, and their reporting methodology for 'new business' and for the fact that more recent or comprehensive information is available from some countries than others. Except where stated, all figures for business volume are on a net cost of acquisition basis, approximate, and for domestic finance leasing only.

Malaysia

Leasing was first established in 1974. Equipment Leasing Association of Malaysia (ELAM) formed in 1979. Of approximately 150 members, comprising merchant banks, finance companies and leasing companies, 11 are major lessors. Business volume in 1986 estimated at US$600m.

Hong Kong

Leasing first established in mid-1970s. Hong Kong Leasing Association founded in November 1980. Some 60 lessors are estimated to have produced new business volume of US$250m in 1986. (Possibly includes one aircraft.)

India

Leasing first established in 1973 though not much active involvement in leasing until 1978. Estimated to be more than 400 leasing companies in existence, though 75 per cent of business volume is generated by 30–40 lessors. Representative body is Equipment Leasing Association of India (ELAI). Business volume in 1986:US$500m.

Indonesia

Leasing first established in 1974. Indonesia Leasing Association (ALI) formed in 1982. Business volume in 1985:US$227m.

Singapore

First equipment leasing company established in 1973, though some finance companies had engaged in leasing business beforehand. Representative body is Leasing Association of Singapore and has 40 full members. Business volume in 1986: US$205m.

Philippines

Leasing industry dates back to 1957 and now comprises about 60 active companies though dominated by some six major lessors. Representative
354

body is Philippine Association of Finance Companies, Inc. (PAFCI) and comprises 29 members. Business volume in 1986 was probably under US$100m.

Sri Lanka

Leasing established in 1981 and Leasing Association of Sri Lanka formed in 1984. Some 10 companies now actively engaged in leasing with between 4 and 5 per cent of investment in equipment believed to be leased.

Thailand

Leasing established in 1978 but as yet no leasing association has been formed. Market still in its infancy and it is believed only three specialist lessors are active. Business volume in 1986 was possibly under US$50m.

Cross-border leasing

Soon after leasing became a favoured form of equipment financing in many domestic markets in the 1960s a number of cross-border leasing facilities were arranged for large assets, particularly mobile items such as aircraft and ships.

The nature of the cross-border leasing market changed dramatically during the 1970s with the realization that tax incentives intended for domestic investments could also be available to overseas users. In some cases these incentives were available on second-hand equipment. Leases were structured so that lessees retained entitlement to tax depreciation and other tax incentives in their own countries, at the same time enjoying reduced rentals arising from tax benefits in the lessor's country. This type of arrangement became known as the 'double dip' and various schemes were developed, initially by Australian, British and US leasing companies. In recent years a large amount of this type of business has been written from Japan.

UNITED KINGDOM

The opportunity to double dip from the UK was short lived. Following the abolition of exchange control in 1979, a number of cross-border lease facilities were arranged for airlines in the United States and for a few other users of major types of asset, such as production plant and railroads. UK cross-border leasing was curtailed by the Finance Act 1982 when the writing-down allowance was reduced from 25 to 10 per cent and several restrictions on the availability of the 10 per cent WDA were introduced, both for leases of British exports and foreign-to-foreign leases (i.e. the leasing of foreign manufactured equipment to foreign users).

In 1987 the ELA commissioned chartered accountants Ernst & Whinney to undertake an international comparison exercise, focused specially on export leasing, to show that under current legislation it is not possible for UK lessors to compete in 'third countries' against those based in competitor countries. The comparison showed that lessors in several OECD countries could achieve full tax write-off on equipment leased abroad over the typical lease periods of the assets concerned. Only in the UK would the tax written-down value remain up to half the original cost, and only in two other countries (USA and Ireland) would it be at any substantial level at all. Accordingly, the ELA has been pressing for a review of the 1982 legislation.

Currently a few lessors, particularly subsidiaries of banks with large international networks, are promoting the benefits of international leasing to both suppliers and users. It is known that some non-tax-based leasing finance packages for exporters containing currency options and incorporating government export credits have been created. Apart from ships and aircraft, among assets which feature in such transactions are construction equipment, computers, photographic and telecommunications equipment, machine tools and vehicles of various categories, e.g. buses, cars, trucks and fork lift trucks.

The restrictive tax rules of export leasing (presently consolidated in Section 42, Capital Allowances Act 1990) are such that export leases are not viable for rapidly depreciating plant. A common alternative structure for UK-based equipment-leasing groups is to lease into the lessee's home state from a third country (such as Switzerland or an off-shore centre) where a subsidiary leasing company can be based, with the parent company or other associates in the UK financing the lease on a hire-purchase basis. Capital allowances can then be claimed at realistic rates in the third country, with a broadly symmetrical flow of taxable income against deductible expenditures in each of the two countries where the finance companies are located.

As referred to in Chapter 13, it remains to be seen whether the UK tax rules on export leasing — as applied in cases where the lessee is in another European Community member state — will be found compatible with the European Single Market after the end of 1992, when the terms of the Single European Act of 1986 will generally preclude discrimination between EC member states by national authorities. It is possible that the European Commission will at some stage have to address the whole question of the tax treatment of cross-border leasing transactions, as part of a Directive to harmonize at least some features of the member states' corporate taxation systems.

AUSTRALIA

In Australia most leasing companies confined their cross-border activities to aircraft until 1982, when the tax authorities announced that deduction for interest, depreciation and investment allowances would no longer be allowed for equipment used by non-residents and the subject of leveraged leasing arrangements. Two years later the Treasury extended the restrictions to non-leveraged finance leases of equipment by non-residents. The demise of tax-based cross-border leasing has not given rise to any sizeable non-tax-based lease market.

UNITED STATES OF AMERICA

The USA is regarded as having initiated the cross-border leasing market in the late 1970s in the form of the leveraged lease for assets such as aircraft, ships and oil-drilling equipment. Although the equipment was for use outside the USA, American lessors were able to pass on domestic investment tax credits and accelerated depreciation allowance advantages to an overseas lessee. A substantial proportion of the business conducted was in the finance of aircraft and most of the world's airlines took advantage of the opportunities available to them. However, following the Pickle/Dole Bill (which became law as the Tax Reform Act 1986) the ability to export tax benefits in cross-border leasing transactions virtually came to an end.

Some leading American banks possess specialist subsidiaries to oversee international leasing and asset-based financing. The operations of these companies are now generally confined to the various domestic markets of the countries concerned and are not 'cross-border' in the transactional sense.

JAPAN

In Japan, investment tax credits and accelerated depreciation allowances have not been used to encourage domestic development of industry on a large scale, though more direct government support in the form of long-term dollar funds at low fixed interest rates by the Export–Import Bank of Japan was forthcoming. The use of these subsidized funds was fundamental to the creation of the 'Samurai Lease' as a very effective cross-border instrument within an overall environment in which the government was promoting international leasing as part of its economic policy.

Following changes in exchange control regulations in 1980, Japanese leasing companies were free to lease assets abroad to non-residents on a purely commercial basis, and these Yen-based transactions came to be known as 'Shogun Leases'. Since 1981 the growth of such business in terms of net acquisition cost is estimated to have risen to between US$15bn and US$17bn.

The larger independent Japanese lessors have an established international network of subsidiary companies. Apart from competing in the leasing scene in which they are domiciled, the overseas subsidiaries assist the parent in its role of lead manager in cross-border financing arrangements. For example, Orient Leasing became the first Japanese leasing company to participate in financing a hotel development in the USA in 1986 and are agent and lead manager for the HK$600m instalment-sale portion of the HK$3bn financing for two new undersea road and rail tunnels in Hong Kong

OTHER COUNTRIES

Most activity receiving publicity has related to the finance of aircraft, particularly for Asian airlines, and most of the well-known Asian carriers have featured in a variety of leases, including Samurai, Shogun, Australian tax-based and US leveraged leases.

Considerable publicity was given in 1981 for a US$109m leveraged lease for an Airbus A300 for Singapore Airlines, but the Leasing Association of Singapore report that no similar transactions have been undertaken since this original aircraft lease, and none is expected.

The Hong Kong Leasing Association has provided estimates that the volume of cross-border leases recorded in Hong Kong in 1986 is approximately HK$1bn — mostly China trade. In addition it is estimated that the volume of business packaged or arranged in Hong Kong, but not recorded there, amounts to HK$3bn, all of it in respect of aircraft.

FUTURE OUTLOOK

While cross-border leasing employing the exportation of taxation advantages is now confined to a few aircraft transactions, there remain considerable opportunities for the major lessors of the world to develop related cross-border financing techniques. The size and complexity of such transactions will require the best tax and legal expertise. There are a number of major problems with which they will have to contend, such as the laws in different countries relating to leasing and instalment financing; establishing title to the goods; obtaining possession of goods; withholding taxes on rentals and foreign exchange risks, etc. The peripheral expenses of the operation added to customary overheads are often very high, with the former tending to escalate beyond the original estimates.

There have been forecasts that diminishing margins on the financing operations will necessitate substantial growth in business volume to make the aggregate financial returns worth while; but, increasingly, lessors who are creating lease/finance packages and acting as lead managers will be looking to fee income to supplement lending income.

While there are still some formidable barriers to be overcome before cross-border opportunities can be fully exploited, there are encouraging signs in some directions. The move in the EC towards financial harmonization by 1992, for example, may well be the most momentous.

Index